France on the TGV

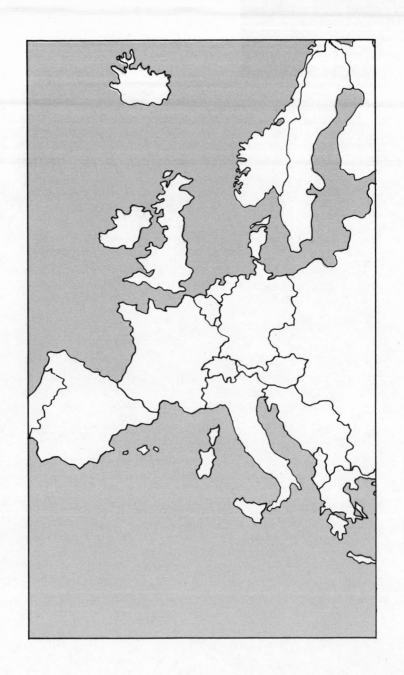

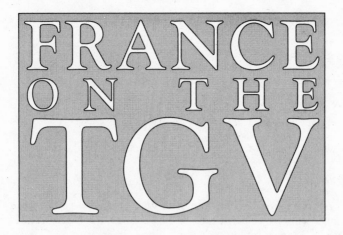

FRANCE ON THE TGV

How to Use the World's Fastest Train to Get the Most out of France

MARK BEFFART

Mustang Publishing Co.
Memphis, TN

Distributed in the USA by National Book Network, Lanham, Maryland. For information on distribution elsewhere, contact Mustang Publishing.

Photographs by Mark Beffart.

Maps by Ortelius Design, Inc.

Library of Congress Cataloging in Publication Data

Beffart, Mark, 1953-
   France on the TGV : how to use the world's fastest train to get the most out of France / Mark Beffart.
      p.   cm.
   Includes index.
   ISBN 0-914457-47-0 (pbk.)
      1. France–Guidebooks.   2. Railroad travel–France–Guidebooks.
   I. Title.
   DC16.B43   1993
   914.404 ' 839–dc20   91-50885
                                                                              CIP

Printed on acid-free paper. ∞

10 9 8 7 6 5 4 3 2 1

Acknowledgments

I am grateful to the following people, who helped make this book possible:

A special thanks to Gwendolyn van Essche, Michele Topper, and the communications staff at Rail Europe, who kept me informed about the latest developments in the TGV system; the *Office de Tourisme* employees in every city in this book, who patiently answered my questions about their city and gave me street directions that made the walking tours more interesting; SNCF ticket clerks, who supplied valuable information about TGV scheduling and regulations; the amiable conductor Jacques, who allowed me to explore the TGV Atlantique train on the Paris to Angers route; the many friendly French citizens I have met throughout my journeys in France, who, despite our language barriers, provided tidbits of information only the locals would know; and my family and friends, who gave me valuable encouragement when needed.

Above all, I thank the SNCF designers and engineers, French government officials, and other involved parties who made the TGV possible. Without them, this book would not exist.

Mark Beffart
Atlanta, GA

CONTENTS

INTRODUCTION

Imagine traveling nearly 200 miles per hour on a train in complete comfort and safety. The ride is so quiet and smooth, you hardly notice you're moving. As you observe your fellow passengers, you see no one alarmed by the high speeds.

Across the aisle, two businessmen with portable computers conduct a meeting as though they were in the office. Four seats ahead, in the center of the car where the seats face each other, a mother and father quietly entertain their two children. At the end of the car, through the sliding glass door, a man talks on a telephone. Other passengers read, relax, eat, and sleep in the firmly padded, spacious seats.

It's almost as if you never left the comfort of your own home—at least until you look out the large window by your seat. That's when you realize the train's velocity, as the lush countryside, narrow highways, and small villages pass in a streak of colors and shapes.

Two hours later, the train slows and your destination appears. You are 400 miles from where you started, and you saved more than two hours over slower trains plying the same route.

This is what it's like to travel on the **TGV** (an acronym for *Train à Grande Vitesse*), the fastest train in the world. Created by the **SNCF** (*Société Nationale des Chemins de Fer Français*, the French National Railroad) to provide faster and more efficient rail service throughout France, the TGV set a world speed record for trains of 320.2 mph on May 9, 1990 while testing the high-speed track from Paris to Vendôme.

However, the French were rather cavalier about the accomplishment. After all, setting speed records was a common occurrence for the TGV.

Since September 27, 1981, when the first high-speed line opened from Paris to Lyon, the TGV has been eclipsing its own speed records and those of its challengers regularly.

Although the TGV does not reach 300 mph speeds on its commercial routes (because it has more cars attached than the test train), it still holds all speed records for passenger train travel. Designed for a top speed of 250 mph with two engine units and 10 cars attached, its current peak speed is limited to 168 mph on its high-speed lines to east and southeast France, and 186 mph on its newer Atlantic routes. At these speeds, you can travel in half the time a conventional SNCF train requires. By using the TGV, you are rewarded with extra hours at your destination, instead of wasting time in transit.

About This Book

The purpose of *France on the TGV* is to show independent travelers how to use the TGV network to see more of France. Section One details how to plan a trip to France—what to take, when to go, how to organize an itinerary of TGV cities, how to survive in France with minimum difficulty, and how to use the TGV system. You'll learn how to buy TGV tickets, make reservations, use rail passes, decipher a train schedule, and find your way around a train station.

Although this book does not go into great detail about Paris—there are many fine books on the city alone—it will discuss Paris' role in the TGV system and how to use the city as a base to explore France via the TGV. Since most travelers enter France by flying into Roissy-Charles de Gaulle or Orly airports, all transportation links from these airports to the Paris TGV train stations are discussed.

Section Two explores the best of France. Organized into 11 regional chapters, this section will help you discover the historic sights and major attractions of 53 cities currently served by the TGV, plus suggest a walking tour of each city. Also included for each city are TGV schedule information, directions to the tourist information office from the train station, and a hotel and restaurant listing with directions.

No matter what cities you choose to visit, each will give a unique view of France—and a lasting memory. By following this book's recommendations, you will definitely increase your sightseeing in France, no matter how long your trip. As *France on the TGV* illustrates, no destination in France is too far away when traveling on the TGV.

A prime example is the Paris to Nice TGV route. Before the TGV, it took 10-12 hours to connect these cities by train. On the TGV, you can leave Paris in the morning and still have a few hours to get a suntan on the French Riviera that afternoon.

For visitors to France—so rich in history, art, architecture, cuisine, culture, and natural attractions—this time savings is a windfall. Wherever you travel in France, you'll find a unique juxtaposition of the past with the present. Down one road, there's a medieval town, complete with castle and country château. Down another road, there's a modern city with a world-renowned jazz festival. With so much to choose from, the biggest problem in France is deciding what to see and do under the inevitable time constraints.

No matter what those constraints are, the TGV should become your main method of transportation through France. With over 200 million satisfied passengers since 1981, the TGV has become the fastest and most efficient method of rail transportation in the world. When you ride the TGV, you ride the train of the future—today.

Bon voyage!

General Information for TGV Travel in France

You are about to embark on one of the most memorable adventures you'll ever have—riding the TGV, the fastest train in the world. For new travelers to France, the first three chapters give useful information on preparing for a trip to France, including packing and budget suggestions, creating an itinerary, transportation links from the Paris airports to the TGV train stations, and general knowledge about France. Unless you're a frequent TGV user, veteran travelers should read this section too, since important information about the TGV system is woven into the chapters.

All travelers should read the final chapter in this section, since it offers the most comprehensive information about the TGV anywhere. Along with details on getting tickets, reservations, rail passes, and other train services, it offers an overview of the TGV's short history, a look at its phenomenal technology, a tour of an SNCF train station, and a car-by-car tour of the TGV Atlantique, the train that set the world speed record.

Planning a Trip to France

France is such an alluring country that I've known travelers to buy an airline ticket on Thursday and leave for Paris on Friday. With modern travel (and a credit card), nothing is impossible.

However, unless a free ticket is thrust into our hands, most of us need a little more time to plan an international trip. After all, you'll be several thousand miles from home in a new culture and language, where even veteran travelers can find themselves in confusing situations. The more prepared you are, the more smoothly you can expect your trip to go.

Don't make your trip a misadventure by holding the wrong documents, bringing inappropriate clothes for the climate, carrying insufficient funds, and having a negative attitude towards the French TGV conductor who does not speak any English. By following the advice in this chapter, you'll be able to determine how to organize your trip and be prepared for most circumstances when on French soil.

When to Go
Every month is appropriate for visiting France, since the country offers something of interest to everyone. Each winter, the ski resorts in the French Alps are packed with skiers who wouldn't consider spending their vacation elsewhere. In the summer, the French Riviera is body-to-body with sun worshippers. And in a small Breton town on the west side of France, far away from these locations, business and local customs happen as usual year-round, without a throng of tourists. France can be what you want it to be.

Weather-wise and crowd-wise, the spring and fall months are the best seasons to visit France. The weather is usually mild at 60°- 75° F (though I've seen it snow in the Loire Valley in April), and the tourist population is manageable most everywhere. May is a pretty month to be in France, as all the flowers are in full bloom, but it also has the most holidays to plan around. During the winter, although much colder with more chance for rain and snow, crowds and long lines disappear except at ski resorts. Airline, hotel, and restaurant prices are also heavily discounted.

In the peak season from June to September, count on large crowds and higher prices at all the popular tourist attractions, especially in August, when most French go on holiday. Excluding the month of August (when Parisians take their vacation), expect crowds in Paris anytime, even in the winter, when the city is host to many European conventions.

Where to Go

Chapter 2 will help you plan a self-guided tour of France based on the cities described in *Section Two*. Chapter 2 also provides five sample tours for different lengths of stay in France, which can be modified to suit your interests. For exclusive use of the TGV system, this guidebook is all you need. When your trip itinerary includes cities beyond the TGV network, Chapter 2 gives you other sources of information that will help.

The Necessities

Passport: To enter France and return home, Americans will need a valid passport. Even if a TGV trip is just on your vacation "wish list," it's wise to order a passport far in advance of your trip. Depending on the U.S. Passport Agency's backlog, it might take a few weeks or several months to process your form. In emergencies, the passport agency can provide express service, but you must show them proof of an airline ticket with a confirmed seat. If an agency office is not located near you, you may have to reschedule your flight.

U.S. citizens over age 17 may apply for a 10-year passport at a federal courthouse or post office that accepts passport applications, or by going to the Passport Agency office (located in Boston, Chicago, Honolulu, Houston, Los Angeles, Miami, New Orleans, New York, Philadelphia, San Francisco, Seattle, Stamford [CT], and Washington D.C.).

If you're getting your first passport, you'll need to give the official a completed application, proof of U.S. citizenship (a certified copy of your birth certificate or naturalization papers), two identical passport-size photographs, and a personal check or money order for $65 (which includes a one-time processing fee of $10). You must also show your driver's license or other official document to identify your signature.

For a passport renewal, you can apply by mail or in person without having to prove your citizenship and signature, since that information is on your old passport. After completing the new application, return your old passport, two new photographs, and a check or money order for $55 to the nearest Passport Agency listed on the form.

For more information about passports, including regulations for children under age 18, contact your Passport Agency or call their 24-hour information line at 202-647-0518.

Passport regulations for citizens in other English-speaking countries including Canada, Great Britain, Australia, and New Zealand are similar to those in the U.S. (except Canadian passports are valid only five years).

Airline Ticket: Once you receive your passport, all you need to get to France is an airline ticket. In the U.S., **American** (for reservations call 800-433-7300), **Continental** (800-231-0856), **Delta** (800-221-1212), **Northwest** (800-225-2525), **TWA** (800-221-2000), **United** (800-241-6522), and **Air France** (800-237-2747) airlines currently fly directly to Paris from the major East Coast cities and other travel hubs, including Atlanta, Chicago, Cincinnati, Dallas, Houston, and Raleigh. In Canada, there are direct flights to Paris from Montreal and Toronto. Travelers departing from western locations usually stop in one of these cities before continuing to Paris.

To save money, fly during the off-season (November 1-March 14), when prices might drop by half. With airline prices changing constantly, it's best to book your flight through a competent travel agent, who should know of any specials an airline may offer.

Before returning from France, reconfirm your flight. Some airlines request that you do this at least 72 hours prior to departure. Failure to do so may result in the cancellation of your reservation by the airline.

Optional Documents

Visa: If you're staying in France more than 90 days, you will need a visa. An application for a temporary-stay visa, long-term visa, or residence card is available from the **French Embassy**, 4101 Reservoir Road N.W., Washington, D.C. 20007 (phone 202-944-6000) or the **French Consulate**, 935 Fifth Avenue, New York, NY 10021 (phone 212-606-3653).

Rail Passes: The most economical way to travel on the TGV and other SNCF trains is to buy a rail pass, which offers significant discounts over the price of single tickets. The passes are available for second- and first-class seating and for different periods of travel, and they give discounts for other tourist-related services. Chapter 4 gives complete information about the rail passes accepted by the SNCF.

Driver's License: If you plan to take side trips from TGV locations by car, don't forget your driver's license. Both U.S. and Canadian driver's licenses are valid in France. For driving in other European countries, it's best to get an **International Driver's License**, since it's written in several languages. To get one, take $5.00, two passport-size photographs, and your U.S. driver's license to the nearest American Automobile Association (AAA) office. If there isn't an AAA office nearby, send a check or money order for $5.00, two passport photographs, and a photocopy of the front and back of your driver's license to AAA, 1133 21st Street N.W., Lafayette Center 2, Suite 110, Washington, D.C. 20036 (phone 202-331-3000). In Canada, it costs $7.00 from the Canadian Automobile Association (CAA), 2 Carlton Street, Toronto, Ontario M5B 1K4 (phone 416-964-3170). In other English-speaking countries, contact your nearest automobile association office.

Clothes

The type of clothes you take to France depends partially on the region in which you'll spend most of your time, the season of the year, and whether you want to blend in with the French or stand out as a tourist. The French, on the whole, dress conservatively and very fashionably, though recently they've taken to wearing more casual clothes. It's common to see people (except the elderly) wearing jeans, sweatsuits in flashy colors, and stylish walking and running shoes. However, unless you're in a beach or resort area, do not wear shorts to churches, cathedrals, or restaurants. It's considered disrespectful by the French, and you may be denied entry.

No matter what month you travel in France, you'll appreciate a raincoat and an umbrella. Pack at least one dressy outfit or suit with proper accessories, in case you visit an upscale restaurant, nightclub, or a French person's home. For travel during the spring and fall months, pack a sweater or warm jacket. While the daytime temperatures are mild, morning and evening can be chilly.

Unless you're staying at hotels with an on-site laundry and dry cleaning service, most hotels will let you wash clothes in the bathroom sink (if you hang them to dry in the bathtub or shower, not in the room where they'll drip on the carpet and furniture). Woolite and other liquid detergents are available in small travel packets for this task.

Therefore, it's unnecessary to take a lot of clothes with you. Even if your hotel has a "no clothes washing in the room" policy posted, wash them in the early evening before you go to supper. Your clothes should be dry by the next morning. But don't wash heavy clothes like sweaters, jeans, and coats unless they're badly stained, since they can take a few days to dry.

Luggage

The critical factor when traveling is the size and weight of your baggage. The bigger the suitcase, the more you'll be tempted to fill it up. For organization and security, buy luggage with double zippers that can be locked and with several outer pockets to better distribute your load.

Unless you can afford to hire a personal porter, you'll be the one carrying your luggage most of the time. You'll need to be strong enough to heave your bag(s) from the train station platform onto the train, then above your seat into the overhead racks. Plus, your hotel may lack an elevator or porter, so you'll have to carry your bags up the stairs. If you're training for the next Olympics, pack a few bricks in your bags. Otherwise, don't ruin your trip by wearing yourself out with your luggage.

Each TGV passenger car has a continuous overhead rack above the seats, which can accommodate one large or two small suitcases per passenger. Shoulder bags, purses, and camera cases will fit under the seat. If the train isn't full, there will be room for another suitcase overhead, plus there are floor-to-ceiling compartments between some of the cars. But with the TGV's popularity, most seats will be occupied, so don't count on extra luggage space. Never put luggage in the aisle. The conductors will make you remove it.

Each TGV train has a small compartment for excess luggage. Request space when you buy your ticket or make your reservation, and the sooner you make arrangements for extra luggage, the better. Depending on room, you're allowed a maximum of three bags not more than 66 pounds each, or one bag not more than 88 pounds. You'll be charged 60 francs per suitcase for extra luggage, and 120 francs per bag if it's delivered from the train station to your hotel by SNCF personnel. If you can't find a porter to help you, use a luggage trolley to transport your bags to the taxi queue. In this age of economic cutbacks, porter service is being reduced or eliminated entirely in the smaller stations.

To add to the time savings you'll gain with the TGV, avoid airport/train station baggage areas entirely by taking one large, lightweight, carry-on suitcase and a large shoulder bag (men) or purse (women). You'll lighten your load and be able to exit immediately, while your fellow passengers are still waiting at the baggage claim area. You'll also save money on taxis, which often charge extra for each suitcase.

Carry-on luggage also gives you peace of mind, since you'll always know where your baggage is. But if traveling light is impossible, at least travel smart by bringing a couple changes of clothes in a small shoulder bag and a few toiletries in case your luggage is delayed or lost.

International Airline Luggage Regulations

On international flights, regulations for luggage are fairly strict. Each passenger may check for free two suitcases not to exceed 62 square inches in total size (length plus width plus height) and 70 pounds in weight. You can also carry on one bag not exceeding 45 square inches in total size and 40 pounds in weight. The carry-on bag must fit under an airline seat or in an overhead bin, or the airline will make you check it.

In addition to your large carry-on, you can take a purse, shoulder bag, portable computer, briefcase, or camera bag onto the plane. Often though, this rule is overlooked, as you'll see people carry on huge shopping bags overflowing with goods. But when the flight is full, you're taking a risk if you exceed the allowed amount.

Another useful travel item is a portable luggage cart that folds up. When my wife travels with me, our luggage doubles. Since we rarely use taxis or buses for transportation to our hotel unless it's raining or far away, the cart lets us easily wheel our luggage through the streets, airports, train terminals, and subway stations. The only time we have to carry our luggage is when the location has many stairs—a common occurrence in old subway and train stations. When we get to the train or hotel, it only takes a minute to unload the luggage from the cart. Although not listed in their regulations, no airline has ever refused to allow my cart on board as an extra piece of carry-on luggage. Since the stewardesses and stewards have used them for years, it's an accepted item.

Additional Supplies

In small quantities, take whatever toiletries you use at home that you can't be without for the length of your vacation. Most hotels provide free soap, but don't expect complimentary shampoo, conditioner, and toothpaste from every hotel. When toiletries are unavailable in small packages, plastic 35mm film containers work well for bringing small amounts taken from larger bottles. If you run out of toiletries, buy replacements from a **Prisunic**, **UniPrix**, or **MonoPrix** store, France's version of Kmart, all with a small supermarket and bakery on their premises.

Although tap water is safe to drink throughout France, new foods and drinks can still make your body rebel. So pack small quantities of basic medications like aspirin, mild antihistamines, motion sickness medicine, laxatives, and anti-diarrhea tablets. If you run short of over-the-counter medications, head to a Prisunic or most French pharmacies, the stores with the big green neon cross on the storefront.

For prescribed medications, take your written prescription with you so customs officers do not suspect you of smuggling drugs into the country. If you bring vitamins, make sure they are properly identified.

Another useful medical item is a **FeverScan**. Created by the American Thermometer Company (125 Bacon Street, Dayton, OH 45402), it's a thin plastic strip that you hold to your forehead if you suspect you have a fever. It's available in most North American drugstores.

Since France operates on 220-volt AC electricity, you'll need a two-prong voltage converter with proper adapters if you bring any American-made appliances operating at 120-volt AC. Make sure you buy a voltage converter that will handle the maximum wattage of your appliance (listed on its handle or in the instruction manual). To be on the safe side, buy a high voltage converter that handles any appliance in the 50-1600 watt range. Unless you have a dual wattage appliance, don't use the adapter plugs by themselves, since they won't convert the electricity and may damage your appliance in the process.

Appliances to consider taking on your trip are a travel iron or clothes steamer, portable coffee pot or hot coil, electric shaver, hair dryer, and curling iron/curlers for women. Also consider a small flashlight, sunglasses, a tiny sewing kit, a compass if you'll be hiking, and a small alarm clock. If you wear contact lenses or glasses, definitely bring an extra pair.

For picnicking in the park or on the train (as the French do all the time), pack a small water bottle (a half-liter of mineral water with a screw top can be bought in France), utensils, small table cloth, a few paper plates, a small cup for hot drinks, and a Swiss Army knife.

Leave expensive watches and jewelry at home, unless you can afford to lose them. Although France is not overrun with crime, local thieves and pickpockets watch transportation hubs and hotels for easy targets. Solo travelers may want to pack a small container of Mace or a whistle. A money belt, neck pouch, or similar device worn beneath your clothes will keep your money, passport, and credit cards more secure.

To eliminate hassles in case of theft, make a photocopy of all your important documents—passport, rail pass, credit cards, airline ticket, etc.— before you leave on your trip. Leave one copy with a friend at home, and pack a copy in your suitcase. An extra set of passport-size photographs will speed the replacement of your passport, and a photo is necessary for some rail and Métro (subway) passes bought within France.

Photography Equipment

Avid photographers should decide how much equipment they want to carry on a daily basis. A large camera bag filled with lenses and accessories can become tiresome fast. It also marks you as a tourist. Unless you're on a professional assignment, consider bringing one camera body and a zoom lens or by buying one of the new 35mm zoom lens, auto-focus, auto-everything cameras. Add a small flash and clamp (in place of a tripod) if you plan a lot of interior or night shots.

If your homeowner's insurance doesn't extend coverage outside your country, consider upgrading your policy if you're bringing a lot of camera equipment or other working supplies (laptop computer, FAX, copier, etc.). Be sure to register such equipment with your country's customs office before you leave so you won't have to pay duty when you return, in case a customs officer thinks you bought it in France.

As you reduce your equipment load, don't skimp on film. French customs is fairly liberal about the amount of film you can bring, as long as you don't intend to sell it. Film in the U.S. is usually cheaper and fresher, and there's a better variety. If you buy film in France, check the expiration date on the box and purchase it from a department store, where it will be the cheapest.

For best results, bring film home for processing in your carry-on luggage, requesting that it be hand-inspected at airport security checkpoints. According to photography experts, most film under 1,000 ISO won't be harmed by airport x-ray machines, but why take a chance?

Put the film in a clear bag and arrive early at the checkpoint, since you'll be asking the security officer to perform an extra task. If hand inspection is refused (signs in the Paris airports state that X-rays will not harm your film), don't argue. You'll hold up other passengers and may cause yourself more trouble than you bargained for. Pass your film through and hope for the best.

Lead foil bags, boxes, tubes, and wrapping sold in photo stores will provide some protection, though the X-ray machine's radiation may be increased to try to see through them. If you use a lead foil bag, send it through separately so the security inspector doesn't wonder about the unknown blob inside your camera bag. Unless you're conducting an experiment for a film manufacturer, *never* pack film in your checked luggage. To combat terrorism, airports x-ray checked luggage several times with maximum amounts of radiation.

Money
The basic unit of French currency is the **franc**, which breaks down into 100 **centimes**. Coins come in 5, 10, 20, and 50 centime denominations, plus ½, 1, 2, 5, and 10 franc units. Paper money comes in 10, 20, 50, 100, 200, and 500 franc bills. By the end of the decade, France and other members of the European Economic Community (EEC) will convert to the European Currency Unit (ECU). The ECU will probably usurp the U.S. dollar and Japanese yen as the most influential currency in the world.

Currently, one franc equals about 17 U.S. cents (or six francs = $1.00). France's Value Added Tax (VAT) adds 6%-33% onto the price, making some items like rental cars and gas extremely expensive. Fortunately for tourists, lodging, food, and public transportation are at the low end of the tax scale. In Paris, the French Riviera, ski resorts, and other prime tourist locations, expect prices to be 20%-40% higher.

Creating a Costs Budget
For each day you'll spend in France, estimate what goods and services you'll purchase. After your hotel room, the next big cost is food. Breakfast in France, usually croissants or hard bread and coffee, ranges from 15-60 francs per person. French hotels often over-price breakfast; the café down the street might offer the same food for half as much. Stand-up

food counters in train stations have good breakfast prices, so keep them in mind if you have an early train.

A typical American lunch of soup, sandwich, and a beverage ranges from 20-90 francs in a café. Traditional French lunches served in restaurants (often the main meal for the day) cost more, last two or three hours, and sometimes require a reservation.

For supper, excluding cocktails and expensive wines, it's possible to get a good, three-course meal for less than 60 francs. For moderate spenders, there are numerous restaurants in the 90-180 franc range. If wine is a necessity, buy a small pitcher of the restaurant's house wine.

After estimating food and lodging costs, decide what museums and sights you'll visit. The average admission fee is 25 francs per person, though the range is 10-45 francs. Churches and cathedrals are free but request donations. Also factor in other things like entertainment and tours.

Using the TGV as your primary transportation, take enough money for tickets if you don't have a rail pass. The cost of a one-way second-class ticket ranges from 104 francs (Paris to Vendôme, the closest TGV location from Paris) to 445 francs (Paris to Nice). First-class tickets cost 50% more. For each TGV trip, whether you have a rail pass or a single ticket, you'll need money for the mandatory seat reservation/supplement card known as a **RESA**. They range from 14-120 francs, the higher prices for long distance trips during peak travel periods.

If you plan to rent a car, gas in France costs 5-6 francs a liter, equivalent to $3.15-$3.88 per gallon (one gallon = 3.79 liters). It's easier and cheaper to arrange for a rental car from the U.S. **Avis**, for example, has offices in 200 SNCF train stations and 55 airports and offers rental car packages in conjunction with the France Railpass. The Eurailpass offers similar deals with **Hertz**.

Other transportation costs include getting to and from the airport in your arrival and departure cities. From Roissy-Charles de Gaulle Airport, you can ride an express train into Paris for as little as 29 francs or take a taxi for 150-200 francs (plus charges for additional bags and the tip). Some hotels offer a courtesy van, bus, or limousine to and from the airport, so check with your hotel. After getting to the city, bus and subway transportation within most TGV cities varies from 2-6 francs per ticket.

The final part of your budget should include souvenirs. Most travelers will buy something to remind them of their trip, even if it's just a postcard. Although French stores sometimes have more "Made in America" goods than U.S. stores, budget money for that unique French item.

Credit Cards

If you have a major credit card, you won't need a lot of cash if you can eat, sleep, and shop mainly at establishments that accept your card. The primary cards issued in North America and accepted in France are **Visa**

(*Carte Bleue* in France), **MasterCard** (*EuroCard*), **American Express**, and **Diner's Card**. Most of the hotels and restaurants listed in Section Two take at least one of these cards, and the SNCF accepts these cards as payment for TGV tickets, reservations, and other train services.

When you need cash, credit cards will work at some automatic teller machines (ATMs) in France, which work exactly like the ones in the U.S. (punch in your Personal Identification Number and follow the instructions), except your monetary choices are in francs instead of dollars. If the ATM accepts only credit cards issued in France, your card will be returned with an explanation message on the screen.

Traveler's Checks

After determining the credit card percentage of your "costs budget" and making sure you have enough available credit, bring the bulk of your money in traveler's checks, available at banks or directly from American Express, Citicorp, MasterCard, Thomas Cook, and Visa—all of which have locations in France to replace your checks if lost or stolen.

If you're visiting only France, buy traveler's checks in French franc denominations. Many establishments in France will take the "franc" checks directly for purchases. If you need cash, most of the large French banks (BNP, Crédit Lyonnais, Crédit Agricole) won't charge a commission to convert them into cash. Although the conversion rate for buying traveler's checks is a little lower than buying cash, you'll save money on commission fees, and a declining U.S. dollar won't affect you. You'll also save time, since you can often go to regular bank windows instead of waiting in line at the Foreign Exchange booth.

If the franc is fluctuating severely before you leave, buy a few traveler's checks in French francs and the rest in U.S. dollars (or your own currency). When the rate rises while in France, trade U.S. dollar traveler's checks for francs. When it drops, wait until the next day unless you need instant cash. For travel to other European countries, it's easiest to get all traveler's checks in U.S. dollars.

When you buy traveler's checks, purchase a small amount of francs in cash for immediate purchases like transportation from the airport to the city. If you're arriving during the weekend, the banks will be closed, so get enough cash to cover transportation, meals, and hotel costs for a day or two.

You can exchange traveler's checks at the airport during specific hours or in some hotels, but expect a worse conversion rate than a bank's, plus a high commission. And unless you collect foreign money, spend your French coins before leaving France, since banks won't convert coins into U.S. money.

Using Travel Agents

Independent travelers get as much joy from planning the trip as going. Nonetheless, travel agents can be very useful. You can still plan your entire trip, but use a travel agent to put it into action. With airline ticket prices fluctuating madly and numerous hotel discounts available, they can help locate the best prices. They also have a wealth of information about lodging, rental cars, and sightseeing at their fingertips. But, of course, exercise caution. You may discover you know more about travel in a certain area than the agent, and some unscrupulous agents might reserve expensive hotel rooms and tours because they pay a better commission.

If you're shopping for travel agents, test their knowledge by asking questions whose answers you know. Some examples: Does the TGV go from Paris to Lille? Do I need a reservation to travel on the TGV? Does the TGV accept rail passes? When I land in Paris, how do I get from Orly to the Gare Montparnasse? Does the France Railpass give me unlimited travel in France? All these questions are answered in this book.

Whatever travel agency you choose, make sure the agent is working for *you* and wants to get the best deal. When booking far in advance of your travel dates, ask the agent to watch for better prices, since you can cancel one flight (unless it's a non-refundable ticket) for another. (Some airlines may charge you a penalty for canceling at a late date.)

Next, decide if you need advance hotel reservations. Except in very popular destinations, reservations aren't necessary, but they're helpful for your first and last night in France, for a late arrival in a city, or for using a city as a base for several days. When time is a factor, a travel agent can speed the reservation process, and when the hotel needs a cash deposit, the agent can get a French franc money order (also available on your own from larger banks or a currency exchange company). Also, agents can get rail passes fast, since they have regular contract with the European railroads.

A Final Word

Good planning is the key to a successful trip, whether you're traveling for a weekend or a month. Take care of all the necessities before you leave and let adventure take care of the rest.

Itinerary Planning & Suggested Tours of France

A successful TGV trip starts weeks before your departure date to France, when you create an itinerary with the sights and attractions that interest you most. Whether you enjoy art museums, military forts, or beaches, you need to estimate how much time you'll want to spend at each sight, then string the TGV cities together in a sequence that will let you see the most in your available time.

The suggestions in this chapter and the information found in *Section Two: TGV Routes & Cities* will help you make these choices. To help simplify planning, there are five sample tours at the end of this chapter, based on varying lengths of stay. Each can be used as is or modified to fit your specific interests.

Holidays

French national holidays (*jours fériés*) are an important consideration when planning an itinerary. Depending on the holiday, a city may become a ghost town or a tangle of parades and crowds. On May 1, the French Labor Day, you may witness an occasional riot, as political factions confront each other in demonstrations.

On every holiday, tourist offices, shops, museums, banks, historic sites, government offices, service businesses, and a large percentage of restaurants are closed. Train stations, airports, public transportation, and hotels operate with a minimum staff. When the holiday occurs on a Thursday, Friday, Monday, or Tuesday, expect longer closures, as people combine the holiday and weekend with their vacation schedule.

If you're in France during a holiday, join the festivities, take a scenic TGV trip, or explore the nearby countryside. The 13 national holidays in France are:

- January 1 (New Year's Day)
- Easter Sunday (late March or early April)
- Easter Monday
- May 1 (Labor Day)
- May 8 (Victory in Europe Day)
- Ascension Day (40 days after Easter)
- Pentecost (seventh Sunday after Easter)
- Pentecost Monday
- July 14 (Bastille Day)
- August 15 (Assumption of the Virgin Mary Day)
- November 1 (All Saints Day)
- November 11 (Armistice Day)
- December 25 (Christmas Day)

There are also regional holidays, plus several annual celebrations, festivals, and religious pilgrimages held throughout France. The French Government Tourist Office (see *Additional Information* in this chapter) can supply you with a list of these events. You might also want to consult *Festival Europe!* by Margaret M. Johnson, a guide to hundreds of fairs and celebrations all over Europe. Ordering information is in the back of the book.

Fine Tuning Your Itinerary

After preparing your list of cities, estimate how long you'll need to visit each sight, including time off for meals. In France, many historic sights, museums, and retail shops close at noon for lunch and open again at 2:00pm. When the sights on your walking tour are closed, do as the French: eat! After lunch, continue the tour until 5:30-6:00pm, when most sights close for the day.

Most of the city tours in *Section Two* are designed for a full day's exploration, with less time for the smaller towns. If you know you'll spend extra time in art museums or tarry at other attractions, either drop some attractions from the suggested tour or add another day for that city to your itinerary, deleting a lesser-liked city.

Paris in Your Itinerary

Make sure you also allow time within your itinerary to see Paris, one of the world's most beautiful cities, the most popular tourist location in France, and the headquarters of the TGV. It's the ultimate French destination, a conglomeration of all that defines the country.

Paris has so much to offer, a chapter or two in this book could never do it justice. There are many excellent guidebooks to Paris alone, and I recommend you get at least one. My own "highlights list" for Paris includes watching the cars race madly around the *Arc de Triomphe*, the views from atop the Eiffel Tower, a picnic in one of the small squares spread throughout the city, pastry shops, quaint no-star restaurants serving excellent food at reasonable prices, Gothic church architecture, street markets, the elegant covered passages of the 2nd *arrondissement*, the quiet atmosphere of the *Jardin du Palais Royal*, a night cruise on the Seine, the narrow, cobblestone streets of the Left Bank and *Montmartre*, a slow walk down avenue des Champs-Elysées, the elaborate Métro system that takes you almost everywhere in Paris, afternoons lingering at a Left Bank cafe over a meal while watching the animated street crowd, shopping at *La Samaritaine* (the working-class department store) with its store-top view of the Seine, and the city's numerous art museums.

Even veteran travelers to France never assume they've seen all of Paris. Like other large cities, it spawns new attractions every year and keeps renovating its historic sites. By the time you read this book, the Louvre will have more buildings extending underground from its pyramid entrance, and Euro Disney will be open in the Paris suburb of Marne-la-Vallée, the last stop on the RER A-4 line.

As you can surmise, one of the most difficult decisions to make when planning an itinerary is deciding how many days to spend in Paris. Truthfully, you could spend your life exploring this beautiful city! It's tough to reduce it to a few days' experience, but if you want to see the rest of France, you'll have to. For most Francophiles, there will be return trips.

Paris As a Base

One way to spend more time in Paris but still tour France is to use it as a base for half-day or one-day excursions. Until you venture southwest beyond Poitiers or southeast past Lyon, you can explore most TGV cities from Paris in 4-8 hours and have time to return to the city for the rest of the day or evening. If you hate to look for a new hotel in every city, using Paris as a base lets you book only one hotel and eliminates the burden of luggage.

You can apply this base concept to other cities if you want to see a region thoroughly, or you can go from region to region using multiple bases.

Hotel Reservations

When using one or more bases, make advance hotel reservations to guarantee a room and to save time. If you arrive without a reservation, the hotel may not have a room for every night of your stay. During peak season travel and at popular locations, reservations four to six months in advance are not uncommon.

To obtain an advance reservation, hotels usually request a deposit in French francs equal to one- or two-nights' stay, sent via wire transfer or international money order, or they ask that your reservation be guaranteed by a major credit card. When making reservations, ask the hotel about its cancellation policy, which can vary from 0-30 days advance notice prior to the arrival date. For reservations guaranteed by a credit card, you won't be charged anything if you notify the hotel before 6:00pm of the booked date, unless stated otherwise by the hotel. Some hotels will charge you for one night if you don't arrive.

Paris & the TGV

When planning trips on the TGV from Paris, it's important to go to the correct train station. There are six train stations in Paris serving major cities; the **Gare de Lyon** and the **Gare Montparnasse** are the only stations with TGV trains. (When the TGV Nord line opens in mid-1993, there will be TGV service to northern France and other countries from the **Gare du Nord**.) If you are heading immediately for the provinces, these stations are easy to reach from Paris' two international airports (see *Chapter 3: When in France*).

Gare de Lyon

The *Gare de Lyon*, where the TGV began service in 1981, is the home of the **TGV Sud-Est**. From this station, located a few blocks north of the Seine River in east Paris (12th *arrondissement*), the TGV travels to 45 locations in eastern and southeastern France, plus five cities in western Switzerland. All TGV services, including tickets, reservations, waiting area, and departure/arrival boards, are located on the station's lower level. Numbered stairwells lead upstairs to the TGV trains. Direct access to this area, bypassing the upper level, is available from rue de Chalon, rue de Bercy, or the Métro beneath the station.

Similar services for non-TGV routes are duplicated upstairs, where you'll also find **Le Train Bleu**, a famous Paris restaurant designated as a historical monument for its flamboyant belle époque decor. If you stay in Paris on the first leg of your itinerary, public transportation to the *Gare de Lyon* includes Métro line 1, RER line A, and buses #20, 57, and 63.

Gare Montparnasse

The *Gare Montparnasse* is home to the **TGV Atlantique**. From this station, located on the south side of Paris next to the 56-story *Tour du Montparnasse* (the tallest office building in Europe) where the 6th, 14th, and 15th *arrondissements* converge, the TGV travels to 48 locations in west and southwest France, as far as the border of Spain.

As one of the largest train stations in France, the five-level *Gare Montparnasse* is a city unto itself. Besides the standard SNCF services, you'll find cafés, restaurants, a branch of the *Office de Tourisme de Paris*, retail shops, a small police department, a beauty parlor, suburban rail lines, and various offices.

The *Gare Montparnasse* is well-served by public transportation. At its lowest level, you'll find one of the largest Métro stations in Paris. Complete with moving sidewalks and escalators, the station is served by lines #4, 6, 12, and 13, for access throughout the city. Along boulevard de Vaugirard (to the left of the building when exiting from the main street entrance [level 3]) are public buses #91, 92, 94, 95, and 96 for transportation to several destinations north of the station, taxis, and Air France buses to the Roissy-Charles-de-Gaulle Airport. Along avenue du Maine on the other side of the station is the stop for the Air France bus to Orly Airport.

Numerous word and picture signs on every level point the way to locations within the station. There are also large signs illustrating the entire station layout with a color-coded index in English, French, and German. Since TGV services in this station are intermingled with other SNCF major line services, don't look for TGV signs. Instead, when entering the station from the main street entrance or Métro station levels, follow the signs for *Grandes Lignes* up the escalators or stairs until they end in the middle of an open waiting area on level 5. On this floor, there are over 40 ticket booths, some in an enclosed waiting area, where you'll also find racks of train schedules and an information booth staffed by English-speaking clerks. If you haven't purchased your ticket and/or RESA yet, do it there. Otherwise, go to the track area.

When departing, verify that you're on the correct track platform, since the *Gare Montparnasse* is divided into three sub-stations. The main station accommodating both TGV and other SNCF trains is called the **Gare Montparnasse 1 Porte Océane**. It contains track lines (*voies*) 3-24 at the south end of the building's fifth level. The **Gare Montparnasse 2 Pasteur** station, with lines 1 and 2, is for the TGV. Located halfway down the east side of the *Gare Montparnasse* 1 tracks, it is also accessible from the *Pont des 5 Martyrs*, which crosses the tracks south of the *Gare Montparnasse* at place de la Catalogne. The **Gare Montparnasse 3 Vaugirard** is a short distance south of this bridge off rue de Cotentin. Its three lines (25-28) were created primarily for the *Trains Auto Accompagnées*, the double-decker auto transports.

Coordinating Cities on the TGV

After determining the number of days you need to explore Paris, choose your other destinations and read *Chapter 5: An Overview of the TGV Routes* to determine if your chosen cities are on the same TGV line. As you'll discover from this chapter, most TGV lines are tied to Paris.

For instance, you can't travel straight west nonstop from Dijon in eastern Burgundy to Nantes near the Atlantic Ocean. You have to go first to the *Gare de Lyon* in Paris and transfer to the *Gare Montparnasse* to catch a TGV to Nantes. The only TGV lines bypassing Paris are the direct north-south routes to Lyon from Lille and Rouen and a new feeder line through the Paris suburb Massy that connects the TGV Atlantique with the TGV Sud-Est. (This line has opened travel from Rennes, Nantes, Angers, and Le Mans to Lyon.)

If you plan well, you won't have to return to Paris until the end of your trip for the flight home. When the TGV line on which you're traveling ends, use a non-TGV train to connect to a new TGV route. For example, a common connection is from Beziers, where the TGV Sud-Est ends, to Bordeaux, where you can join the TGV Atlantique. Of course, to retain your time savings, use non-TGV trains only when the connection is relatively short.

Getting TGV & SNCF Train Schedules

In North America: To determine the exact time a TGV train runs, get the free TGV schedule and information booklets published by the SNCF twice a year for the periods September 30-June 1 and May 27-September 29. The *Guide du Voyageur TGV Sud-Est* covers TGV travel from Paris to east and southeast France, plus the two Lyon to northern France lines and the connections through Massy. For journeys from Paris to west and southwest France, get the *Guide du Voyageur TGV Atlantique*. Each guide has complete schedule and ticket information for the route system, including ticket/reservation prices to each location from Paris, instructions for purchasing TGV services in France, phone numbers for information and reservations throughout France, various regulations, and information about changes in the system, including new locations and renovations.

Unfortunately, the booklets are written entirely in French (except for a short explanation section in English and other languages). But if you don't read French, don't fret. By following the instructions given for the sample schedule in *Illustration 1* (end of chapter), you should be able to interpret the schedule and pricing. And from the color photographs and station maps illustrating the booklets, you'll get a good idea of what to expect from the TGV. Everything else you need to know about the TGV is in this book.

Note: The train schedules in the *Guide du Voyageur* are created several months before the booklets are distributed and are subject to change by the SNCF without notice. When in France, be prepared to adjust your itinerary to fit new departure times. Sometimes the times are changed by just a few minutes, but it may be enough for you to miss your planned connection. Occasionally, a route is dropped from the system or its service is drastically shortened when there aren't enough regular passengers to merit a specific time slot.

For both guides, call a local **Rail Europe** office or their toll free number, 800-345-1990. (Residents of Connecticut, New Jersey, and New York must call 914-682-5172.) The France Railpass, TGV tickets, RESAs, and other SNCF services discussed in detail in *Chapter 4* can be purchased from Rail Europe, too.

Offices in the U.S.:
- 230 Westchester Ave. (headquarters), White Plains, NY 10604 (phone 914-682-2999).
- 800 Corporate Dr., Suite 108, Fort Lauderdale, FL 33334 (305-776-2729).
- 11 East Adams St., Suite 906, Chicago, IL 60603 (312-427-8691).
- 6060 North Central Expressway, Suite 220, Dallas, TX 75206 (214-691-5573).
- 100 Wilshire Blvd., Suite 435, Santa Monica, CA 90401 (213-451-5150).
- 360 Post St., On Union Square, Suite 606, San Francisco, CA 94108 (415-982-1993).

Offices in Canada:
- 643 Notre Dame Ouest, Suite 200, Montreal, Quebec H3C 1H8 (514-392-1311).
- 2087 Dundas East, Suite 204, Mississauga (suburb of Toronto), Ontario L4X 1M2 (416-602-4195).
- 409 Granville St., Suite 452, Vancouver, BC V6C 1T2 (604-688-6707).

Train schedules for the TGV and the rest of the SNCF network, excluding commuter and suburban routes from the big cities, are also listed in the *Thomas Cook European Timetable*, the bible of European railroad itinerary planners. This 500-page passenger rail service schedule (published monthly in England) is helpful for finding a connection to a TGV city on a non-TGV train if TGV departures don't fit your schedule or you're in a city outside the TGV network. You can buy it from the **Forsyth Travel Library** (9154 West 57th Street, Shawnee Mission, KS 66201; phone toll free 800-367-7984) for $23.95 plus $4.00 for priority shipping. Forsyth also distributes the guide to retail outlets, so try your local bookstore as well. In France, it's sold at the **Thomas Cook Bureaux de Change** office in Lyon (*Gare de la Part-Dieu*), Bordeaux (*Gare St-Jean*), Nice (*Gare Nice-Ville*), and all offices in Paris. Elsewhere in Europe, contact Thomas Cook Ltd., Timetable Publishing Office, P.O. Box 36, Peterborough, PE3 6SB, England.

In France: In France, the same TGV booklets, plus single route schedules, are available from any French railroad station or SNCF ticket outlet. The most current schedules are displayed on large posters in key locations in every train station. Departures are listed on separate posters with a yellow background, arrivals on posters with a white background.

Each poster contains the departure or arrival of each train (beginning with the first train of the day), the train number, the type of train (fast trains are highlighted in red), a list of stops, information on special services the train offers, track number, and the platform for boarding. In stations with minimal rail traffic, the posters are only in one color, so make sure you're looking at the correct column for departures or arrivals.

For the most current schedule, always check the computerized boards in the waiting areas. These boards repeat the information on the posters for all trains arriving or departing in the next hour (or longer, depending on the size of the board). When one train leaves the station, it's automatically deleted from the board, and a new train is added at the bottom. When a train is delayed, it will be noted on the board and announced over the loudspeaker. Since track assignments are subject to change, make sure you check this board when your train is listed. In Paris, Marseille, Lyon, and other large cities that have trains leaving nearly every minute, the overhead boards may list trains for only the next 15-30 minutes. Smaller video monitors on the platforms and station walkways repeat similar information. Arriving and departing trains are also announced over the loudspeaker (though you probably won't understand the rapidly spoken words).

Those planning a long stay in France should consider buying the large paperback *Indicateur Official Ville à Ville: SNCF,* which lists all SNCF routes, schedules, prices, and related information. Used primarily by French ticket agents, it costs 60 francs and is available at train station magazine kiosks and SNCF offices in France. This book is also available in four smaller regional schedule books. The *Horaires du Reseau de l'Est* (*Timetable for the East System*) contains schedules for all train travel east of Paris. There are also guides for the SNCF networks in north (*du Nord*), west (*l'Ouest*) and southeast (*de Sud-Est*) France, plus a series of guides for the suburban Paris networks.

Scheduling Tips
Since SNCF trains arrive and depart within minutes of each other, read the train schedules carefully so you don't miss a connection. One of the hallmarks of the SNCF is exceptional punctuality. Unless delayed by weather or equipment malfunction, trains depart exactly when the schedule says they will. If you ask the station master (the official roaming the rail platforms with a clipboard) about a departure or arrival, he/she will give you the time—down to the tenth of a second!

Missing a TGV train may leave you stranded for a few hours. If you have individual tickets, definitely don't miss the train. Although you can get a refund for unused tickets up to one year after their purchase, trying to explain your predicament to a harried ticket clerk can be a major hassle if you don't speak fluent French. If you have a rail pass and you miss a train, just buy a new reservation for the next TGV with vacant seats if you can't communicate with the ticket clerk.

When using one city as a base, make sure all your day-trip destinations are easily accessible from your base, with adequate return service. On some routes, the trains don't return after a certain hour. A good example is direct TGV travel between Paris and Nice, the longest distance between two TGV cities. The first direct TGV train from Paris arrives in Nice at 5:38pm. The last TGV train departing from Nice to Paris leaves at 1:00pm. Of course, popular routes like this will have return service on other SNCF trains, but it will be *slooooow*.

Your Last Night in France
It's wise to reserve a hotel room in Paris or your departure city for the night preceding your flight home. However, if you time it well, you can return to Paris from most TGV locations in time to reach the airport. But for morning flights, it's best not to chance it. Even with perfect timing, a weather delay or railroad union strike could leave you stranded.

Final Itinerary Tips
Most of all, be flexible. No itinerary should be so tight that you can't adjust to fit the circumstances. A fellow train passenger may enlighten you about a new attraction in a city, and making new discoveries is one of the reasons we travel.

On my first trip to Europe, before the TGV was created, I was traveling by train from Barcelona to Nice. With my thoughts focused on the glamorous French Riviera, I couldn't wait to get there.

A British couple sitting across from me raved about a small fishing village on the northeast coast of Spain called Tossa de Mar. With the French border approaching soon, I pondered whether to make a detour, especially since I'd have to transfer to a local bus at the next train stop to get there. It seemed like a lot of trouble for such a small town, but since I had a Eurailpass, I decided it was worth at least a half-day excursion. If it didn't excite me, I'd go back to the station on the next bus and continue on to France.

I stayed in Tossa de Mar for five days. Complete with a Roman fort and ruins, enough to keep the tourist in me happy, yet extremely quiet and relaxing, it far surpassed my original choices. So I strongly advise: when an opportunity appears, take advantage of it.

Don't feel you must follow the suggested city tours in *Section Two* step-by-step. The streets mentioned are the most direct and easiest way to reach the sights, and by following the directions, you won't get lost. But, if you find a more interesting street or prettier route, or discover an intriguing restaurant not listed in this book, by all means manipulate the tour to create your own adventure.

Vacations shouldn't exhaust you either, so plan time for relaxation. Between every three or four days of heavy touring, plan a day to rest and do chores like laundry, grocery shopping, and banking. France is a big country. Even with the TGV, you can't cram every sight into one trip. Leave room for last minute changes in plans such as an unexpected dinner invitation, a tour of a private château, or just getting off the beaten track to relax.

Additional Information

If you're traveling beyond the TGV network of cities, the best source for information about France is the **French Government Tourist Office.** When requesting information from them, be specific about the destinations and the sights you want to see; otherwise, they'll send regional brochures that give only brief descriptions of major attractions. Also, tell them your approximate date of arrival in France so the information reaches you before you leave.

If you don't live near a French Government Tourist Office or don't have time to write, use their "French on Call" hotline in the U.S.: 900-990-0040 (50-cents per minute). In the U.S., French Government Tourist Offices are at:

- 610 Fifth Ave., New York, NY 10020-2452 (mail requests only) (phone 212-757-1125)

- 628 Fifth Ave., New York, NY 10020-2452 (public information office for street traffic) (900-990-0040, 50-cents per minute)

- 645 N. Michigan Ave., Suite 630, Chicago, IL 60611-2836 (312- 337-6301)

- 2305 Cedar Springs Blvd., Dallas, TX 75201 (214-720-4010)

- 9454 Wilshire Blvd., Beverly Hills, CA 90212-2967 (213-271-6665)

In **Canada**, addresses are Maison de la France, 1981 ave. McGill College, Tour Esso, Suite 490, Montreal, Quebec H3A 2W9 (514-288-4723) and 1 Dundad St. West, Suite 2405, Box 8, Toronto, Ontario M5G 1ZE (416-593-4723). In **England**, the address is 178 Piccadilly, London W1V 0AL (01-629-9376), and in **Australia**, the address is Kindersly House, 33 Bligh St., Sydney, New South Wales 2000 (612-233-32-77).

Maps

For navigating large cities like Paris, buy a detailed map, since the maps from tourist information offices, hotels, and department stores usually list only main thoroughfares. Three excellent maps in book form (with an alphabetized index for every street) for Paris are Michelin's *Paris Index Plan* and the pocket-size books *Paris by Arrondissement* and *Plan de Paris.* Although you can order these books from any North American bookstore, they are considerably cheaper in Paris. For other French cities, the *Plan Guide Blay* maps offer excellent detail.

Sample Tours of France

The following tours, ranging from 7-21 days, offer you the possibility of seeing a variety of France or just the highlights. All the cities listed in these itineraries are served by the TGV, but you'll have to coordinate the type of schedule you want. If you don't mind late-night suppers and have hotel reservations in the next city, you can leave on later trains. Other travelers may prefer to arrive in a new city at an earlier hour. Just be sure the cities you need to travel to each day have enough service so you're not stranded for the night.

Although you can follow these tours verbatim, they are best used as a guide to show the possibilities of TGV travel and to help you plan an efficient and fun tour of France. Of course, the arrival and departure times (using the 24-hour clock) listed in these tours may be different when you take your trip. Always obtain a current TGV schedule and check it against the poster schedules in the station.

Tour 1: The Best of France, Including Paris

Allow 21 days for this tour, plus two flight days. Since this is a circular route of France, some connections to TGV cities will be on non-TGV trains. Unless otherwise noted, you'll spend the night in the last city mentioned each day.

Day 1: Fly to Paris on an evening flight.

Day 2: Arrive in Paris the next morning, check into your hotel, and explore Paris for the rest of the day.

Day 3: Leave Paris from the *Gare de Lyon* on the 7:14 or 8:05 TGV Sud-Est to Dijon for a full day of exploration.

Day 4: Travel from Dijon to Besançon on the 8:50 TGV for a full day of exploration.

Day 5: Today is a long travel day. From Besançon, you'll travel south to Annecy in the foothills of the French Alps via the 9:04 non-TGV train to Bourg-en-Bresse. From there, take the 12:48 TGV to Aix-les-Bains (just southwest of Annecy) or the 16:40 direct TGV to Annecy. Since you'll have a layover in Bourg-en-Bresse, see its most famous sight, the *Église de Brou*. If you go to Aix-les-Bains, you'll have a two-hour layover until the next TGV comes for Annecy (or you can take a non-TGV train).

Day 6: Spend the morning and early afternoon exploring Annecy. Take the 18:20 TGV train back to Aix-les-Bains to make a connection on a non-TGV train to Lyon. Arrive in Lyon in the early evening.

Day 7: Explore Lyon for the entire day.

FRANCE

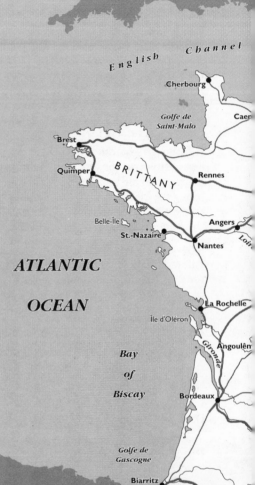

English *Channel*

Cherbourg

Golfe de
Saint-Malo

Caen

Brest

BRITTANY

Quimper

Rennes

Belle-Île

Angers

St.-Nazaire

Nantes

Loir

ATLANTIC

OCEAN

La Rochelle

Île d'Oléron

Gironde

Angoulên

Bay

of

Biscay

Bordeaux

Golfe de
Gascogne

Biarritz

Pau

Gers

Lourc

PYRÉNÉE

SPAIN

CORSICA

Bastia

Calvi

Golo

Corte

Ajaccio

Taravo

Propriano

Sartène

Porto-
Vecchio

Bonifacio

| 0 | 50 | 100 miles |
| 0 | 50 | 100 kilometers |

Day 8: Travel to Grenoble on the 8:45 TGV from Lyon's *Gare de la Part-Dieu* to explore this historic and modern city in the shadow of the French Alps. If you finish your tour before mid-afternoon, take a non-TGV train to Valence to explore for a few hours. Return to Lyon on the last TGV train for the day from either city.

Day 9: Leave Lyon on the 9:00 TGV for Marseille, connecting on a non-TGV train to one of the four French Riviera cities served by the TGV. Spend the rest of the day exploring your chosen city (including overnight).

Day 10: Spend the entire day exploring the Riviera, gradually working your way back to Marseille. Take the 18:20 and last daily TGV from Marseille to Avignon.

Day 11: Explore Avignon's papal palace and other historic sights for a half-day, then take the 11:40 or 14:03 TGV for a short ride to explore Nîmes' wealth of Roman architecture for the rest of the day.

Day 12: Today it's cross-country travel. Leave Nîmes on an early non-TGV train traveling south to Narbonne then west to Bordeaux. There are some direct trains to Bordeaux from Nîmes; some require a transfer in Narbonne. For late risers, take the 12:12 TGV south to Montpellier, where you'll make connections to Narbonne or Bordeaux. Not far from Narbonne on this east-west route is Carcassonne, location of the largest medieval fortress in Europe. If this interests you, spend the afternoon there, then continue onto Bordeaux.

Day 13: Explore Bordeaux in the morning, then travel north on the 11:53 TGV Atlantique to Angôuleme for another half-day of exploration, continuing north after an early supper on the 20:24 or 21:09 TGV for a 50-minute ride to Poitiers.

Day 14: From Poitiers, travel to La Rochelle on the Atlantic coast for the day, returning to Poitiers for the night.

Day 15: Explore Poitiers for a half-day, then travel to St.-Pierre-des-Corps and Tours on the 15:01 TGV, a 47-minute ride. If you still have some daylight, explore historic Tours.

Day 16: Rent a car or take a tour of nearby Loire Valley châteaux.

Day 17: Spend another day exploring Loire Valley châteaux.

Day 18: After a late breakfast, take the 11:39 non-TGV train from Tours to Angers or Nantes. If you continue to Nantes, transfer to a TGV in Angers. Explore the sights in either city for the rest of the day.

Day 19: If you spent yesterday in Nantes, take the 6:32 or 8:19 non-TGV train for a 90-mile trip north to Rennes. If you're in Angers, take the 7:13 TGV to Le Mans, arriving at 7:53, then transfer to the 7:59

TGV to Rennes. After getting a room for the night in Rennes, rent a car and drive an hour to the famed island cathedral *Mont St.-Michel*, returning to Rennes for the evening.

Day 20: Take an early TGV from Rennes to Vannes or Quimper for the day. Return to Rennes for the evening.

Day 21: Take an early TGV from Rennes to Paris, a mere two-hour trip. Check into your hotel, eat lunch, and spend the rest of the day exploring Paris.

Day 22: Explore Paris for the entire day.

Day 23: Fly home.

Tour 2: The Best of France, Excluding Paris
Allow 21 days for this tour, plus two flight days.

After arriving in Paris, go directly from the airport to the *Gare de Lyon* (see instructions in *Chapter 3*) to board a TGV for Dijon. Follow the same itinerary of Tour 1, but you now have an extra three days to explore provincial France instead of Paris.

I suggest taking an extra day on the French Riviera, sampling rough-and-tumble Marseille, or spending half-days in Montpellier and Beziers. In Bordeaux, spend another day in the region by taking a day trip south to Bayonne and Biarritz. After traveling north on the TGV Atlantique, spend an extra day in Tours for further Loire Valley exploration, another day exploring Brittany, or half-days in Laval and Le Mans.

Tour 3: The Mini-TGV Trip
Using Paris as a base, you can explore the city and still see a small piece of France within the confines of a one-week trip. Allow seven days for this trip, plus two flight days.

Day 1: Fly to Paris on an evening flight.

Day 2: Arrive in Paris the next morning, check into your hotel, and explore Paris for the rest of the day.

Day 3: Leave Paris for Besançon on the 7:14 TGV Sud-Est, arriving at 9:47. Explore this city until late afternoon, returning on the 17:42 TGV to Dijon for an early supper. Return to Paris from Dijon on the 21:53 TGV.

Day 4: Explore Paris for the entire day.

Day 5: Leave for Annecy on the 7:24 TGV Sud-Est, arriving at 11:01. Get an early lunch, then explore the city for the rest of the day, returning to Paris on the 19:27 TGV. If you're traveling in first class, book a dinner at your seat.

Day 6: Explore Paris for the entire day.

Day 7: Leave the *Gare Montparnasse* on an early morning TGV Atlantique to Angers or Tours, and rent a car for a full day of exploring Loire Valley châteaux. Return to Paris on a late TGV—21:14 from Angers, 20:59 from Tours, or 22:07 from St.-Pierre-des-Corps.

Day 8: Explore Paris or take a day trip to Brittany or Lyon.

Day 9: Fly home.

Tour 4: Highlights of France, Using Paris as a Base

Tour 4 begins where Tour 3 left off. Using Paris as a base, this tour is for 14 days of travel in France. Use days 1-7 exactly as they are above, and add this new itinerary from day 8:

Day 8: Leave the *Gare Montparnasse* on the 7:15, 7:50, or 8:50 TGV Atlantique for Nantes, arriving two hours later. Explore Nantes for the day, with a possible side-trip to the ocean resort of La Baule. Return to Paris for the evening on any of eight TGVs leaving from 18:23-21:48.

Day 9: Explore Paris for the entire day.

Day 10: Go to Tours or Angers, whichever you didn't visit on Day 7, to continue exploring the Loire Valley. See Day 7 for return times.

Day 11: Explore Paris for the entire day.

Day 12: Take the 7:05 TGV Atlantique to Rennes to pick up a rental car for the drive to *Mont St.-Michel*, or continue to Vannes or Quimper. Return to Rennes for an early supper, leaving on the last TGV for Paris at 21:19.

Day 13: Leave the *Gare Montparnasse* on an early TGV Atlantique for Le Mans. Explore for a half-day and return to Paris. If you're getting your fill of Paris, continue west on the TGV to the pretty city of Laval.

Day 14: Take the 6:45 or 7:54 TGV Sud-Est to Grenoble or Lyon for the day. After an early supper, return to Paris on the last TGV at 20:33 from Grenoble or 21:49 from Lyon's *Gare de la Part-Dieu*.

Day 15: Explore Paris for the day.

Day 16: Fly home.

Tour 5: Highlights of France, Using Multiple Bases

This tour extends the base camp concept by using Lyon, Avignon, Bordeaux, and Tours as short-term bases, with one night in Beziers and Paris. The tour gives a good exploration of France and eliminates the hassle of looking for a new hotel in a new city nearly every night. Allow 14 travel days, plus two flight days.

Day 1: Fly to Paris on an evening flight.

Day 2: After arriving in Paris the next morning, go directly from the airport to the *Gare de Lyon* to board the TGV Sud-Est to Lyon's *Gare de Perrache*. Spend the rest of the afternoon exploring Lyon's old quarter, with dinner in one of its outstanding restaurants.

Day 3: Explore Lyon for the entire day.

Day 4: Travel to Grenoble on the 8:45 or 9:30 TGV from Lyon's *Gare de la Part-Dieu*. Explore Grenoble's variety of sights and attractions for the day, returning to Lyon as late as 20:33.

Day 5: Take the 9:00 TGV from Lyon's *Gare de la Part-Dieu* to Avignon for a day of exploration and your next base.

Day 6: Spend a leisurely morning in Avignon shopping at the market for your lunch for the next two days, then board the 11:40 TGV for a 32-minute trip south to Nîmes. After eating lunch in a Nîmes park, explore the city for the afternoon. The last TGV with return service to Avignon from Nîmes is at 18:50. Non-TGV service from Nîmes to Avignon is as late as 3:05.

Day 7: Take the 10:50 TGV from Avignon to Marseille, arriving at 11:46 in time for a short lunch at its *Vieux Port*. Unless you want to visit this large city, wait until 15:55 when the first TGV train to Nice arrives, or take a non-TGV train to the French Riviera city of your choice. Return to Marseille by 18:20 to catch the last TGV heading north to Avignon. Other non-TGV trains travel the same route if you prefer to start earlier and return later.

Day 8: Leave Avignon on an early non-TGV train south to Montpellier. Explore this university city for a half-day, then continue to Beziers for an afternoon of sightseeing. Spend the night in Beziers, since the next day you'll travel west to Bordeaux.

Day 9: Leave Beziers on an early non-TGV train for Bordeaux, with a possible transfer in Narbonne. On the way, stop in Carcassonne for the afternoon if you wish.

Day 10: Spend a few hours exploring Bordeaux, then travel on the 11:08 TGV Atlantique to Bayonne and Biarritz in the southwest corner of France. (Several non-TGV trains leave earlier for these locations.) Return to Bordeaux on the last TGV departing Biarritz at 18:59 or Bayonne at 19:09, or return on a later non-TGV train.

Day 11: Take the 11:08 TGV southeast to Pau or Lourdes for a day of exploration. Pau is two hours away, Lourdes a little farther. Return to Bordeaux on the last TGV train, leaving Lourdes at 17:38 (18:06 from Pau).

Day 12: Leave Bordeaux on the 7:11 TGV Atlantique for Tours, arriving at the suburban St.-Pierre-des-Corps station at 10:40. After checking into your hotel, rent a car and explore the Loire Valley châteaux.

Day 13: Rent a car for a second day or take a guided bus tour of more Loire Valley châteaux.

Day 14: Transferring to the St.-Pierre-des-Corps station on a commuter train, take the 7:56 or 9:57 TGV Atlantique a short distance southwest to Poitiers or La Rochelle. Return to St.-Pierre-des-Corps and Tours from Poitiers on the 21:21 TGV Atlantique.

Day 15: Take the 7:04 TGV Atlantique to Paris, with the option of stopping in Vendôme. The next TGV from Vendôme to Paris leaves at 12:36. After checking into a hotel, explore Paris for the rest of the day.

Day 16: Fly home.

Reading a TGV Schedule

To the beginning rail traveler, a train schedule looks complex and confusing. Fortunately, most of them are logical if you take time to read everything about a specific route, from new connections to days it doesn't run. The abbreviated schedule on the next page, explained line by line, is similar to the routes found in the *Guide du Voyageur TGV Sud-Est*.

Line 1 is a title bar showing where the train begins, its final stop, and its stops in major cities.

Line 2 is the number of the TGV train. The number in parentheses by the last train number indicates that this particular train has something you should note before you buy your ticket. Dropping to line 26, the message says, "TGV 845 has only first-class cars on Saturdays and on December 24, 31, March 31, and May 8, 19; first- and second-class the other days."

Line 3 line indicates the kind of food service available on the train. A symbol of a fork, plate, and knife on a tray means that meals are served in first class. A crossed fork and knife means only snacks are served. Light meals are always available for both classes from the BAR car.

Line 4 shows the TGV's departure city indicated by the capital **D** symbol, followed by the departure times for each train.

Lines 5-15 are the cities to which the TGV travels from Paris on this specific route. As you will note, not every train stops in every city. Some departures are more direct, others stop at several locations.

The small "a" and "b" listed in the timetable note connections you must make to non-TGV trains to reach the final destination on the schedule if the TGV train stops short. For trains 803 and 807, the TGV ends at Marseille, while 811 goes one more stop to Toulon. If you wanted to reach Nice earlier than 17:38 (when TGV 845 goes the entire distance from Paris), you'd travel on either of the first two TGV trains to Mar-

1 **Paris**		Valence	Marseille	Toulon	Nice
2 **Nº du TGV**		803	807	811	(1)845
3 Restauration		X	X	X	X
4 Paris-Gare de Lyon	D	7:00	7:40	10:23	10:41
5 Le Creusot-TGV	A		9:05		
6 Lyon-Part-Dieu	A	9:00			12:43
7 Valence	A	9:55	10:39		
8 Montélimar	A		11:02		
9 Avignon	A	10:50	11:40	14:08	
10 Marseille	A	11:46	12:37	15:03	
11 Toulon	A	a	a	15:51	15:55
12 Saint-Raphaël	A		a	b	16:46
13 Cannes	A		a	b	17:10
14 Antibes	A		a	b	17:22
15 Nice	A		a	b	17:38
16 **Lundi** (Monday)		4	2		4
17 **Mardi au Jeudi**		2	1		4
18 **Vendredi** (Friday)		2	1	1	4
19 **Samedi** (Saturday)			1		1
20 **Dimanche** (Sunday)			1	1	4
21 **Octobre** Vendredi 26		2	1	1	4
22 Samedi 27			1		4
23 Mercredi 31		2	1	1	4

24 **A** Arrivée **D** Départ   a Correspondence á Marseille
25   b Correspondence á Toulon
26 (1) TGV 845, en 1ʳᵉ classe uniquement les samedis et **24, 31 décembre, 31 mars, 8** et **19 mai**; 1ʳᵉ et 2ᵉ classes les autres jours.

seille, then transfer to a non-TGV train to complete your trip.

Lines 16-20 indicate the slow and peak travel periods for every day of the week—essential for determining the cost of reservations. (In the actual schedule booklet, peak periods are color-coded over the number for easier identification.) The mandatory TGV reservations (RESA) vary in cost according to the seating class, destination, and departure time. The least-traveled period is noted by number 1, the heaviest period by number 4. If the box is blank, the train does not travel on that day. In the case of TGV 811, it runs only on Sundays and Fridays, whereas TGV 845 is a heavily used train every day except Saturday.

Lines 21-23 show peak periods of travel for specific days. When the day is a holiday, the number may be higher than normal due to extra passengers on vacation. The actual schedule lists specific days for every month covered by the booklet's time parameters.

Lines 24-26 define the abbreviations found in the schedule.

The schedule board at Paris' Gare Montparnasse.
Note the numerous TGV routes.

When in France

Most people arriving in France will experience some form of culture shock. Not only is there a new language, but also the French do business differently than other cultures. Restaurant meals are served in specifically defined courses, matronly women guard the public rest rooms, retail stores close for a two-hour lunch, and the second floor is actually the first floor. These are just a few oddities you can expect.

However, the following information will help keep your trip fairly trouble-free:

Arriving at the Airport

International airports are notorious for inducing cultural shock. You exit the security of an airplane into unknown sights and sounds. Loudspeakers blare messages in rapid-fire French, passengers from around the world rush around you, there's chaos at passport control, and your new suitcase has a new dent.

Don't turn back! Accept the fact that large airports anywhere can be confusing. Use a little extra patience, follow the multilingual signs from the concourse to passport control, and continue to the baggage claim, money exchange, and tourist information areas as needed.

When you're finally ready to leave the airport, you'll need transportation into the city. Fortunately for travelers flying directly to Paris, there's excellent public and private transportation between its two international airports and the two Paris TGV train stations. These transportation links and the airports are described below.

Roissy-Charles-de-Gaulle Airport

The Roissy-Charles-de-Gaulle Airport, located 15.5 miles northeast of Paris near the small town of Roissy-en-France, is divided into two terminals. The round **Aérogare 1**, featuring ascending/descending moving sidewalks and crisscrossing escalators in Plexiglass tubes, handles all trans-Atlantic flights (except Air France). In brochures and schedule information in France, this terminal is simply identified as **CDG 1**.

From the airplane concourse (or "satellites," as they're called), take the moving sidewalk or walkway down to the transit level of the building. If you're transferring to another flight beyond, follow the signs to the Connecting Flights desk. Otherwise, go to Passport Control, where you'll need to get into the correct line—one for declaring items brought into the country, the other for people with nothing to declare. After getting your passport stamped and answering any questions the border police may have, take an escalator up to the arrival level, where you'll find the baggage claim area and other services. To exit the building, follow the *Sortie* signs (French for "Exit") to the outer ring of the building, where each exit is identified by even numbers from 2 to 36.

Aérogare 2 (or **CDG 2**) consists of three small, crescent-shaped terminals. **CDG 2-A** handles Air France flights, including the Concorde. **CDG 2-B** and **-D** service other French domestic airlines and foreign carriers. When exiting planes from these terminals, go to the lower level if you have a connecting flight. Otherwise, follow the signs to Passport Control, then to the baggage claim area and other services. The exits in these terminals are numbered A3-A8, B3-B11, and D3-D12. All the terminals for CDG 2 are linked to CDG 1 by a free *navette* (shuttle bus).

A Paris Métro Primer

Whether you travel directly from the airport to a TGV train station or use Paris as base, you'll probably use the Paris **Métro** at least once. This elaborate subway system has 13 lines, totaling 123 miles of tunnels spread throughout Paris and its closest suburbs. The system also includes four **RER** *(Réseau Express Regional)* lines, a combined subway-railroad network providing faster travel through Paris on Métro lines, then commuter rail travel to suburbs and towns up to 40 miles beyond Paris.

Métro stations from the street and inside buildings are identified by signs with a large "M" inside a circle, the word *Métro*, or the word *Métropolitain* written in scroll letters over the few glass-and-iron, Art Nouveau entrances still left in the city. For the RER, look for the "RER" inside a blue circle.

Shortly after entering a Métro station, you'll come to ticket booths, where you can buy single tickets (second-class, 5.20 francs each) or a *carnet* (10 tickets) for second- or first-class travel. These tickets are also valid for travel on city buses. For long stays, consider buying a weekly or monthly Métro pass.

Since you can leave the city on the RER, its tickets are priced according to your destination. From the center of Paris going outward, the RER system is divided into eight travel zones. You may travel on its trains with only a Métro ticket if you stay within the Paris city limits (zones 1 and 2).

To ride the Métro/RER, insert your narrow yellow ticket into the turnstile slot to open the gate, and retrieve it when it shoots out the top of the turnstile. Sometimes a Métro official will ask for your ticket to verify that you aren't riding for free or in the incorrect class. From the turnstile area, or when exiting any Métro/RER car for a transfer, begin looking for the orange and white signs saying *Correspondence*, the interconnecting passages/tunnels/moving sidewalks that lead you to the available Métro lines in the station. After following the signs to the line you want, look for a *Direction* sign indicating the passage/tunnel you need to walk through to reach the correct platform.

The name listed after a Métro line is the last stop in the direction you need to travel. For example, Line 1 ends at *Château de Vincennes* (east) and at *Pont de Neuilly* (west). Large maps of the entire Métro/RER system are displayed throughout the station, and free pocket-size editions are available at the ticket counter. In some stations, electronic boards can show the route you need. Punch the button for your destination and the board lights up, showing any connecting routes.

For Roissyrail and the other methods of transportation listed below, allow 60-90 minutes travel time from the airport to the TGV stations. If you have a TGV reservation on your arrival day, schedule it at least three hours after you arrive at the airport. For the transportation links listed below, all transfers and connections are in bold type for easy reference.

Roissy-Charles-de-Gaulle Airport Transportation to Paris TGV Stations

Roissyrail and Métro to Gare de Lyon or Gare Montparnasse:
Combining speed and economy, the best way to reach the **Gare de Lyon** from the Roissy-Charles-de-Gaulle Airport is on Roissyrail, an RER train (line B). To ride, buy a ticket at the airport's SNCF desk (opposite Gate 28 in CDG 1 and Gate B6 in CDG 2) or exchange your railpass voucher for a free, first-class RER ticket. If you're going to ride the TGV today, get your railpass validated from this official. Then, go outside Gates 28 and 30 at CDG 1 (Gates A7 and B6 at CDG 2) to board the free *navette* (shuttle bus) to the Roissy RER station. If the SNCF desk is closed (common on weekends), buy your ticket at the station and get your pass validated at the *Gare de Lyon*. Roissyrail costs 29 francs for a second-class ticket, 38 francs for first-class.

When you reach the Roissy RER station, proceed to the turnstile area, making sure you retrieve your ticket, since you'll use it to exit the *Gare de Lyon* RER station. On the other side of the turnstiles, stairs lead down to the Roissyrail trains labeled ECHO, EDEN, ERAN, ERIC, ETAL, and ETEL. RER service begins at 5:00am, running every 15 minutes until 11:59pm.

Approximately 35 minutes later, after several stops, you'll exit the RER train at the large Châtelet-les Halles Métro/RER station in the center of Paris. Since stops aren't announced on the RER as they are on an SNCF train, pay attention to the route map posted above each car's doors. At this station, transfer to **RER line A**, next to the track you arrived on. The overhead signs listing the *Gare de Lyon* and other major stops show the correct direction you need to go. **Métro line 1** passing through the Châtelet-les Halles station will also take you to the *Gare de Lyon* if line A's cars are full (common during rush hours). For this line, go to the **Château de Vincennes** direction platform.

When you arrive at the Gare de Lyon Métro/RER station located beneath the train station, look for signs directing you to the TGV or *Grande Lignes*. All TGV services are on the lower level of the train station, so it's unnecessary to exit to the street level—unless you need fresh air and natural light after being underground for a while.

To reach the **Gare Montparnasse**, take Roissyrail to the Châtelet-les Halles station, transferring to **Métro line 4-Porte d'Orleans**, exiting the subway at the Montparnasse-Bienvenüe Métro station. From the platform of this large station, follow the *Grande Lignes* or *Gare Montparnasse* signs up several levels on escalators or stairs to the main hall of the train station and the TGV tracks.

Bus #350 & Métro to Gare de Lyon or Gare Montparnasse:

The cheapest way to travel into Paris from the CDG airport, but less direct than the above scheme, is on public bus #350. Operating from 6:00am-11:51pm, it leaves every 15-30 minutes from CDG 1 at the RATP (*Régie Autonome des Transports Parisiens*; operator of the Paris RER, Métro, and bus systems) sign on the *Boutiquaire* level and from gates A5 and B6 at CDG 2. The trip takes 50 minutes during normal traffic and costs six second-class Métro tickets. (Ticket machines are near the exit gate.) The drawbacks: this consistently crowded bus lacks room for luggage and makes several stops, and you must transfer to two Métro lines before you reach the *Gare de Lyon* station.

To reach the **Gare de Lyon**, travel on bus #350 to either the *Gare du Nord* or *Gare de l'Est*, the last two stops on this bus route, transferring to **Métro line 5-Place d'Italie** to the **Bastille** station. Transfer there to **Métro line 1-Château de Vincennes**, exiting the subway at the *Gare* *de Lyon.*

To reach the **Gare Montparnasse**, take bus #350 to the *Gare du Nord* or *Gare de l'Est*, transferring to **Métro line 4-Porte d'Orleans**, exiting the subway at the **Montparnasse-Bienvenüe** station.

Bus #351 & Métro to Gare de Lyon or Gare Montparnasse: With only one Métro transfer, bus #351 is more convenient for reaching the **Gare de Lyon**. Stopping at the same CDG airport exits as bus #350 and costing the same, bus #351 takes a different route into Paris, with its final stop at **place de la Nation**. Beneath this busy traffic intersection is a large Métro station serving lines 1, 2, 6, 9, and RER line A. From there, take **Métro line 1-Pont de Neuilly** or **RER line A** to the Gare de Lyon station.

To reach the **Gare Montparnasse**, take bus #351 to place de la Nation bus stop, transferring to **Métro line 6-Charles-de-Gaulle-Étoile** for a long subway ride to the **Montparnasse-Bienvenüe** station. Bus #351 begins service at 6:13am, running every 30 minutes until 9:15pm. The trip from the CDG airport to the Nation stop takes 55 minutes.

Air France Bus to Gare de Lyon or Gare Montparnasse: Excluding taxicabs, the most convenient way to travel into Paris is on the Air France bus, which leaves every 15 minutes from Gate 36 at CDG 1 and every 20 minutes from Gates A5-6 and B6-7 at CDG 2. Air France provides this shuttle for travelers from all airlines. The modern, air-conditioned buses have lots of luggage space and provide a comfortable, 40-minute ride into Paris. The bus costs 38 francs and runs from 6:00am-11:00pm. (Discounts are available for small groups: four people can travel on one ticket together for 115 francs.) Stops are at the corner of avenue Carnot and rue de la Tilsitit (near the *Arc de Triomphe*), and at Porte Maillot, opposite the *Palais des Congrès*, a huge convention center, hotel, and shopping complex.

Although these bus stops are on the opposite side of Paris from the **Gare de Lyon**, both are near entrances for **Métro line 1**. At Porte Maillot, go to the corner of boulevard Pereiré and avenue de la Grand Armée (the west extension of avenue des Champs-Elysées). For passengers stopping at the *Arc de Triomphe*, enter one of the Charles-de-Gaulle-Étoile station (Métro lines 1, 2, and 6 and RER line A) entrances along this hectic traffic circle. **Métro line 1-Château de Vincennes** or **RER line A** will take you to the *Gare de Lyon* station from there.

To reach the **Gare Montparnasse**, you have two options. The first is to take the Air France bus that travels directly to the west side of the Gare Montparnasse on boulevard de Vaugirard, near the main street-level entrance. It departs from Gates A5-6 and B6-7 at CDG 2. (CDG 1 passengers can take the free *navette* to these gates.) This bus runs every 20 minutes, takes an hour in normal traffic, and costs 62 francs per ticket. (Discounts available for three or more people traveling together.) The drawback: it operates only from 7:00am-7:30pm.

The second option is to take the Air France bus to the *Arc de Triomphe* and Charles-de-Gaulle-Étoile station, transferring to **Métro line 6-Nation** and exiting the subway at the **Montparnasse-Bienvenüe** station. The main advantage of this option is that it saves you money. Besides your 38-franc bus ticket, all you need is one Métro ticket. In rush-hour traffic, this method also saves time, since the subway doesn't have to stop for traffic lights and other road mania.

Taxi to the Gare de Lyon or Gare Montparnasse: A taxi ride to the **Gare de Lyon** from the Roissy-Charles-de-Gaulle Airport costs 150-200 francs and takes 50-80 minutes, depending on the traffic. After 8:00pm, the fare will be higher. When you enter the cab, be sure the last passenger's fare has been removed from the meter, lest it be added to your fare. Also, note that some Paris taxis have a three-passenger limit.

A taxi ride to the **Gare Montparnasse** will cost more and take longer, since the station is on the south-central side of town. Since Paris is always congested with traffic, taxi drivers usually follow the 22-mile express belt line (boulevard Périphérique) around the city from CDG to reach this station. When you're on a tight schedule, the other methods of transportation described above will be faster.

Roissy-Charles-de-Gaulle Airport Shuttle to Orly Airport: An Air France shuttle bus connecting the two airports stops every 20 minutes at CDG 1 (Gate 36) and CDG 2 (Gates A3 and B10). At the Orly Airport, the bus stops at Orly-Sud (Porte B) and Orly-Ouest (Porte C). It operates from 6:00am-11:00pm, costs 64 francs, and takes 50 minutes in normal traffic.

Paris' Orly Airport

Orly Airport is eight miles south of Paris in the suburb of Orly. International flights are handled at Orly-Sud (south), domestic flights at Orly-Ouest (west). Both terminals are linked by a shuttle bus.

After landing at the five-level Orly-Sud, you'll exit the plane through the transit area (a round satellite building on each end of the building) on a narrow walkway connecting the main terminal on the building's second level. If you're transferring to another flight, follow the signs to the Connecting Flights desk. Otherwise, go through Passport Control, then down one level to the baggage claim area and other services, finally exiting the building. Orly-Sud exits are identified by the letters D-N. Similar instructions apply for navigating the Orly-Ouest terminal.

Orly Airport Transportation to Paris TGV Stations

Orlyrail & Métro to Gare de Lyon or Gare Montparnasse: The Orly Airport is also linked with Paris through the RER system. You can buy RER tickets for Orlyrail (plus get voucher redemption/railpass validation) from the SNCF desk located on the Arrivals level opposite Gate H in Orly-Sud. After getting a ticket, take the free *navette* (shuttle bus) from Gate H or from Orly-Ouest's Gate F to the **Pont de Rungis** RER station (line C). Trains heading into the city are marked ROMI and MONA. Orlyrail service from this station begins at 5:35am, running every 15 minutes until 11:17pm. From this location, RER tickets into Paris cost 23 francs for second-class, 33 francs for first-class.

To reach the **Gare de Lyon**, exit Orlyrail at the **Gare d'Austerlitz** station on the south side of the Seine River. If you have a little extra time and light luggage, take a short, scenic walk to the *Gare de Lyon* across the river. To reach it from the main entrance of the *Gare d'Austerlitz*, cross quai d'Austerlitz to your right, then walk left alongside the river to the *Pont d'Austerlitz*. After crossing the Seine, stay on avenue Ledru for one long block, then turn right on rue de Bercy, which takes you directly to the *Gare de Lyon* and a TGV entrance.

To reach the *Gare de Lyon* by Métro from the *Gare d'Austerlitz*, you'll have to make two transfers. After exiting Orlyrail, transfer to **Métro line 5-Bobigny-Pablo Picasso**. Two stops later, get off at the **Bastille** station, transferring to **Métro line 1-Château de Vincennes**, exiting the subway at the *Gare de Lyon* station.

To reach the **Gare Montparnasse**, stay on Orlyrail one stop past the *Gare d'Austerlitz* to the **St. Michel-Notre Dame** Métro/RER station. Transfer there to **Métro line 4-Porte d'Orleans**, then exit the subway at the Montparnasse-Bienvenüe station.

OrlyVal & Métro to Gare de Lyon, Gare Montparnasse, or CDG: The newest transportation link between the Orly Airport and Paris is the OrlyVal RER train. From the **Pont de Rungis** RER station, this train runs a short distance northwest of the Orly Airport to the **Antony** RER station, where it joins RER line B, which travels north into Paris. Even more important than reaching the city, OrlyVal provides direct RER access from the Orly Airport to the CDG Airport.

From the Pont de Rungis RER station, OrlyVal service operates from 5:45am-11:50pm, runs every seven minutes, and costs 55 francs for any trip to Paris, no matter where you get off (40 francs for passengers with a current Air Inter ticket). The 61-minute trip to CDG from Orly costs 69 francs (54 francs for passengers with an Air Inter ticket). OrlyVal service from the Roissy RER station begins at 5:14am, terminating at 10:57pm.

To reach the **Gare de Lyon** by OrlyVal, travel on **RER line B** to the **Châtelet-les Halles** station (29 minutes), transferring to **RER line A** or **Métro line 1-Château de Vincennes**, exiting at the _Gare de Lyon_ station.

To reach the **Gare Montparnasse** by OrlyVal, travel on **RER line B** to the **Denfert-Rochereau** Métro/RER station (21 minutes), transferring to either **Métro line 4-Porte de Clignancourt** or **Métro line 6-Charles-de-Gaulle-Étoile**. Both lines make two stops before reaching the Montparnasse-Bienvenüe station.

Orlybus & Métro to Gare de Lyon or Gare Montparnasse: Public bus #215 (known as the "Orlybus") travels to **place Denfert-Rochereau**, two miles southeast of the _Gare Montparnasse_, from Porte F at Orly-Sud and Porte R at Orly-Ouest. It runs every 15 minutes from 6:30am-11:30pm, takes 30 minutes during normal traffic, and costs 20 francs. Like the other public buses, this one lacks luggage space, makes many stops, and is crowded.

To reach the **Gare de Lyon** from place Denfert-Rochereau, descend into its Métro station to take **RER line B** to the **Châtelet-les Halles** station, transferring to **RER line A** or **Métro line 1-Château de Vincennes**, exiting the subway at the Gare de Lyon station.

To reach the **Gare Montparnasse**, follow the instructions given for OrlyVal.

JetBus & Métro to Gare de Lyon or Gare Montparnasse: Slightly quicker and cheaper than the Orlybus is the privately owned JetBus, which travels from the Orly Airport in only 12 minutes to the **Villejuif-Louis Aragon** station, the southern terminus of Métro line 7. With longer operating hours and better frequency, this bus is great if your hotel is near these Métro stops: Jussieu on the east edge of the 5th _arrondissement_, Châtelet (_not_ Châtelet-les Halles), Palais Royal-Musée du Louvre, Opéra, and Gare de l'Est. The JetBus runs every 12 minutes from 5:48am-11:36pm and costs 17 francs.

To reach the **Gare de Lyon** from the Villejuif-Louis Aragon station, take **Métro line 7-La Courneuve-8 Mai 1945** to the **Châtelet** station, transferring to **Métro line 1-Château de Vincennes**, and exit the subway at the _Gare de Lyon_ station.

To reach the **Gare Montparnasse**, take **Métro line 7-La Courneuve-8 Mai 1945** to the **place d'Italie station**, transfer to

Métro line 6-Charles-de-Gaulle-Étoile and exit the subway at the Montparnasse-Bienvenüe station.

Air France Bus & Métro to Gare de Lyon or Gare Montparnasse: Air France also provides bus transportation to Paris from Orly. The buses leave every 12 minutes from Orly-Sud Gate J and Orly-Ouest Gate E. The trip takes 30 minutes in normal traffic, costs 31 francs, and runs from 5:50am-11:10pm. (Reduced rates are available for small groups traveling together.) This bus stops first on the south edge of Paris at *Porte d'Orleans*, then travels to the **Gare Montparnasse**, stopping on avenue du Maine near the main street entrance to the station. From there, it continues to the **Duroc** Métro station (serving lines 10 and 13) and the **Gare des Invalides** Métro/RER station (serving lines 8 and 13, and RER line C). From these stations, you can reach the **Gare de Lyon** by taking the **Métro line 13-St. Denis-Basilique** to the **Champs Elysées-Clemenceau** station, transferring to **Métro line 1-Château de Vincennes.**

You can also reach the **Gare de Lyon** by getting off the Air France bus at either *Porte d'Orleans* or *Gare Montparnasse* to board **Métro line 4-Porte de Clignancourt.** Go to the **Châtelet-les Halles** station and transfer to either **RER line A** or **Métro line 1-Château de Vincennes,** exiting the subway at the *Gare de Lyon.*

Other Public Bus Options: Other public buses traveling from Orly to Paris include bus #183A directly from the airport to **Porte de Choisy,** a Métro line 7 stop on the southeast edge of Paris. Buses #131, 185, and 285 travel from the Pont de Rungis RER station to **Porte d'Italie,** the next stop on line 7. Unless you want to sightsee in the blue-collar 13th *arrondissement* where these stops are located (or if your hotel is nearby), you'll do better sticking to the buses already mentioned.

Taxi to the Gare de Lyon or Gare Montparnasse: A taxi to the *Gare de Lyon* or *Gare Montparnasse* from Orly costs 75-100 francs and takes 20-30 minutes, depending on the traffic. Both stations are about equal distance from the airport.

Parlez-vous Français?
If possible, learn some French before you arrive. Even if you lack the proper accent, just trying to communicate in their language will make the French more receptive to you. Don't assume they speak English because it's the international business language. Most know as many English words as you know French. If you try speaking French, they may try their English words on you. Stumbling through each other's language becomes a

unique learning experience for both parties.

If you don't speak French, your trip may not be as interesting and occasionally frustrating, but you can still get through France with relative ease. If you need a service from a French person, or if someone begins talking to you, ask in French if they speak English by saying "*Parlez-vous anglais?*" (sounds like "Par lay voo Awng-lay?"). If they say no, do the best you can with sign language or show them words from a phrase book. In a restaurant, point at something on the menu that sounds exotic. It might be a pleasant surprise!

The French People

Many tourists hold the misconception that the average French person is rude and arrogant. This bad word-of-mouth usually comes from tourists who visit only Paris and never stray far from their tour buses. If you're part of a busload of tourists descending on an unsuspecting restaurant, you may indeed get a surly waiter—but he's probably just stressed-out from dozens of unreasonable demands, such as asking for a menu in English or ordering hard liquor with your supper meal, a definite no-no in French dining etiquette. Try to view the situation from his perspective.

Paris is a fast-paced city like New York and Los Angeles, and Parisians take pride in their efficiency. They have little time for foolishness from their neighbors, much less from foreigners. Parisians, who see themselves as being the best at everything in France, are sometimes condescending toward their countrymen from the provinces. As one cynical citizen said, "Parisians don't necessarily like Parisians, so why should they like anyone else?"

But, even in Paris, there are many extremely hospitable people, and outside Paris, the French tend to be more open, helpful, and friendly to foreigners. Most of them are proud of their home and are glad they don't live in Paris with its problems, pollution, and craziness.

In most French shops, hotels, and even restaurants, you'll find a high standard of politeness, and you'll usually be greeted by the owner or an employee. When was the last time you entered a store in a big city and were immediately greeted with a "Good Morning" or "Good Day" and then thanked profusely after your purchase, followed by more salutations? In French retail stores, this is the norm. Most shopkeepers go overboard to help you make a good selection from their merchandise. In large department stores such as Printemps, a well-dressed greeter is at every entrance of the store to answer your questions.

From my experience, it's usually tourists who are rude, demanding everything according to the fast service they expect at home, criticizing a culture that has been doing business a certain way for over a thousand years. Most of the French are willing to help you with your needs, but let them do it on their terms. ⌐ ⌐ demand to be served supper at 6:00pm, because that's not the way it's done in France. Relax and be flexible. If you don't get frustrated with them, they probably won't get frustrated with you, either.

Business Hours

France uses the 24-hour clock, starting with 1:00am or 0100 hours (also listed as 100 or 1.00 hours). Midnight is 2400 hours. So, to figure the pm time (after noon), subtract 12 from the listed hour. (I.e., when a store's closing time is listed as 1630 hours, it closes at 4:30pm.)

Except in the largest cities—where many businesses open early and close late—and on national holidays, when nearly everyone closes shop, businesses in France usually keep the following hours:

• **Banks** in Paris are open Monday-Friday 9:00am-4:30pm. Banks in the provinces are open the same hours Tuesday-Saturday and may be closed during the lunch hour. Currency exchange offices in airports and train stations are open every day for long hours, some even on national holidays.

• **Cafés** open from 6:00am-noon and close anytime from the mid-evening hours to 2:00am.

• **Bistros, brasseries**, and some **restaurants** serve lunch from noon-2:30pm. Supper is served from 7:30pm-10:30pm, though it is more fashionable to eat after 8:30pm.

• **Churches/Cathedrals** are open 7:00am-7:00pm every day. Remember not to explore a church when a service is in progress. Service hours are posted at the entrance.

• **Museums** and **historic sites** are open 9:30am-noon and 2:00pm-5:30pm. National museums are open Wednesday-Monday; local museums open Tuesday-Sunday. Very popular museums like the Louvre stay open during the lunch hours. Some museums have longer evening hours one or more nights per week, and some offer free or half-price admission one day a week.

• **Post Offices (P.T.T.)** are open Monday-Friday 8:00am-7:00pm, and 8:00am-noon on Saturdays.

• **Retail shops** and **service businesses** are open Monday-Saturday 9:00am-noon and 2:00pm-6:00pm. Stores selling food have longer hours, often from 7:00am-8:00pm and sometimes Sunday mornings from 8:00am-noon. Department stores and essential service businesses remain open during lunch.

• **Street markets** are open Tuesday-Saturday from 7:30am-1:00pm. Some markets are open from 4:00pm-7:30pm, and on Sunday mornings.

- **Tourist information offices** are open Monday-Saturday 9:00am-noon and 2:00pm-5:00pm. In very popular destinations, the office will be open on Sunday and for longer hours during the peak season.
- **Train station ticket counters** are open Monday-Saturday 6:00am-10:00pm, with slightly shorter hours on Sundays. In large cities with frequent service, at least one ticket counter will be open 24-hours.

Dining in France

In France, dining is the national pastime. Food is supposed to be carefully enjoyed, served course-by-course, and not rushed but savored slowly. For a good sampling of French cooking, it's important to know what to expect from the types of eating establishments in France. While all types overlap, they are also very different from each other. They are explained as follows:

Bar: Emphasizes alcoholic drinks, snack foods, and sometimes musical entertainment. They rarely serve coffee and full-course meals.

Bistro: The best way to identify a bistro from a restaurant is to examine its menu; all eating establishments in France post a menu in a front window or on a doorway stand. A bistro serves basic, home-style food like *pot-au-feu* (beef roast simmered with vegetables), *poulet rôti* (roasted chicken), and *tarte tatin* (caramelized upside down apple pie) in hearty portions. The cuisine isn't fancy, but it's filling.

Although some bistros in the larger TGV cities are famous because of their celebrity chefs and clientele, most are small, family-run, neighborhood restaurants preferred by the locals for their delicious food, affordable prices, and homey atmosphere. Bistros are often open for lunch, and reservations are rarely necessary.

Brasserie: When a restaurant's menu has many German-sounding dishes on it and offers several different types of beer and white wine, it's probably a *brasserie* (French for brewery). These lively restaurants, often a combination café, beer hall, and stylish restaurant, are usually open for lunch and serve earlier and later than restaurants and bistros.

Buffet: Usually found in railroad stations and airports, the food and drink in buffets ranges from basic fare to exceptional cuisine, from cheap to expensive. If you see a crowded buffet, the food's probably good.

Café: When I think of France, one of my best visions is of the café, a lively, smoke-filled room with hustling, white-aproned waiters serving boisterous patrons who lounge more than eat in sleek booths or at sidewalk tables. The café in France is more of a neighborhood meeting place than an eating and drinking establishment. It's a place to share gossip with friends, people-watch, play pinball, have a coffee break, buy a lottery ticket, cigarettes, and stamps, and in some, even cast a vote in an election. Usually opening at dawn for workers stopping in for breakfast and closing in the wee hours of the next morning, cafés offer light meals: *Croque Monsieur* sandwiches (toasted ham and cheese), soup, salads, meat terrines, quiche, and all types of beverages.

Cafeteria: Quick and basic ready-to-eat meals with several choices of food, the same as in North America.

Crêperie: A café or small restaurant serving primarily meal and dessert crêpes.

Fast Food/Chain Restaurants: Since the early 1980's, American-style pizza/hamburger franchises and various chain restaurants have grown across France. Like their American counterparts, the menu offers basic food for inexpensive prices. Most chains have longer dining hours, so you can get dinner at 6:00pm or a midnight snack.

The most popular French chain restaurant is **Flunch**. With 113 locations in France, plus a few in Spain and Italy, it offers a satisfactory, cafeteria-style meal with a small bottle of wine for under 40 francs. They have everything from salads, sandwiches, vegetables, and casserole-style dishes to made-to-order steaks and lamb chops.

Restaurants: A restaurant serves meals only at set times, usually requires reservations, offers an extensive menu with several types of food and wine, and is more formal and stylish in decor, food preparation, and service. Although there are many types of restaurants in all price ranges—some specializing in specific types of food or regional cooking—the ambiance of better restaurants tends toward a sedate, leisurely meal that can easily last three hours. An **Auberge** is a restaurant usually in a country inn, while a **Rôtisserie** specializes in grilled and roasted meats.

Salons de Thé: More sedate and stylish than a café or wine bar, tea salons are primarily places to eat dessert over a cup of coffee or tea. Although some feature light meals for lunch, the emphasis is on satisfying the sweet tooth. Many tea salons are extensions of pastry shops, where the exquisite desserts are made. Most are open mid-morning to early evening.

Wine Bar: Often looking like a café, wine bars emphasize wine by the glass or bottle, with light meals and platters of cheese to complement the wine. Most are open from the lunch hour until the late evening.

French Floor Numbering System

The French number the floors of their buildings differently than other countries. The street-level or ground floor of a building in France is essentially floor zero or the *rez-de-chaussée*, marked on elevators as "RC". The first floor (or *premier étage*) is actually the second floor up from the street. The basement is called the *sous-sol* ("SS" on elevators).

Hotels

Hotels in France, whether privately owned or part of a chain, are rated by the government from zero to four stars, plus a four-star deluxe class. Hotels must adhere to certain standards to retain a ranking. When the letters "N.N." are on the ratings sign posted by the front door, the hotel has been upgraded recently by expansion or renovation.

In recent years, the government has given hotels more flexibility in setting room prices, although one- to three-star hotels must post their prices by the front desk. Most two-star hotels in France have similar amenities to those found in North American hotels: a modern bathroom with bathtub or shower, television, telephone, closet, and writing desk. Breakfast is served in a main-floor dining room in most French hotels but usually costs extra.

Above two stars, expect your hotel to have bigger rooms with more furniture, private bathroom facilities in every room, and other comforts like a mini-bar and a hair dryer. The service will also be better, but you're expected to tip. Four-star deluxe hotels are luxury all the way. Pack a trunk full of money, since breakfast will cost as much as a night at a one-star hotel.

On the lower end of the scale, one- and no-star hotels usually have small rooms and lack modern conveniences. They may not have a toilet, shower, and/or bathtub in the room, modern mattresses, an elevator, or a decent breakfast.

Check out time for hotels in France is noon. Since rooms go fast at popular establishments, the earlier you arrive in a city, the better chance you'll have for a good room. If you expect to arrive after 6:00pm and don't have an advance, pre-paid reservation, the hotel will hold a room if you reserve it with a major credit card. If you don't arrive, you'll be charged for one night's stay.

When you arrive, ask to see the room before you commit, since rooms vary in size, cleanliness, and amenities. If you don't like the room, ask for another, and leave the hotel if you aren't satisfied. Sometimes you won't have a choice if all the hotels are fully booked because of a convention or festival in town.

Public Rest Rooms

Public rest rooms, identified by the letters "W.C." (Water Closet) or the word *Toilettes*, are fairly abundant in France, though their type and cleanliness—ranging from the primitive hole in the floor to ultra-modern—varies widely. Privacy also varies; the men's toilets/urinals are often separated from the women's toilets only by a narrow divider. In some locations, you'll also find self-contained, cement blockhouse facilities and the new unisex, space capsule-looking *Toilettes* placed randomly on street-corners in the larger cities. Costing two francs, these easy-to-operate contraptions are one of France's best recent inventions.

Many of France's public rest rooms, especially those in train stations, subway stations, museums, department stores, and public parks, are overseen by stout, middle-aged women, who require 1-4 francs from you before you leave. Don't try to avoid paying—the attendants can be fierce! If a public W.C. is not nearby, a café will let you use its toilet, though it's proper to buy some food or drink before using the facilities.

Public Telephones and Minitel

Most public telephones in France operate only with a *télécarte*, France Telecom's telephone debit card. The size of a credit card, it's inserted in a slot on the phone, and the charge for the call is automatically deducted from the card. When you finish talking, the cost of your call and the credit remaining on the card is displayed on the phone's video monitor. Sold in a 50- and 120-unit card, *télécartes* are available from a Post Office, café, train station, or bus/subway ticket booth. A few older telephones still take coins or *jetons* (tokens).

To call from Paris to a city in another region of France, dial 16, wait for the low-pitched dial tone, then dial the eight-digit number. To call from a French region to Paris, dial 16, wait for the dial tone, then dial 1 plus the eight-digit Paris number. To call province-to-province or within Paris, just dial the eight-digit number.

To reach North America, dial 19, listen for the dial tone, then dial 1 (the country code), the area code, and the seven-digit number. To get an English-speaking operator in France, dial 19-3311 or 19-0011 for an AT&T operator.

Minitel is a small computer connected through the telephone lines that gives access to many different services in France, including airline and TGV train information, theater and art events, and retail shops advertising their current products. You can purchase many services from Minitel with a major credit card (some services require that your credit card be issued in France). Although many French people have this system in their homes, the Minitel is available to the public in large Post Offices and libraries. If you can't read French, you can access an English directory on the system by punching 3614 on the keyboard. After you hear a beep, press the Connection button, then type ED. Minitel costs two francs per minute to use and accepts *télécartes*.

Tipping

To tip or not to tip? Since the French usually tip for any service rendered, follow their lead when the service is good. When the service is lousy, don't bother tipping unless you're a repeat visitor to an establishment that will recognize you. You should tip for the following services:

• **Restaurants:** Most restaurants in France already add a 12%-15% service to each dish. This is indicated on the menu by the words "*service* *compris.*" When the menu says "*service non compris*," a service charge will be added to the total wine and food bill. Tip wine stewards 10 francs.

- **Hotel Porter:** Tip 5-10 francs per bag.
- **Hotel Chambermaid:** Tip 5-10 francs per day when the room is fixed up nicely, including new towels and soap.
- **Taxi Driver:** Tip 10%-15% of the amount on the meter, plus 3-4 francs per bag if not already added into the charge.
- **Cloakroom Attendant:** Tip 5 francs per item.
- **Rest Room Attendant:** Tip 3 francs if a price is not posted.
- **Museum or Tour Guide:** Tip 5-10 francs.
- **Movie and Theater Usher:** Tip 2-5 francs, depending on the establishment.

Value-Added Tax (VAT)

France adds a value-added tax ranging from 6%-33% to the price of its products and services. You can get a refund of the VAT on merchandise if 1. you spend 1,200 or more francs at a single store, 2. your purchases are taken out of France, and 3. your stay in France does not exceed six months. Each store, upon request, has VAT refund forms and instructions.

CHAPTER 4

A Guide to the TGV
& SNCF Services

Traveling on the TGV and using SNCF services is simple once you understand a few key regulations governing the system. After an overview of TGV history and technology, this chapter gives information about buying tickets, reservations, and rail passes in North America and France, a tour of an SNCF train station, and a car-by-car description of the TGV's latest high-speed marvel, the TGV Atlantique.

History & Technology of the TGV

Always fascinated by speed, SNCF engineers began experimenting with high-speed trains in the mid-1950's, breaking the world speed record in 1955 when they ran a test train at 206 mph in the Landes region of southwest France. By the end of the 1960's, several SNCF commercial lines were speeding to their destinations at 125 mph.

After 1964, when the Japanese ushered in high-speed (130 mph) commercial rail travel with the "Bullet" train from Tokyo to Osaka, the SNCF accelerated development of a high-speed train, including investigating magnetic levitation vehicles. "Maglev" trains, although technologically advanced and capable of high speeds, require a very heavy, often elevated concrete runway to travel upon, whereas the TGV can operate safely and achieve high speeds on conventional tracks built on a new type of ground-hugging infrastructure made specifically for high-speed travel. The TGV can also run on existing tracks at slightly lower speeds, as long as there are no severe curves in the route. When SNCF officials examined the maglev system in the late 1960's, they determined its problems outweighed its advantages. Constructing such a system would be very expensive and difficult to build through some of France's historic neighborhoods to reach train stations, often located near the center of the city.

After government approval and funding in 1974, SNCF designers and engineers decided to create a new high-speed train run by electric traction, based on the simple wheel-and-rail concept used for over 150 years. The choice of electricity as fuel was based on two primary factors: cost and environmental impact. By using non-polluting electricity produced cheaply in France, the TGV does not harm the environment and saves the country money by reducing the need to import petroleum. Compared to airplanes and automobiles, the TGV is 25% cheaper to operate on a per-passenger basis, saving an estimated 200,000 tons of oil a year. This exceptional profitability has given government transportation officials the impetus to approve SNCF expansion proposals without major reservations.

Basic TGV Technology

After creating a powerful motor to achieve high speeds, the SNCF began designing a train set (engine cars plus passenger cars) that would be aesthetically pleasing and energy efficient. Since high speeds equal increased energy consumption, the SNCF created a low-profile train with a streamlined nose (built from lightweight metal alloys), capable of hugging the track and cutting through the air.

The next key to achieving high speeds was to determine how to collect enough electrical energy to consistently turn its 12,000 horsepower engines. The SNCF engineers solved this problem by developing an aerodynamic, two-stage pantograph (the plunger-looking device connecting the car to the overhead electrical wires) that gathers enough current to power the engines yet won't bounce off the wires at high speeds or be affected by crosswinds.

Another critical factor: a smooth track that hugged the terrain, had few curves, a minimal gradient, and no level automobile crossings (all traffic goes under or over the tracks). On the Sud-Est high-speed track through the rolling Burgundy countryside, the maximum gradient is only 3.5%. On the Atlantique routes to Vendôme and Le Mans, where the terrain is flatter, the average maximum gradient is 1.5%, with a few places at 2.5%. Since the continuous-weld rails are placed in a relatively straight line, the travel distance to many cities is reduced. When the Paris to Lyon high-speed track was completed, the curving route formerly used by slower trains was shortened by 56 miles.

Nonetheless, it's not always easy to find placement for a straight line. Before any tracks are laid, the SNCF insures the line won't disrupt the environment and ecosystem. When you ride the train, you'll notice the TGV travels primarily through farmland instead of forests, unless it's using a right-of-way previously created for existing tracks. And to prevent disruption of animal migration patterns, tracks have frequent underpasses.

With safety in mind, the SNCF opted for a driver-run train over an automated train, which would have been easy to create. With a good safety record throughout its history, the SNCF decided that the experience of its drivers, who can react immediately to abnormal situations, was more valuable than a computerized train, where decisions would be made from a centralized controller. Each driver, sitting in a specially designed seat that insures the same angle of view no matter his height, has a panoramic view of the tracks before him from the two windows above the engine car's slanted nose. Smaller side windows on the cab extend the driver's field of view.

However, computers are essential to the TGV's efficient operation. At every driver's desk, there's a computer console alerting him to any variance in the TGV's system. The computer tells the driver what's wrong, provides solutions, and advises him of everything he must do to stay operational. Most of the troubleshooting can be done from the engine cab as the driver types instructions into the computer. All this data is simultaneously transmitted to a control center in Paris, where additional advice is available when needed.

Computers also play a big role in the safety of the TGV. Since drivers can't identify conventional land signals while zipping along at 160 mph, these signals are conveyed to the driver on his computer screen. On the ground, the rail line is divided into blocks, each 2,000 meters (6,561.68 feet) long with large section markers and track circuits. As the train passes a section border, information about the upcoming block is instantly sent to the driver. The signals also tell the driver where changes occur in the track, so he'll know when to adjust the train's speed. If this computer fails, another computer trips emergency brakes when the train goes 15 kph (9.32 mph) over the block's recommended speed.

For extra safety, all TGV tracks have fences on each side. All crossings run above or beneath the track, with electronic devices notifying the train if an animal or debris has fallen onto the tracks. With these features, the TGV can continue traveling at high speeds even during dense fog or a heavy rain/snow storm.

Beyond high technology and safety, TGV designers were also challenged to create a smooth and stable ride at high speeds, similar to the comfort passengers experienced traveling on a Corail train, an SNCF train that travels 100-125 mph. They devised a pneumatic suspension system that keeps the suspension stiffer and the cars stable as wheel/rail vibrations increase, and they put shock absorbers or dampers within the frame of the cars in both vertical and horizontal positions. The bogies—the assembly holding the axle, wheels, brakes, dampers, and suspension system together—were placed between the cars so that no one would sit above a wheel. A smoother ride is also provided by lowering the floor of the cars and fitting the traction motors to the body of the train instead of the bogies, which helps reduce the forces acting between the wheel and rail.

Other comforts include carpeted passenger cars with rubberized tiles in the connecting gangways, well-padded seats (pneumatically adjustable in first class), automatic opening doors to the gangways, clean bathrooms, and an air-conditioning system that automatically adjusts the temperature and provides two-speed ventilation so you never feel air moving. Since the cars are fully coupled without any breaks to the outside, climate and acoustic control is assured throughout the entire train set. This also eliminates the click-clack sound of the wheels and other rail noise.

A Short History of the TGV Routes

While the TGV train was being constructed, refined, and tested, the SNCF also had to decide what cities it would serve. Since the heaviest business passenger concentration was from Paris to Lyon, they made France's third largest city the first location served by the Sud-Est route. In the past, a Paris to Lyon train ride took four hours, but on the TGV, it takes two. With TGV trains departing every 30-45 minutes (beginning at 6:15am) and return service operating from Lyon until 9:49pm, business people can get back to Paris in the same day at a reasonable hour, even if their meeting runs into the early evening.

Shortly after the Lyon line began service in 1981, the SNCF created new routes to the rest of France. From 1982-84, the SNCF added TGV service to Dijon and eastern France, Geneva, Lausanne, and Vallorbe in western Switzerland, Aix-les-Bains and Annecy in the foothills of the French Alps, and south of Lyon to the Languedoc and Provence regions, as far as Montpellier, Marseille, and Toulon. And to further serve the business needs of France, it opened a direct line from Lyon to four cities in northern France, which bypassed Paris. By the end of 1985, the TGV added a Paris to Grenoble route, with further expansion into the foothills of the French Alps. In 1987, the TGV conquered the French Riviera, providing service to four cities along the Mediterranean coast, as far as Nice.

Since 1987, the TGV Sud-Est network has expanded rapidly. Today, its trains travel deep into the French Alps to several ski resorts. For people in need of exercise, therapy, and relaxation, a line travels from Paris along picturesque Lac Léman to the spa cities of Thonon-les-Bains and Evian-les-Bains. Across Lac Léman, two more Swiss cities north of Lausanne are part of the TGV network. The line through the Languedoc coastal region now travels as far as Beziers, only 82 miles north of Spain. With the demand for more direct travel, another line bypassing Paris provides service from Lyon to Rouen, and several shorter lines from Dijon and Lyon have made the network even larger.

From its very first trip, the TGV quickly became the most popular train in France. As the TGV Sud-Est proved itself, the Transportation Ministry's proposals to provide TGV service to west and southwest France were approved. In 1989, the SNCF introduced the TGV Atlantique, with a new route running from Paris' *Gare Montparnasse* to Le Mans, Angers, and Nantes on the edge of Brittany. Today, the TGV Atlantique travels as far west as Brest and southwest to Spain.

From its sleek new silver and blue color scheme, the TGV Atlantique was created to be better than the TGV Sud-Est. Having studied the TGV Sud-Est carefully, the SNCF wanted to improve anything even slightly negative about the first system. To give the Atlantique even higher speeds, despite its having more and larger cars than its predecessor, the SNCF changed from a DC electrical motor to a three phase, synchronous AC motor (which can also run on DC current) that gives the Atlantique 1,000 more rpm's than first-generation TGV engines. By using new technology, the SNCF improved all the operating systems and designed a complete interior make-over. From its complex microprocessor to the high-tech suspension system that insures a smooth ride, the TGV Atlantique is a train 20 years ahead of its competition.

TGV Tickets, Reservations, and Rail Passes

Buying Tickets and Reservations in France

To travel on the TGV, you need a ticket or rail pass accepted by the SNCF and a combination reservation/supplement card known as a **RESA** (discussed below). You can buy TGV tickets and RESAs up to two months before your travel date from any train station in the SNCF system (even if it's not served by the TGV) or other ticket vendors. Since train stations are often located in unsafe neighborhoods, the SNCF has opened several branch offices (boutique SNCF) in Paris, Rennes, Tours, Marseille, Lille, and other large cities. You can also buy train tickets and RESAs from French travel agencies, over the telephone, or through the Minitel system (3615-SNCF) for pickup, mailing, or delivery to your hotel—though it helps to be fluent in French for these options. Telephone numbers for information and reservations are listed for TGV cities in the schedule booklets. The SNCF accepts cash, traveler's checks (in francs), and major credit cards.

When buying a TGV ticket and/or RESA at the train station, make sure you're in the correct line. The larger the station, the more specific the lines. Some stations have ticket windows for TGV tickets and reservations only. Other stations have windows saying **Grande Lignes**, which means they sell tickets and reservations for all city-to-city lines in France and to other European countries (includes the TGV, EC, TEE, TEN, IC,

Rapide, Express, and Corail trains). At small stations, all train services are sold from the same windows. It's also important to read the small print on any signs, since some lines may be only for ticket refunds or same-day departures.

At the *Gare Montparnasse* in Paris, you'll find over 40 ticket windows divided between Grande Lignes and **Banlieue** (suburban commuter lines) train service. To help keep order and to give the clerks a chance for a coffee break, each window has a light on a short pole above the ticket booth. Pay attention to the color, or you'll feel the wrath of the clerk and other people in line! When the light is green, the line is open to anyone. A white light means the line will be closing soon, but you can still get in line until it turns red. When the light turns red, the line is frozen. Customers already in line will be served, but no one else can join it. When the last customer is through, the clerk will put a Closed (*Fermé*) sign in the window.

If you have money to burn, take the ultimate adventure and rent the TGV for a party. You can rent a car or the whole train. The cost varies, but, for example, you can rent an entire TGV (eight cars, seating 386) for a Paris-to-Lyon round trip for a mere $36,000. (I tried to talk my publisher into this for a book premier party, but he declined.) For more information, contact the SNCF headquarters at least two months before your travel date at 162 rue du Faubourg-Saint Martin, Paris 75010 (telephone 42-02-50-20). They'll send you a free estimate.

The RESA Reservation/Supplement Card

Before you board a TGV, you must buy a **RESA TGV** (for Sud-Est line) or **RESA 300** (for Atlantique line), a combination seat reservation and supplement card that varies in price from 14-120 francs, depending on the class of seating and the peak demand for the train. (Current RESA prices are listed in the TGV schedule booklets.) The RESA is non-refundable and valid only on the train for which you bought it, so if you change your mind about departure time or destination, you must buy a new RESA. You may purchase a RESA in France or North America up to two months before your travel date.

For people who have rail passes, the RESA is of special significance. Although the Eurailpass, for example, lets you ride most trains in Europe without reservations, you must have a RESA to board the TGV. Otherwise, the conductor will levy a fine (which must be paid immediately) and might order you off the train at its next stop. Some people try to keep moving through the train to avoid paying for a RESA, but conductors usually catch them. Some rail passes state that supplements are waived for their owners. In the past, when reservations and supplements were purchased separately for the TGV, this was possible. But with the RESA, it's no longer valid.

A woman makes a purchase from a self-service ticket machine at Paris' Gare Montparnasse.

TGV Seat Selection for Reservations

Wherever you buy a TGV ticket and/or RESA, there are several items you must request to get the correct seat. If you're in France and your French is poor, hand the ticket agent a piece of paper with all the information discussed below, preferably written in French as noted in the parentheses.

The information needed for a RESA includes your **name** (for groups, list everyone's name and the number of tickets you need), the **date** and **day of the week** you are traveling, the **TGV train number**, your **departure city** and **departure time**, and your **destination city** with **arrival time**. Next, tell the clerk whether you need a one-way (*aller-simple*) or round-trip (*aller-et-retour*) ticket (*billet*).

The last part of your request list determines the type of seat you'll get. You can choose a first class (*première classe*) or second class (*deuxiéme classe*) car (*voiture*), smoking (*fumeur*) or non-smoking (*non-fumeur*) car in either class, and an aisle (*couloir*) or window (*fenêtre*) seat (*place assise*). For travel through scenic areas like the Mediterranean coastline, request the side of the car that will give the best view; *droit* is right, *gauche* is left.

You should arrange for any other service in advance, preferably at the time you buy your ticket or RESA. This includes getting space in the baggage car for extra suitcases, reserving a meal at your first-class seat, and reserving special seating for business meetings, families, groups, and disabled people.

After the ticket agent receives your payment, you'll receive a computer-printed ticket and/or RESA listing all the above information, along with the number of the TGV car, your seat number, the names of the stations the TGV will depart from and arrive at, the supplemental period in which you're traveling, the price, and any price reductions.

Although you can buy a ticket and RESA a few minutes before the train leaves, you'll rarely find a ticket counter without a long line. Also, of course, if you wait until the last minute, you won't get the best seating. If you're in a group, each person might have to sit in a different car—sometimes in a smoking section (even if you don't smoke, and vice-versa).

It's not unbearable if the trip is short, since you can stay in the snack car. (But keep eating and drinking, since the conductors discourage loitering and don't like passengers walking around a lot, especially if you have a second-class ticket and you're lingering in the first-class sections.) But for a long trip with few stops, seat assignments are more critical, especially for smokers. Smoking is forbidden anywhere in the train except in smoking cars—a rule strictly enforced. Even if the train makes several stops, you won't have enough time to get off to finish a cigarette.

Automatic Ticket/Reservation Machine

When the ticket counter lines are too long, you'll see people forming lines at the **Billetterie Automatic Grande Lignes**, the large, yellow, ATM-like boxes found in most stations. But before you rush to one of these machines, beware that they only accept Carte Bleue, Eurocard, and Visa credit cards issued in France, or coins (to a maximum 100 francs). Since no TGV tickets cost less than 100 francs, you won't be able to buy tickets from this machine unless you have the correct credit card. Second-class passengers can buy a RESA for all travel periods from these machines. But first-class passengers, whose RESAs cost 30%-90% more, can buy them only for the less-traveled periods.

The easy-to-use, multi-lingual machines give instructions and questions on a large screen that you touch to move to the next screen and series of questions. After you touch the British flag on the screen for instructions in English, the screen offers several choices regarding schedules, tickets, reservations, and other services. If you touch the square for tickets or reservations, the machine asks about your destination by presenting a new screen with several small squares, one for each letter of the alphabet. For travel to Angers from Paris, for example, touch the letter "A." The screen will list all towns beginning with "A" for train service from Paris. Scroll to Angers and select it. The screen will change to a train schedule for Paris-to-Angers service, followed by questions on your name, departure date and time, etc. When the screen shows the price of the ticket or RESA, insert your coins in the slot on the top right-hand corner, and your ticket will be printed in a few seconds, dropping onto the shelf below the screen. If you're using a credit card, there's a slot by the screen with a keypad for typing in your secret code.

Validating Tickets & Reservations in France

Since conductors no longer stand at the entrance to the train to check tickets, it's very important before you board any SNCF train to have your ticket and RESA validated (date-stamped) by inserting it into a *composteur*, one of the narrow, orange pedestals at the entrance to the train platforms. If you're transferring to another train, have a round-trip ticket, or go into the station during a short stopover, you need validation every time you board a train. The *Compostez Votre Billet* signs over the track areas remind you of this task. If you fail to do this, the conductor will fine you 20% the value of your ticket and RESA. If you can't pay the fine, expect to be removed from the train at its next stop, with a possible visit from the local *gendarmerie*.

If you validated your ticket and RESA but missed your train, return to the ticket counter, where you can have the date-stamp annulled, get a refund, or exchange your ticket for a new train. Although you can trade in your ticket, you must buy a new RESA, since it's non-refundable.

Please note: For TGV tickets and reservations bought outside of France from an SNCF sales representative like Rail Europe, you do **not** have to put them in the *composteur*, since they are already validated. In this situation, **never** place your rail pass in a *composteur*, since it will punch a hole in the ticket, rendering it invalid for further travel! Rail passes require only a one-time validation, performed by an SNCF ticket agent or representative. Only tickets and RESAs bought in France need validation.

Tickets & Reservations Bought in North America
TGV tickets purchased from Rail Europe are valid for six months from their issuance date. You can buy a RESA from them up to two months in advance of your travel date.

If you're on a tight budget and a flexible itinerary is important, buy tickets and RESAs in France, since Rail Europe adds a $10-$15 service fee to every order in North America. Unless you're making several reservations at once, save money by buying them in France.

Refunds in France & North America
You can get a refund for an unused or partially used ticket up to one year from its purchase, as long as the ticket is endorsed by an SNCF official at the station of origin indicated on the ticket. Unless otherwise noted, SNCF train tickets are valid for travel up to two months from the time of purchase. Endorsement at one of the destination cities is not proof of non-use. Whenever a ticket agent asks you to surrender your old ticket, make sure you get a receipt if refunds aren't given from this ticket window. The larger stations have specific windows for refunds and exchanges.

All ticket refunds, minus any special services added, are subject to a 15% cancellation charge. Special services are refundable, too, with cancellation charges ranging from a set fee to 15% of the service's cost—if you cancel at least 24 hours before the departure time on the ticket. Short-notice cancellations for special services get a steep 50% fee.

Lost or stolen tickets, passes, and reservations are neither replaceable nor refundable.

For unused or partially used TGV tickets purchased from Rail Europe, refunds are available only from the U.S. corporate office (230 Westchester Ave., White Plains, NY 10604).

Rail Passes
Rail passes can provide a substantial savings, eliminate the hassle of ticket lines, and are convenient for last-minute travel plans. With a train pass, you can change your itinerary at random and travel on several trains a day if you wish.

The **France Railpass**, **BritFrance Railpass**, and **Eurailpass** sold in North America are accepted by the TGV in combination with a RESA. Order these passes from your travel agent or Rail Europe (call 800-345-1990; CT, NJ, and NY residents call 914-982-5172). Rail Europe accepts American Express, MasterCard, or Visa for your pass and any other TGV services. The prices listed for these passes in this chapter are effective to 12/31/92. After this date, request Rail Europe's *Europe on Track* brochure, which gives current prices and information about every rail pass available. Since rail passes usually increase in price $20-$120 every January, you can save money by buying your ticket in December if you're planning a spring trip.

In France, the SNCF sells several rail passes, most of which favor heavy train users or travelers spending several months in France. Since most SNCF passes provide a full year of travel, they are too expensive for short-term travel.

France Railpass

For TGV travel, the **France Railpass** is the most economical pass to have if you make at least one long distance trip. For comparison, the cheapest second-class pass for four days of travel costs about $125. A round-trip ticket from Paris to Nice costs $148 (890 francs). With a France Rail-pass, you'd save $23 *and* have two days of travel left on your pass.

For short trips, however, the pass won't save you money.

Validating & Using Your France Railpass

You have up to six months (beginning with its date of purchase) to begin using your France Railpass. When you receive it—usually about a week from your order—check it carefully for errors. The upper right corner of the pass should contain an issuing stamp. If you find a problem, call Rail Europe or your travel agent immediately. If the pass is correct, write your passport number and signature on it in ink. Don't write anything else on the pass until you begin to use it.

Before using the pass, you must get it validated (date-stamped) by a ticket agent or SNCF representative at a train station, boutique SNCF, or the Paris airports' SNCF desks. Train conductors do not validate passes; they only check to see if they're valid. The SNCF official will stamp your pass and write the first and last days of its use in the boxes on the pass. To avoid mistakes (which will invalidate your pass), write the correct dates on a piece of paper for the ticket clerk. (Be sure to write the dates as the French do: day, month, year—so April 21, 1993 would be 21-04-93.) If there's a mistake, ask the clerk to make the correction. Don't write the dates yourself, as any sign of alteration will render the pass invalid. And be sure to keep the pass in a safe place, since some passes can't be replaced if lost or stolen.

Aside from the spaces for your signature and passport number, the only place you may write on the pass is in a set of boxes located below the date information. This is where you list your travel days. Before boarding the first train for the day, write the date in ink in the first box, keeping all dates in sequential order. For each pass day, you have unlimited travel on SNCF trains until midnight. When your trip starts after 7:00pm, it's counted as travel for the next day. (Therefore, you can travel in the late evening, stop, and continue traveling the next day within the same time slot.) If you fail to write these dates before boarding the train, the conductor might demand that you to buy an individual ticket. If you transfer to more than one TGV train in a single day, you must buy a separate RESA for each TGV train.

Types of France Railpasses

The basic France Railpass comes in six variations for both second- and first-class travel. In each variation, you have a maximum number of rail travel days to use within a one-month period. With this flexibility, you don't have to travel every day to receive the full monetary benefit of the pass. If you want to explore a city a few more days, you can, traveling on the train whenever you want.

Besides rail travel, all passes include special bonuses for use in France. Attached to the pass are coupons for RER rail tickets (transfers between the airports and Paris), a free second-class pass for one day of unlimited travel on the Paris Métro system, a gift from a Paris department store, and discounts on tickets for various museums and attractions in Paris. (*Note:* Detaching the coupons before using them will make them void.)

The France Railpass is available for children age 4-11 at half the adult price. Children under 4 may travel for free on SNCF trains, as long as they sit on a parent's lap.

Pass Duration	1st class	2nd class
• 4 rail travel days	$ 175	$ 125
• Addl. rail days (5 maximum)*	$ 38	$ 27

*For example: A six-day pass will cost $251 for first-class travel and $179 for second-class travel, based on $38/$27 extra per day.

The **France Rail'N Drive Pass** allows you to combine the above rail passes with an Avis rental car for three days of unlimited mileage within the same parameters on the rail pass. The only stipulations are that drivers be at least 21 and have a valid North American driver's license issued at least one year before the rental, and a major credit card. The rental fee, VAT, basic liability insurance, and drop-off at any Avis rental location in France are included in the price. However, gasoline, collision damage insurance, and personal accident insurance are not included.

With this pass, you may use both train and auto transportation on the same day if you wish. Since Avis has 200 offices in France located inside SNCF train stations, you have a lot of flexibility to visit sights near TGV cities. For example, you can travel to Tours in an hour from Paris in the early morning, where you can get a car at the station and tour the nearby châteaux for the day. From there, you could spend the night in the Loire Valley, or return the car and catch the night TGV back to Paris.

You can also get five more days at a discount when you purchase the pass from an Avis office in North America. Additional days arranged in France are charged a higher rate.

Since rental cars are subject to availability, Avis recommends you make reservations at least seven days before leaving home. In the U. S., call Avis at 800-331-1084; in Ontario and Quebec, call 800-387-7600; and elsewhere in Canada, call 800-268-2310.

The chart below describes the different Avis rental car groups available in France, with the prices based on a four-day rail pass. All cars have manual transmission except Group D.

Car Category	2 Adults* 1st Class Railpass	2 Adults 2nd Class Railpass	1 Adult 1st Class Railpass	1 Adult 2nd Class Railpass	Addl. Car Day**
• Group A (Opel Corsa)	$ 199	$ 159	$ 279	$ 229	$ 35
• Group B (VW Golf)	$ 225	$ 185	$ 329	$ 279	$ 50
• Group C (Renault 21 GTS)	$ 255	$ 215	$ 389	$ 339	$ 70
• Group D (Renault 5)	$ 239	$ 199	$ 359	$ 309	$ 60
Additional rail day**	$ 38	$ 27	$ 38	$ 27	—

*Price per person, based on two people traveling together.
**Five additional days maximum.

The **France Rail'N Fly Pass** allows you to combine a France Railpass with one day of unlimited air travel within France on Air Inter, the French domestic airline that serves 23 TGV cities. Included with your train pass will be a voucher for a ticket at an Air Inter counter. If you don't use the voucher, you can get a refund for it (within 12 months of its issuance date) only if none of your pass package has been used.

If your itinerary includes long-distance travel, the Rail/Fly pass option is advantageous. For example, after flying into Paris, you could transfer to an Air Inter flight for Toulouse or Nice, explore there, then work your way north to Paris on the TGV. Although the extra cost for this pass is about the same as a long-distance TGV ticket, you'll save at least half a day of travel. For an Air Inter flight schedule, call them in New York at 212-245-7578 (address: 888 Seventh Ave., New York, NY 10106).

Pass Duration	Adult fares		Child fares*	
	1st Class	2nd Class	1st Class	2nd Class
• 4 rail travel days + 1 day air travel	$ 249	$ 199	$ 160	$ 135
• Addl. rail days, add	$ 38	$ 27	$ 19	$ 13.50
• Addl. air travel, M class (1 day max.)	$ 75	$ 75	$ 75	$ 75

*Fares for children age 2-11. Children under 2 travel free on Air Inter.

For an elaborate itinerary that includes long-distance travel and side trips to sights outside the TGV periphery, buy the **France Fly Rail'N Drive Pass**, which combines all three methods of transportation discussed above. The basic pass includes four rail days, one air day, and three car rental days.

To determine the price, add $70 to the cost of a France Rail'N Drive Pass. For example: In Category A, the pass will cost $269 for first class rail holders and $229 for second class rail holders. Additional rail, car, and air days cost the same as the other passes and have the same limits for maximum number of days. The costliest pass has nine rail days, eight car days, and two air days, for use within a one-month period.

BritFrance Railpass

In anticipation of the late-1993 opening of the English Channel Tunnel ("Chunnel") connecting France and Great Britain, the SNCF and British Rail introduced the **BritFrance Railpass** for both first- and second-class travel. A bonus of this pass, which offers unlimited rail travel in both countries within two different time periods, is a free round-trip Channel crossing by catamaran or on the Hovercraft operated by Hoverspeed between Boulogne, France and Dover, England. You must make reservations ($3-$6 per crossing) through Rail Europe, at a train station in England or France, or at the Hoverspeed office in Paris (135 rue La Fayette; phone 42-85-44-55). When the Channel Tunnel opens, you'll be able to travel on the TGV from Paris to London in under three hours. (Note: Boulogne is not served by the TGV, but there is frequent service on express trains from Paris, Amiens, Arras, and Lille.)

This pass has similar regulations as the France Railpass. The BritFrance Railpass is available for children age 4-11 at half the adult price.

| Pass Duration | Adult | | Youth 12-25 |
	1st Class	2nd Class	2nd Class
• 5 rail travel days used within 15 days	$ 335	$ 249	$ 199
• 10 rail travel days used within 1 month	$ 505	$ 385	$ 299

Travelers exploring England and France should also investigate the **Brit-France Rail Drive Pass,** which provides five days of unlimited train travel and three days of rental car through Avis, with unlimited mileage—good in either or both countries—within a 15-day period. The pass also grants a round-trip Channel crossing on the Hovercraft or catamaran between Dover, England, and Boulogne, France. With first-class rail travel, the pass costs $399 per person (based on two people traveling). With second-class rail travel, it's $315 per person. For more information, contact Rail Europe.

Eurailpass

For extensive travel in France and other European countries, the **Eurailpass** is a good buy if you're going long distances and prefer first-class seating. (There's no second-class Eurailpass for people over age 26.) Offered by the European railroads since 1959, with rules similar to those of the France Railpass, the Eurailpass is currently valid for rail travel in 17 countries. You must buy it outside Europe and North Africa, and it's not refundable once used. Before it's good for travel, it must be validated at a European railroad ticket counter within six months of purchase. Eurail-passes are available for children age 4-11 at half the adult fare. Children under 4 can ride free on European trains.

Eurailpass holders also get several bonuses for use in specific countries. Since these bonuses change often, read the information sent with your pass carefully before you plan your itinerary. Recent bonuses for France included free ferry crossings (except for a small port tax) on the luxurious Irish Continental Line from Le Havre and Cherbourg to Ireland, a free one-day ticket on the private railroad *Chemins de Fer de la Provence* (based in Nice), Europabus discounts, and car rental discounts.

For more information on the Eurailpass, call 900-990-7245 (50-cents per minute).

Types of Eurailpasses

The Eurailpass comes in six variations. The standard Eurailpass resembles a credit card and is good for unlimited first-class travel. The **Eurail Youthpass,** for people under age 26, offers a similar deal, except it's for second-class travel. (It's still valid if your 26th birthday occurs after the pass has been validated.)

Pass Duration for Unlimited 1st Class Travel	Eurail Price	Eurail Youthpass Price
• 15 days	$ 430	N/A
• 21 days	$ 550	N/A
• 1 month	$ 680	$ 470
• 2 months	$ 920	$ 640
• 3 months	$ 1,150	N/A

Another option, the **Eurail Flexipass**, offers varying travel time in first class, but buy it only if you're going to other European countries, since similar France Railpasses are cheaper and also offer second-class seating. A **Youth Flexipass**, with the same regulations as the Eurail Youthpass, is available for 15 days of second-class in two months ($420).

Pass Duration	Eurail Flexipass price
• 5 days of travel in 15 days	$ 280
• 9 days of travel in 21 days	$ 450
• 14 days of travel in 1 month	$ 610

For two or more people traveling together, the **Eurail Saverpass**, with unlimited first-class travel for 15 days, can save you almost 27% off the standard Eurailpass. Most Saverpass regulations are the same as the other passes, but there are a few different requirements to note. First, each pass needs a minimum number of travelers, which varies depending on peak travel seasons. Second, each person pays the pass fee listed below. One person in the party receives a **master pass**; the rest get a supporting ticket cross-referenced to the master. With this pass, the group must sit together in the same car, since the number of people in the group is listed on the pass. Children count toward the number of passengers needed for this pass, with free and half fares still in effect. The Saverpass is an excellent buy if you plan to be on the train nearly every day and cover a lot of territory.

Pass Duration Unlimited 1st Class Travel	Saverpass Price per person	Minimum number required to travel together	
		(4/1-9/30)	(10/1-3/31)
• 15 days	$ 340	3 people	2 people

In conjunction with Hertz, the Eurail system also offers a rail-auto package **EurailDrive Pass**, which offers a minimum plan of four days unlimited first-class rail travel, plus three days of car rental (to be used within 21 days). You may also buy up to five additional train and/or car days at a discount. Hertz, with 350 offices in France, has regulations similar to Avis (described above), except that different drop-off charges apply. The prices below are charges per person.

Car Category	2 adults	1 adult	Extra Days
• Group A (economy)	$ 269	$ 439	$ 50
• Group B (compact)	$ 299	$ 489	$ 65
• Group C (mid-size)	$ 309	$ 509	$ 75
• Addl. rail day	$ 40	$ 40	—
• 3rd person sharing car	$ 179	—	—

Rail Pass Refunds

Rail Europe will issue refunds for totally unused, non-validated France Railpasses and BritFrance Railpasses still in the ticket jacket with all the coupons attached. All refunds are subject to a 15% cancellation charge. You must return the pass to the issuing office within 12 months from the date of issuance, unless otherwise noted on the pass. There are no refunds for partially used passes. If you get the pass validated and then can't use any of it, you can't get a refund. Nor can you get a refund for lost or stolen passes.

Eurailpasses have the same refund regulations except that in the case of loss or theft, a Eurail Aid Office in Europe will replace the standard Eurailpass for a fee, after you present the original validation slip (no photocopies) and a police report. (You'll get a list of these offices with your pass.) For $8, the Eurail Flexipass will be replaced during the first eight days of validity and for a pro-rated number of days.

Eurail offers **pass protection insurance** (about 3% of the pass price) through Travel Assistance International. This insurance, which you must buy within 72 hours of receipt of your Eurailpass, will reimburse you when you return home for the cost of a replacement pass from a Eurail Aid Office. For more information on this and other forms of travel insurance, call 800-821-2828 in the U.S., or 800-368-7878 (ext. 422) in Canada.

SNCF Rail Passes/Discounts Bought in France

The SNCF sells several rail passes that offer substantial discounts on "blue days" (low capacity passenger travel days) and "white days" (slightly heavier capacity travel) tickets. To know when these days occur, get the brochure *Calendrier Voyageurs* from an SNCF train station schedule rack or a ticket agent. Blue days range from noon Saturday to 3:00pm Sunday, and from noon Monday to noon Friday. White days run from noon Friday to noon Saturday, and from 3:00pm Sunday to noon Monday, plus a few public holidays. A few "red days" indicate heavy travel, such as December 20-22, when many people are traveling for the holidays.

For the younger set, a **Carte Kiwi** gives children age 4-16 a 50% discount during blue and white days. Up to four children can travel on the same card, and they must be accompanied by an adult. The card costs 395 francs and is good on any SNCF train one year from the date of purchase. Children under 4 ride free on SNCF trains as long as they sit on a parent's lap.

The **Carte Jeune** gives youths age 12-26 (with an I.D. card) a 50% reduction during blue days from June 1-September 30. Discounts are also given for other services, including one free *couchette* (a fold-out seat for sleeping, available only on non-TGV trains) and half off the Dieppe-Newhaven, England ferry. The **Carte Carré**, valid for one year, gives the same age group a 50% reduction for four rail trips during blue days, or 20% off for trips on a white day. Both passes cost 190 francs.

The **Carrissimo Pass** has the same stipulations as the Carte Carré, except that up to four people can travel on the same pass, and its holders have a choice of up to eight rail trips. A four-trip pass costs 190 francs, an eight-trip pass costs 350 francs. This pass is not good on the TGV during its peak periods (indicated by #4 in the TGV schedule booklets).

The **Carte Vermeil**, valid for one year, gives men over 62 and women over 60 a 50% reduction during blue days. It costs 165 francs.

A slightly different pass, the **Carte Couple** can be used only when two adults over 26 travel together. With this free pass, valid for five years, one person pays the full fare, and the other gets a 50% discount during blue periods. The **Carte Famille** operates similarly: when one person pays full fare, family members get 50% reductions.

For frequent travel on the same route, the economical **Carte Demi-tarif** offers 50% discounts for specific routes or for travel within certain rail traffic zones. With France divided into 16 zones, this pass is a bargain for travelers staying long-term in one or more connecting regions. It has six-month or one-year validity periods for as many routes and zones you want. A similar pass is **L'Abonnement à Libre Circulation**, which offers unlimited monthly travel in one or more traffic zones—another bargain if you're doing heavy exploring in specific regions. French businesspeople often buy this pass for all 16 zones. Seat reservations and supplements are included in its price.

A **Billet Séjour** ("excursion ticket") offers a 25% discount for a round-trip under 1,000 kilometers (621.39 miles). You must travel on blue days, and you must return within two months of your departure.

Other Rail Passes Valid in France

European and North African residents under age 26 can buy an **Inter-Rail Card**, which entitles them to one month of unlimited second-class travel in 23 countries, including France. Discounts of 50% are available in the country where you buy the card and in countries not in the Inter-Rail system. The **Inter-Rail + Boat Card** adds free travel on some ferries, and the **Inter-Rail-Flexi Card** lets you choose ten days of travel within a 30-day period. The **Inter-Rail 26 + Card**, sold only in Scandinavian countries, allows those over age 26 the same benefits as the Inter-Rail Card for youth.

Permanent European residents age 60 or older who have a European national senior citizen card can buy the **Rail Europe Senior Card** (RES Card), which gives 30%-50% reductions for travel in 21 European countries. The pass, sold at train stations in the participating countries, does have strict regulations. In France, for example, it's invalid for travel from noon Friday to noon Saturday, noon Sunday to noon Monday, on "red" days, and on certain holidays.

The **Rail Europe Family Card** (REF Card) allows family groups (3-8 people residing at the same address) similar travel, except that the first person listed on the card pays full fare, while the others get up to 50% off. The RES and REF cards are valid for one year from their issuance date and are accepted in France.

Discovering the SNCF Train Station

For some TGV travelers, the train station is simply a place to board the train. For others, it's a major cultural experience. Often located in the heart of the city, the SNCF train station is a center of French life. Excluding the markets, parks, and department stores, it's where you'll find a large percentage of the local population. Many are fellow passengers, while others are there to meet relatives, use the services (package delivery, newsstands, rental cars, and restaurants), or just hang out with a regular group of loiterers (from teenagers to the homeless).

In large cities, the train station is a city unto itself, with services and products as diverse as a shopping mall. In all stations, there are crowds of people, noise, and loud-speaker announcements that can't be heard above the din. Train after train unloads its passengers and takes on new people. In the arrival hall—slightly calmer but not necessarily quieter—people examine schedules, wait for tickets, and kill time in the shops.

It can be quite confusing if you don't know what to expect. Since every train station in France offers similar services, the following—based on the station in Tours—is a basic tour of the floor plan and essential services found in any SNCF station.

As you'll see on page 82, the tracks dead-end inside the station. This is common in cities where the train goes deep into the center of the city. One of the SNCF's early goals for the TGV was to connect city centers with city centers. To do this, the TGV developed a train with an engine car on each end for easy reversals.

In cities where the train lines pass completely through the city or on the edge of town, the tracks are usually on one side of the station, connected to each other through underground passageways. There will be poster schedules or video monitors on every level and track platform.

Please note: The older stations have a lot of stairs and lack escalators and elevators, making it difficult for elderly and handicapped passengers. If you need assistance, have a porter, *Agent d'Accueil* (SNCF information officer), policeman, or fellow passenger help you. As the TGV continues a renovation program to expand and modernize all the stations it serves, there will be better accessibility.

The Gare SNCF in Tours, France

When you exit the train in Tours, the first thing you'll see are more tracks and trains. At the end of each track, toward the terminal, are orange *composteurs* and signs indicating the track number and destinations of the current train. Other services in the station are identified by word or picture signs (pictogram).

Directly opposite the track signs in the center of the station, there's a waiting area. In winter, when this unheated station is very cold (there's no way to enclose the track area), this room is often packed with people and luggage. In small stations, the waiting room is usually a few chairs along the wall or in the middle of the hall where the ticket counter and other services are. Waiting areas are identified by the words "*salle d'attente*" or pictograms showing a person sitting, sometimes with a clock and baggage in the picture.

Next to the waiting room, the baggage collection area offers temporary storage of your suitcase(s) for 10-15 francs per bag per day. If porters aren't in the track area, you'll usually find them here. Baggage areas (*bagage*) are identified by a pictogram of a suitcase. A suitcase on a scale represents the area for baggage forwarding (*enregistrement*). A suitcase on an upright cart indicates baggage carts. A tilted cart represents porters.

For cheaper storage, coin-operated lockers (*consigne automatique* or a picture of a suitcase with a key beneath it) are spread throughout the station. A small (12 x 17 x 29) locker costs 5-10 francs; large (24 x 34 x 58) lockers cost 10-20 francs. Each locker, which accepts ½-, 1-, 5-, and 10-franc coins, releases a numbered key after you insert the proper fee.

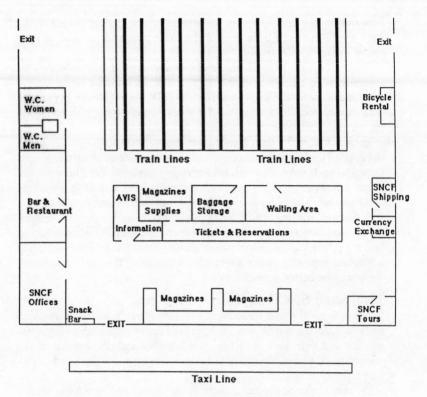

Gare SNCF in Tours, France

A few stations have computerized lockers that eject a piece of paper with a set of numbers instead of a key. To open this locker, you have to punch in the code.

Most locker rentals are valid 24 hours. If you return later than 24 hours and find your locker empty, don't panic! Your bags were probably moved to the baggage collection area, where you can claim them after paying the standard per-item fee. The rental period, noted in each locker's instructions, is 72 hours for some electronic lockers (but they cost 10-15 francs more than the 24-hour lockers).

To the right of the baggage area, a newsstand sells magazines, newspapers, paperback books, SNCF schedule books, postcards, souvenirs, maps, cigarettes, stamps, film, candy, snacks, and other supplies. Occasionally, the kiosks will have English-language publications. Except for pre-marked literature, prices are steep, and most items are 50% cheaper at the grocery store a half-block from the station. Hanging overhead, in the open area fronting these services, is a large, computerized schedule board showing current departing and arriving trains with their track numbers, times, and major destinations.

If you need to use a toilet or take a shower, the W.C. for both men and women is along the right side of the station (facing away from the tracks). Most stations charge a small fee for the rest rooms to keep them clean—a tough job due to the heavy use. If the shower cabinets and toilet stalls are locked, you must deposit your money first to get a key from the attendant. Towels are usually included in the cost, but soap, shampoo, shaving cream, and razor blades are extra.

Along the same wall, closer to the main entrance, is a bar and restaurant. When you see a lot a people in the restaurant, don't assume they're all passengers, since many stations have fine eateries, popular with the locals. As long as you eat or drink something, you can stay in the restaurant until your train arrives—a more pleasant atmosphere than the waiting room. A full-scale restaurant is identified by a crossed knife and fork pictogram, whereas a bar is identified by a wine goblet.

The other doors on the right side of the building beyond the restaurant are SNCF administrative offices. In the corner by this office, there's a snack bar serving hot and cold beverages, croissants, and bread and jam in the morning, and sandwiches and light food the rest of the day.

On the left side of the building (returning to the track area) is the Train+Vélo office, where you can rent a bicycle for touring châteaux—many within easy pedaling distance of Tours. Halfway to the main entrance on this side of the building, there's an office for baggage car reservations and shipping services. Next to it is a small currency exchange office with a high commission rate. Before entering one, identified by the word *Exchange* or a pictogram of money, know the prevailing exchange rate, since a bank with a better rate is likely nearby. In Tours, there are six banks within three blocks of the station.

In the corner of the station next to the main entrance is the small *Services Touristiques de Touraine*. Operated by the tourism services branch of the SNCF, it offers inexpensive bus tours of Loire Valley châteaux in several languages. In other cities, this office is also called the *Bureaux de Tourisme de la SNCF* or *Service de Tourisme SNCF.*

Opposite this office, in the center of the building (the other side of the waiting room), there's a long counter where you buy tickets, reservations, and other SNCF services, with special windows for TGV trains. For quicker service, use the two *Billetterie Automatic Grande Lignes* machines in the same area. In SNCF train stations, ticket counters are identified by pictograms of tickets or the word *billet* (ticket) or *guichet* (ticket office). Reservation windows are denoted by a large "R" and words specifying the items you can reserve.

Next to the ticket area is a combined Avis rental car office and train services information office (identified by a pictogram with a white, lower-case "i" in a blue circle or the words *Information* or *Renseignements*), where you can get the small SNCF timetables (*horaire*) and current information about smaller rail lines. Since the timetables are printed in advance and can change, check with the clerk or read the poster schedules outside the office for the most current times. This office will also handle your complaints and offer help for emergencies. In the larger stations, small train information and *Accueil* (welcome or reception) booths are scattered throughout the building. The multilingual *Agent d'Accueil* officers roaming the station (identified by an orange band on their caps or sleeves, or orange scarfs for female agents) can also help.

A pictogram with a white, lower-case "i" in a green circle indicates a city tourist information booth or annex. The Tours' *Office de Tourisme* is only two blocks from the station, so it doesn't have an annex.

Directly across from the ticket area are two newsstands with the same supplies as the kiosk in the track area. Scattered throughout the building are pay telephones and a few postal boxes imbedded into the wall.

Beyond the kiosks are the main entrances/exits of the station. Directly outside is a long taxi line and bus stops. At the Paris, Marseille, Lyon, and Lille train stations, there's direct access within the station to the city's subway system. The *Gare Routière* (bus station) in most TGV cities is near or next to the train station.

In every city, a ring of shops, food stores, restaurants, and hotels surrounds the station. Multi-level stations like Paris' *Gare Montparnasse* and Lyon's *Gare de la Part-Dieu* have many of these services within the station. Serving both travelers and residents, these shops are usually open longer than street-level shops.

Comparing TGVs

When the TGV Sud-Est began running in 1981, it quickly became the standard for other trains to copy. Unlike traditional European trains—with their boxy seating compartments that cram 6-8 people in like sardines, luggage spilling everywhere, and an aisle that runs along one side of the train—the TGV has an open seating arrangement like airplanes. With their large windows, the bright and spacious cars are a delight.

In 1989, the SNCF introduced the TGV Atlantique, which increased ride quality and passenger comfort and offers more variety in seating than any other train in Europe. Its second class is better than first class on many European trains, and its first class is luxurious.

In the TGV Atlantique's second-class cars, there are two pairs of padded, fabric-covered seats on either side of a carpeted aisle. Although the seats aren't as fancy as those in first class, each seat has lots of leg room, a fold-up tray (in the back of the forward seat), and an adjustable headrest.

In the roomier first-class cars, you'll find a configuration of a seat, the aisle, and two seats (except in the club cars). The wide, adjustable seats are covered in a plush velvet pile.

From the outside, the two TGVs are distinguished by their colors. The TGV Sud-Est is bright orange with a wide gray stripe, accented by smaller white stripes down the middle of the length of the train. In a small pocket window at each door, the number of the train is listed, with the car number and destinations. Bracketed by two engine cars, the TGV Sud-Est pulls eight trailers (passengers cars) holding 386 passengers (111 first-class seats, 275 second-class seats). With the ability to couple two train sets together, the passenger capacity can be doubled during peak periods.

The TGV Atlantique—slightly wider than the TGV Sud-Est, 122.7 feet longer, and 72 tons heavier (due to two more trailers)—is silver with a dark blue band, accented by white stripes down the middle of the length of the train. Each TGV Atlantique train set consists of ten trailer cars with a power car at each end. It holds 485 passengers—116 in first class, 369 in second class. Like the TGV Sud-Est, it can be coupled with another complete train set during peak periods, doubling its passenger capacity.

The bright yellow TGVs with gray and white stripes are postal trains that don't carry passengers except postal and SNCF employees. Patterned after the Sud-Est, this train has the words *La Poste* and an emblem of a letter on its nose.

A Car-by-Car Tour of the TGV Atlantique

Whether you travel in second or first class on the TGV Atlantique, the service and comfort will be the best in Europe for a daily passenger train. Between engine cars, passenger cars are designated R1-R10 (the "R" stands for *remorque*, French for "trailer"). When two TGV train sets are coupled for peak travel periods, the second set of cars is numbered R11-R20.

To help passengers identify their car, each trailer door is color-coded. Doors in first class are cherry red with a large "1" printed on them. The BAR car door is bright yellow with the word BAR in large letters above the door handle. Doors for second-class cars are blue-green with a large "2". A small display window by the door shows the number of each car. Inside, seat numbers are printed on metal tags attached to the lower bar of the overhead baggage rack or on the frame of the seat.

The first three cars, R1-R3, offer first-class seating only. At the beginning of R1 (closest to the engine car), there's a small baggage compartment accessible only from the outside. On the other side of the baggage car wall is the "business meeting room" section—an eight-seat, semi-circular lounge with television monitors for video tapes. For a more flexible arrangement, the seats in this section fold up. The rest of the car, divided by luggage racks and a small area/rest room for the disabled (who ride in first class at second-class prices), features open seating with all passengers facing the same direction. The entire R1 car has 44 first-class seats. The next two first-class cars, R2 and R3, reflect a new concept in first-class seating. When the SNCF examined the weaknesses of the TGV Sud-Est, they found that some passengers missed the privacy of compartment-style seating. So the SNCF created "club" cars, with 36 first-class seats. Some seats are arranged in pairs facing each other, separated by a large wall-to-aisle table with a reading lamp and overhead lights, semi-enclosed by floor-to-ceiling dividers that offer partial privacy from the aisle and the next set of seats. Across the aisle from each compartment, two facing, single seats are separated by a small table with a reading lamp.

Between the R1 and R2 cars are galleys for preparing the "at seat" meals for first-class passengers and a semi-enclosed booth with a cellular telephone. The three telephones on every TGV train set (one each for first- and second-class cars, plus one in the BAR car) accept only *télécartes* for payment. A unisex rest room and a luggage rack are located at the ends of R2 and R3, and R3 and R4. The R3 is the only first class smoking car.

The entire R4 car, separating first from second class, is the BAR car. This brightly lit car open to all passengers features hot and cold food, snacks, drinks, cigarettes, magazines, newspapers, *télécartes*, and souvenirs. You can stand at elevated tables or sit on bar stools and eat while watching the countryside zip by. A television above the ordering area provides additional entertainment. You can stay in the snack area as long as its open, or you can take your food to your seat.

Although Europeans usually bring a picnic lunch to avoid the train's high prices and often mediocre food, the fare on the TGV is tastier than most train and airline food. A typical breakfast (*petit déjuner*)—served to first-class passengers at their seats by waiters/waitresses—consists of two croissants or brioches with jam, mixed fruit, cheese, and coffee. Both lunch (*déjuner*) and dinner (*dîner*) menus include a meat dish with vegetables, fruit, salad, bread, dessert, and bottled water. Cheese, soft drinks, wine, beer, coffee, and tea cost extra.

By using regional foods relating to the train's route, the menu is varied, with choices that should satisfy all palates. On the down side, meals in first class are fairly pricey. An average lunch or dinner costs 150-200 francs. But, if you bought a first-class ticket (50% higher than second class), you're probably not on a tight budget. Meals are served in first class during standard French eating hours on all but very short routes and must be reserved before the departure date.

In the BAR car, the emphasis is on healthy, high-energy dishes for immediate purchase. A garnished sandwich or mixed salad with dessert and drink costs 50-70 francs. In addition, an attendant pushes a cart with snacks, beverages, cookies, and candy through both classes of the train. But be warned—the prices are ridiculous. A 12-ounce can of Coca-Cola, for instance, costs 30 francs.

Trailers R5-R10 have seats for 369 second-class passengers. Each trailer in R5-R7 has 60 seats facing the same direction. In the middle of these cars, two pairs of seats face each other over a large table extending from the window to the aisle. The R5 is the only second-class smoking car. There are unisex rest rooms at the end of each second-class car.

Especially for families with children, the TGV Atlantique has special seat layouts. In trailers R8 and R9, each holding 56 passengers, there are four semi-enclosed compartments at the end of each car. Each compartment has two seats facing each other with enhanced sound insulation, acrylic dividers, and a small fold-out table. There's also a small, enclosed nursery between R8 and R9, equipped with a bottle-warming device and a large changing table. A tip-up seat lets a parent sit in the nursery with a baby as long as needed. The rest of R8 and R9 have the open seating arrangement.

Trailer R10 provides open, one-direction seating for 60. At the end of the trailer, after passing three tip-up seats and a luggage rack, there's a large, semi-circular compartment with 17 tip-up seats, part of which has a sub-compartment with floor-to-ceiling dividers. Designed mainly for children, the compartment can be reserved by small school groups or others who need room for a play area. On certain days, this area is reserved for the *Jeune Voyageur Service* (JVS), which provides an SNCF hostess for children age 4-13 traveling alone. JVS costs 219 francs per child, which includes the RESA but not the ticket price.

PART 2

TGV Routes & Cities

The next 12 chapters will trace all the present TGV routes in France and introduce the regions and major cities served. To assist your planning and use of this book on location, the cities, listed according to their departure order from Paris, are placed within regional chapters. The only exception is Chapter 16, which describes the towns in northern France linked directly to Lyon.

Small villages, ski resorts, and towns with very limited appeal are mentioned in Chapter 5. A good example of the latter is the port of St.-Nazaire, where the primary industry is ship building. Unless you're a ship builder, you won't find much of interest there, since most of St. Nazaire was leveled during World War II.

To aid you while you're in France, the cities are described in a standard format, discussed below, that will help you find the information you need quickly.

Introduction: Each city gets a brief overview noting its past and present importance. (When appropriate, there are more facts about the city's history later in the section *Tour of Historic Sights & Major Attractions*.) Throughout the book, cities are occasionally ascribed to specific regions or departments. To give more autonomy to local governments,

France is divided into 96 departments and 22 regions. The Basque, Dordogne, Loire Valley, French Riviera, and Savoie regions mentioned are not official governing regions, but rather areas of France commonly recognized by these names, which come from their geography or heritage.

TGV Travel from Paris: This section includes the name of the train station you need to arrive at (most stations in France are simply known as the *Gare SNCF*), its location in the city, the frequency of TGV service between Paris and the city, trip mileage (railroad miles), the fastest travel time to each city from Paris, and, since many travelers will use Paris as a base, the departure time of the last TGV back to Paris. Bear in mind that travel time will decrease to many locations as the TGV continues to convert its routes to high-speed lines. And always remember that train schedules are subject to change.

Tourist Information Office: Every TGV city has at least one tourist information office, where you can get a free map to aid you in the walking tours (see below), and this section gives directions there from the train station. Although you won't get lost if you follow the tour directions, a map is always helpful.

Tourist information offices usually have one person who speaks some English to assist you if all the brochures are in French or you have questions. If no one speaks English, try the French for "I would like": "*Je voudrais.*" Follow these words with your request, ending with *s'il vous plaît* (please). For example, if you want a city map of Bordeaux, say, "*Je voudrais une plan de ville pour Bordeaux, s'il vous plaît*," which sounds like "Zher voo-dray oon plaan de veel poor Bore-doe, seel voo pleh."

Most tourist information offices in France are called *Office de Tourisme* or *Syndicat d'Initiative,* but they're also called *Maison de Tourisme, Bureau de Tourism, Municipal de Tourisme, Information Touristique,* or *Comité de Tourisme.* All are identified by pictograms of a white, lower case "i" inside a green circle. Sometimes the *Office de Tourisme* is combined with the *Accueil de France,* a national organization with offices in 45 French cities that helps travelers (for a small commission) find lodging.

Besides having maps and brochures, tourism offices will often change money when banks are closed, act as brokers for commercial tour companies, and sell tickets for local events. In some TGV cities, there's a small tourist information booth in the train station or at major sights—convenient for day-trippers. Annexes are listed when the main *Office de Tourisme* is far from the train station.

Tour of Historic Sights & Major Attractions: This section offers a street-by-street walking tour of the city's historic sights and major attractions from the train station or tourist information office. After the last sight, directions guide you back to the train station. Although it's possible to complete most of these walking tours in eight hours or less, you'll need an extra day (or more) for the largest cities.

Public transportation to the sights is noted when available, and in the larger cities, you should get a public transportation map/schedule from the tourism office. Most TGV cities have a bus system, and Paris, Lille, Lyon, and Marseille have subways.

Since street names in France can change several times for the same thoroughfare, try to be on the same side of the street for the turns in the walking tours. For example, if you're walking down boulevard Peyrou and the next direction says "Turn left on rue Dunay," then stay on the left side of boulevard Peyrou. When you reach rue Dunay, its name will be posted on the building ahead of you. If you were on the right side of the boulevard, there's a good chance the street will have a different name. A street with multiple names for the walking distance needed is indicated with slashes: "Walk down avenue de la Tessvoire/rue Robert/rue Bernais for seven blocks. . ."

For easy reference, the sights and attractions are set in bold first, then italic if they're mentioned again. Landmarks and buildings are, mostly, in italic. Streets are in regular type, and everything is spelled in French. Common terms include *rue* (street), *cours, allée, traverse,* and *chemin* (other names for streets), *quai* (street alongside a body of water), *place* (intersection of several streets, either open or with a land mass with fountains, monuments, or park benches), *pont* (bridge), *Ile* (island), *musée* (museum), *Gare Routière* (bus station), *Hôtel* "Name" (lodging, prices by the front door), *Hôtel* "Name" (a city mansion known as a *Hôtel Particulier*), *Hôtel de Ville* (city hall; called *Mairie* in smaller towns), *Hôtel-Dieu* (public hospital), *Palais de Justice* (courthouse and law offices), *Palais de Congrès* (convention hall), *Préfecture* (government administrative offices), *Bibliothèque* (library), *Jardin* (large park, often with elaborate landscaping), *Église* (church), *Vieille* or *Vieux Ville* (old town), and *Vieux Port* (old port).

The inflection marks (è, é, â, ï, î, etc.) over the vowels in French words are pronunciation guides best explained by a French language dictionary. As you'll notice in the street directions, the French hyphenate words often and offer spellings that look incorrect in English. The words *cathédrale, parc,* and *quartier* are French for cathedral, park, and quarter, plus there's both a Loir and Loire River.

All sights and attractions in the walking tours are open to the public, unless otherwise indicated. Hours (see Chapter 3) and admission fees aren't listed since they are similar across France. Bear in mind that inflation continues to push admission fees higher; 25 francs per person is average. Some regional museums are free, and historic sights are free when viewed from the outside, but their museums usually charge a fee. Public gardens and churches are free, though they sometimes charge a small fee to climb the belfry or see the treasury.

Restaurants: Although restaurants are included for every type of budget, this book emphasizes those near the train station or city attractions. When the restaurant is on a street already discussed in the text, directions to it are not repeated under this listing. Unless noted otherwise, the restaurants serve traditional, regional fare. If you want more variety, most two-star (or higher) hotels have a restaurant.

The cost ratings are based on the average cost of a three-course *à la carte* supper meal with a small carafe of house wine. Using a 6-francs-per-dollar conversion rate, the restaurants are rated as follows:

Inexpensive: Under 90 francs per person
Moderate: 90-180 francs per person
Expensive: 180+ francs per person.

To keep costs down, order the *menu prix fixe* (set price menu) instead of individual entrees. The *prix fixe* allows you to sample regional meat and vegetable specialties, plus dessert and a small carafe of wine. Some restaurants give you even more variety by offering multiple *prix fixe* menus.

Expensive and popular restaurants will require advance reservations.

Hotels: This section lists comfortable hotels, most within a mile of the train station. The hotels at the beginning of the list are closest to the train station. When the hotel is on a street already mentioned in the text, directions to it are not repeated under this listing.

Hotel costs are based on the daily charge for a double room with toilet and shower, excluding breakfast. Rooms with bathtubs are more expensive; single rooms less expensive. When a hotel has more than one cost rating, it's because it doesn't have uniformly sized rooms (typical of older hotels). You can save money by asking for a room without a shower and/or toilet, more common in the inexpensive hotels. Using a 6-francs-per-dollar conversion rate, the hotels were ranked as follows:

Inexpensive: 240 francs or less
Moderate: 241-540 francs
Expensive: 541-900 francs.

Sights Worth Seeing Nearby: Nearby attractions not served by the TGV but easily reached from a TGV city are described in this section, with details on how to get there.

An Overview of TGV Routes

The TGV has two major route systems in France. The **TGV Sud-Est**, which began service from Paris to Lyon in 1981, now serves 45 cities in east and southeast France, plus five in Switzerland. The TGV also operates two rail lines in this route system that bypass Paris completely and directly connect Lyon, Grenoble, and several villages in the French Alps to cities in northern France.

The newer **TGV Atlantique**, opened in 1989, serves 44 cities in west and southwest France, and one in Spain. When the Poitiers-La Rochelle high-speed line opens in late 1993, four more cities will join this route.

The travel times noted below are based on the TGV's stopping at every location along the route, so actual travel time may be less on non-stop trains. Also, the frequency of travel from Paris to a location varies from a single daily trip to 33 daily trips, depending on demand.

The TGV Sud-Est to Eastern France

Sliding out of the *Gare de Lyon*, the bright orange TGV Sud-Est gradually accelerates as it passes through the congested suburbs of Paris, then turns up the speed as it heads east across the gentle hills and plains of the Ile de France region. Less than an hour outside Paris, the high-speed line splits in two directions, one to eastern France, the other south to Lyon and beyond.

Shortly after the split on the east line, the TGV stops at **Montbard**, a small town between the Burgundy Canal and Brenne River. Although you can tour the town's restored mansion and park (formerly belonging

FRANCE
TGV Routes

English Channel

Caen

Golfe de Saint-Malo

Brest — 4.02 — 3.42 — Guingamp
Morlaix
3.13 — St.-Brieuc
2.55

Quimper
4.21 — Lorient
3.44 — Vannes
3.11 — Redon
la Baule
le Croisic — 3.15
2.57
St.-Nazaire — 2.40

Rennes — Vitré — Laval
2.05 — 1.35

Angers — 1.29
2.00
Nantes

ATLANTIC

OCEAN

Niort
La Rochélle — 3.00

Île d'Oléron

Angoulême
3.04

Bay

of

Biscay

Libourne
2.58
4.08

Arcachon — 4.05
Bordeaux

Golfe de Gascogne

Bayonne — 4.33 — Dax
Biarritz — 4.48
Hendaye — 5.00 — Pau — Tarbe
5.08 — St. Jean-de-Luz — 4.54
5.20 — 5.36
Lourde

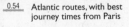

0.54 — Atlantic routes, with best journey times from Paris

1.05 — Southeast routes, with best journey times from Paris

3.16 — Paris bypass routes, with best journey times from Lyon

SPAIN

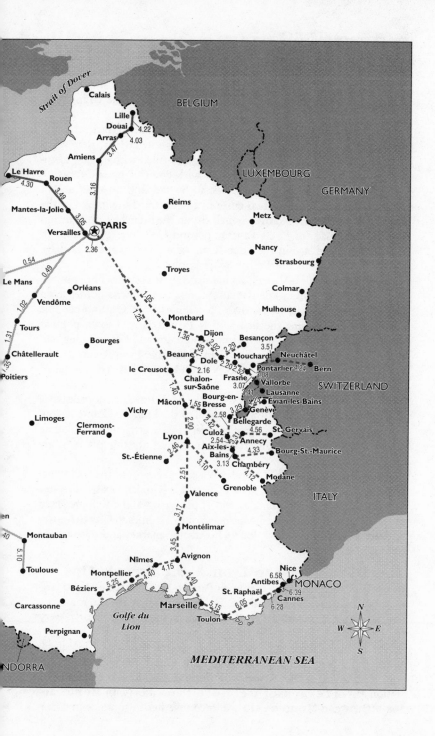

to the 18th-century naturalist George Louis Leclerc de Buffon), most travelers visit the 12th-century *Abbaye de Fontenay*, four miles east of town. Take a taxi there or go for a pleasant walk in the countryside on the D905 highway or GR 213 hiking trail.

From Montbard, the TGV travels east on conventional tracks through the hilly, vineyard-laden Burgundy countryside to **Dijon**. Renowned for its mustard, Dijon is a large, charming city filled with elegant townhouses and buildings, many decorated with colorful mosaic roofs.

From Dijon, you can continue east to Switzerland on the line out of Paris, or head south to two cities in east-central Burgundy. On the east line, the first stop is **Dole**, a small city in the Franche-Comte region and the birthplace of Louis Pasteur. Beyond Dole, the TGV stops in **Mouchard**, a village in the Loue River valley, and **Frasne**, a village about 25 miles from the French-Swiss border.

From Frasne, the TGV enters Switzerland at two points. The continuation of the Paris-Dijon line slants southeast to the Swiss border town **Vallorbe**, arriving in **Lausanne** 35 minutes later. On another line northeast from Frasne, the first stop is **Pontarlier**, a town popular with those exploring the nearby Jura Mountains and GR 5 hiking trail along France's eastern border. Less than eight miles from Pontarlier, the TGV crosses the border, going to **Neuchâtel** and **Bern**, capital of Switzerland.

On a separate line northeast of Dole, the TGV travels a short distance to **Besançon**, the administrative capital of the Franche-Comte region. Off the beaten track, this large city offers many attractions, including a large fort and an excellent art museum. The only thing it lacks are crowds of tourists.

South of Dijon, the TGV travels on a short section of the traditional Dijon-Lyon line through the famed Côte-d'Or (Golden Coast) vineyards to **Beaune**, the wine-trading capital of the region and a well-preserved medieval city. The train then continues south 19 miles to **Chalon-sur-Saône**, a busy city known for its fur-trading market and outstanding photography museum.

The TGV Sud-Est to Lyon & the French Alps

In pre-TGV days, the train trip from Paris to **Lyon** (France's third largest city) took four hours, and the SNCF lost money on the route. Today, the route is one of the great successes of the TGV, as nearly every train to Lyon is full for the two-hour ride.

Not far out of Paris, where the high-speed rail splits, the TGV heads south and zips through central Burgundy. One hour and 25 minutes later, just south of the rugged *Parc Regional de Morvan*, it stops at a station east of **Le Creusot**, the largest of three cities (with **Montceau-les-Mines** and **Montchanin**) jammed together in south-central Bur-

gundy. This urban area is a leader in the steel, glass, and plastic industries. Le Creusot has three separate museums within the *Château de la
Verrerie* dedicated to the French Industrial Revolution.

From Le Creusot, the TGV runs southeast toward the Saône River,
crossing it south of Mâcon, then turns south towards Lyon, through
the fertile Saône basin lined with vineyards, fields of yellow colza, farms,
and villages. Forty-two minutes later, after crossing the wide Rhône River,
the train glides into the *Gare de la Part-Dieu* on the east side of **Lyon**,
then on to the *Gare de Perrache* (a 10-minute ride) on the peninsula
dividing the Saône and Rhône Rivers in west Lyon. From this station,
you'll find most of Lyon's historic sights and attractions.

From Lyon, on conventional rail lines, you can travel 62 miles south
to the pretty Rhône River city **Valence**, head 37 miles southwest to
the industrial city **St.-Étienne** on the edge of the Auvergne region,
or go 65 miles southeast to **Grenoble** in the foothills of the French
Alps—an excellent base for mountain exploration and a city filled with
colorful streets and interesting museums.

On a slightly different route, another TGV traveling on the high-speed
line to Lyon skips Le Creusot and stops in **Mâcon**, an important shipping point for the Beaujolais wines produced in the area. On the southeast
tip of Burgundy on the Saône River, it's the first stop on the TGV's
Paris-Geneva, Switzerland route. A few miles east of Mâcon, the TGV
enters historic **Bourg-en-Bresse**, home of a unique medieval church
and famous among gourmands for the Bresse chicken, considered the
best poultry in France.

From Bourg-en-Bresse, the TGV moves south through hilly terrain
to the village **Culoz** near the north end of pretty Lac Bourget, where the
line splits northeast to Switzerland and southeast to the French Alps.
Heading northeast to Geneva, the train climbs through the southern
end of the Jura Mountains, dotted with small farms and vineyards, to
Bellegarde-sur-Valserine, a small industrial town set on steep hills
above the confluence of the Rhône and Valserine rivers. From the top
of the *Grand Crêt d'Eau*, a 5,300-foot mountain north of town, you
get excellent views of Mont Blanc, the tallest mountain in Europe (15,772
feet) and Geneva on the southwest tip of Lac Léman (a.k.a. Lake Geneva). The TGV then passes through a long tunnel to follow the Rhône
through mountain passes to **Geneva**, the largest French-speaking city
in Switzerland, famous for international banking and diplomacy.

On the same TGV line, there is one daily departure from Paris that
bypasses all the aforementioned cities to serve three French cities on
or near Lac Léman. The first stop (under four hours from Paris) is the
town of **Annemasse**, a former Middle Ages crossroads only five miles
south of Geneva. From there, the TGV heads to **Thonon-les-Bains**

and **Évian-les-Bains**, two resort towns known for their excellent spas (the latter renowned for its mineral water).

Returning to Culoz, the other TGV line travels southeast, climbing through mountain passes and alpine terrain dotted with lakes and farms to three cities in the foothills of the French Alps. The first stop, less than three hours from Paris, is **Aix-les-Bains**, a popular spa city above Lac Bourget, surrounded by snow-capped mountains. Only 12 minutes farther southeast on the same line is the elegant **Chambéry**, the former capital of the House of Savoie.

Thirty-six minutes northeast of Aix-les-Bains on another TGV line is **Annecy**, one of the prettiest cities in France, at the foot of the Savoy Alps on Lac d'Annecy. Farther east on this line, through hilly valleys and then along the narrow Arve River, the TGV goes deep into the French Alps to **Cluses**, **Sallanches**, and **St.-Gervais**. Sixteen miles east of St.-Gervais (via a non-TGV train), in the shadow of Mont-Blanc, is the famous resort Chamonix. Two daily trains from Paris, both bypassing Aix-les-Bains and Annecy, travel directly to these mountain locations. During prime ski season (December 22-April 15), TGV service is increased to these ski resorts.

Beyond Chambéry on the line from Culoz, the TGV parallels the Isère River briefly, then travels south along the Arc River to the alpine villages **St.-Avre-la-Chambre**, **St.-Jean-de-Maurienne**, and **St.-Michel-Valloire**—all good locations for skiers. One hour from Chambéry (4.5 hours from Paris), this line ends at the border town of **Modane**. Though lacking famous sights, Modane is significant as a customs inspection stop for cars and trains entering the Fréjus Tunnel to Italy.

From Chambéry, another TGV line goes east to more alpine towns. Following the scenic Isère River, the train climbs through the river valley rimmed by mountains and quaint villages to **Albertville**, site of the 1992 Winter Olympics. From there, the TGV continues to **Moutiers** (near the popular Courchevel ski resort), the winter resort **Aime-la-Plagne**, and the tiny village **Landry**. Just five hours from Paris, the line ends at **Bourg-St.-Maurice**, located in a deep valley south of Mont Blanc, near the les Arcs ski resort and a few miles from the Italian border.

The TGV-Sud Est to Southeastern France

South of Valence, the TGV follows the wide Rhône River, lined with vineyards and an occasional castle, to the regions of Languedoc-Roussillon, Provence, and the French Riviera. Half of the TGV trains on this line from Paris stop in Lyon; the other half bypass the *Gare de la Part-Dieu* for faster service.

The first stop beyond Valence is **Montélimar**, made famous by its eponymous candy. Thirty-eight minutes later, the TGV stops in the former papal city **Avignon**, easily recognized by its *Pont St.-Bénézet*, an unfinished medieval bridge across the Rhône. Avignon is also a major TGV hub. The main line from Lyon splits there, with one route going southeast to Marseille and the Mediterranean coast, the other southwest to the Languedoc region.

Thirty-two minutes from Avignon on the southwest line is **Nîmes**, a city with more Roman buildings and monuments intact than any other in France. Not far beyond Nîmes, across the heavily farmed plains of northern Languedoc, the TGV stops at the business and university city **Montpellier**, a few miles from the Mediterranean Sea. The final stop on this line is historic **Beziers**, on a plateau above the *Canal du Midi* and Orb River.

On the southeast line, just under an hour from Avignon, the TGV stops in rough-and-tumble **Marseille**, France's largest port and second-largest city. From there, the line follows the rocky Mediterranean coast to **Toulon**, a bustling port and home of the largest French naval fleet. On the fringe of the French Riviera, Toulon makes an inexpensive base from which to explore the area. Fifty-one minutes beyond Toulon, the TGV enters the heart of the French Riviera, stopping first at the village **St.-Raphaël**, then at the resort cities **Cannes**, **Antibes**, and **Nice**.

The TGV Sud-Est from Lyon to Northern France

Before the TGV, train travelers from northern locations had to stop at either the *Gare du Nord* or *Gare St.-Lazare* in Paris, then take a taxi, bus, or subway to the *Gare de Lyon* for a southeast rail connection. Today, the TGV from Lyon to northern France travels on the high-speed line to Paris, then swings around the capital's east side on a feeder line to connect with the conventional north line. North of Paris, the train enters Picardy, one of the most prosperous agricultural regions in France, where it dashes across its gentle hills and plains to **Amiens**, home of the largest Gothic cathedral in France. From there, the TGV continues north, crossing into the industrial Nord-Pas-de-Calais region en route to **Arras**, the site of numerous battles from the Middle Ages to World War II and the most Flemish-inspired architecture in France.

After Arras, the TGV stops in **Douai**, capital of French coal mining, then rushes north to **Lille**, the largest city in northern France, near the Belgium border. Be sure to visit Lille's excellent fine arts museum and its massive, Vauban-designed citadel. By mid-1993, the TGV Nord route will provide service from Paris and its Charles-de-Gaulle-Roissy airport to these cities, plus Calais on the north coast. By 1994, the TGV Nord will travel from Paris to London via the English Channel Tunnel at Sangatte (six km. south of Calais).

The TGV's second northern France line bypassing Paris from Lyon stops first in the Paris suburb of **Massy**, where a feeder line switches TGV Sud-Est trains onto the TGV Atlantic line and vice versa, making

At Paris' Gare Montparnasse, travelers prepare to board a TGV to Le Mans, Laval, and Rennes.

it possible to travel from Rennes, Nantes, Angers, and Le Mans to Lyon without going into Paris. There are currently two daily trains in each direction between these cities. Beyond Massy, the TGV skirts Paris' south side to head west toward Normandy. Its second stop, within shouting distance of Paris, is **Versailles**, where you'll find the most spectacular palace in Europe.

Just past Versailles, on the west edge of the Ile de France region, the TGV stops in **Mantes-la-Jolie**, an industrial town on the Seine River. Bombed heavily in World War II, there's little of interest to tourists except the *Église Collégiale-Notre-Dame* (patterned after the *Cathédrale de Notre-Dame* in Paris) and a museum with the work of Post-Impressionist artist Maximilien Luce. Following the Seine, the train heads for **Rouen**, immortalized as the site of Joan of Arc's execution and home of a beautiful Gothic cathedral, often painted by Claude Monet. The third-largest port in France, Rouen offers many historic sights, museums, churches, and pedestrian malls. The final stop on this line is **Le Havre**, France's second-largest port, which also suffered heavily in World War II. Today it's a modern city with few attractions, unless your hobby is watching large ships and sailors at work.

The TGV Atlantique to Le Mans, Angers, and Southeast Brittany

Running parallel to the A10 expressway south of Paris for a short distance after leaving the *Gare Montparnasse*, the silver TGV Atlantique crosses the plains and marshes of the Ile de France region and zips toward southwest France. Halfway to Tours and a few miles west of Courtalain, the high-speed line splits west to Le Mans and south to Vendôme.

In just 54 minutes from Paris, the train arrives in **Le Mans**, home of the famous auto race and a historic city worthy of a stop even if the race isn't in progress. Beyond Le Mans, the line switches to conventional tracks, splitting in two directions as it heads for Brittany. On the southwest branch, it stops at **Sablé-sur-Sarthe**, known for its château and biscuits (*sablés*), then speeds to **Angers**, a city anchored by a fortress-château on the Maine River, on the west edge of the Loire Valley region.

From Angers, the TGV heads west to the port **Nantes** and the southeast coast of Brittany. One of France's largest cities, Nantes has many interesting sights, including a château near the train station. From there, the train goes a little further west to the ship-building city **St.-Nazaire** at the mouth of the Loire River and Atlantic Ocean. Nearly leveled by World War II bombing, it's a modern city with few sights except for large ships.

Next, the TGV briefly follows the coast north to the towns **Pornichet**, **La Baule**, **Le Pouliguen**, and **Le Croisic**, all within a few minutes of each other. Of the four, La Baule is the largest with 15,000 residents, and it's a famous Atlantic Ocean resort. Lined with luxury hotels, its five-mile-long beach with fine sand—one of the most beautiful in Europe—lures thousands of European tourists in the summer.

The TGV Atlantique from Le Mans to Brittany

On the other branch from Le Mans, across a fertile farming area, the TGV travels northwest to **Laval**, a town with an interesting château on the Mayenne River, just east of the Brittany border. From there, the train heads straight west, stopping twice daily in the village **Vitré**, dominated by a fascinating castle. Most trains continue to **Rennes**, Brittany's second largest city. Rennes' rail hub makes it an excellent base for exploring the region.

West of Rennes, the line splits in two directions. The route from Vitré continues northwest through rural Brittany, making stops in the small towns **Lamballe, Guingamp, Plouaret-Tregor, Morlaix**, and **Landernau**. These market towns are fun to explore if you're interested in rural Breton life or want a less-congested base to the beaches on the north coast of Brittany. Between Lamballe and Guingamp, the TGV also stops at **St.-Brieuc**, an industrial town of 52,000, where you can rent a car to explore the nearby *Côte d'Emeraude* (Emerald Coast), a gorgeous, 68-mile section of north Brittany from St.-Malo to Val-André. Angling south from Morlaix, this line ends at the port city **Brest**, the furthest west any TGV travels in France. Partly obliterated during a 43-day siege following D-Day in 1944, Brest is one of the most modern cities in Brittany.

The second TGV line from Rennes runs briefly south, then west, paralleling the southern coast of Brittany as far as Quimper. The first stop, less than 45 miles from Rennes, is the small, agricultural community **Redon**, featuring a 14th-century Gothic bell tower and the remains of a 12th-century Romanesque church. The *Canal du Brest á Nantes*, formerly a major link between the two cities, is just south of the Redon train station. Today, it's used primarily by small pleasure craft and fishing boats.

From Redon, the TGV heads west to historic **Vannes**. Set at the back edge of the Gulf of Morbihan, its narrow, twisting streets surrounded by ancient ramparts are evidence of a medieval past. Next stop: the small town **Auray** on the banks of the Loch River, and then onto **Lorient**, a mid-size city and Atlantic Ocean port. Home of one of France's largest fishing fleets, Lorient has grown steadily since the 17th century, when the French East India Company claimed it as a base. But unless you're going to the excellent beaches outside Lorient, there's little reason to stop there, since the more interesting **Quimper** is only 41 miles west. On the Odet River, a few miles from the Atlantic Ocean, Quimper has an excellent Gothic cathedral, many old homes and narrow streets, a museum focusing on the artists of the School of Pont-Aven, and fame for faïence-style ceramic production. You can get a glimpse of the centuries-old ceramics industry by touring one of the factories on the outskirts of town.

The TGV Atlantique to the Loire Valley and Southwestern France

The TGV Atlantique's second high-speed line barrels straight south from the Courtalain split to **Vendôme**, with an interesting monastery and the ruins of a feudal château, then angles southwest to **Tours**, the largest city in the Loire Valley and an excellent base for exploring the numerous châteaux in the area. Although several trains travel daily to Tours, even more stop at **St.-Pierre-des-Corps**, an industrial suburb two miles east of Tours.

From Tours, heading southwest toward the Atlantic coast, the TGV soon enters the hills of rural Poitou, an agricultural region known for its cognac. The first stop, a half-hour from Tours, is **Châtellerault**, a town on the Vienne River and former residence of 17th century philospher René Descartes. Often bypassed for Loire Valley sights, it's worth a short stop for its automobile museum and Descartes' home (now a museum). Just southwest of Châtellerault, **Poitiers** is home to more churches per square mile than any city in France. The site of many religious pilgrimages and military battles, it has become the region's most prosperous city.

By the winter of 1993, the TGV will travel (91 miles) on a high-speed line from Poitiers to the picturesque port **La Rochelle** on the Atlantic coast, a prime summer resort for the French. Before La Rochelle, the TGV will stop at the rural communities of **St.-Maixent-l'École** and **Surgères**, and at **Niort**, a mid-sized city dominated by the insurance industry. Between Niort and La Rochelle, the TGV will travel along the south edge of the flat *Marais Poitevin*, a marshy area known as "the green Venice." Evolving from an island-dotted gulf, it was drained for agriculture in the Middle Ages by monks from a local abbey. In this scenic setting, you may see residents gliding down tree-lined canals in small, flat-bottomed boats called *yoles*.

Southwest of Poitiers, the direct TGV line from Paris crosses the hills and agricultural Charentes countryside for 63 miles to **Angoulême**, an ancient city overlooking the Charente River. From there, the next stop is **Libourne**, a small, 13th-century town that's the primary shipping point for Bordeaux wines from nearby St.-Émillion, Pomerol, and Fronsac vineyards. After Libourne, the TGV enters the east side of sprawling **Bordeaux**, a large port on the Garonne River. With a variety of sights, Bordeaux is a good base for exploring southwest France.

From Bordeaux, the TGV travels on one line to the southwest corner of France, and on another line southeast to **Toulouse**, one of France's largest and most progressive cities. On the way to Toulouse, the TGV also stops at the small market town **Agen** and at **Montauban**, a pretty city on the Tarn River, with a museum dedicated to the artist Jean-Auguste-Dominique Ingres.

On the other line from Bordeaux, the TGV heads south for a few miles, then slips off the main line to travel west to **Arcachon**, a small, often crowded resort just inland from the Atlantic Ocean on the Arcachon Basin. Known by gourmets for its oysters and by tourists for its beaches, the town also features the *Dune du Pilat*, the tallest sand dune in Europe (384 feet above sea level). The dune is reached by following the coastal boulevards south for six miles to the village Pyla-sur-Mer.

Returning to the main line, the TGV travels south across the marshes of the Gironde and Landes regions to **Dax**, a major crossroads for travel into the French Basque and Pyrénées regions—and the best spa city in the region. From Dax, you can travel on the TGV south on the same line or switch to a line going east through the scenic Gave de Pau River valley to **Pau**. In the foothills of the Pyrénées Mountains, Pau features a royal château among its various sights. From Pau, the TGV is often crowded with senior citizens, invalids, and nuns, as it climbs south to the Catholic pilgrimage town of **Lourdes** and the Pyrénées Mountains. A surprisingly small town (only 18,000 permanent residents), Lourdes receives five million visitors a year. Beyond Lourdes, the TGV travels north to the market city of **Tarbes**.

South of Dax on the north-south line from Bordeaux, the TGV heads to **Bayonne**, at the intersection of the Adour and Nive Rivers, a few miles from the Atlantic Ocean. It features a Gothic cathedral, Vauban-designed ramparts, pretty river quais, and some outstanding museums. A few minutes away, the resort **Biarritz** offers famous beaches, waves that will challenge the best surfers, and a casino worthy of James Bond. It's a fun, though expensive, city to visit.

The final stops for the TGV Atlantique on this line are the fishing villages **St.-Jean-de-Luz**, dominated by tuna and anchovy fisheries, and **Hendaye**, which rises steeply above the Bidassoa River at its intersection with the Atlantic Ocean. More Spanish than French in character, both towns boast excellent beaches and have become small resort communities to rival Biarritz. Three of the five daily TGV trains to Hendaye travel one mile further to **Irún, Spain**.

Eastern France

Dijon

World-famous for its mustard, Dijon has consistently been one of France's most industrious and wealthy cities. Although it lacks the prestige it had in the 14th and 15th centuries, when the Grand Dukes of Burgundy reigned from northern Holland to Lyon, Dijon is still powerful as the administrative capital of Burgundy.

A growing city of 220,000, Dijon reflects an aristocratic heritage in its elegantly restored churches, palaces, and mansions. Near the famed Côte-d'Or vineyards, which produce some of France's best wine, and home to a number of France's best chefs, Dijon's cuisine alone attracts thousands of tourists every year.

TGV Travel from Paris

Fifteen TGV trains travel daily from Paris to Dijon. The 176-mile trip takes one hour, 36 minutes. The *Gare Dijon-Ville* is along rue Docteur-Albert-Rémy on the west side of town. Currently, the last TGV back to Paris leaves at 21:15.

Tourist Information Office

Dijon has two tourist information offices. The *Office de Tourisme* and *Accueil de France* are in a building on a triangular block opposite the busy place Darcy. To reach it, follow the left side of avenue du Maréchal-Foch, which enters the *Gare Dijon-Ville* parking area, for less than two blocks. The office has a money-exchange service at no commission and a wealth of information about Dijon and the Burgundy region.

The second *Office de Tourisme* is at 34 rue des Forges in the 15th-century *Hôtel Chambellan*, a former mansion of a Dijon nobleman. (It's on the tour route below, a few steps west of the *Palais des Ducs de Bourgogne*.) From this office, concerned primarily with Dijon tourism, you can buy an inexpensive "one-for-all" ticket that allows entry into the main museums and sights of Dijon.

Tour of Historic Sights & Major Attractions

After visiting the first *Office de Tourisme*, cross the street to the right side of place Darcy, continuing past the large stone arch *Porte Guillame* to the beginning of the pedestrians-only rue de la Liberté, a lively street anchoring Dijon's market and shopping district, including the Grey Poupon mustard store (#32). About a mile down this street, where the pedestrians-only section ends, you'll enter the spacious, semi-circular place de la Libération, a beautiful square bordered on the south by 17th-century townhouses and on the north by the **Palais des Ducs de Bourgogne**. Built in the 1300's for the Dukes of Burgundy, the palace has been altered so much over the years that its original Gothic architecture is barely evident. Bus #1 runs from the *Gare Dijon-Ville* to the palace, and buses #2, 3, 4, 9, and 12 go there from place Darcy.

Today, the former palace is home to Dijon's city government, with its east wing housing the **Musée des Beaux-Arts**, one of the oldest (opened 1799) museums in France. To get to the museum entrance at place de la Ste.-Chapelle, continue through place de la Libération for a brief walk on rue Rameau along the palace's south side and turn left when the building ends.

The museum's large collection features French, Swiss, Italian, German, Dutch, and Flemish art from the 15th to 20th century, with its best work from 19th- and 20th-century artists like Corot, Manet, Monet, Delacroix, Rodin, Picasso, and Kandinsky. Unlike the haphazard exhibits of some art museums in France, the *Musée des Beaux-Arts* groups pieces in galleries by national schools or styles, making it easy to choose what you want to see. Also, this museum has the elaborate 15th-century tombs of the Dukes of Burgundy (Philip the Bold and John the Fearless), the ducal kitchens and banquet hall, and several carved and painted altarpieces.

After getting your fill of art, walk to the north side of the building to place des Ducs-de-Bourgogne, where you'll find the original 14th-century palace. If you're in good shape, climb to the top of the 170-foot **Tour de Philippe-le-Bon** for a great view of Dijon's colorful rooftops.

Descend the tower and follow the exterior of the palace west to rue des Forges, a narrow street with several restored mansions. The **Hôtel Chambellan** at #34 has an interesting interior courtyard, with open galleries on the first and second floors. (The other *Office de Tourisme* is on the second floor.) At #38 is the **Maison Milsand**, built in 1561; at #40 is the 13th-century **Exchange**; and at #56 is the elegant, 15th-century **Hôtel Morel-Sauvegrain**.

When the street ends at place François-Rude, a lively square featuring half-timbered buildings and a fountain with a statue of a naked man treading grapes, turn right onto rue François-Rude and right at the next street onto rue Mussette. One long block down this street (just north of the palace), the **Église Notre-Dame**, a 13th-century, Gothic-inspired church, features a gargoyle-covered façade and a *Jacquemart*, a mechanical chiming clock brought from the Flemish town of Courtrai in 1389 by Duke Philip the Bold as a spoil of war. The church contains ancient stained glass windows, an 11th-century Virgin Mary of black wood, and a Gobelins tapestry celebrating Dijon's 1944 liberation by the Allies.

Surrounding the church to the east and north are several streets lined with buildings and houses from the 15th to 17th centuries. Just behind the church to the north, at 8 rue de la Chouette, is the **Hôtel Vogüe**, a 1614 Renaissance mansion. The pedestrians-only rue Verrerie, the first street to the left beyond the *Hôtel Vogüe*, is a good place to begin a random tour of the old houses in the area, as are the rues Auguste-Comte, Jean-Jacques Rousseau, and Vannerie, all of which enter rue Jeannin (continuation of rue de la Chouette) in subsequent blocks.

After exploring, you might want to get lunch in the area. Then, turn right off rue Jeannin onto rue Vannerie, walking a short block to admire the exterior of the **Église de St.-Michel**, which features a unique combination of Gothic and Renaissance styles. Take a brief look inside to see its ancient bas-reliefs of Biblical scenes, then follow rue Vaillant away from the church entrance, turning left a block later through the parking area at the *Bourse de Commerce* building. One block later, turn right at rue des Bons-Enfants. At building #4, you'll find the **Musée Magnin**, a small art museum half a block from place de la Libération in the former *Hôtel Lantin*. Even if you aren't an art lover, step inside to see the gorgeous room settings, including a grand staircase and formal salon. The museum's collection, given to the city in 1938, includes the Hieronymous Bosch masterpiece *Christ Crowned by Thorns*.

Next, follow rue des Bons-Enfants to its end at place de la Libération. If your time is limited, you can easily return to the *Gare Dijon-Ville* from there by retracing your steps. Otherwise, explore this area's numerous 16th- to 18th-century mansions. At the far end of rue du Palais (which enters the south side of place de la Libération) is the **Palais de Justice**, former home of the Parliament of Burgundy.

From this point, turn right off rue du Palais onto rue Admiral-Roussin, on which you'll find the **Hôtel Liégeard**, a sumptuous mansion stretching from the corner of rue Jean-Baptiste-Liégeard to the next corner at rue Vauban. From rue Vauban, continue a block across the small place Jean-Macé to rue Piron, which leads to rue and place Bossuet.

Turn left there, then take an immediate right at the small *Église St.-Jean*, following rue Danton past the even smaller 12th-century *Église St.-Philibert* to the **Cathédrale St.-Bénigne**. This 13th-century Gothic cathedral with a glazed tile roof is built over the site of a 9th-century Romanesque church, which was built over a 6th-century abbey. Be sure to see its circular crypt, which dates to 1007. A few steps behind the Cathédrale, housed in the dormitory of a former Benedictine abbey, is the **Musée Archéologique**, containing Gallo-Roman and medieval artifacts.

From this quarter, on rue Bossuet or rue Docteur-Maret (in front of the Cathédrale), you can return to rue de la Liberté to shop or to the Gare Dijon-Ville, a short distance away. To reach the station, follow rue Mariotte away from the Cathédrale entrance for three long blocks, then cross the wide boulevard de Sévigné to rue Docteur-Albert-Rémy.

If you're interested in flowers, natural history, or medieval art, take one more detour before the train station. When you reach boulevard de Sévigné, turn left under the railroad tracks and proceed straight ahead across a wide intersection to the huge **Jardin de l'Arquebuse** and **Musée Botanique** along avenue Albert 1er. Founded in 1525, it's the oldest and largest park in Dijon. The botanical garden (founded in 1770) features thousands of flowers and trees from around the world.

About half a mile past the park on avenue Albert 1er (N5 highway) are the remains of the **Chartreuse de Champmol**, a Carthusian monastery built in the 14th century. All that's left of the original structure (destroyed in 1793 during the French Revolution) is a circa-1390 chapel doorway and the remains of the sculpture Well of Moses by Claus Suter. Bus #18, which travels on avenue Albert 1er, goes to the Gare Dijon-Ville.

Restaurants

Melodine, 6 avenue du Maréchal-Foch, inexpensive, tel. 80-45-51-00.

Flunch, 24 boulevard des Brosses (the wide street off the northeast corner of place Darcy), inexpensive.

Le Pré-Aux-Clercs et Trois Faisans, 13 place de la Libération, moderate, tel. 80-67-11-33.

Chasse Royale, 15 place de la Libération, moderate, tel. 80-30-13-45.

Moulin à Vent, 8 place François-Rude, inexpensive, tel. 80-30-81-43.

La Chouette, 1 rue de la Chouette, expensive, tel. 80-30-18-10.

Au Bec Fin, 47 rue Jeannin, inexpensive, tel. 80-66-17-77.

Le Duche, 52 rue Verrerie, inexpensive-moderate, tel. 80-72-30-50.

Le Grilladou, 29 rue Jean-Jacques Rousseau, moderate, tel. 80-74-42-33.

Le Rallye, 39 rue Chabot-Charny (one block past rue des Bons-Enfants), moderate, tel. 80-67-11-55.

Le Vinarium, 23 place Bossuet (behind the Église St.-Jean), moderate-expensive, tel. 80-30-36-23.

St. Jean, 13 rue Monge (continuation of the rue/place Bossuet past Église St.-Jean), moderate, tel. 80-30-06-64.

Le Charbrot, 36 rue Monge, moderate-expensive, tel. 80-30-69-61.

Hotels

Relais Arcade, 15 avenue Albert 1er (past the *Jardin de l'Arquebuse* and *Musée Botanique*), moderate, tel. 80-43-01-12.

Hôtel Jura, 14 avenue du Maréchal-Foch, moderate, tel. 80-41-61-12.

Hôtel Nord, place Darcy at rue de la Liberté, inexpensive-moderate, good restaurant on premises, tel. 80-30-58-58.

Hôtel Pullman-La Cloche, 14 place Darcy, moderate-expensive, tel. 80-30-12-32.

Hôtel Poste, 5 rue du Château (2nd street to the left off rue de la Liberté), inexpensive, tel. 80-30-51-64.

Hôtel Central Urbis, 3 place Grangier (turn right off rue du Château), moderate, tel. 80-30-44-00.

Hostellerie du Chapeau Rouge, 5 rue Michelet (short street connecting rue Bossuet with the *Église St.-Philibert*), moderate-expensive, good restaurant on premises, tel. 80-30-28-10.

Sights Worth Seeing Nearby

Throughout history, Dijon has been the place where all Burgundy roads cross. The SNCF provides rail service to most cities and villages in the Burgundy region, including **Beaune** and **Chalon-sur-Saône** on the TGV running south. With easy access to Paris, Lyon, the Alps, and the nearby Franche-Comte region, Dijon is an excellent base for day trips.

Dole

A small, working-class city, Dole was founded in the 14th century as a monastic village and university center. Fiercely independent, it has been invaded by French, Spanish, Prussian, and German armies attempting to gain its strategic location on the Doubs River. In 1668, it became a part of France after succumbing to the army of Louis XIV. Despite the destruction in its past, Dole retains much of its old-world flavor, with shaded squares and narrow streets lined with ancient buildings.

TGV Travel from Paris

Five TGV trains travel daily from Paris to Dole. The 205-mile trip takes two hours, two minutes. The *Gare SNCF* is along rue des Messageries on the north side of town. Currently, the last TGV back to Paris leaves at 19:10.

Tourist Information Office

The *Office de Tourisme* is more than a mile from the *Gare SNCF* at place Jules-Grévy. To reach it, exit left from the station across the parking area to avenue Aristide-Briand. At the next major intersection, turn left onto boulevard Président-Wilson for several blocks, then turn right on avenue de la Paix, which leads to the square.

Tour of Historic Sights & Major Attractions

From the *Office de Tourisme*, walk across place Jules-Grévy to rue de Besançon at the top right corner of the square. At 44 rue de Besançon, stop to admire the exterior staircase at the 16th-century **Hôtel Terrier de Santans**. A little further down, you'll come to a short side street on the left that takes you to the **Cathédrale Notre-Dame**. This town landmark features a tall steeple and broad nave, plus interesting statues and furniture from the 16th century.

From the *Cathédrale*, venture south on one of the short side streets to rue Pasteur, where you'll find the **Maison Natale de Louis Pasteur** at #43, the birthplace of the renowned chemist who developed pasteurization. The tiny museum inside the house documents his life and scientific pursuits.

Just south of this street is the **Canal du Rhone-au-Rhine**, which connects the Doubs and Saône Rivers. (North of Besançon at Mont-béliard, the canal breaks away from the Doubs River to join the Rhine River on the France-Germany border, 12 miles north of Basel, Switzerland.) There are good views of the city from the bridges spanning the canal and river. To reach them, exit the *Maison Natale de Louis Pasteur* to the left, then turn left again at the Grande-Rue. The first two bridges cross the narrow canal; the third bridge goes over the river.

From the south side of the first bridge, turn left (facing the city) on rue du Vieux-Château, following it for half a mile to rue des Arènes. A half-block to your left is the **Musée Municipal** at #85, a combination fine arts and archaeology museum, featuring paintings by Vouet, Lebrun, and Courbet, plus a display of Gallo-Roman artifacts from the region.

Returning to the city center on rue des Arènes, note on your right, about three blocks from the museum, the **Palais de Justice** set back from the street through an alley in a former 16th-century convent. To return to the *Gare SNCF* from the alley, turn left one long block later at rue du Mont-Roland, then right on rue du Collège-de-l'Arc, where you'll pass the **Collège de l'Arc**, a Jesuit school started in 1582 that's still in use. When you reach avenue Aristide-Briand, a left turn takes you back to the station. Staying on rue des Arènes (the extension of rue de Besançon) will take you back into the city center near the *Cathédrale*.

Restaurants

Buffet de la Gare, at the *Gare SNCF*, moderate, tel. 84-82-00-48.
La Bucherie, 14 rue de la Sous-Préfecture (street entering rue de

Besançon north of the *Cathédrale*), inexpensive pizza, tel. 84-82-27-61.
La Demi-Lune, 39 rue Pasteur, inexpensive, tel. 84-72-65-17.
Les Templiers, 35 Grande-Rue, moderate-expensive, tel. 84-82-78-78.
Clemenceau, 62 bis rue Arènes, moderate-expensive, tel. 84-79-16-47.

Hotels
Hôtel Moderne, 40 avenue Aristide-Briand, inexpensive, tel. 84-72-27-04.

Hôtel Cloche, 1 place Jules-Grévy, inexpensive-moderate, tel. 84-82-00-18.

Nouvel Hôtel, 2 place Jules-Grévy, inexpensive-moderate, tel. 84-79-12-11.

Grand Hôtel Chandioux, 2 rue de Besançon, moderate, tel. 84-79-00-66.

Sights Worth Seeing Nearby
Same as Besançon and Dijon, where you'll find better train service.

Besançon

Though Besançon is one of the most interesting and picturesque cities on the TGV system, it does not experience heavy tourist traffic. In the heart of the Franche-Comte region—a mountainous area more popular with European outdoorsmen than with tourists, who flock to the nearby Burgundy region instead—Besançon is often overlooked by travel guidebooks. However, the town is an easy day trip from either Dijon or Paris, and it's a great discovery for travelers who give it a chance.

The administrative capital of the Franche-Comte region, Besançon's 120,000 residents live along the pretty Doubs River, which forms a narrow loop through the middle of town. Anchored by a massive *Citadelle* that protected the city from invaders, Besançon today is prosperous, with a major university and several industries. For visitors, it has numerous museums, forts, historic sights, river walks, a great pedestrians-only street mall, and a cuisine blending Burgundian and Alsatian cooking.

TGV Travel from Paris
Four TGV trains travel daily from Paris to Besançon. The 233-mile trip takes two hours, 29 minutes. The *Gare de la Viotte* is along avenue de la Paix on the north side of town. Currently, the last TGV back to Paris leaves at 17:40.

Tourist Information Office
The *Office de Tourisme* and *Accueil de France* are at 2 place de la 1ere Armée-Française, about a mile from the *Gare de la Viotte*. To get there,

cross avenue de la Paix to avenue Maréchal-Foch, which becomes avenue d'Helvétie as it curves left beside the Doubs River. The office is across the busy traffic area at the beginning of the *Promenade Micaud*, a narrow park along the river. Bus #31 travels there from the station.

Tour of Historic Sights & Major Attractions

From the *Office de Tourisme*, exit left across the *Pont de la République* to central Besançon, then right on avenue Élisée-Cusenier, following the ancient ramparts bordering the Doubs River. Shortly after the street becomes rue Claude-Goudimel, you'll reach Besançon's acclaimed **Musée des Beaux-Arts**, the oldest (1694) public art museum in France, with major works by Rubens, Goya, Renoir, Matisse, and Picasso. The museum also has archaeological exhibits and a section devoted to clock- and watch-making, a big industry in Besançon until the advent of quartz technology.

After the museum, exit left through place de la Révolution (where a market may be open) to the **Grande-Rue**, Besançon's large, pedestrians-only shopping area that runs several blocks through the oldest quarter of town. (It's also the main route to the *Citadelle*.) After rue de la République, buses may travel on the street. At this junction on the left is the 18th-century **Église St.-Pierre**. To the right is the 16th-century **Hôtel de Ville**, with the 16th-century **Palais de Justice** one street behind it. Behind these buildings, you'll see university students traveling to classrooms in the area.

One long block beyond this intersection on the Grande-Rue, after crossing rue de la Prefecture, is the entrance to the **Palais Granvelle**, the former residence of Nicolas Perrenot de Granvelle (1486-1550), who rose from peasant stock to become a doctor of law and chancellor to Emperor Charles V. His son Antoine (1517-86) continued the family's success by becoming Cardinal-Prime Minister of the Lowlands, Viceroy of Naples, and Minister to Philip II of Spain.

Inside the palace is the **Musée d'Historique et d'Ethnographie**, containing exhibits about Besançon's history, a 17th-century Bruges tapestry illustrating Charles V's life, items of the Granvelle family, and mementos from Victor Hugo, born two blocks away in the house at 140 Grande-Rue. Behind the palace is a courtyard and gardens.

At the end of the Grande-Rue is the **Porte Noire**, a 2nd-century Roman arch—the original entrance to the city. Opposite, nearly built into the street, is the **Cathédrale St.-Jean**. Begun in the 12th-century but not completed until the 1700's, the *Cathédrale* has a unique 4th-century circular altar, a Renaissance masterpiece entitled *Virgin with Saints*, and a treasury with a gold crafts collection. Behind the church, the **Horloge Astronomique**, a 30,000-piece clock built by local craftsmen, features a mechanical Christ leaping from a tomb every day at noon. The figures on the clock begin moving ten minutes before every hour.

From the *Porte Noire*, walk past the *Cathédrale*, cross the street (bearing slightly to the right), then turn left onto rue des Fusillés-de-la-Résistance, a steep and winding road climbing to the **Citadelle**, a massive fortress on a cliff 400 feet above the Doubs River. Designed by Louis XIV's military architect and engineer Sébastien de Vauban (1633-1707), it was built in 1674 on the ancient site of a Gallo-Roman acropolis to thwart invading Swiss armies. The fort was an integral part of Vauban's 20-year building plan to fortify France's borders.

From the top of the *Citadelle*'s walls, you can see all of Besançon, plus the Doubs River as it flows through deep river valleys. The *Citadelle* contains a small zoo on its grounds (you probably noticed deer along the fence, following you up the main road), an aquarium, and three museums. The **Musée de la Resistance et de la Deportation** presents a painful reminder of the Nazi occupation of France. Exhibits explain the history of the French Resistance in the area and the role of the Vichy government during World War II. The four stakes outside the building mark the spot where the Nazis shot four members of the local resistance. The **Musée Populaire Comtois** is a folklore museum highlighting regional arts, crafts, and agricultural techniques. The **Musée d'Histoire Naturelle** displays the animals and plants of the Franche-Comte region.

After exploring this large complex, return to central Besançon. When you reach the *Cathédrale*, continue past it on rue du Chapitre, then turn left at rue Vieille-Monnaie, which ends at faubourg Tarragnoz at the river's edge, directly below the *Citadelle*. (This is a main highway, so watch out for speedy drivers!) There, board bus #31 or walk a mile to the left to cross the *Pont Passere Ile de Mazagran* to chemin de Mazagran. Bus #31 travels from the bridge through the city to the *Office de Tourisme* and the train station.

Follow chemin de Mazagran along the river back to the city and the *Pont de Gaulle* (the next bridge). After passing the small island in the middle of the river, note the stone walls on the other side—more of the original ramparts circling the city from the base of the *Citadelle*. When you reach the *Pont de Gaulle*, cross it to the **Promenade Chamars**, a large park along the river. If you need to return to the station, take bus #4 from the *Promenade*. If not, cross to the opposite side of the *Promenade*, following the paths or quais by the river for half a mile to the Grande-Rue. From the Grande-Rue, you can shop, return to your hotel, or walk to the station by crossing the *Pont de Battant* (past quai de Strasbourg), then going right on rue Battant to avenue Maréchal-Foch. The station is one block to the left from this intersection. The *esplanade de la Gare Viotte*, across from the station, is a pretty park to explore while waiting for the train.

Restaurants

Le Chaland, *Promenade Micaud* at the *Pont de Bregille* (opposite end of the *Promenade Micaud* from the *Office de Tourisme*), moderate-expensive, tel. 81-80-61-61.

Mungo Park, 11 rue Jean-Petit (backtrack from the *Musée des Beaux-Arts* for two blocks on rue Claude-Goudimel, then turn right), moderate-expensive, tel. 81-81-28-01.

Poker d'As, 14 square St.-Amour (three blocks from the *Pont de la République,* turn left off rue de la République onto rue Proudhon, then left two blocks later at this small square), moderate-expensive, tel. 81-81-42-49.

Tour de la Pelote, 41 quai Strasbourg (connects avenues Maréchal-Foch and d'Helvétie with the *Pont de Battant*), moderate-expensive, tel. 81-82-14-58.

Restaurant Carnot, 73 quai Veil-Picard (continuation of the quai Strasbourg past the *Pont de Battant*), inexpensive.

Restaurant Mégavand, rue Mégavand (walking toward the *Citadelle,* turn right off the Grande-Rue onto rue de la Préfecture, then left), inexpensive.

Le P'tit Loup, 9 rue du Lycée (at the *Pont de Battant* and Grande-Rue, with your back to the river, turn right on rue Claude-Pouillet, then left one block later), inexpensive, tel. 81-83-19-19.

La Boite à Sandwiches, 21 rue du Lycée, inexpensive, tel. 81-83-47-46.

Hotels

Hôtel Urbis, 5 avenue Maréchal-Foch (faces the *Gare de la Viotte*), moderate, tel. 81-88-27-26.

Hôtel Carnot, 8 avenue Carnot (at the foot of place de la 1ere Armée-Française, turn left instead of crossing to the *Office de Tourisme,* following the street as it curves left), inexpensive, tel. 81-88-06-23.

Hôtel Parc, 12 avenue Carnot, moderate, tel. 81-80-60-70.

Hôtel Mercure, 4 avenue Carnot (between *Office de Tourisme* and *Casino Municipal*), moderate, tel. 81-80-33-11.

Hôtel Altéa Parc Micaud, avenue Édouard-Droz (runs along east side of *Promenade Micaud*), moderate, tel. 81-80-14-44.

Hôtel Gambetta, 13 rue Gambetta (first left off avenue Elisée-Cusenier), inexpensive, tel. 81-83-50-54.

Hôtel Arcade, 21 rue Gambetta, moderate, tel. 81-83-50-54.

Sights Worth Seeing Nearby

Besançon is in the foothills of the **Jura Mountains,** which run along the France-Switzerland border from the Alsace region through the Franche-Comte region to Geneva. Similar in elevation and landscape to the Appalachian Mountains in the U.S., the lakes, wild rivers, caves, and hiking trails make the area very popular for outdoor recreation. The *Office de Tourisme* has basic trail maps and more information.

Beaune

For travelers interested in medieval history and premium wines, Beaune is the place. Over 2,000 years old, this town offers a good look at the past and, literally, a taste of the present.

Just 24 miles south of Dijon, Beaune was a Roman outpost and a residence of the 14th-century Dukes of Burgundy. Beaune's economy turned to wine production in the 17th century, and it has become the wine-trading center of the region and one of the best-preserved medieval towns in Europe. With only 20,000 residents, its compact size makes it easy to explore in a half-day, unless you visit several wine cellars.

TGV Travel from Paris
Three TGV trains travel daily from Paris to Beaune. The 219-mile trip takes one hour, 58 minutes. The *Gare SNCF* is at avenue de 8-Septembre on the east side of town. Currently, the last TGV back to Paris leaves at 14:22.

Tourist Information Office
The *Office de Tourisme*, where you can arrange visits to the city's wine caves and nearby vineyards, is almost two miles from the *Gare SNCF* in the center of town, across from Beaune's most famous site, the *Hôtel-Dieu*. To get there, follow avenue du 8-Septembre three blocks to the turreted **Bastion St.-Jean**, the former first line of defense, connected to the 14th-century ramparts that still enclose most of the town. Immediately after passing through the entrance, turn left onto a narrow, pedestrians-only passage bordering the interior walls, following it until you reach rue de l'Hôtel-Dieu. The *Office de Tourisme* is on the right. You can also get there by turning left off avenue du 8-Septembre onto boulevard Jules-Ferry, one of the names for the street that circles the city outside the ramparts, until you reach rue de l'Hôtel-Dieu.

Tour of Historic Sights & Major Attractions
The first thing you notice about the **Hôtel-Dieu** is the tile roof, a multi-colored, intricate design commonly found in Burgundian architecture. This historic building, which also features multiple turrets, steeply pitched dormer windows, and a beautiful cobblestone courtyard, was used as a charity hospital from 1443-1971. Today, half of it is a retirement home, though it's better known as the site of the annual **Burgundy wine auction**. Held the third Sunday in November to

determine the year's prices for specific vintages, the proceeds from the auction provide upkeep for the building and support other local charities. The sale is opened to the public, but reservations are required—often two years in advance!

Inside the *Hôtel-Dieu*, you'll find most of the hospital's original furnishings, including period costumes like those still worn by the nursing sisters who tend the residents. In the halls off the courtyard hang several ancient paintings and tapestries, including Rogier van der Weyden's *The Last Judgment*, commissioned as an altarpiece during the building's construction.

Wine aficionados should make time for at least one trip to a wine cave. Across the street before you reach the *Hôtel-Dieu* is the **Marché aux Vins**, Beaune's most prestigious cave, housed in a former 15th-century church. The 40-franc entrance fee lets you sample its 37 different wines. Another good cellar, **Maison Calvert** at 6 boulevard Perpreuil, offers a tour explaining the whole process of wine storage. To reach it, follow rue de l'Hôtel-Dieu outside the ramparts, then turn left on boulevard St.-Jacques/boulevard Perpreuil.

Not far north of the *Hôtel-Dieu* in a pedestrians-only zone (turn right off avenue de la République onto rue d'Enfer), the **Musée du Vin de Bourgogne** covers the history of local wine production from its beginnings to the 20th century. Housed in a medieval mansion (a residence of the Dukes of Burgundy), this wine museum has many interesting exhibits, including a 14th-century wine press house with vats and fermentation room.

A few blocks north of the museum in a large open square, the 12th-century **Église Collegiate-Notre-Dame**, modeled after the abbey at Cluny, features some exceptional art, including a 15th-century Flemish tapestry entitled *Life of the Virgin*, 15th-century frescoes, and a 12th-century statue of the Virgin.

North of the church, Beaune's small **Musée des Beaux-Arts** is housed in the chapel of a 17th-century convent. Although it has a variety of European art, the best paintings are by 19th-century landscape artist and Beaune native, Félix Ziem. In a separate gallery of the same museum, the **Musée Marey** showcases the work of Étienne-Jules Marey, a 19th-century scientist and pioneer of motion picture photography. To reach the museum, exit the rear of the church to rue Marey, turn right to place Monge, then left at rue de Lorraine, a street lined with many 16th-century homes. When rue de Lorraine splits a few blocks later, take the right fork, rue de l'Hôtel-de-Ville. Don't be alarmed to see police cars parked in front of the museum. The convent is also the *Hôtel de Ville* and police headquarters.

From the museum, wander through the interior of town and visit another wine cave. If you need to return to the *Gare SNCF* quickly, walk down rue de Lorraine to the old city gate *Porte St.-Nicolas*. Pass through the gate, then turn right onto boulevard Maréchal-Joffre. Stay on this street (another section of the street that circles the old city) until you come to avenue du 8-Septembre, the street that goes to the station.

Restaurants
Brasserie de la Gare, 33 rue de 8-Septembre, inexpensive.
Auberge St. Vincent, place Halle (north of the *Hôtel-Dieu*), moderate-expensive, tel. 80-22-42-34.
Rôtisserie La Paix, 47 rue du Faubourg Madeleine (exit left from the *Gare SNCF* on rue Celler, then turn right on rue de Seurre/rue du Faubourg Madeleine), moderate, tel. 80-22-33-33.
Brelinette, 6 rue du Faubourg Madeleine, inexpensive, tel. 80-22-63-94.
L'Eschelier, 2 rue du Faubourg Madeleine, inexpensive, tel. 80-22-22-40.
Auberge Bourguignonne, 4 place Madeleine (a large square to the right, halfway down rue du Faubourg Madeleine), moderate, tel. 80-22-23-53. (Also has eight moderately priced rooms.)
Maxime, 3 place Madeleine, inexpensive-moderate, tel. 80-22-17-82.
Les Gourmets, 17 rue Monge (to the right of the *Office de Tourisme*), moderate, tel. 80-22-15-99.
Au Petit Pressor, 15 place Fleury (just beyond the *Hôtel-Dieu* at the foot of avenue de la République), inexpensive-moderate, tel. 80-22-07-31.

Hotels
Hôtel de France, 35 avenue du 8 Septembre, inexpensive, tel. 80-22-19-99.
Hôtel la Cloche, 42 rue du faubourg Madeleine, moderate, tel. 80-24-66-33.
Hôtel Rousseau, 11 place Madeleine, inexpensive, tel. 80-22-18-59.
Central Hôtel, 2 rue Millot (short street near the *Hôtel-Dieu* connecting place Carnot with rue Poterne/rue Thiers), moderate, tel. 80-24-77-24.

Sights Worth Seeing Nearby
The *Office de Tourisme* can arrange tours of the nearby **Côte de Beaune** vineyards. Other Burgundy attractions are more accessible by train from Dijon.

Chalon-sur-Saône

Since its more popular neighbors Beaune and Dijon aren't far to the north, Chalon-sur-Saône is often bypassed by tourists. But then, this town doesn't rely much on tourism. Instead, it has cultivated the fur trade since the Middle Ages, coupled today with a few modern industries. Despite its commercial character, it's worth a short visit for an outstanding photography museum, a busy river quarter lined with 18th-century houses, and its waters filled with boats and barges.

TGV Travel from Paris

Three TGVs travel daily from Paris to Chalon-sur-Saône. The 209-mile trip takes two hours, 16 minutes. The *Gare SNCF* is at place de la Gare on the southwest side of town. Currently, the last TGV back to Paris leaves at 14:04.

Tourist Information Office

The *Office de Tourisme* is a few blocks from the *Gare SNCF* in a circular building at square Chabas, a small park at the intersection of boulevard de la République and rue Michelet. To reach it, exit the station onto avenue Jean-Jaurès (which enters place de la Gare), pass beneath a highway bridge, then cross rue Michelet to square Chabas.

Tour of Historic Sights & Major Attractions

From the *Office de Tourisme*, walk down boulevard de la République for three blocks and turn right on rue Denon. Almost five blocks later at the corner of place de l'Hôtel-de-Ville, you'll come to the **Musée Denon**, named for Vivant Denon, who organized the museum system in France under Napoléon. Housed in a former 18th-century convent, this combination fine arts/archaeology museum features Bronze Age implements and paintings from French, Italian, and Dutch artists.

From the *Musée Denon*, exit to the other side of place de l'Hôtel-de-Ville, veering left past the large *Hôtel de Ville*, then right on rue du Port-Villiers, which leads to the Saône River. Before you cross the street to see the river, walk left half a block to 28 quai des Messageries, home of the **Musée Nicéphore-Nièpce** (a.k.a. *Musée de la Photographie* or *Maison Européene de la Photographie*).

Born in Chalon-sur-Saône in 1765, Nièpce is the scientist credited with inventing photography in 1826. The museum, housed in the 18th-century *Hôtel des Messageries*, contains an interesting collection of cameras dating to the early 19th-century, the first camera used on the U.S.A.'s Apollo space mission, and cameras used by spies. The second floor offers a small collection by 20th-century European photographers.

For a good view of the city, exit the museum to the left on quai des Messageries to the short *Pont St.-Laurent*, which crosses to the triangular *Ile St.-Laurent*. Immediately after crossing the bridge, turn right on quai de l'Hôpital and walk past the 16th-century hospital to the **Tour de Doyenne** on the tip of the island. From the top, you can see all of Chalon-sur-Saône and nearby vineyards.

Cross back to the city, staying on rue du Pont for a block, then turn right on rue St.-Vincent to view the 12th-century **Cathédrale St.-Vincent**, which contains some interesting statues, Renaissance tapestries, and a 16th-century altarpiece.

To return to the *Gare SNCF,* backtrack down rue St.-Vincent to rue du Pont and cross to rue du Châtelet, a street lined with 17th- and 18th-century townhouses. House #37 is the most interesting, with a façade of bas-relief sculpture and gargoyles. When this short street ends at place du Châtelet, continue to the left to the Saône River, following it to the right on quai des Messageries/quai Gambetta, then right onto rue Michelet, then left at the corner of boulevard de la République and square Chabas. Bus #2 also travels along the quais to the *Gare SNCF.*

Restaurants

Gourmets, 15 avenue Jean-Jaurès, moderate, tel. 85-48-37-25.

Ribert, 31 rue St.-Georges (walk away from the river on rue Port-Villiers, turn right on rue au Change, then turn left two blocks later), inexpensive-moderate, tel. 85-48-89-20.

Marché, 7 place St.-Vincent (opposite the *Cathédrale St.-Vincent*), inexpensive-moderate, tel. 85-48-62-00.

Didier Denis, 1 rue du Pont, moderate-expensive, tel. 85-48-81-01.

Le Bourgogne, 28 rue de Strasbourg (after crossing *Pont St.-Laurent* to *Ile St.-Laurent*, veer left), moderate-expensive, tel. 85-48-81-01.

L'Ille Bleue, 3 rue de Strasbourg, moderate, tel. 85-48-39-83.

Hotels

Hôtel St.-Georges, 32 avenue Jean-Jaurès, moderate, tel. 85-48-27-05 (excellent restaurant on premises).

Nouvel, 7 avenue Boucicaut (turn left off avenue Jean-Jaurès before reaching the highway bridge), inexpensive, tel. 85-48-07-31.

Hôtel St.-Régis, 22 boulevard de la République (two blocks beyond the *Office de Tourisme*), moderate, tel. 85-48-07-28.

Royal Hôtel, 8 rue du Port-Villiers, moderate, tel. 85-48-15-86.

Hôtel St.-Jean, 24 quai Gambetta, inexpensive, tel. 85-48-45-65.

Sights Worth Seeing Nearby

The small medieval town of **Autun** is 33 miles west on the D978 highway.

CHAPTER 7

East Central France

Mâcon

Although officially in Burgundy, Mâcon has buildings with the curved, red-tiled roofs more common in the Midi region near Toulouse. Because Mâcon is far from most Burgundian sights and close to Lyon, tourists often skip this town, whose trade revolves around the wine industry. However, it's worth a short stop to see a commercial French city on a smaller scale and to make a base for side trips to the medieval abbey of Cluny and to nearby vineyards.

TGV Travel from Paris

Eight trains travel daily from Paris to Mâcon. The 226-mile trip takes one hour, 40 minutes. The *Gare TGV Mâcon-Loché*, built specifically for the TGV, is four miles south of Mâcon in the country, just west of the A6 expressway. Currently, the last TGV back to Paris leaves at 22:15.

Tourist Information Office

The *Office de Tourisme* is at 187 rue Carnot in the center of the city, one block west of the Saône River. Since it's a considerable distance from the *Gare TGV Mâcon-Loché* via several busy highways, the best way to get there is by taxi.

Tour of Historic Sights & Major Attractions

From the *Office de Tourisme*, continue down rue Carnot to rue Sigorgne. Two blocks to the left, housed in the elegant 18th-century *Hôtel Senéce*, is the **Musée Lamartine**, containing 19th-century art, furniture, and other mementos of the poet Lamartine, famous for proclaiming the founding of the second French Republic. From this small museum, backtrack on rue Sigorgne to its end at quai Lamartine and the **Saône River**, where you can view barges and boats being loaded with wine and other goods for shipment. For an overall view of Mâcon, cross the 14th-century *Pont St.-Laurent* over the river to the suburb of St.-Laurent-sur-Saône. Returning to central Mâcon, walk straight ahead from the *Pont St.-Laurent* on rue du Pont to rue St.-Vincent, and turn right to the remains of the **Vieux St.-Vincent**, a small Romanesque church partly destroyed in 1795. Not far from there, walking left away from the church to the intersection of place de la Baille and rue des Ursulines, is the **Musée Municipales des Ursulines**, housed in a 17th-century Ursuline convent. This combination art and archaeology museum open since 1971 has paintings by Courbet, Monet, de Chavannes, and several lesser-known artists of the 17th to 20th centuries.

To return to the *Gare TGV Mâcon-Loché*, take a taxi.

Restaurants

La Perdrix, 6 rue Victor-Hugo (in the *Grand Hôtel de Bourgogne*; exit left from the *Office de Tourisme*, then right on rue Gambetta to rue Victor-Hugo, then right for half a mile), moderate, tel. 85-38-36-57.

Rocher de Cancale, 393 quai Jean-Jaurès (the street along the river, north of the *Pont St.-Laurent*), moderate-expensive, tel. 85-38-07-50.

Auberge Bressane, 114 rue 28-Juin 1944 (follow quai Jean-Jaurès until it becomes avenue de Lattre de Tassigny, then turn left), moderate-expensive, tel. 85-38-07-42.

Le Saint Laurent, 1 quai Bouchacourt (turn left after crossing the *Pont St.-Laurent*), moderate-expensive, tel. 85-38-32-03.

Hotels

Hôtel Terminus, 91 rue Victor-Hugo (on the right at the corner of rue Gambetta), inexpensive-moderate, tel. 85-39-17-11.

Hôtel Genève, 1 rue Bigonnet (turn left from the intersection above), inexpensive-moderate, tel. 85-38-18-10.

Hôtel la Promenade, 266 quai Lamartine, inexpensive, tel. 85-38-10-98.

Hôtel Bellevue, 416-420 quai Lamartine, moderate, tel. 85-38-05-07.

Sights Worth Seeing Nearby

Cluny, 15 miles northwest of Mâcon, is the former medieval seat of a Benedictine order (founded in 910 A.D.) that exercised religious, intellectual, and artistic control over most of Europe during the Middle Ages. Although little remains of the abbey (built 1088-1130), which was the largest in Europe at the time, the restored Gothic façade and the town's narrow, winding streets with old houses evoke Cluny's medieval past. There is frequent bus service to Cluny from Mâcon's *Gare Routière* (at the intersection of rues Gambetta, Victor-Hugo, and Bigonnet).

The **vineyards** on the outskirts of Mâcon produce the Pouilly-Fuissé white wines. For red wine fans, the famed *Route de Beaujolais* starts in **Juliénais**, five miles south of Mâcon. The *Office de Tourisme* can arrange visits to the vineyards.

Bourg-en-Bresse

Just 21 miles east of Mâcon on the southeast tip of Burgundy, this small city is well-known by gourmets as the major market for the Bresse chicken raised in the area. Each week, thousands of chickens and capons are sold at the poultry market. According to the buyers, it's the best chicken in the world. With several outstanding restaurants featuring chicken specialties, Bourg-en-Bresse is also worth a stop for the medieval *Église de Brou*, an early 16th-century church and monastery like no other in France.

TGV Travel from Paris
Seven TGV trains travel daily from Paris to Bourg-en-Bresse. The 250-mile trip takes one hour, 55 minutes. The *Gare SNCF* is along avenue Pierre-Sémard on the west side of town. Currently, the last TGV back to Paris leaves at 18:25.

Tourist Information Office
The *Office de Tourisme* is at 6 avenue Alsace-Lorraine in the center of the city. To reach it, cross avenue Pierre-Sémard to avenue Alphonse-Baudin. When the street splits a few blocks later, take the left fork, which is avenue Alsace-Lorraine.

If you only want to see the *Église de Brou*, skip this office, since it's on the opposite side of town. In July and August, a small *Office de Tourisme* annex is open next to the church.

Tour of Historic Sights & Major Attractions
The **Église de Brou** is one of France's greatest medieval treasures. Built from 1506-32 in the wildly decorative, Flamboyant Gothic-style, this small, squat church was commissioned by Margaret of Austria to house the tomb of her husband Philibert le Beau, Duke of Savoy. The interior, designed as a cross with three naves, features sculpture by Van Boghem, an ornate Renaissance doorway, Carrera marble statues, 74 oak choir stalls carved with Biblical scenes, and the tombs of Margaret of Austria, Duke Philibert, and Margaret of Bourbon, grandmother of King François I. The chapel features a marble altar depicting "The Seven Joys of the Madonna" and a stained-glass window patterned after a Dürer engraving. Nowhere in France will you find so much ornament in such a small space.

Next to the church in the monastery, the small **Musée de l'Ain** displays paintings, sculpture, furniture, and ceramics. The most interesting paintings are by Jan "Velvet" Bruegel, son of Pieter Bruegel, the greatest Dutch painter of the 16th-century, and portraits by Alphonse Baudin, a native of Bourg-en-Bresse. On a humorous note, the *Salle du Coq* (Hall of the Chicken) features artistic renditions of poultry.

For the most direct route to the *Église de Brou*, exit right from the *Gare SNCF* on avenue Pierre-Sémard for a half-mile, then turn left on boulevard Jules-Ferry/boulevard Emile-Huchet/boulevard Paul-Valéry for over a mile, until you come to rue Tony-Ferret, which enters the street at a left angle. Follow it to its end at boulevard de Brou. The *Église de Brou* is directly across the street. If you'd rather not walk, take bus #1 from the *Gare SNCF.*

Additional Bourg-en-Bresse sights worth seeing include the **Église Collégiale-de-Notre-Dame**, the city's oldest church (1505), and several 15th-century buildings in the center of town. To reach these sights, board bus #1 or follow boulevard de Brou to rue des Bons-Enfants. Turn left, then right at rue Samaritaine, which crosses in front of the church.

For a short circular detour, continue for another block on rue des Bons-Enfants until it ends at rue Victor-Basch, a street with several well-preserved 15th-century homes. From there, walk one block to the right to rue Gambetta, which also has several old homes. A right turn takes you back to rue Samaritaine. After a look inside the church at its finely carved, 16th-century choir stalls, follow rue Notre-Dame away from the church to rue Bichat. Two blocks to the right is the oddly-shaped **place de la Grenette** and more old buildings.

To return to the *Gare SNCF* from the rue Bichat intersection, cross the street to the *Hôtel de Ville*, then turn left around the corner to avenue Alsace-Lorraine, retracing the directions to the *Office de Tourisme*.

Restaurants

Mail, 46 avenue du Mail (exit left from the *Gare SNCF*, then left beneath the tracks), moderate, tel. 74-21-00-26 (also has nine moderately priced rooms).

Restaurant de l'Église de Brou, across from the *Église de Brou*, moderate, tel. 74-22-15-28.

Ermitage, 142 boulevard de Brou, moderate, tel. 74-22-19-00.

Auberge Bressane, 166 boulevard de Brou, moderate, tel. 74-22-22-68.

Chalet de Brou, 168 boulevard de Brou, moderate, tel. 74-22-26-28.

Le Français, 7 avenue Alsace-Lorraine (near the *Hôtel de Ville*), moderate, tel. 74-22-55-14.

Brasserie du Theatre, 1 rue Paul-Pioda (turn right off rue Notre-Dame onto rue Pasteur/rue Paul-Pioda) moderate, tel. 74-23-35-72.

Hotels

Hôtel Terminus, 19 avenue Alphonse-Baudin (across from the *Gare*

SNCF), moderate, tel. 74-21-01-21.

Hôtel Prieuré, 49 boulevard de Brou, moderate, tel. 74-22-44-60.
Le Logis de Brou, 132 boulevard de Brou, moderate, tel. 74-22-11-55.
Hôtel Ibis, boulevard Charles-de-Gaulle (first major road past the *Église de Brou* to the left for a short distance), moderate, tel. 74-22-52-66.

Sights Worth Seeing Nearby

For some fresh country air, venture 35 miles east of Bourg-en-Bresse to the village of **Nantua**, located on a pretty lake. At this popular summer resort, you can hike around the fir-lined shore or climb to the top of the 3,698-foot Mont d'Ain for a panoramic view. Before leaving, duck into the church to see a Renaissance altar and Delacroix's *Martyrdom of St. Sebastian*. A few non-TGV trains travel there daily, or you can drive there on the D979 highway.

Lyon

Tourists, dashing from Paris to the French Riviera, often skip Lyon, the third largest city in France—a shame, since there's plenty to see and do there. It's worth at least a day to see the major sights, and two or more days to include a few of its outstanding museums in your itinerary.

At the convergence of the rushing Rhône and Saône Rivers, Lyon has been one of France's most important cities since the Romans claimed it in 43 B.C. Valued for its central location and easy access to the Mediterranean Sea (via the Rhône, one of the longest navigable rivers in France), Lyon quickly became a progressive, commercial city.

Today, with over 1.2 million residents, Lyon leads France in the silk production, publishing, and banking industries. It's also a popular site for trade conventions, a major university center with schools comparable to those in Paris, and the gastronomic capital of France. Some of France's finest chefs have a restaurant or *bouchon* (bistro) in the city or a nearby village. Although it will lighten your wallet, a meal in Lyon could become the highlight of your entire trip.

TGV Travel from Paris

Thirty-three TGV trains travel daily from Paris to Lyon. The 265-mile trip takes two hours to the *Gare de la Part-Dieu* and another 10-15 minutes to the *Gare de Perrache*. There are also direct lines bypassing Paris to Lyon from Amiens, Arras, Douai, and Lille in northern France and a line to Lyon from Versailles, Mantes la-Jolie, and Rouen.

The TGV serves two Lyon train stations. From Paris, the first stop is usually the *Gare de la Part-Dieu* on the east side of Lyon, in the heart of the city's business district. This modern station was built specifically for the TGV. You enter the main terminal at place de la Gare de la Part-Dieu, off boulevard Marius-Vivier-Merle. The entrance to a smaller terminal on the east side of the tracks is off rue de la Villette.

The TGV's other stop, *Gare de Perrache*, is south of the *Pont Galliéni* and *Pont Kitchener-Marchand* on the narrow peninsula in west Lyon that divides the Rhône and Saône Rivers. This station is in the older section of town, near most of the sights described in the tour below.

Note: Not all TGV trains stop at both stations. If your train stops only at the *Gare de la Part-Dieu*, you must take the Lyon Métro or a taxi to the *Gare de Perrache* to start the tour described below. (The stations are four miles apart.) It's also important to make reservations for the TGV to Lyon a few days in advance. It's the TGV's most popular route, and it's usually filled with business people and travelers going south to the Riviera or the Alps.

Currently, the last TGV back to Paris leaves at 21:49 from the *Gare de la Part-Dieu*.

Tourist Information Office

The *Office de Tourisme* and *Accueil de France* are a mile north of the *Gare de Perrache* at the spacious place Bellecour, one of the largest open squares in France. To get there, exit the upper level of the *Gare de Perrache* by the ticket counters through an overhead concourse to the *Centre d'Echanges*, a multi-use complex above the street just north of the station. From this building, take the escalator down to place Carnot, crossing it to the pedestrians-only rue Victor Hugo, a lively shopping street that ends at place Bellecour. The *Office de Tourisme* is on the lower right corner of the square, behind the flower market in the *Pavillon Est*. You can also take the Lyon Métro there from the *Gare de Perrache*.

Small *Office de Tourisme* annexes are inside the *Gare de la Part-Dieu* and *Centre d'Echanges*, and at 25 cours Émile-Zola in the eastern suburb Villeurbanne.

Tour of Historic Sights & Major Attractions

The most interesting sights to explore in Lyon are west of the Rhône River on the peninsula and across the Saône River in *Vieux Lyon*.

From the *Office de Tourisme*, cross place Bellecour to admire the equestrian statue of Louis XIV and the 18th-century buildings around the square. From the statue, continue across the top of place Bellecour to the *Pont Bonaparte*, which crosses the Saône River to **Vieux Lyon**, where you'll find the most 15th-century Renaissance buildings in one location in France.

Straight ahead from the bridge, there's the station for a **funicular** that runs to two locations in the steep hills above *Vieux Lyon*. Buy a ticket at the vending machine and board the car on the right marked

"Fourvière" for a ride to the **Basilique Notre-Dame-de-Fourvière**, a fortress-like cathedral begun in 1870 over the site of a Romanesque church. Considered ugly by some critics, this cathedral offers a unique blend of architectural styles, from Romanesque to Classical, and is visible throughout Lyon. From its terrace and towers, you'll get superb views of the city, and on clear days you can see Mont Blanc and the Alps.

Just south of the cathedral on rue Cléberg via montée de Fourvière, the **Musée Gallo-Romain ou Archéologique**, built in 1975, illustrates the history of Lyon from the Neolithic Era to the Middle Ages. Numerous Roman artifacts—art, jewelry, money, and weapons—enhance its collection.

From the museum, you can see the excavation of two Roman theaters (**Théâtres Romains**) discovered in the 1930's. The larger dates to 15 B.C., making it the oldest theater in France. For a closer look, follow rue Cléberg to place de l'Antiquaille, where a right turn takes you to the theater entrance at 6 rue de l'Antiquaille.

After visiting the Roman sites, return to the streets near the river via the funicular at the cathedral, or, using a good map, follow the roads down the hill. Facing the river in front of the funicular station, turn left through place Édouard-Commette to the **Cathédrale St.-Jean**, which features a combination of Romanesque/Flamboyant Gothic architecture. Check out the front portals decorated with zodiac signs and statues telling the story of creation, then duck inside to see the Bourbon chapel, 13th-century stained glass windows, and the treasury with Lyonnais silk and jewels. If you arrive at the top of the hour, you'll hear a 16th-century clock announce the time with a herald of roosters and angels.

North of the *Cathédrale*, at the foot of the Fourvière hill, lies the heart of the **St.-Jean Quartier**, the most interesting part of Lyon. Off the pedestrians-only rue St.-Jean, numerous alleys, courtyards, spiral stairs, and hanging gardens give a true picture of medieval Lyon. In the same area, over 100 *traboules* (covered passageways) connect the streets through courtyards and buildings. Since the entrances to many *traboules* are hidden behind large doors, ask the *Office de Tourisme* for their *Les Traboules* map or take one of their guided *traboule* tours. During World War II, the French Resistance used the *traboules* to harrass and avoid Nazis.

The best way to explore this area is to wander down rue St.-Jean, investigating side streets at will. Don't worry about getting lost, since any downhill direction will return you to the river. Halfway down the street, rue de la Fronde on the left leads to the **Musée Historique de Lyon**, housed in the 15th-century *Hôtel de Gadagne*. This small museum at 12 rue de Gadagne depicts Lyon's history through exhibits of furniture, ceramics, and paintings. In the same building, the **Musée de la Mari-**

onette displays one of the world's best collections of marionettes and puppets, including Guignol, the best-known French marionette.

Beyond this museum, rue de Gadagne empties into the pedestrians-only place du Change, former site of the Renaissance drapery market, now occupied by a small church and several mansions with Gothic arcades. (It's also the north end of rue St.-Jean, if you want to return to the *Gare de Perrache* from there.) A few blocks further north on rue Lainerie/rue François-Vernay, the small **Église St.-Paul** features an octagonal lantern tower from the 12th-century and a Flamboyant Gothic chapel. Although this church has been rebuilt, there has been a church on the site since the 6th century.

From there, backtrack one block to place St.-Paul, go left across the Saône River on the *Pont de la Feuillée*, and angle slightly to the right to rue de Constantine. Two long blocks down this street will bring you to Lyon's *Musée des Beaux-Arts* and *Hôtel de Ville* on adjacent ends of place des Terreaux, which is dominated by a fountain created by Frédéric Bartholdi, creator of the Statue of Liberty.

The large **Musée des Beaux-Arts**, housed in a 1659 Benedictine abbey, contains a diverse collection of paintings and sculpture: Etruscan, Egyptian, Phoenician, Sumerian, and Persian art, plus masterpieces by non-French artists like Rembrandt, Picasso, and Rubens. But it excels most in its collection of 19th-century paintings, which rivals the collections in Paris. Delacroix, Corot, Daumier, Manet, Degas, Renoir, Gauguin, Van Gogh, and Rodin are all represented. Many of the 90-plus galleries are filled with unique treasures confiscated by Napoléon during his military campaigns.

At the east end of the square opposite the *Musée des Beaux-Arts*, the **Hôtel de Ville** is considered one of the most beautiful town halls in Europe. On the second floor you'll find several opulent reception rooms with parquet floors, crystal chandeliers, and walls lined with murals.

From there, you have different options. If you're not in a hurry to leave Lyon, enter the *Hôtel de Ville*'s Métro stop at the east end of the building and take Line C to the Croix-Rousse stop. The hilly **Croix-Rousse neighborhood** is home of the French silk industry and the scene of riots in the 1830's between workers and the local militia. Until recently, most of the weavers lived and worked in this area.

After exiting the Croix-Rousse Métro stop, head to the far north end of place de la Croix-Rousse, entered via the Grande-Rue de la Croix-Rousse. One block later, turn right onto rue d'Ivry, stopping at #10-12 for the **Musée de Canutes**. This small museum devoted to the silk industry has examples of woven silk, looms from the past and present, and a small workshop where weavers still make their exquisite creations.

From there, backtrack to the Métro stop and ride back to the *Hôtel* de Ville, where you can change to Line A to return to the *Gare de Perrache*. If you'd rather walk, cross the wide boulevard de la Croix-Rousse to rue des Pierres-Plantées/montée de la Grande Cole/rue Ste.-Marie-des-Terreaux, which eventually leads to place des Terreaux. If you have time, explore the narrow side streets jutting into this avenue. Like *Vieux Lyon*, the area is full of *traboules*.

Whether you toured the Croix-Rousse neighborhood or not, continue the walking tour by following the wide, pedestrians-only rue de la République south from the east end of the *Hôtel de Ville*. Seven blocks later at 13 rue de la Poulaillerie (a short street opposite the *Palais de la Bourse*), the **Musée de l'Imprimerie et de la Banque** highlights Lyon's role in the printing and banking industries. Housed in a 15th-century mansion, the printing portion of the museum includes pages from a Gutenberg Bible, 17th- to early 20th-century printing presses, and books dating to the 1500's, including the first book printed in French. The banking section offers exhibits on banking from the 16th-century to the present.

After this museum, you can return to the *Gare de Perrache* via the Cordeliers Métro stop (just past the *Palais de la Bourse*) or continue walking down rue de la République for several blocks to place Bellecour. Skirting its east side, walk on rue de la Charité, a pretty street lined with elegant homes, shops, and restaurants. At #30, in the 1739 *Hôtel Lacroix-Laval*, the **Musée des Arts-Decoratifs** has exhibits of 17th- and 18th-century furniture, musical instruments, and decorative objects. Next door (#34), the **Musée Historique des Tissus** contains a priceless collection of international fabric and textile creations spanning 2,000 years. Even if the collections of these two museums don't interest you, the interior decoration and architecture are worth seeing for a good look at past wealth in Lyon. A single ticket gives admission to both museums.

A half-mile from these museums is the *Gare de Perrache*. When rue de la Charité ends, walk right for one block to place Carnot. Bus #44 traveling down this street will take you to the station.

Lyon Outside the Old Quarter

If you're staying more than a day in Lyon, be sure to explore the city east of the Rhône River. Although this modern part of Lyon doesn't compare with the old quarter or the sights on the peninsula, it does have some interesting museums, the city's largest park, and a huge shopping mall.

On the north edge of Lyon, bordering the Rhône River, is the 350-acre **Parc de la Tête d'Or**. (The TGV parallels its eastern border after crossing the Rhône when entering the city.) Used by residents for centuries, it features a lake with islands, a zoo, botanical gardens, a mini-golf course, and a 19-acre rose garden. The fastest way to reach the park from the

Gare de Perrache is on Métro Line A to the Masséna stop. From this stop, follow rue Masséna or rue Tête d'Or north to boulevard des Belges, which borders the south side of the park. From the *Gare de la Part-Dieu*, ride Métro Line B two stops north to the Charpennes stop and change to Line A, or walk three blocks west of the stop to the railroad tracks, then go right on boulevard des Belges two blocks later.

Since the park's many paths and streets wind all over the place, get a city map showing the park's layout before visiting. The allée du Parc aux Daims takes you directly from boulevard des Belges to the lake. On the way out of the park, stop at 28-30 boulevard des Belges for the small **Musée Guimet d'Histoire Naturelle**.

After the park and/or museum, walk south on rue Boileau, the street entering boulevard des Belges on the west side of the *Musée Guimet*, where you'll find the **Musée de la Resistance et de la Deportation** at #5. This small museum examines Lyon's Resistance movement in World War II and the deportation of area Jews to Nazi concentration camps. Lyon is where the legendary Resistance leader Jean Moulin was imprisoned and tortured by order of Klaus Barbie, the infamous "Butcher of Lyon." The **Montluc Prison**, where the Gestapo held prisoners between torture sessions, is a half-mile south of the *Gare de la Part-Dieu*, via boulevard Marius-Vivier-Merle. It's still a prison today.

One other "must" museum is the **Nouveau Musée**, Lyon's modern art museum and exhibition hall, a mile east of the *Gare de la Part-Dieu* in the suburb Villeurbanne. To get there, exit left from the station's east terminal on rue de la Villette for four short blocks. Turn right at rue de Bonnel/rue St.-Antoine/rue de la Convention, walking to its end at rue du Docteur-Dolard. The museum is across the street to the right.

For a last-minute souvenir, head for the modern **La Part Dieu Centre Commercial**, the large office/cultural/shopping complex across the street from the *Gare de la Part-Dieu*. The home of many French companies, it also has a concert hall, exposition and convention space, one of the largest libraries outside Paris, and the largest shopping mall in Europe.

Restaurants

Bistrot de la Mère, 26 cours de Verdun-Perrache (a two-blocks-long street east of the *Gare de Perrache* concourse to the *Centre d'Echanges*), moderate, tel. 78-42-16-91.

Brasserie Georges, 30 cours de Verdun-Perrache, moderate, tel. 78-37-15-78.

La Tassee, 20 rue de la Charité, moderate, tel. 78-37-02-35.

Tante Alice, 22 rue des Rempart-d'Ainay (crosses rue Victor-Hugo), moderate, tel. 78-37-49-83.

Vivaris, 1 place Gailleton (turn right off rue Victor-Hugo onto rue Ste.-Hélène to this place opposite the *Pont de l'Université* and *Rhône River*), moderate, tel. 78-37-85-15.

Restaurant La Voûte, 11 place Antonin-Gourju (opposite the *Pont Bonaparte* at the Saône River), moderate, tel. 78-42-01-33.

Bouchon de Fourvière, 33 quai Fulchiron (turn left in *Vieux Lyon* after crossing the *Pont Bonaparte*), moderate, tel. 72-41-85-02.

Boeuf d'Argent, 29 rue du Boeuf (in *Vieux Lyon*, turn left off rue St.-Jean onto rue de la Bombarde, then take the next right), moderate, tel. 78-42-21-12.

Café des Federations (*bouchon*), 8 rue Major-Martin (across from the west side of the *Musée des Beaux Arts*), moderate, tel. 78-28-26-00.

La Meuniere (*bouchon*), 11 rue Neuve (crosses rue de la République five blocks south of the *Hôtel de Ville*), inexpensive-moderate, tel. 78-28-62-91.

Savoy, 50 rue de la République, moderate, tel. 78-37-69-25.

Café du Jura (*bouchon*), 25 rue Tupin (crosses rue de la République two blocks south of the *Palais de la Bourse*), moderate, tel. 78-42-20-57.

Chez Sylvain (*bouchon*), 4 rue Tupin, moderate, tel. 78-42-11-98.

Grand Café des Négociants (*bouchon*), 1 place Francisque-Régaud (at the intersection of rues Tupin and Président-Édouard-Herriot), moderate, tel. 78-42-50-05.

Chez Rose (*bouchon*), 4 rue Rabelais (exit right from the *Gare de la Part-Dieu*, then left on rue de Bonnel, right on rue Du Guesclin, left two blocks later), moderate, tel. 78-60-57-25.

Hotels

Grand Hôtel Bordeaux, 1 rue du Bélier (two-blocks-long street east of the *Gare de Perrache* concourse to the *Centre d'Echanges*), moderate, tel. 78-37-58-73.

Hôtel Normandie, 3 rue du Bélier, inexpensive-moderate, tel. 78-37-31-36.

Hôtel Berlioz, 12 cours Charlemagne (wide street running beneath and directly south of the *Gare de Perrache*), moderate, tel. 78-42-30-31.

Hôtel Charlemagne, 23 cours Charlemagne, moderate-expensive, tel. 78-92-81-61.

La Résidence, 18 rue Victor-Hugo, moderate, tel. 78-42-63-28.

Hôtel Bayard, 23 place Bellecour (across from the *Office de Tourisme*), moderate, tel. 78-37-39-64.

Hôtel Royal, 20 place Bellecour, moderate-expensive, tel. 78-37-57-31.

Hôtel Globe, 21 rue Gasparin (one block north of place Bellecour), moderate, tel. 78-42-58-95.

Hôtel Mercure, 47 boulevard Marius-Vivier-Merle (extension of the *Gare de la Part-Dieu*), expensive, tel. 72-34-18-12.

Ibis, place Pierre-Renaudel (across the street from the *Gare de la Part-Dieu*, then left for two long blocks), moderate, tel. 78-95-42-11.

Sights Worth Seeing Nearby

A little over five miles north of Lyon, in the village Collonges-au-Mont-d'Or, is the three-star restaurant owned by the famous chef **Paul Bocuse**. If you can afford it (600-plus francs), you'll have one of the premier dining experiences in the world. To get there by car, follow the D51 highway north along the left bank of the Saône River. Bus #40 travels to the village from the quai Pêcherie, just south of the *Pont de la Feuillée*. Of course, you must make reservations several months in advance (tel. 78-22-01-40).

St.-Étienne

Although St.-Étienne is ringed by factories and warehouses involved in metallurgical industries, it's worth a stop for its fine art museum and for a classic French meal. The town is in the same gastronomic region as Lyon, and several area restaurants have earned Michelin stars and other accolades from food critics. And soccer fans take note: St.-Étienne is home of *Les Verts*, one of the country's best teams.

TGV Travel from Paris

Four TGV trains travel daily from Paris to St.-Étienne. The 314-mile trip takes two hours, 46 minutes. The *Gare de Châteaucreux* is at square Stalingrad on the east side of town. Currently, the last TGV back to Paris leaves at 18:01.

Tourist Information Office

The *Office de Accueil et d'Information* is at 12 rue Gérenet across the street from the *Hôtel de Ville*, slightly over a mile from the *Gare de Châteaucreux*. To get there, cross square Stalingrad to avenue Denfert-Rochereau, following it to place Fourneyron. From there, turn right onto the wide rue de la République, then another right onto rue Gérenet. The office is two blocks further on the right.

Tour of Historic Sights & Major Attractions

To reach the fine arts museum from the station, follow the walking route above for the *Office de Accueil* one block beyond rue Gérentet on rue de la République, then left on rue du Général-Foy. After the turn, you'll come to place du Peuple (trolleybus #10 from the *Gare de Châteaucreux* stops there, too), the heart of St.-Étienne's **Vieux Quartier**. This primarily pedestrians-only area includes numerous buildings from the 16th century and the 15th-century *Église St.-Étienne*, three blocks west of place du Peuple on rue Ste.-Catherine.

After exploring this area, continue through place du Peuple onto rue Gambetta (or ride the tram down the street) for about a mile, then turn right onto cours Jovin-Bouchard, which leads to the **Palais des Arts** (8 place Louis-Comte), home of the **Musée d'Art** and the **Musée d'Industrie**. Housed within a 19th-century palace in a hillside park, the highlights of the art museum's collection are paintings and sculpture by 20th-century French and American artists, including Picasso, Matisse, Warhol, Calder, Nevelson, and Stella. Another section of the museum is dedicated to the Symbolist artists (including Meunier and Maurin), plus a few paintings by 17th-century Dutch, French, and Italians. Like most museums in France, it has a Rodin sculpture. The *Musée d'Industrie* displays objects and documents relating to the local mining industry. It also has a collection of guns, motorcycles, bicycles, and silk—other prosperous industries of the city.

To return to the *Gare de Châteaucreux*, you can retrace your steps or take a more scenic walk by exiting the *Palais des Arts* across place Louis-Comte and rue Gambetta to rue de la Badouillière. (Also, bus #7 crossing this street at rue Fougerolle goes to the station.) When this street ends at cours Gustave-Nadaud, cross it veering right, then fork left onto rue Arago. A few steps later, turn left on the short streets leading into the **Jardin des Plantes**, a large park and botanical gardens.

If you have time, wander through this beautiful park. Otherwise, walk left on allée Chantegrillet to the **Maison de la Culture**, a building used for local art shows and cultural happenings. Beyond it, allée Chantegrillet continues straight for a short distance, angles to the right, then takes a twisting left, twisting right, and a hard left to become rue Chantegrillet. After passing a technical school on the left, the street ends at the intersection of place Locarno (the southern extension of place Fourneyron) and rue de la République. Avenue Denfert-Rochereau across place Locarno leads to the station.

Restaurants

Le Regency, 17 boulevard Jules-Janin (exit right from the *Gare de Châteaucreux* past several railroad buildings, follow the street going beneath the tracks, then turn left at the second street on the other side), moderate, tel. 77-74-27-06.

Le Bouchan, 7 rue Robert (three blocks beyond the *Office de Accueil*), expensive, tel. 77-32-93-32.

Praire, 14 rue Praire (continuation to left of rue Robert, above), expensive, tel. 77-37-85-74.

Le Gratin, 30 rue St.-Jean (pedestrians-only street off rue de la République, two blocks before rue Général-Foy), moderate, tel. 77-32-52-60.

Pierre Gagnire, 3 rue Georges-Teissier (one block to the right off rue Général-Foy), expensive, tel. 77-37-57-93.

Andre Barcet, 19 bis cours Victor-Hugo (street paralleling rue Gambetta), expensive, tel. 77-32-43-63.

Hotels

Hôtel Terminus du Forez, 31 avenue Denfert-Rochereau, moderate, tel. 77-32-48-47.

Hôtel Carnot, 11 boulevard Jules-Janin, moderate, tel. 77-74-27-16.

Hôtel Cheval Noir, 11 rue François-Gillet (crosses rue de la République), moderate, tel. 77-33-41-72.

Hôtel Touring Continental, 10 rue François-Gillet, moderate, tel. 77-32-58-43.

Hôtel Arts, 11 rue Gambetta, inexpensive, tel. 77-32-42-11.

Sights Worth Seeing Nearby

Le Puy, 55 miles southwest of St.-Étienne, is easily recognized by its three rocky volcanic peaks with small churches, statues, and monuments atop their narrow summits. It's one of the most unusual sights in France. A few non-TGV trains travel to Le Puy daily.

Valence

Valence, 62 miles south of Lyon on the east bank of the Rhône River, is the gateway to the Midi and Provence regions and a major business center for this agricultural/wine production area. With 80,000 residents, this former Roman outpost is a relaxing haven from congested Lyon. Although Valence has no renowned historic sights, you'll enjoy wandering the narrow streets of its old quarter, seeing a 12th-century cathedral, and dining at a gourmet restaurant.

TGV Travel from Paris

Twelve trains travel daily from Paris to Valence. The 332-mile trip takes two hours, 51 minutes. (When the high-speed line from Lyon to Valence opens in 1994, this time will be less.) The *Gare SNCF* is on rue Denis-Papin on the southeast side of town. Currently, the last TGV back to Paris leaves at 20:21.

Tourist Information Office

The *Office de Tourisme* is about four blocks from the *Gare SNCF* off avenue Felix-Faure on a large, L-shaped traffic island/park. To get there, exit right from the station on rue Denis Papin and cross boulevard du-Général-de-Gaulle to the park.

Tour of Historic Sights & Major Attractions

From the *Office de Tourisme*, backtrack to boulevard du-Général-de-Gaulle, following it toward the Rhône River. Turn right at rue des Repenties, opposite the east corner of the *Parc Jouvet* across the street. On this corner, the **Musée Bibliothèque** contains 100 red chalk drawings by the 18th-century artist Hubert Robert, plus a collection of Greco-Roman artifacts. The **Cathédrale St.-Apollinaire**, next to the museum, was commissioned by Pope Urban II in 1095 and restored in the 17th century. This Romanesque cathedral contains the tomb of Pope Pius VI, who died there as a prisoner at the end of the 18th century. Bus #20 travels to these locations from the *Gare SNCF* and the *Office de Tourisme*, continuing across the Rhône River to the suburb Granges-les-Valence.

From the *Cathédrale*, explore the narrow streets spreading north and east for a good look at Valence's **Vieux Quartier**. Using your *Office de Tourisme* map, wander at random or follow the series of pedestrians-only streets connecting the *Cathédrale* with the *Office de Tourisme*. To take this route, walk to the rear of the *Cathédrale* and follow rue Championnet to the pedestrians-only Grande-Rue. At #57, the busts of Homer, Hippocrates, Aristotle, and other famous Greeks adorn the entrance to the **Maison des Têtes**.

To continue the pedestrians-only route, turn right off the Grande-Rue onto rue Vernoux. At its end, turn left onto rue Emile Augier, which leads to place de la Liberté, a large square containing Valence's municipal theater. Cross the square and turn right on rue Madier-de-Montjau to reach the *Office de Tourisme* (to the right across place Général Leclerc). A left turn in the middle of place de la Liberté returns you to an automobile traffic street, which leads to the north end of the Grande-Rue.

After exploring these streets, relax in the beautiful **Parc Jouvet** bordering the Rhône River off boulevard du-Général-de-Gaulle, followed by a walk across the **Champ de Mars**. From there, cross place Aristide-Briand and avenue Victor-Hugo to avenue Pierre-Sémard, which ends at the *Gare SNCF.*

Restaurants

La Licorne, 13 rue Chalamet (turn left off rue Denis-Papin one block before boulevard du-Général-de-Gaulle), moderate, tel. 75-43-76-83.

Flunch, 19-21 boulevard Maurice-Clerc (opposite side of the traffic island from the *Office de Tourisme* and avenue Félix-Faure), inexpensive.

Le Coelacanthe, 3 place de la Pierre (near the *Cathédrale* via rue Pérollerie, which begins at the foot of rue Championnet), moderate, tel. 75-42-30-68.

La Petite Auberge, 1 rue Athènes (go one block past the *Office de Tour-*

isme on avenue Félix-Faure, turn right on rue Faventines, then left two blocks later), moderate, tel. 75-43-20-30.

Chaumont, 79 avenue Sadi-Carnot (continuation of avenue Félix-Faure), moderate, tel. 75-43-10-12.

Restaurant Pic, 285 avenue Victor-Hugo (on south edge of city—take a taxi or bus #1 from the intersection of avenues Pierre-Sémard and Victor-Hugo), expensive—but the most affordable three-star restaurant in France, with *prix fixe* menus of 250, 500, and 750 francs, tel. 75-44-15-32.

Hotels
Hôtel Lyon, 23 avenue Pierre-Sémard, moderate, tel. 75-41-44-66.

Hôtel les Negociants, 27 avenue Pierre-Sémard, moderate, tel. 75-44-01-86.

Hôtel de Paris, 30 avenue Pierre-Sémard, moderate, tel. 75-44-02-83.

Hôtel France, 16 boulevard du-Général-de-Gaulle, moderate, tel. 75-43-00-87.

Hôtel de l'Europe, 15 avenue Félix-Faure, moderate, tel. 75-43-02-16.

Sights Worth Seeing Nearby
Grenoble, also accessible by TGV, is 60 miles east of Valence on non-TGV trains. To its south, you can travel to several cities in the **Provence** and **Languedoc-Roussillon** regions on the TGV and other SNCF train lines. If you prefer less populated locations, Valence is a good alternative base instead of Lyon or Grenoble for exploring the same areas.

CHAPTER 8

The Foothills
of the French Alps

Évian-les-Bains

Famous for its bottled mineral water, Évian-les-Bains is a relatively new French town. On the south side of Lac Léman, 26 miles east of Geneva, it belonged to Switzerland until 1860. Today, people come to the festive resort to enjoy its spa, casino, flowered-lined streets, water sports, and the nearby French and Swiss Alps. Its modern convention center is a popular site for European business people desiring a relaxing retreat from the large cities.

TGV Travel from Paris
One TGV train travels daily from Paris to Évian-les-Bains. The 370-mile trip takes four hours, 23 minutes. The *Gare SNCF* is at the intersection of place and avenue de la Gare on the west side of town. Currently, the last TGV back to Paris leaves at 14:03.

Tourist Information Office
The *Office de Tourisme* and *Accueil de France* are off avenue du Lac in the middle of the L-shaped place d'Allinges. To get there, exit right from the *Gare SNCF* on avenue de la Gare, veering right a few blocks later after crossing boulevard Jean-Jaurès. When you reach place Charles-Cottet (the center of town), turn left at avenue du Lac. The *Office de Tourisme* is two blocks away.

Tour of Historic Sights & Major Attractions
A small village (6,200 permanent residents) and resort community, Évian-les-Bains does not abound in historic sights. Its buildings date mostly from the 19th and 20th centuries, and its oldest sight is the 15th-century bas-relief of the Virgin Mary in the church across the street from the *Office de Tourisme*.

So instead of sightseeing, Évian-les-Bains is a place for resting and relaxing. If you can afford it, spend a few days at the spa, try to win back the cost of your trip at the casino, and take a boat ride on Lac Léman. To reach these sights, turn right off avenue du Lac onto quai Baron-de-Blonay, bordering the flower-lined lake. The **Casino Royale** is a short distance on the right, set back from the street across a sweeping lawn. After paying a 55-franc entrance fee, you can try your luck at blackjack, baccarat, roulette, and other games of chance. From February to mid-December, the Casino offers elaborate floor shows five nights a week in its cabaret/disco *Le Régent* for no additional charge, though there is a minimum drink order.

Just beyond the Casino, also set back from the quai, are the **Hôtel de Ville** and the large spa **Etablissement Thermal**. At Evian's **port** (at the far end of the quai at place du Port), you can buy a ticket for a boat tour or night cruise (summer) on **Lac Léman**, the largest lake in central Europe (362 square miles). The *Compagnie Générale de Navigation*, which runs these tours, also has daily boat service to 46 locations on both the French and Swiss sides of the lake.

Across from the port at the **Parc Thermale**, you'll find the beautiful, 19th-century headquarters of the **Évian Company**. Behind the building, you can get a free glass of the water from the *Buvette Cachat*, the spring discovered in 1789 by French nobleman Marquis de Lesert. According to company history, Lesert found his kidney ailments disappearing a few days after drinking the delicious water he saw bubbling from Mr. Cachat's garden. Others felt the water's healing properties, so a spa was built over the garden in 1859, and a company was formed to bottle the water for local sales. Beginning as melted snow from the slopes of Mont Blanc, Évian water is today the best selling bottled mineral water in the world.

From there, you can return to the center of town on the pedestrians-only rue Nationale, the main business street, which begins behind the *Parc Thermale* at place de la Libération. Since rue Nationale is the east extension of avenue de la Gare, it's an easy route to the *Gare SNCF.*

For the best view of Évian-les-Bains, Lac Léman, and the Alps, walk one block down rue Nationale from the *Parc Thermale*, turn left on avenue de Neuvecelle, then right one block later on avenue des Sources, which skirts a small park. At the west end of the park, a funicular runs up the steep hills south of town for a panorama of the area. The funicular also stops near the *Hôtel de Ville.*

To return to the *Gare SNCF* from the funicular station, walk to the south end of the park, then go right on boulevard Jean-Jaurès to its intersection with avenue de la Gare. You can also follow avenue des Sources through the center of the town to its end at place Charles-Cottet. From there, retrace your steps on avenue de la Gare. For conventioneers, the **Palais des Festivities et Ville des Congrès**, built in 1956, is on these routes between boulevard Jean-Jaurès and place Charles-Cottet.

Restaurants

Restaurant Le Bourgogne, place Charles-Cottet, moderate-expensive, tel. 50-75-01-05.

Toque Royale, in the *Casino Royale*, moderate-expensive, tel. 50-75-03-78.

Da Bouttau, quai Baron de Blonay, moderate-expensive, tel. 50-75-02-44.

Brasserie Regence, place du Port, moderate, tel. 50-75-13-75.

Hotels

Hôtel Terminus, place de la Gare, inexpensive-moderate, tel. 50-75-15-07.

Hôtel Continental, 65 rue Nationale (near place Charles-Cottet), inexpensive-moderate, tel. 50-75-37-54.

Hôtel Palais, 69 rue Nationale, inexpensive-moderate, tel. 50-75-00-46.

Hôtel Bellevue, place de la Libération, moderate, tel. 50-75-01-13.

Sights Worth Seeing Nearby

In **Lausanne**, directly across Lac Léman to the north, you can transfer to the TGV to return to eastern France. There is frequent boat service there. Trips into the **Alps** (south) require a rental car; see the *Office de Tourisme* for more information.

Aix-les-Bains

Since the 16th century, Aix-les-Bains has been famous for its thermal baths constructed by the Romans 2,000 years ago. Nestled in the foothills of the French Alps on Lac du Bourget, Aix is the largest and most fashionable spa in eastern France and a popular vacation site for Europe's rich and famous. Even if you can't afford it, Aix is worth a stop to enjoy the scenery and rub elbows with a *haute* crowd.

TGV Travel from Paris

Eight trains travel daily from Paris to Aix-les-Bains. The 315-mile trip takes two hours, 54 minutes. The *Gare SNCF* is at place de la Gare in the center of town. Currently, the last TGV back to Paris leaves at 20:00.

Tourist Information Office

The *Office de Tourisme* is next to the *Hôtel de Ville*, a 16th-century château formerly belonging to the Marquis d'Aix. It's less than a mile from the *Gare SNCF.* To get there, cross place de la Gare to avenue Charles-de-Gaulle/avenue Lord-Revelstoke and turn left when you see the *Thermes*

Nationaux. If you feel lucky on the way, stop at the *Casino Grand Cercle* in the former *Palais de Savoie* (go left at rue du Casino).

Tour of Historic Sights & Major Attractions

The **Thermes Nationaux**, across the square from the *Office de Tourisme*, is the main draw to Aix-les-Bains. However, treatment at the spa requires advance appointment and great sums of money. There are guided tours of the facility, including the remains of the Roman baths, the thermal caves, and the modern spa. Outside the *Thermes Nationaux*, you can view bubbling sulphur springs and a Roman triumphal arch (*Arc de Campanus*). The former **Temple of Diana**, another Roman relic, is behind the *Hôtel de Ville*.

About six blocks from the spa, the **Musée du Docteur Fauré** contains an art collection bequeathed to the city in 1942. Housed in a 19th-century villa, it features excellent paintings by Sisley, Pissarro, Renoir, and Cézanne, plus two rooms of Rodin sculpture. The **Bibliothèque Municipale** is in the same building. To reach them, exit right from the spa on rue Davat/boulevard des Côte.

Certainly no visit to Aix-les-Bains would be complete without a close look at the beautiful **Lac du Bourget**. To reach the lake on foot from the museum, cross boulevard des Côte to the steps (*montée Cléry*) leading down to boulevard de Paris, then turn left on this street, which becomes rue Claude-de-Seyssel after it goes around a corner to the right. After it crosses rue de Genève to become rue de la Dent, it ends at rue du Temple. From there, walk right for one block, then left on avenue du Petit-Port. About a mile later at the junction of boulevard Lepic, the avenue bears right, crosses avenue de Lattre two blocks later, then bears left at place Jean-Lahor for a half-mile to its terminus at the *Esplanade du Petit-Port* at the lake's edge. (For a slightly longer walk with less turns, turn right on rue de Genève, which becomes avenue du Grand Port, and follow it to the lake.) Unless you're in very good shape, take a taxi for the uphill return trip.

From this lake location, follow boulevard du Lac from the *Petit Port* to the *Grand Port*. For a unique experience, travel across the lake by boat from the *Grand Port* to the **Abbaye d'Hautecombe**, founded in 1125. It's best to visit this working abbey during morning mass or evening vespers to hear Gregorian chants and to see the formal gardens and mausoleum containing the Princes of Savoie. Several tour boats also make a four-hour loop of this narrow, 11-miles-long lake.

To return to the *Gare SNCF* from the *Grand Port* (three miles, mostly uphill), follow avenue du Grand-Port away from the lake. About a mile after the avenue curves to the right after passing over a canal, walk along the right side of the traffic circle (fronted by the *Hôpital Léon Blanc*) to avenue Alsace-Lorraine/boulevard Président Wilson, and follow this street back to the station. If you've got francs to spare, stop at the **Nouveau Casino** on the corner of avenue Victoria, two blocks before the station.

Restaurants
Cafeteria Casino, 8 rue du Casino, inexpensive.

La Quimperoise, 4 rue Albert-1er (turn left off avenue Lord-Revelstoke behind the *Hôtel de Ville*), inexpensive, tel. 79-88-99-45.

Brasserie de la Poste, 32 avenue Victoria, moderate, tel. 79-35-00-65.

La Petite Auberge, 76 rue de Genève, moderate.

Au Temple de Diane, 11 avenue d'Annecy (looking toward the lake, turn right off rue de Genève), moderate, tel. 79-88-16-61.

Restaurant Davat, 21 chemin des Bateliers (enters boulevard du Lac at place du Président-Édouard-Herriot, opposite the *Grand Port*), moderate, tel. 79-35-09-63.

Lille, Grand Port, moderate, tel. 79-35-04-22.

Hotels
Hôtel Beaulieu, 29 avenue Charles-de-Gaulle, moderate, tel. 79-35-01-02.

Cécil Hôtel, 20 avenue Victoria, moderate, tel. 79-35-04-12.

Hôtel le Dauphinois, 14 avenue de Tresserve (exit right from the *Gare SNCF*, then left three blocks later), inexpensive, tel. 79-61-22-56.

Hôtel Parc, 28 rue de Chambéry (turn right off avenue Charles-de-Gaulle at place du Revard, opposite the large park), moderate, tel. 79-61-29-11.

Hôtel Vendôme, 12 avenue de Marlioz (east extension of rue de Chambéry), moderate, tel. 79-61-23-16.

Hôtel Palais des Fleurs, 17 rue Isaline (turn left off avenue Marlioz), moderate, tel. 79-88-35-08.

Sights Worth Seeing Nearby
Mont Revard, a few miles east of Aix-les-Bains, offers panoramic views of Mont Blanc and the French Alps. Buses travel there daily from the *Gare Routière*, located on rue de Genève at the tip of place Georges-Clemenceau.

Annecy

Annecy, on the west shore of Lac d'Annecy in the foothills of the Savoie Alps, is one of the prettiest cities in France. Its narrow passages, arcaded townhouses, cobblestone streets, island fortress, and flower-lined canals have earned it the nickname "Venice of France." But unlike Venice, Annecy is relatively unpolluted, thanks to local environmentalists, who have encouraged its industries to locate factories in the suburbs, far from the picturesque old quarter.

As the largest city (52,000 residents) near Mont Blanc, Annecy makes an excellent base for outdoor adventure and the exploration of the Savoie region's delightful towns. Due to its proximity to ski resorts and its status as a transportation hub, expect crowds year-round.

TGV Travel from Paris

Five TGV trains travel daily from Paris to Annecy. The 339-mile trip takes three hours, 31 minutes. The *Gare SNCF* is along rue de l'Industrie on the west side of town. Currently, the last TGV back to Paris leaves at 19:27.

Tourist Information Office

The *Office de Tourisme* is in the **Centre Bonlieu**, Annecy's modern civic center, less than a mile from the *Gare SNCF* off place de la Libération. This large building also has an auditorium, meeting facilities, offices, shops, and public bathrooms. To get there, exit the *Gare SNCF* to the parking lot across rue de l'Industrie, then go left down rue Sommeiller for a half-mile to rue du Président-Favre. The *Centre Bonlieu* is across the street, one block to the right. Buses #1-6 travel from the station and rue Sommeiller to place de la Libération.

Tour of Historic Sights & Major Attractions

Annecy's major attraction is its **Vieille Ville** along the flower-lined canals of the Thiou River, which flows through the center of the city. Since this area is compact and only a short distance from the *Gare SNCF,* it won't take long to explore. For a quick tour, cross rue de l'Industrie to rue de la Gare, walk three blocks, then go left at rue Royale, right on rue de la République, and then follow the rest of the tour below. But most visitors will want a longer time to explore this picturesque city and wander through its narrow streets.

From the *Centre Bonlieu*, you can reach the *Vieille Ville* easily by crossing rue du Président-Favre to the pedestrians-only rue du Pâquier/rue Royale. A half-mile down this street, turn left at rue de la République and cross the Thiou River where it splits into two canals. (The pedestrians-only quai de l'Évêché on the left side of the second canal leads directly to Lac d'Annecy, in case you don't want to visit the *Vieille Ville* and château immediately.) Stay on rue de la République, ignoring the modern office/shopping complex on the right, until the street ends at the lively rue Ste.-Claire, the main street of the *Vieille Ville* and site of a large food market every Tuesday. To the right is Annecy's original medieval gateway, and the street beyond is full of interesting shops and small cafés.

To reach the **Château d'Annecy**, angle across rue Ste.-Claire to the right, then go left up one of the narrow cobblestone passages to the top of the hill, where the *Château* overlooks the city. Begun in the 11th century, the *Château* was primarily a castle-fortress until the 16th century, when the Dukes of Nemour added living quarters—now the **Musée de Château**, a museum showcasing the art, folklore, archaeology, and natural history of the Savoie region. The top floor has an excellent display on the geology of the Alps and a good view over the old quarter's rooftops.

From the *Château*, exit right to follow the narrow rampe du Château down the hill across rue de l'Isle (continuation of rue Ste.-Claire), then right on quai Palais de l'Isle, where you'll find the **Palais de l'Isle**, Annecy's most-photographed sight. Hardly resembling a palace, this austere building on an island in the *Canal du Thiou* has served as a prison, a mint, and a courthouse.

Watch the swans and ducks circle this building, then follow the quai to the last bridge over the canal, where it widens to enter **Lac d'Annecy**. Cross the bridge, then go right and follow the quai around the outside edge of the **Jardin Public** (a.k.a. *Jardins de l'Europe*), which has excellent views of the lake and the distant Savoie Alps.

If you have time, take a boat trip on the lake from the vendor **La Compagnie des Bateaux à Vapeur**, located off the quai near the bridge. Their boats dock at several villages along the lake's nine miles, including a stop beneath **Mont Veyrier**, where you can take a cable car to the top for a great view. (But make sure you know the boat's departure time, or you'll be stranded overnight!) The average lake tour (with no departures) takes two hours. If you prefer to be the captain, you can rent surfboards, paddle boats, canoes, kayaks, sailboats, and other craft at the lake front during the warmer months.

At the north end of the park, cross the foot bridge over the *Canal du Vasse* to the **Champ de Mars**, a large park and promenade along the lake and avenue d'Albigny. The rectangular building on the left is Annecy's old theater and casino.

After passing two buildings on the *Jardin Public*-side of the *Canal du Vasse*, turn left at place de Hôtel de Ville, where you'll find the 1848 **Hôtel de Ville** (which also contains the *Bibliothèque Municipale*). Opposite the place, Annecy's largest church, the 15th-century **Église St.-Maurice**, has a fresco from 1458 and lovely stained glass windows.

Across the street to the left is the small, 17th-century **Église St.-François**, with the *Canal du Thiou* on its south side. From there, follow the canal back to rue de la République—lots of interesting quai-side shops along the way. When you reach it, turn right, then go right a block later at rue Jean-Jacques Rousseau. Just down the street on the left is the current police headquarters and former **Palais Épiscopal**, built in 1784 on the site of the house where Rousseau met his lover, the Madame de Warrens, in 1728. Next to the palace, the historic but uninspiring **Cathédrale St.-Pierre** was the seat of Bishop François de Sales, a leader in the 16th-century Catholic Reformation movement, which prevented Europe from being overrun by Protestantism.

At the rear of the *Cathédrale* and palace, cross a short bridge over a narrow canal to a park behind the **Église Notre-Dame-de-Liesse**. If you pass through the park, you'll be back on rue Royale, or you can follow the outline of the church to place Notre-Dame. From there, follow the pedestrians-only rue Notre-Dame across rue Royale where it widens to become rue Carnot, another pedestrians-only street filled with shops and restaurants. Two blocks further, turn left onto rue Sommeiller to return to the *Gare SNCF.*

Restaurants
Buffet Gare TGV, inside the *Gare SNCF*, inexpensive.
Fer á Cheval, 21 rue Sommeiller, moderate, tel. 50-45-13-35.
Flunch, 23 rue Sommeiller, inexpensive.
Cafeteria Le Petit Pierre, 8 rue de l'Annexion (narrow street connecting rue Sommeiller to rue Royale), inexpensive.
Le Boutae, 10 rue Vaugelas-impasse Pré Carré (near *Centre Bonlieu*; street between rue Sommeiller and rue Royale), tel. 50-45-62-94.
Garcin, 11 rue Pâquier, moderate, tel. 50-45-20-94.
Au Lilas Rose, passage de l'Évêché (off quai de l'Évêché), moderate, tel. 50-45-37-08.
Auberge du Lyonnais, 9 rue de la République, moderate-expensive, tel. 50-51-26-10.

Hotels
Hôtel Allobroges, 11 rue Sommeiller, moderate-expensive, tel. 50-45-03-11.
Hôtel Nord, 24 rue Sommeiller, moderate, tel. 50-45-08-78.
Hôtel Carlton, 5 des Glières (street on the left side of the parking lot across from the *Gare SNCF*), moderate, tel. 50-45-47-75.
Hôtel des Alpes, 12 rue de la Poste (right off rue Sommeiller), inexpensive, tel. 50-45-04-56.
Ibis Hôtel, 12 rue de la Gare (about seven blocks from *Gare SNCF* across the Thiou River), moderate, tel. 50-45-43-21.
Touring Hôtel, 24 avenue Berthollet (behind the *Gare SNCF*; exit left, staying on the left side of avenue de Brogny, and at the traffic circle, turn left onto avenue Berthollet), moderate, tel. 50-57-16-97.

Sights Worth Seeing Nearby
Gorges du Fier, a canyon west of Annecy near the village Lovagny, features a magnificent waterfall crashing over cliffs to a river far below.

144 / Foothills of the French Alps

Just five minutes up the hill from the gorge's entrance, the **Château de Montrottier** contains a museum with regional pottery, Oriental costumes, 16th-century art, military armor, tapestries, and antiques. From the top of the château's tower, you can see Mont Blanc on a clear day. Three non-TGV trains travel daily to Lovagny, as does the *Voyages Crolard* bus line from Annecy's *Gare Routière* (next to the *Gare SNCF*).

Chambéry

Like its neighbors Annecy and Aix-les-Bains, Chambéry is another gateway to the French Alps. Just south of *Lac du Bourget* in a large valley, this city of 55,000 has guarded the strategic entrance to the mountain passes to Italy for centuries. Formerly the capital of the House of Savoie in the Middle Ages, it is today an important business, government, and cultural center of the region. Many of Europe's wealthy, who prefer city life over the crowded mountain resorts, keep a winter residence in Chambéry.

TGV Travel from Paris
Seven TGV trains travel daily from Paris to Chambéry. The 324-mile trip takes three hours, 13 minutes. The *Gare SNCF* is at place de la Gare on the north side of town. Currently, the last TGV back to Paris leaves at 20:35.

Tourist Information Office
The *Office de Tourisme*, at 24 boulevard de la Colonne (rear entrance off avenue des Ducs-de-Savoie), is less than a half-mile from the *Gare SNCF.* To get there, walk left from the station on the right side of rue Sommeiller until you reach a large intersection. At the end of this triangular block, angle to the right across the divided rue Freizier to the parking island, then diagonally left across place du Centenaire to the divided boulevard de la Colonne. The office is a few steps to the left.

Tour of Historic Sights & Major Attractions
Just a few blocks from the *Office de Tourisme* down boulevard de la Colonne is the **La Fontaine des Éléphants**, honoring the memory of Comte de Boigne (1741-1830), who helped build Chambéry into a prosperous city after making his fortune with the French East India Company. This unique fountain, built in 1838, consists of the front halves of four life-size elephant statues projecting from each side of a stone base, from which rises a tall column with a statue of the Comte at the top.

Past the fountain a few blocks on the right, set back from the street on the square de Lannoy-de-Bissy, a former Franciscan convent now houses the **Musée Savoisien**. Established in 1864, this combination history, ethnography, and archaeology museum documents 14th- to 16th-century mountain village life through displays of farm implements, furniture, paintings, costumes, and other artifacts. Next to the museum in the former convent church is the **Basilique Métropolitaine** (a.k.a. *Cathédrale de St.-François-de-Sales*). Although the exterior is nothing special, be sure to go inside to see the 10th-century Byzantine diptych in the treasury and the 19th-century *trompe l'oeil* wall paintings imitating the twisting shapes of Flamboyant Gothic architecture. Behind the cathedral is the 1824 **Théâtre Municipal**.

From the cathedral entrance, cross the small, enclosed place Métropole to rue Métropole, and walk a block to the pedestrians-only **place St.-Léger**, the hub of Chambéry's nightlife, filled with cafés and restaurants. The narrow streets, alleys, and vaulted passages in this quarter evoke the Chambéry of medieval times. For the city's best mansions, proceed a short distance south of place St.-Léger to **rue Croix d'Or**.

After exploring the side streets and perhaps enjoying a meal in this quarter, walk to the north end of place St.-Léger, then left down rue de Boigne until it ends at the **Château des Ducs de Savoie**. This palace was built in 1232 for the Dukes of Savoie—and to house the "Holy Shroud" of Christ. But when the Dukes chose Turin as their regional capital in the 16th century, they took the controversial linen with them, where it remains today. Although the building is old, its furnishings are primarily 18th- and 19th-century. The Savoie Department government now uses the *Château*, so you can't tour it independently. There's a daily afternoon tour year-round, plus extra tours in the summer.

Next to the *Château*, the small **Ste.-Chapelle** has hosted many royal weddings, including Louis XI to Charlotte of Savoie. The chapel features stained glass windows from the 16th century, *trompe l'oeil*, and a panorama of the city from the **Tour Yolande**.

On the other side of the *Château* and chapel are the **Grand Jardin**, a large park and botanical garden, and the **Muséum d'Histoire Naturelle**, a small natural history museum, in operation since 1844.

From the *Château* or Ste.-Chapelle, go left on rue de la Trésorerie for two blocks, then right on the long rue Derrière-les-Murs, crossing through place de Genève to rue Doppet, which leads to the **Musée des Beaux-Arts**. Housed on the top floor of a 19th-century grain market, this small art museum contains an impressive collection of Italian art, including work by Titian, and a large 19th-century sculpture collection, with a bust by David d'Angers. The rest of the museum consists of rather unexceptional 17th- and 18th-century paintings by various artists.

To return to the *Gare SNCF* from there, turn left at the corner of rue Doppet and boulevard du Musée, and walk past the *Palais de Justice* and the *Jardin du Verney*. When the park ends, turn right, crossing to avenue Maréchal-Leclerc, which leads to the station.

Restaurants
Flunch, avenue des Ducs-de-Savoie, inexpensive.

La Chaumiere, 14 rue Denfert-Rochereau (follow boulevard de la Colonne to a series of short streets behind the *Théâtre Municipal*), moderate, tel. 79-33-16-26.

Le Sporting, 88 rue Croix-d'Or, moderate, tel. 79-33-17-43.

Le Tonneau, 3 rue St.-Antoine (south from place du Centenaire), moderate, tel. 79-33-78-26.

La Vanoise, 44 avenue Pierre-Lanfrey (borders the west side of the *Jardin du Verney*), moderate, tel. 79-69-02-78.

Note: There are many restaurants—too numerous to list—in the St.-Léger quarter.

Hotels
Hôtel Ducs de Savoie le Grand Hôtel, 6 place de la Gare, moderate, tel. 79-69-54-54.

Hôtel Lion d'Or, 1 avenue de la Boisse (exit right from the *Gare SNCF*), moderate, tel. 79-69-04-96.

Hôtel le France, 22 faubourg Reclus (turn left off rue Sommeiller), moderate, tel. 79-33-51-18.

Hôtel des Princes, 4 rue de Boigne (at *La Fontaine des Éléphants*, turn right off boulevard de la Colonne), moderate, tel. 79-33-45-36.

Sights Worth Seeing Nearby
Albertville, site of the 1992 Winter Olympics, and several other smaller ski resorts are about 50 miles east of Chambéry on the TGV. **Grenoble,** where TGV connections to Lyon and Paris are available, is 39 miles south of Chambéry on non-TGV trains.

Grenoble

Grenoble, the former capital of the ancient Dauphine region, is the largest city near the French Alps. At the junction of the rushing Drac and Isère Rivers, it has grown steadily in size and prosperity since it became part of France in 1349. Until 1791, when the Dauphine region was divided into three departments, the city was ruled by the eldest son (the "Dauphin") of the King.

Grenoble is known for its independent character. Indeed, Napoléon found allegiance from Grenoble's soldiers, who were sent to arrest him when he marched to Paris in 1815, in defiance of his exile on Elba. Following the Napoléon era, Grenoble experienced rapid growth, as the railroad brought new industries to the city.

Today, Grenoble is a sprawling, modern metropolis of nearly 400,000, including a university with 30,000 students. It is also headquarters for many businesses and the site of professional winter sports events.

TGV Travel from Paris

Nine TGV trains travel daily from Paris to Grenoble. The 345-mile trip takes three hours, 10 minutes. The *Gare SNCF* (or *Gares Europole*, as it is identified on bus lines) is at place de la Gare on the west side of town. Currently, the last TGV back to Paris leaves at 20:33.

Tourist Information Office

The *Maison du Tourisme* and *Accueil de France* are at 14 rue de la République, in the center of the city—almost two miles from the *Gare SNCF.* The quickest way there is on tramline A in the "Grand Place" direction, departing at the "Maison du Tourisme" stop. From there, follow rue La Fayette north one block and turn right on rue de la République. Maps of tram and bus routes are available at the TAG (*Transports de l'Agglomération Grenobloise*) office to the right of the train station.

By foot from place de la Gare, follow the tram along avenue Alsace-Lorraine (one of Grenoble's primary business/shopping streets) for several blocks to the beautiful place Victor-Hugo, then continue on a series of pedestrians-only streets to the office.

Tour of Historic Sights & Major Attractions

Grenoble's most popular attraction, the **Téléphérique de la Bastille**, is an exhilarating, six-minute ride in a clear, bubble-like cable car that whisks passengers high across the Isère River to the **Fort de la Bastille**, 1,594 feet above the city's north end. Formerly a military installation, the fort today contains a restaurant and café for leisurely dining. From its terraces, you get a marvelous panorama of Grenoble and the snowy peaks of the Grand-Chartreuse Range of the French Alps.

To reach this attraction, exit left from the *Maison du Tourisme* on rue de la République. Three blocks later, pass through **place Grenette**, Grenoble's liveliest café and shopping district, to the *Jardin de Ville*. Enter the park through a vaulted passage on its southeast corner as the street begins to curve left. The *Téléphérique* is at the other end of the park on quai Stéphane-Jay.

If you skip the *Office de Tourisme*, you can get to the *Téléphérique* directly from the *Gare SNCF.* Exit left across place de la Gare toward the *Église Sacré-Coeur*, then follow rue Casimir-Brenier to the Isère River. Turn right at the river and follow the quais until you reach the cable cars.

Fans of author Stendhal (pseudonym for Marie Henri Beyle) should return via the *Téléphérique* to visit the **Musee Stendhal** at the northeast corner on the *Jardin de Ville*. The small museum contains mementos and original manuscripts. Directly behind the museum is the Dauphin's private chapel, the 13th-century **Église St.-André**. Next door, along the riverfront, the 15th-century **Palais de Justice** combines Gothic and Renaissance architecture for a beautiful building.

If you have sturdy legs, descend the mountain from the fort on the marked paths that pass through tunnels and across bridges, winding through the terraced **Parc Guy-Pape**, which leads to the **Jardin des Dauphins**. Depending on the path, you'll eventually hit an Isère River quai. Before crossing the river to central Grenoble, check out the **Musée Dauphinois**, reached by following the winding rue Maurice-Gignoux up the hill from quai Perrière. This museum contains historic items, art, and crafts concerning the folk traditions of the Dauphine region. One mile beyond quai Perrière on the same side of the river (via a left turn on rue Sappey), the **Église St.-Laurent** boasts a 6th-century Merovingian crypt, one of the oldest Christian relics in France.

From the church, cross the river on the *Pont de la Citadelle* (or take bus #32 from the church), following the quais back to the *Jardin de Ville* to visit its nearby sights or to return to place Grenette. After exploring the shops around place Grenette, walk north past the fountain onto the pedestrians-only Grande-Rue for one block, then go right at the pedestrians-only rue Jean-Jacques Rousseau. At building #14, in the heart of Grenoble's oldest quarter, the **Musée de la Résistance** explains anti-Nazi activity in Grenoble and the region during World War II. (If you continue on the Grand-Rue, you'll come to the rear of the *Palais de Justice* and the *Église St.-André*.)

From the museum, follow rue Jean-Jacques Rousseau a few blocks east to the oddly-shaped place Ste.-Claire, with a covered market in the center, then go left about four blocks to place Notre-Dame and the 12th-century **Cathédrale Notre-Dame**. Its main feature is a 46-foot, 15th-century Flamboyant Gothic tabernacle.

Two blocks south of the *Cathédrale*, turn left off place Notre-Dame onto rue Bayard, walk about six blocks to rue Cornélie-Gémond, then go right for a block to place de Verdun, where you'll find the **Musée de Peinture et de Sculpture** (a.k.a. *Musée de Grenoble*). This museum has an outstanding modern art collection and numerous masterpieces, including work by Picasso, Matisse, Rubens, Goya, Klee, Gauguin, and Monet. There's a tram stop one block south of the entrance, on the other side of place de Verdun.

Also south of the museum and place de Verdun, via rue Haxo, is the **Musée d'Histoire Naturelle**, fronting the **Jardin des Plantes** (a.k.a. *Jardin Botanique*). Behind this park and across boulevard Jean-Pain, there's the modern **Hôtel de Ville** and the **Parc Paul-Mistral**, home of several Olympic facilities from the 1968 Games.

If you're staying overnight, consider attending an event at the **Maison de la Culture**, Grenoble's cultural and entertainment center, less than two miles south of the *Parc Paul-Mistral* in the suburb Malherbe. (There's a tram stop for it.) You'll find a schedule of events at the *Maison du Tourisme*.

To return to the *Gare SNCF* from the *Parc Paul-Mistral*, walk to the park's west edge (to the right when facing the *Hôtel de Ville*), where you can board the tram. For a long (or partial) walk, fork right off boulevard Jean-Pain onto boulevard Maréchal-Lyautey/Agutte-Sembat, staying on it until you see the tram and avenue Alsace-Lorraine at place Victor-Hugo, which anchors another business/shopping district. From there, take the tram or follow avenue Alsace-Lorraine to the station.

If you have time, visit **MAGASIN**, the National Center for Contemporary Art, at 155 cours Berriat. Housed in a former warehouse, this museum presents exhibitions of modern artists, with an emphasis on the hottest European artists and sculptors today. To get there, take the tram to the Berriat stop, walk down boulevard Gambetta one block, then turn right onto cours Berriat. Also, bus #50 travels this street en route to place Victor-Hugo.

Restaurants

Brasserie le Strasbourg, 11 avenue Alsace-Lorraine, moderate, tel. 76-46-18-03.

Au Bon Petit Coin, 48 avenue Alsace-Lorraine, inexpensive-moderate, tel. 76-87-54-27.

Au Madelon, 55 avenue Alsace-Lorraine, moderate-expensive, tel. 76-46-36-90.

Concorde, 9 boulevard Gambetta (six blocks from the *Gare SNCF,* turn left off avenue Alsace-Lorraine), inexpensive-moderate, tel. 76-46-63-64.

Restaurant de la Plage, 2 rue St.-Hugues (first street south of the *Cathédrale*, off place Notre-Dame), inexpensive, tel. 76-51-38-85.

Le Cantilène, 11 rue Beyle-Stendhal (short street entering the south corner of place de Verdun, opposite the pedestrians-only rue Fantin-Latour), inexpensive, tel. 76-43-05-19.

Le Berlioz, 4 rue de Strasbourg (crosses rue Beyle-Stendhal at place de Metz; also enters boulevard Jean-Pain across from the *Parc Paul-Mistral*), moderate-expensive, tel. 76-56-22-39.

Thibaud, 25 boulevard Agutte-Sembat, moderate-expensive, tel. 76-43-01-62.

La Poularde Bressane, 12 place Paul-Mistral (across from the west entrance to the *Parc Paul-Mistral*), moderate-expensive, tel. 76-87-08-90.

Hotels

Hôtel Savoie, 52 avenue Alsace-Lorraine, moderate, tel. 76-46-00-20.

Hôtel Lux, 6 rue Crépu (first street to the right off avenue Alsace-Lorraine, or left off rue du 4 Septembre), inexpensive-moderate, tel. 76-46-41-89.

Hôtel Porte de France, 27 quai Claude-Bernard (turn left off rue Casimir-Brenier onto rue Aristide-Berges, go to its end at the river, then left), inexpensive-moderate, tel. 76-47-39-73.

Hôtel Bellevue, quai Stéphane-Jay and rue de Belgrade (two blocks south of the *Téléphérique)*, inexpensive-moderate, tel. 76-46-69-34.

Hôtel Bastille, 25 avenue Félix-Viallet (runs into the *Gare SNCF,* one street to the left of avenue Alsace-Lorraine), inexpensive-moderate, tel. 76-43-10-27.

Hôtel des Alpes, 45 avenue Félix-Viallet, inexpensive-moderate, tel. 76-87-00-71.

Hôtel Angleterre, 5 place Victor-Hugo, moderate, tel. 76-87-37-21.

Hôtel Gambetta, 59 boulevard Gambetta, moderate, tel. 76-87-22-25.

Sights Worth Seeing Nearby

Several ski resorts, campgrounds, lakes, and hiking trails are near Grenoble, including the **Parc Naturel Regional du Vercors**, which has three *Grande Randonnée* (GR) long-distance paths, offering moderate to strenuous hikes in mountains from 5,000-8,000 feet. The *Club Alpin Français* at 32 avenue Félix-Viallet and CIMES (*Centre d'Information Montagne et Sentiers*) in the *Maison du Tourisme* building have information about hikes in the area. There is bus service from the *Gare Routière* (next to the *Gare SNCF*) to many of the trail heads and ski resorts.

In Voiron, 17 miles north of Grenoble, you can tour the **Caves de la Chartreuse** distillery, where the fiery green liqueur is made. It's a short walk south of Voiron's train station (exit right) along the N75 highway. There is bus and non-TGV train service there.

Provence & Languedoc-Roussillon

Avignon

On the western edge of Provence, Avignon is famous for its papal history and the narrow *Pont St.-Bénézet* stretching halfway across the Rhône River. Built in 1117, the bridge experienced several disasters, and half of it finally collapsed in 1669. Other sights include the fortress-like palace of the 14th-century Popes and the ancient ramparts surrounding the old city. Walking through the narrow streets will transport you to medieval times, when cardinals, archbishops, and visiting royalty were the norm.

With 92,000 residents, Avignon's economy revolves around tourism, conventions, and numerous annual festivals, especially the *Festival d'Art Dramatique et de Danse*, an international theater and dance event from mid-July to mid-August that features outdoor performances throughout the city.

TGV Travel from Paris
Fifteen TGV trains travel daily from Paris to Avignon. The 409-mile trip from Paris takes three hours, 45 minutes. The *Gare SNCF* is at place de la République, directly across boulevard St.-Roch (part of the ring road circling the ramparts) from the *Porte de la République*, an ancient city entrance on the south side of town. Currently, the last TGV back to Paris leaves at 19:17.

Tourist Information Office
The *Office de Tourisme* and *Accueil de France* are at 41 cours Jean-Jaurès (inside the ramparts), about a half-mile from the *Gare SNCF.* To get there, go through the *Porte de la République* to cours Jean-Jaurès (the old city's main street).

Tour of Historic Sights & Major Attractions

At the end of cours Jean-Jaurès/rue de la République (less than a mile beyond the *Office de Tourisme* and near the *Palais des Papes*), the lively **place de l'Horloge** has been a popular meeting place for centuries. Cafés and restaurants abound. The large building on the left is the rebuilt **Hôtel de Ville**, and the city theater is next to it. Bus A also runs from the *Gare SNCF* to these sights.

To reach the *Palais des Papes* from there, walk to the far end of place de l'Horloge to rue Gérard-Philipe, skirting along the left side of the *Banque du France* building into the narrow place du Palais, which fronts the palace. Before entering, note the 16th-century **Hôtel des Monnaies**, Avignon's former mint, on the left.

Seven Popes ruled from Avignon from 1309-1403. The **Palais des Papes** was built from 1334-52 during the reign of Benedict XII and Clement VI, who had fled warring factions in Rome to gain closer alliance with France. Designed for defense from assassination, as well as being a church and palace, this building is an excellent example of civil, religious, and military architecture of the Middle Ages. Though the exterior resembles a fortress, the interior reflects the decorating tastes of the various Popes. Part of the palace is simple, even austere, and part is regal, suitable for a king and his court.

Though there are tours of the palace, explore it on your own if you can to save time. (Most of the interior is bare because of looting during the French Revolution.) Since it's one of the largest medieval buildings in the world (surface area of 161,464 square feet), a long tour may cramp the rest of your sightseeing. But don't miss the Gobelin tapestries in the entrance hall and the fabulous frescoes painted by Simone Martini and Matteo Giovanetti from 1345-52.

A few steps north of the palace, the **Cathédrale Notre-Dame-des-Doms**, a 12th-century Romanesque church, features a Baroque interior and the Gothic tombs of Pope John XXII and Pope Benedict XII.

To the left of the *Cathédrale* entrance, at the highest elevation in the city, the **Promenade du Rocher-des-Doms** is a beautiful park with good views of the palace, the Rhône River, and *Pont St.-Bénézet*. Just below the park to the left, the **Musée du Petit-Palais**, a small 14th-century palace and former home of the archbishops who joined the Pope in exile, is now an art museum with over 1,000 works by Italian artists—one of the most important collections of Italian paintings in France. The museum also has medieval paintings from the Avignon School and sculpture from the Roman era.

Follow the sidewalk behind the *Musée*, through the narrow *Porte du Rocher*, to the 12th-century **Pont St.-Bénézet**, which stops halfway across the Rhône River. Famous in the French nursery rhyme about a boy instructed by angels to build the bridge, today's structure has only four of the original 22 arches—the rest washed away in floods over the centuries. For a small fee, you can walk on the bridge (except in winter, when it's icy).

To see the bridge and Avignon together, cross to the **Ile de la Barthelasse** on the other side of the Rhône. To get there from the *Pont St.-Bénézet*, follow boulevard du Rhône to the *Pont Édouard-Daladier*. After crossing, look for an opening that goes down to the street opposite the stadium. Follow the street along the stadium to the river, then go as far left as you need for the necessary view. If you plan to visit the island, you may want to make it your first sightseeing destination, since bus #10 travels from a boulevard St.-Roch stop opposite the *Gare SNCF* to a stop near the stadium.

After visiting the *Pont St.-Bénézet*, tour the **Musée Calvet** and **Musée Réquien** before returning to the *Gare SNCF*. Considered one of the best art museums in Provence, the *Musée Calvet* is set in the former *Hôtel de Villeneuve-Martignan*, an elegant 18th-century palace reflecting a pure French style, as opposed to the Italian-inspired buildings that dominate the city. Within its spacious rooms are outstanding French paintings by Corot, Renoir, and Manet, plus work by other European schools, including the Russian Expressionist Chaim Soutine. There's also an interesting exhibit of wrought iron, tapestries, and ancient Greek sculpture, plus a library. The *Musée Réquien* next door is a natural history museum, also well worth a stop.

To reach the two museums from the *Pont Édouard-Daladier*, cross the busy boulevards outside the ramparts to the *Porte de l'Oulle*, passing through and following the right side of place Crillon to the short, L-shaped rue Mazan. When rue Mazan ends, turn right on rue Joseph-Vernet and stay on this street until you see the museums on your left about a half-mile away. You can also reach them by following rue Joseph-Vernet from its intersection with rue de la République/cours Jean-Jaurès, a few blocks from the *Gare SNCF*.

After seeing the sights, take some time to wander through Avignon's narrow streets, which have changed little since the Middle Ages. (The major difference is cars!) The pedestrians-only streets from place de l'Horloge to the *Église St.-Didier* off rue de la République is a pleasant area to explore. To return to the *Gare SNCF*, retrace your steps on rue de la République/cours Jean-Jaurès, or follow the ramparts.

Restaurants

Le Magnanen, 19 rue du Rempart-St.-Michel (pass through the *Porte de la République*, then turn right at avenue du 7ere Génie/rue du Rempart-St.-Michel), inexpensive, tel. 90-82-21-66.

Flunch, 11 boulevard Raspail (turn left off cours Jean-Jaurès a few blocks from the *Gare SNCF*), inexpensive.

Les Trois Clefs, 26 rue des Trois-Faucons (turn right off cours Jean-Jaurès at rue Henri-Fabre, then take the second left), moderate-expensive, tel. 90-86-51-53.

Arrête des Salades, 4 rue Pavot (first left off rue Henri-Fabre), inexpensive, tel. 90-85-24-34.

L'Aquarelle, 41 rue de la Saraillerie (halfway down rue de la République, turn right on rue Prévôt, going left around the *Église St.-Didier*), moderate, tel. 90-86-33-79.

Hiely, 5 rue de la République at place de l'Horloge, expensive, tel. 90-86-17-07.

Les Domaines, 28 place de l'Horloge, moderate, tel. 90-82-58-86.

L'Isle Sonnante, 7 rue Racine (turn left on rue Molière, which runs along the top side of the city theater from place de l'Horloge), moderate, tel. 90-82-56-01.

La Fourchette II, 17 rue Racine, moderate, tel. 90-85-20-93.

Hotels

Ibis Centre Gare, 42 boulevard St.-Roch at avenue Montclar (a few steps to the right of the *Gare SNCF*), moderate, tel. 90-85-38-38.

Hôtel Bristol, 44 cours Jean-Jaurès, moderate, tel. 90-82-21-21.

Hôtel Splendid, 17 rue Agricol-Perdiguier (turn right off cours Jean Jaurès, five blocks from the *Gare SNCF*), inexpensive, tel. 90-86-14-46.

Hôtel Angleterre, 29 boulevard Raspail, moderate, tel. 90-86-34-31.

Fimotel, 8 boulevard St.-Dominique (continuation of boulevard St.-Roch; exit left from the *Gare SNCF*), moderate, tel. 90-82-08-08.

Hôtel Central, 31 rue de la République, inexpensive, tel. 90-82-15-56.

Le Midi Hôtel, 25 rue de la République, moderate, tel. 90-82-15-56.

Hôtel Danieli, 17 rue République, moderate, tel. 90-86-46-82.

Sights Worth Seeing Nearby

Villeneuve-les-Avignon, a village on a hill overlooking the Rhône River and the *Ile de la Barthelasse*, is easily accessible via bus #10 from the boulevard St.-Roch stop. When the Popes lived in Avignon, the cardinals built palaces and mansions in the village. Sights include an arts center operating from one of the largest 12th-century Carthusian monasteries (a.k.a. "Charterhouse") in France, the medieval *Fort St.-André*, the 1333 *Église Notre-Dame* (part of the *Cloître Collégiale*) containing the "Virgin of Ivory," one of France's greatest art treasures, and the 1292 *Tour Phillipe-le-Bel*. Houses 1, 3, and 53 on rue de la République belonged to cardinals. Get off the bus at the Phillipe-le-Bel stop or the Charles-David stop near the fort.

The small city of **Orange**, 17 miles north of Avignon, features the best-preserved Roman theater in Europe and a triumphal arch from 20 B.C. Non-TGV trains run there frequently.

Nîmes

One of the oldest cities in France, Nîmes was settled by the Romans in 121 B.C. On a rolling plain 15 miles west of the Rhône River in the northeast corner of the Languedoc-Roussillon region, its historic sights seem more Italian than French. Built on seven hills like Rome, Nîmes has large squares surrounded by tall cypresses, wide boulevards, cooling fountains, flower and produce markets, statue-filled parks, and more preserved Roman buildings and monuments than any other city in France.

But Nîmes is not stuck in the past. With over 140,000 residents, it is a bustling, modern city made prosperous by the clothing and footwear companies there. Its textile heritage is well-known: from Nîmes, we get the word "denim" ("*de Nîmes*").

TGV Travel from Paris
Eight TGV trains travel daily from Paris to Nîmes. The 439-mile trip takes four hours, 15 minutes. The *Gare SNCF* is along boulevard du Sergent-Triaire on the south side of town. Currently, the last TGV back to Paris leaves at 18:47.

Tourist Information Office
The *Office de Tourisme* and *Accueil de France* are at 6 rue Auguste on the opposite end of the city from the *Gare SNCF.* Since Nîmes' historic sights are between the *Office de Tourisme* and the station, directions to the office are below in the walking tour. A tiny *Office de Tourisme* annex in the station has city maps, hotel listings, and a current events schedule.

Tour of Historic Sights & Major Attractions
To reach the main sights of Nîmes, cross boulevard du Sergent-Triaire to avenue Feuchéres and go to its end at the traffic circle, place de la Libération (a.k.a. esplanade Charles-de-Gaulle). Cross to the middle of the circle, take a quick look at the fountain, then veer left beyond the circle to the **Roman Arena**. Built in the early first century, this well-preserved oval arena can seat 24,000 in 34 tiers. Renovated in the 19th century, it's used today for bullfights, concerts, and other events. There are guided tours every day except Tuesday in winter.

After visiting the Arena, return to place de la Libération, bearing left on boulevard de la Libération, which becomes the busy boulevard Amiral-Courbet, Nîmes' main business street, lined with shops, hotels, cafés,

156/ Provence & Languedoc-Roussillon

and restaurants. Halfway down this boulevard in an austere, Classical-styled building (#13), the **Musée Archéologique**, housed in a former Jesuit college and monastery, contains a collection of antiquities from the prehistoric age through the Roman era, all found in Nîmes. The city library and a small natural history museum are in the same building.

At the north end of boulevard Amiral-Courbet, where it empties into place Gabriel-Péri and place des Carmes, is the **Porte Auguste**, a Roman gate built in 16 B.C. as part of the city ramparts. Across from it is the 17th-century, Gothic-inspired **Église St.-Baudile**.

Behind the *Musée Archéologique* at place aux Herbes in an old part of the city, the **Cathédrale St.-Castor** is an 11th-century cathedral rebuilt in the 1800's in the Roman-Byzantine tradition. To reach it, exit left from the museum and go left at rue Poise. When it ends two blocks later, turn right on the Grand-Rue, take a quick left on rue du Chapitre, and a right at the next block, which puts you on the south side of the *Cathédrale*.

Adjacent to the *Cathédrale*, the **Musée du Vieux Nîmes**, in a 17th-century bishop's palace, displays regional folk art and crafts, plus several exhibits on bullfighting and the local textile industries. The youths you'll see in the building are students at the city's arts and music schools there.

Nearby, the **Maison Carrée** is the oldest Roman building in France. Built at the end of the first century B.C. on a raised platform, this narrow stone building has a Greek portico with Corinthian columns. Originally constructed as a temple and subsequently used as a fort, home, and church, it's one of the best-preserved Roman buildings in Europe. Today, it's also home of the **Musée des Antiques**, featuring Roman artifacts found in Nîmes and the area. To get there, cross place aux Herbes to rue de la Madeleine. Several blocks later, when you reach boulevard Victor-Hugo (another business street filled with restaurants, pâtisseries, and shops), turn right. The *Maison Carrée* is a few blocks away on the right. You can also get there directly from the Arena on boulevard Victor-Hugo.

A few steps north of the *Maison Carrée*, at 6 rue Auguste, is the *Office de Tourisme*. Next, if you have time for a one-mile walk and are interested in ancient methods of water supply, go to the **Castellum**, which houses the device used by the Romans to distribute water throughout the city. To get there, continue north from the *Office de Tourisme* around the right side of square Antonin to boulevard Gambetta, then turn left at rue du Fort. Two blocks later, bear left to rue de la Lampèze. The *Castellum* is a short distance down this street, next to a fort.

To continue the walking tour, return to square Antonin, cross it to the mansion-lined quai de la Fontaine, which borders a canal filled with murky water. Follow the left side of the canal, and a half-mile later you'll see the main entrance of the **Jardin de la Fontaine**, a beautiful 18th-century formal park, complete with vases, statues, canals, and flowers planned around the ruins of early Roman buildings (including the 2nd-century **Temple de Diane**). On sunny weekends, the park is packed with families and lovers out for a stroll, men playing *boules*, and teens hanging out with their friends.

Beyond the canals and statues, stairs lead to several shady footpaths that wind up a steep hill to the **Tour Magne**. Built in 15 B.C. as part of the defense walls around the city, the view from the top offers a lovely look at Nîmes and the countryside—as far as the Cévennes Mountains in the west. On a clear day, you can also see the Pyrénées to the south. For a more direct route to the tower (it's a long hike to the top), follow the right side of quai de la Fontaine almost to the east edge of the park, and turn right on rue Agrippa/rue de la Tour Magne.

To return to the city center, follow boulevard Jean-Jaurès, the wide, divided street leading away from the park entrance. If you're pressed for time, follow this street to its intersection with boulevard Sergent-Triaire (about two miles from the park), then go left for a mile to the *Gare SNCF*. Several buses also travel on this street.

When time is not at a premium, linger at the open markets along the boulevard and sample the food, flowers, clothes, and trinkets. About a mile from the park, turn left at rue du Cirque-Romain and walk half a mile to place Montcalm. To your left is the small triumphal arch and ancient city gate **Porte de France**. Proceeding across the place, follow rue Bourdaloue to the corner of rue Cité-Foule, where you'll find the **Musée des Beaux-Arts**. This small museum has paintings by Vernet, Watteau, Rubens, and Canaletto, some Rodin and Bourdelle busts, and an interesting Roman mosaic.

To return to the *Gare SNCF* from there, exit right onto rue Cité-Foule for a short distance, then go left on boulevard Sergent-Triaire to the station. (A left on rue Cité-Foule leads you to the south side of the Arena.)

Restaurants

Flunch, 10 boulevard Amiral-Courbet (across from the *Museé Archéologique*), inexpensive.

Brasserie la Courbet, 18 boulevard Amiral-Courbet, moderate, tel. 66-67-25-23.

San Francisco Steak House, 33 rue Roussy (exit right from the *Gare SNCF* on boulevard Talabot, then left two blocks later), inexpensive, tel. 66-21-00-80.

Restaurant le Lisita, 2 boulevard des Arènes (across from the Arena's north side), moderate, tel. 66-67-29-15.

Au Chapon Fin, 3 rue du Château-Fadaise (small street/square behind the *Église St.-Paul*; turn left off boulevard Victor-Hugo almost to the *Maison Carrée*), inexpensive-moderate, tel. 66-67-34-73.

L'Ouef à la Côte, 29 rue de la Madeleine, inexpensive, tel. 66-21-88-55.

Le P'tit Bec, 18 rue de l'Etoile (turn left off rue de la Madeleine one block before reaching boulevard Victor-Hugo), moderate, tel. 66-21-04-20.

Les Jardins du Couvent, 21 rue du Grand-Couvent (one street to the left of rue Auguste; facing the *Maison Carrée*), moderate, tel. 66-67-54-08.

Lou Mas, 5 rue de Saure (second street crossing avenue Jean-Jaurés away from the *Jardin de la Fontaine* entrance), moderate, tel. 66-23-24-71.

Hotels

Novotel Atria Nîmes Centre, 5 boulevard Prague (first street to the right at avenue Feuchéres/esplanade Charles-de-Gaulle), moderate, tel. 66-76-56-56.

Hôtel Tuileries, 22 rue Roussy, moderate, tel. 66-21-31-15.

Hôtel Plazza, 10 rue Roussy, inexpensive-moderate, tel. 66-76-16-20.

Hôtel Louvre, 2 square de la Couronne, moderate, tel. 66-67-22-75.

Nouvel Hôtel, 6 boulevard Amiral-Courbet, moderate, tel. 66-67-62-48.

Hôtel Carrière, 6 rue Grizot (turn right off boulevard Amiral-Courbet onto this narrow, one-way street across from the *Musée Archéologique*), moderate, tel. 66-67-24-89.

Hôtel Cheval Blanc, 1 place des Arènes (across from the south side of the Arena at boulevard de la Libération), moderate, tel. 66-67-20-03.

Hôtel Amphitheatre, 4 rue Arènes (small street entering boulevard des Arènes north of the Arena), inexpensive, tel. 66-67-28-51.

Sights Worth Seeing Nearby

Take time to see the **Pont du Gard**, a Roman engineering marvel 12 miles north of Nîmes. Built over 2,000 years ago, this three-tiered aqueduct/bridge, with a 10-foot-wide water channel in its top tier, was an important part of the aqueduct system that supplied water to Nîmes' *Castellum* from the reservoir in Uzès. With a 902-foot span across the Gardon River, 161 feet above the river, and nary a loose stone in its structure, it's truly an amazing sight. You can walk across it, but at your own risk—there are no guard rails! Several buses travel daily there from Nîmes' *Gare Routière* (behind the *Gare SNCF*).

For more Roman monuments, venture 17 miles southeast of town on a non-TGV train to **Arles**, where you'll find the largest Roman arena in France, a well-preserved Roman theater, and many other ancient buildings built during the Roman Empire. Arles is best known as the former home of Vincent Van Gogh, who painted over 200 canvasses of the city and nearby countryside in the two years he lived there, before his period of insanity. The house he briefly shared with Gauguin was destroyed by a bomb in 1944.

Montpellier

Montpellier is one of the few cities in southern France with no ties to the Roman Empire. Located on the eastern edge of the Languedoc-Roussillon region, only six miles from the Mediterranean Sea, it developed in the 8th century as a trading post on the spice route from the Near East. During the 13th century, the town was ruled by the Spanish Kings of Aragon and Majorca, and it was a center of French Protestantism until Louis XIII's armies quelled the movement in 1622. In the wake of this revolt and several violent protests against Spanish rule, Montpellier and other area towns were restored to France under the Pyrénées Treaty of 1659.

After this tumultuous period, Montpellier became a French business center, thanks mainly to a thriving wine export industry. The 17th- and 18th-century mansions are evidence of the prosperity the city enjoyed until a disease in the 1800's destroyed the vineyards. (The wine trade was revived in the mid-20th century with disease-resistant vines from the U.S.)

Today, Montpellier is a sprawling city of over 200,000, the administrative seat of the Languedoc-Roussillon region, and the intellectual, cultural, and university center of southern France. Its medical school, founded in 1000 (!) and confirmed as a university in 1289, is the oldest in France.

TGV Travel from Paris
Eight TGV trains travel daily from Paris to Montpellier. The 470-mile trip takes four hours, 40 minutes. The *Gare SNCF* is at place Auguste-Gilbert on the southeast side of town. Currently, the last TGV back to Paris leaves at 18:23.

Tourist Information Office
Montpellier has two tourist information offices within walking distance of the *Gare SNCF*. The *Office du Tourisme* at 6 rue Maguelone is three blocks from the station on the wide street that begins at place Auguste-Gilbert. To obtain a city bus map, stop first at the **SMTU** (*Société Montpellieraine de Transport Urbain*) office at 23 bis rue Maguelone, a few steps north of the station.

The *Bureau de Tourisme* is in *Le Corum*, a large office building at the north end of the esplanade Charles-de-Gaulle (see the walking tour, below). This office has more information about the region and a currency exchange open evenings and weekends.

Tour of Historic Sights & Major Attractions

With 50,000 university students, Montpellier is a lively town with a wide choice of cultural activities and entertainment. Although most of its university classrooms have been relocated to a modern section north of the city, the main meeting place for students and other residents is **place de la Comédie**. This large pedestrians-only area in the city center, just beyond the *Office de Tourisme* at the north end of rue Maguelone, is filled with shops, hotels, cafés, and restaurants. Arrive in the morning and plan your sightseeing over café au lait and a croissant at an outdoor café.

At the southwest end of place de la Comédie is the **Opéra Municipale**, a 19th-century theater where plays, opera, concerts, and other events are held regularly. To the northeast of the place, take a pleasant walk down **esplanade Charles de Gaulle** to its end at *Le Corum*. Paralleling its east (right) side is the **Jardin du Champ-de-Mars**, bordered by a 17th-century **Citadelle**, now used as a secondary school and government offices. Just south of the *Citadelle* and at the far end of the northeast pedestrians-only extension of place de la Comédie, the **Centre Commercial le Polygone**, a modern business/government complex with the city's *Hôtel de Ville*, offers shops, movie theaters, restaurants, and even a few hotels.

Halfway along the west (left) side of the esplanade, cross boulevard Sarail to rue Montpellieret to visit the **Musée Fabre**, one of the oldest regional art museums in France. Opened in 1803 after an exhibition of the Royal Academy was sent to Montpellier by Napoléon, most of its art comes from its namesake, local artist François Fabre, who donated his collection to the city in 1825. The museum features outstanding work by Courbet and Delacroix, paintings from Dutch, Flemish, and Italian artists, modern work by Utrillo and Matisse, several paintings by Fabre (a student of David), and paintings by area artists.

After the museum, follow boulevard Sarail back to place de la Comédie. Halfway down the place, turn right at the pedestrians-only rue de la Loge and go north through the center of Montpellier's **Vieux Quartier**, where you'll find over 100 17th- and 18th-century Italianate mansions (*Hôtel Particuliers*), many with ornate balconies, grand staircases, and magnificent courtyards. The *Office de Tourisme* has a walking tour of these homes.

One block after the covered market, where rue de la Loge ends at place des Martyrs-de-la-Résistance (the large building across the place is the *Préfecture*), turn left onto rue Foch. In less than a mile you'll pass the **Arc de Triomphe**, erected in 1691 to honor Louis XIV, who named Montpellier the capital of Languedoc.

Across the boulevard from the Arc is the **Promenade du Peyrou**. Begun in the 17th-century, it's one of Montpellier's prettiest areas, with reflecting pools, tree-lined paths, and a large statue of Louis XIV. At its west end, the **Château d'Eau**, an 18th-century Classical pavilion, marks the terminus of Montpellier's aqueduct system, which brought water from a spring nine miles away. You can see about 800 meters of the original aqueduct stretching westward from the monument. Also from there, the highest elevation in the city, you can see (on clear days) the Cévennes Mountains and the Mediterranean coast.

Two blocks north is the peaceful and colorful **Jardin des Plantes**. Originally created for the medical school's study of herbs, it was the first botanical garden in France, created in 1593, and today contains an outstanding collection of exotic plants.

Across the street, on the corner of boulevard Henri IV and rue de l'Ecole-de-Médecine, the **Musée Xavier-Atger**, housed in the Faculté de Médecine's library, displays 300 drawings and sketches by 16th- and 17th-century artists, including Watteau, Caravaggio, and Puget. The large, 14th-century **Cathédrale St.-Pierre** is directly behind the *Faculté de Médecine* building.

To return to the *Gare SNCF* through the *Vieux Quartier*, follow the curvy rue St.-Pierre/Vieille-Intendance away from the *Cathédrale* entrance to rue Cambacères, then go right along the west side of the *Préfecture* to place des Martyrs-de-la-Résistance. From there, retrace your steps on rue de la Loge or create your own route back to place de la Comédie.

For a more direct route to the station, stay on the wide boulevard skirting the west side of the city, walking south from the *Arc de Triomphe*, then east. Although the boulevard undergoes several name changes, it eventually ends at the station as rue de la République. Buses #3, 5, 7, 8, 9, and 11 travel from *Promenade du Peyrou* to the *Gare SNCF*.

Restaurants

Janus, 11 rue Aristide-Ollivier (go halfway down rue Maguelone, turn right at rue du Clos-René for one block, cross an open intersection, then go right), moderate-expensive, tel. 67-58-15-61.

L'Ollivier, 12 rue Aristide-Ollivier, moderate, tel. 67-92-86-28.

Flunch, inside the *Centre Commercial le Polygone*, inexpensive.

Chez Marceau, 7 place de la Chapelle-Neuve (exit right from the *Musée Fabre* for two blocks, then go right on rue de l'Aiguillerie to its end), inexpensive, tel. 67-66-08-09.

Au Vollier Nommé Désir, 10 rue du Collège-Duvergner (turn right one block past place de la Chapelle-Neuve), inexpensive, tel. 67-66-34-15.

Le Menestrel, place des Martyrs-de-la-Résistance (past the covered market on rue de la Loge), moderate, tel. 67-60-62-51.

Isadora, 6 rue due Petit-Scel (short street off rue Foch, halfway to the *Arc de Triomphe*), moderate-expensive, tel. 67-66-25-23.

Taverne du Peyrou, 17 rue Terral (south of promenade du Peyrou; turn left off boulevard Ledruc-Rollin), inexpensive, tel. 67-60-56-73.

La Table Sainte Anne, 20 rue Terral, inexpensive, tel. 67-60-45-35.

Hotels

Hôtel des Princes, place Auguste-Gilbert, moderate, tel. 67-58-93-94.

L'Hôtel, 6 rue Jules-Ferry (street in front of the *Gare SNCF*), inexpensive-moderate, tel. 67-58-88-75.

Hôtel Escargot, 14 rue Jules-Ferry, moderate, tel. 67-92-64-38.

Hôtel Angleterre, 7 rue Maguelone, moderate, tel. 67-58-59-50.

Royal Hôtel, 8 rue Maguelone, moderate, tel. 67-92-13-36.

Hôtel Commerce, 13 rue Maguelone, moderate, tel. 67-58-36-80.

Hôtel Édouard-VII, 10 rue Aristide-Ollivier, moderate, tel. 67-58-37-11.

Hôtel Paris, 15 rue Aristide-Ollivier, moderate, tel. 67-58-37-11.

Sights Worth Seeing Nearby

The modern seaside resort **La Grande-Motte** is 12 miles east of Montpellier. Known for its triangular and blockhouse-shaped buildings, it's the largest of a series of holiday centers created by the French government to promote tourism along the Mediterranean coast from the Spanish border to the Provence region. Each center features well-kept beaches, a boat harbor, sports facilities, and a variety of accommodations. There's regular bus service to La Grande-Motte and several small fishing ports with beaches from the *Gare Routière* (next to the train station).

The port of **Sète**, second to Marseille in Mediterranean shipping, is 21 miles south of Montpellier and the eastern terminus of the Midi canal. You'll enjoy this mid-size city's picturesque harbor—if you can stand the industrial smell. Non-TGV trains runs there frequently from Montpellier.

Béziers

Situated on a high plateau above the Orb River, just inland from the Mediterranean Sea, Béziers marks the last stop on the TGV line branching southwest from Avignon. Linked to the Mediterranean and the Atlantic by the *Canal du Midi*, the town is the business and production center for Languedoc wines, exporting more table wine than any city in the world.

Although Béziers has nearly 100,000 residents, this former Roman colony reflects the slower pace found in most southern French towns. However, this casual atmosphere changes whenever its champion rugby team whips an opponent, and in August during the *feria*, when bull-fights, parades, dancing, and all sorts of festivities occur throughout the city.

TGV Travel from Paris

Two TGV trains travel daily from Paris to Béziers. The 515-mile trip takes five hours, 25 minutes. The *Gare du Midi*, between boulevard de Verdun and the *Canal du Midi*, is on the south side of town. Currently, the last TGV back to Paris leaves at 16:22.

Tourist Information Office

The *Office de Tourisme* at 27 rue du 4-Septembre is in the center of the city, just south of the 18th-century *Hôtel de Ville* and less than two miles from the *Gare du Midi*. To get there, cross the open traffic area in front of the station to avenue Gambetta, a wide street on your left, near the top of the intersection. Walk on this street, which becomes avenue Alphonse-Mas after it curves left at place Garibaldi, until you see the *Hôtel de Ville* on the right (off place Gabriel-Péri). Rue du 4-Septembre is the first street on the right before the *Hôtel*. Bus #7 travels from boulevard de Verdun to the left of the *Gare du Midi* up the length of these streets.

Tour of Historic Sights & Major Attractions

Skipping the *Office de Tourisme* for now, go to the top of the open traffic intersection one street to the right from avenue Gambetta and follow rue de la Rotonde, which borders the **Plateau des Poétes** (Béziers' public gardens). When you reach rue Bayard shortly after the park, turn right. At the end of this short street, a left turn takes you to the south end of the beautiful **allées Paul Riquet**, a shady esplanade named for the rich landowner Pierre-Paul Riquet (1604-80), who conceived and directed the building of the *Canal du Midi*. Although commercial craft rarely use the canal today, Béziers probably would not have prospered without it.

Near the center of the esplanade is a David d'Angers' statue of Paul Riquet. Two miles to the right of the statue on avenue St.-Saëns, the restored, 13,000-seat **Roman Arènes** is still used for bullfights and other events. (Bus #4 goes there.) To the left of the statue is place Jean-Jaurès, a semi-circular area lined with hotels, shops, and the *Gare Routière*. At the far end of the allées Paul Riquet, in front of place de la Victoire, the **Théâtre Municipal** has a lovely façade sculpted by d'Angers.

Just before you reach the *Théâtre*, turn left on the pedestrians-only rue du 4-Septembre. At the end of the next block, check out the Flamboyant Gothic doorway of the **Église Penitents**, then continue to the *Office de Tourisme* at the end of the street. Get a city map, since there are several narrow streets and odd intersections in the last part of our tour.

The next sight is the **Cathédrale St.-Nazaire**, the focal point of Béziers' skyline when viewed from the Orb River. To get to the *Cathédrale*, cross avenue Gambetta and place Gabriel-Péri beyond the *Office de Tourisme* to rue Pépezuc, which takes you across place des Trois-Six to rue Viennet, which empties into place de la Révolution and the *Cathédrale*. A monument there commemorates Mayor Casimir Péret, who died resisting Napoleon III's 1851 *coup d'état*.

The *Cathédrale St.-Nazaire* was rebuilt during the 13th and 14th centuries after being destroyed in the 1209 Albigensian Crusade, when Béziers was burned on orders from Pope Innocent III for refusing to hand over 20 Cathars (Protestant heretics). On the highest point in town, it offers great views of the Orb River valley and the *Canal du Midi* from its towers, as well as good views from the grounds of its cloister and ramparts. The interior features a 12th-century statue of Christ, frescoes dating to 1374, and a 13th-century chapel with interesting bas-reliefs. The adjacent 14th-century cloister houses the **Musée Lapidaire**, with a small collection of precious stones.

After exploring the *Cathédrale*, walk back across place de la Révolution to its southeast corner at rue de Bonsi, where you'll find the *Hôtel Fabrégat*, a former Renaissance mansion now housing the **Musée des Beaux-Arts**. This small museum contains a varied group of works by French, Flemish, Italian, and German artists—including good paintings by Corot, Delacroix, Dufy, and Soutine—plus Greek ceramics.

For an overview of Béziers' history, visit the **Musée du Vieux Biterrois** a few blocks from the *Musée des Beaux-Arts*. Exhibits explore regional dress, archaeological artifacts, and wine production. To get there, walk two blocks further on rue de Bonsi, then go right on rue Massol to building #7.

After the museums, you'll find the remaining sights along the Orb River. To reach them, follow rue Massol/rue Docteurs-Bourguet south to place St.-Cyr. Turn right onto rue Canterelle, which is lined with ancient houses, until you come to an intersection with a teardrop-shaped traffic island. On the other end of the island (via rue du Pont-Vieux) is the 13th-century **Pont Vieux**, the oldest bridge in Béziers. There are impressive views of the city and the *Cathédrale St.-Nazaire* from the **Jardin du Faubourg du Pont** on the other side of the river (turn left at the bridge).

To return to the city and the *Gare SNCF*, walk to the other end of the park, then go left across the river on the *Pont Neuf*, which puts you on avenue du Colonel-d'Ornano. When this street splits several blocks later, the left fork goes to the central city, while the right fork (boulevard de Verdun) leads to the station.

If you have time, continue past the station and turn right on the first street beneath the tracks, then right at quai du Port-Neuf, where you can watch commercial and pleasure craft on the **Canal du Midi**. An interesting sight at the far end of this quai are boats crossing *over* the Orb River on a special viaduct. From Béziers, the canal flows to its east terminus at Sète and west to Carcassonne and Toulouse.

Restaurants

Cigale, 60 allées Paul-Riquet, moderate, tel. 67-28-21-56.

Le Framboiser, 12 rue Boïeldieu (after passing the Paul-Riquet statue and avenue St.-Saëns, angle to the right), moderate, tel. 67-49-90-00.

Chez Soi, 10 rue Guilhemon (turn left off avenue St.-Saëns, two blocks from allées Paul-Riquet), moderate, tel. 67-28-63-34.

Le Jardin, 37 avenue Jean-Moulin (two blocks after passing the *Théâtre Municipal*, turn right on avenue Georges-Clemenceau, then right again three blocks later), moderate, tel. 67-36-41-31.

Le Thé Retrouve, rue Viennet, inexpensive.

Hotels

Hôtel de Paris, 70 avenue Gambetta, inexpensive, tel. 67-28-43-80.

Hôtel Poétes, 80 allées Paul-Riquet (near intersection of rue Bayard), moderate, tel. 67-76-38-66.

Hôtel Nord, 15 place Jean-Jaurès, moderate, tel. 67-28-34-09.

Hôtel Angleterre, 22 place Jean-Jaurès, inexpensive, tel. 67-28-48-42.

Hôtel Imperator, 28 allées Paul-Riquet, moderate, tel. 67-49-02-25.

Sights Worth Seeing Nearby

If you make it all the way to Béziers, by all means visit **Carcassonne**, where you'll find the largest medieval fortress in Europe. It's 55 miles southwest of Béziers on non-TGV trains, with a change in Narbonne when there isn't a direct train. If you have a layover in **Narbonne**, check out its massive cathedral and the pretty canal that runs through the center of town.

The fishing village **Valras-Plage**, less than 10 miles from Béziers, features a seven-mile-long beach. To get there, take bus #1, which leaves frequently from place du Général-de-Gaulle. (At the rear of the *Théâtre*, turn right onto avenue du 22-Août-1944, then left at rue Emile-Suchon to place du Général-de-Gaulle).

CHAPTER 10

Mediterranean Ports & the French Riviera

Marseille

Founded 2,600 years ago by the Greeks, Marseille has been part of France since 1482. Today, it's France's second-largest city and the largest port on the Mediterranean Sea. Almost everything is imported and exported there—including illegal drugs, which bolster Marseille's reputation as one of the seamiest cities in the world. Despite being the crime and underworld capital of France, Marseille is well worth a visit, as long as you exercise caution.

With huge cargo and passenger ships entering its ports constantly, Marseille's streets are always filled with a mélange of sailors and visitors from many nations. Just sitting in a port-side café to people-watch is a great experience. When you get tired of sitting, visit the city's outstanding museums, churches, and parks, and end your tour with a meal of *bouillabaisse*, the seafood stew flavored with saffron, garlic, fennel, and other herbs, served in hearty portions at nearly every bistro in the city.

TGV Travel from Paris

Ten TGV trains travel daily from Paris to Marseille. The 484-mile trip takes four hours, 40 minutes. The restored 19th-century *Gare St.-Charles*, between rue Honorat and avenue Pierre-Sémard on a hill overlooking the city, is two miles northeast of the harbor. Currently, the last TGV back to Paris leaves at 18:18.

The station is on the edge of a notoriously rough neighborhood, so be careful. Be aware of the people near you, don't advertise the fact that you're a tourist, act like you know where you're going—and get there quickly!

Tourist Information Office

The *Office de Tourisme* is at 4 La Canebière (one of the few streets in

France without a street prefix like rue, avenue, etc.), over a mile from the *Gare St.-Charles* at the corner of rue Beauvau, one block from the *Vieux Port* and quai des Belges. The quickest way to reach it is to take Métro Line 1 from the station to the *Vieux Port-Hôtel de Ville* stop. From there, exit to La Canebière.

For an interesting walk, exit left from the station across avenue Pierre-Sémard to a series of steps leading down to the wide boulevard d'Athènes/boulevard Dugommier, which borders the edge of the North African quarter to La Canebière. At La Canebière, cross the street and turn right toward the *Vieux Port*.

At the tourist office, get a bus system/Métro map—very useful for extensive touring. If the tourist office has run out of them, try the *Régie des Transports de Marseille* office at 6 rue des Farbes. It's across La Canebière from the *Office de Tourisme* on a short street heading east from the *Bourse* building.

Tour of Historic Sights & Major Attractions

The first sight you'll encounter after leaving the *Gare St.-Charles* is the large **North African quarter**, an exotic area abounding with inexpensive shops and restaurants that will entice your senses of sight and smell in ways you've never experienced. However, it's not safe for a single person anytime, and you should definitely avoid it at night, unless you're with an area resident who speaks an Arabic language fluently.

If you choose to wander there, take an accurate map, dress plainly with no jewelry, and keep your money and I.D. in a front pocket or neck pouch. Even if you speak Arabic, don't fall for the ploy of joining a local proprietor or street vendor for a cup of tea in his back room, where you may be joined by the local theft committee. The quarter's approximate borders are boulevard Charles-Nédelec (north), rue d'Aix/cours Belsunce (west), La Canebière (south), and boulevard d'Athènes-boulevard Dugommier (east).

Beyond the quarter, the most famous attraction in Marseille is **La Canebière**, affectionately known by sailors as "La Can o' Beer." Lined with bars, cafés, restaurants, and retail shops stretching from quai des Belges at the *Vieux Port* to the intersection at square Stalingrad (where it changes to boulevard de la Libération), the street is crowded during the day with local business people, tourists, and boisterous sailors on leave. After 10:00pm, it becomes a more menacing area, with prostitution, drug-dealing, and other illicit activities. Whether you enter it off boulevard Dugommier en route from the *Gare St.-Charles* to the *Office de Tourisme*, or walk up it from the *Vieux Port*, this street offers the essence of Marseille's personality.

After strolling down La Canebière, visit the busy **Vieux Port**, site of the first Marseille settlement. Unfortunately, the modern buildings surrounding the port don't reflect Marseille's long history, since the area was leveled by the Nazis in 1943, when they dynamited building after building to roust the Resistance. Despite its modernity, it's still Marseille's most interesting and lively district, with numerous museums, two forts guarding the entrance to the sea, the 17th-century *Hôtel de Ville* on the waterfront, a palace in a park at the mouth of the port, and constant boisterous activity from fisherman, street hucksters, black marketeers, and sailors on leave.

The best view of Marseille—from its harbor and coastline to the rugged hills of Provence in the north—is from the terraces of the 19th-century **Basilique de Notre-Dame-de-la-Garde**, located on a steep hill a few miles south of the *Vieux Port*. It's Marseille's most prominent landmark, with a 151-foot gilded statue of the Virgin rising above its main tower. It was also the site of a fierce World War II battle during the liberation of Marseille on August 25, 1944. Near the bus parking area below the *Basilique*, an Allied tank destroyed by a Nazi shell serves as a memorial to the battle.

The quickest way there is via bus #60 from the *Vieux Port*. For some exercise, walk along the south side of the port on quai de Rive-Neuve, then turn left on rue Fort-Notre-Dame/boulevard Notre-Dame. About a mile and a half later, turn right at the *montée de Notre-Dame de la Garde*, a short series of steps up a narrow alley to rue Fort du Santuaire. There, cross the street and bear right for a short distance, go up the next set of steps on the left (where the street splits), then turn left at the narrow driveway that ascends the hill to the church.

The **Parc du Pharo**, overlooking a yacht basin at the entrance to the port, offers good views of the harbor and the château Napoleon III built for the Empress Eugénie. To get there from the *Office de Tourisme*, follow quai de Rive-Neuve/boulevard Charles-Livon past *Fort St.-Nicolas* (one of two forts guarding the port) until you see the park on your right. To get there from the *Basilique*, follow a long series of steps off the left corner of the terrace (looking towards the Mediterranean) down to the curvy chemin du Roucas/rue d'Endoume. Take a right, turn left a half-mile later at avenue de Corse, then turn right on avenue Pasteur to its end at the park.

On the return trip to the *Vieux Port*, turn right off boulevard Charles-Livon opposite *Fort St.-Nicolas* at rampe St.-Maurice, which travels through a short tunnel beside a fort. After exiting the tunnel, turn left on rue Sainte, which leads to the **Basilique St.-Victor**. Inside this small, 11th-century church is a 5th-century crypt and catacombs with the remains of two 3rd-century Christian martyrs.

From the church, rue Sainte goes back to the city, and any side street to the left goes back to quai de Rive-Neuve. Before heading to the other side of the port, consider visiting three museums near the *Office de Tourisme.* The **Musée Cantini et de la Faïence** (19 rue Grignan), housed in a 17th-century palace, is Marseille's modern art museum, with work by Ernst, Bacon, Dubuffet, and others, plus a 600-piece collection of Provençal porcelain. To get there, follow rue Beauvau along the *Office de Tourisme* to the Opéra building. Walk around it to rue Lulli, which ends two blocks later at rue Grignan. The museum is less than two blocks to the left.

From the museum, exit left, then go right on rue Paradis. At place du Général-de-Gaulle, cross La Canebière to the 1559 **Bourse** building, the oldest Chamber of Commerce in France. Inside, the **Musée de la Marine et de l'Economie Marseillaise** illustrates the city's history and its maritime associations. Behind the *Bourse* in the *Centre Bourse* complex, the **Musée d'Histoire de Marseille** traces 2,000 years of local history. Exhibits include Roman pottery, coins, hardware, and a boat recovered from this site. The archaeological garden outside has ongoing excavations.

On the north side of the *Vieux Port*, the 17th-century **Hôtel de Ville** is one of the few area buildings the Nazis did not blow up. Two museums behind City Hall focus on Marseille's past. The **Musée du Vieux-Marseille** at 2 rue de la Prison (turn right past the *Hôtel de Ville*) is a history and folklore museum known for its *santons*, small clay statues of figures from the Nativity. It also includes pottery, old maps, furniture, a model of Marseille in 1848, and a costume room.

Down the street to the left on rue du Lacydon is the interesting **Musée des Docks Romains.** After the Nazis destroyed most of the old quarter around the *Vieux Port*, archaeologists discovered many ancient Greek and Roman artifacts. The museum has remnants from boats, a collection of urns, and other antiquities.

Returning to the *Vieux Port*, follow the quai beyond the *Hôtel de Ville* to the 17th-century **Fort St.-Jean**, the second fort used to control the port's narrow entrance. After strolling around the fort on the pedestrians-only promenade, proceed along the coastal quai to the *Gare Maritime* on the left and the **Cathédrale de la Major** on the right. Built on the ruins of the Temple of Diana, the older (12th century) and smaller church features a Lucca della Robbia bas-relief in white ceramic and a Romanesque altar from 1175. Next door, the "new" cathedral is one of the largest churches built in Europe during the 19th century (1893). Constructed from green and white stone, its interior is an interesting display of mosaic floors and red and white marble banners.

Two blocks inland from the *Cathédrale*, the **Panier Quartier**, the oldest section of Marseille, features some of the narrowest streets in Europe. Though the faded buildings are long past their prime—their balconies lined with either flowers or clothes drying—the quarter is one of city's most picturesque neighborhoods.

After wandering in this area (take a good map), return to the rear of the *Cathédrale*, then follow rue de Mazenod paralleling the coast one block inland to place de la Joliette. At the west end, you can observe the **modern port** at work. At the opposite end of the square (at the Joliette stop), take Métro Line 2 to the *Gare St.-Charles* and transfer to Line 1 to the Cinq-Avenues-Longchamp stop.

Opposite this stop, about three miles inland from the *Vieux Port*, the **Palais Longchamp** fronts a large park and zoo. Built in 1870, the palace features an interesting colonnade and fountain that connects its two wings. The north wing contains the **Musée des Beaux-Arts**, one of the finest collections of European painting and sculpture in southern France, with masterpieces by Corot, David, Rubens, Watteau, Tiepolo, and Vuillard. Two Marseille-born artists are showcased in the museum: Honoré Daumier (1808-79), who has an entire room filled mainly with his lithographs, and Alphonse Monticelli (1824-86), who was a big influence on Van Gogh. The first floor of the museum contains France's first children's museum, a unique series of exhibits on the visual arts. The south wing of the palace contains the **Musée d'Histoire Naturelle**, with an aquarium and displays of birds and animals native to the Provence region.

Another museum worth visiting is the **Musée Grobet-Labadié** at 140 boulevard Longchamp, a block outside the palace's main entrance. This small museum, the former home of violinist and artist Louis Grobet, contains an eclectic collection of paintings by Corot, Monticelli, and Daubigny, medieval sculpture, Louis XV and Louis XVI furniture, antique violins, 17th-century Gobelins tapestries, and a letter from Beethoven. From there, return to the *Gare St.-Charles* or *Vieux Port* on the Métro. For a more scenic route, buses #41 and #80 run to the *Vieux Port* from there.

Fans of modern architecture should not miss the **Cité Radieuse** (a.k.a. *Unité d'Habitation le Corbusier*), a 17-story housing complex designed by Le Corbusier and considered avant-garde during its construction (1947-52). On the south edge of the city, it's easily reached on Métro Line 2 from the *Gare St.-Charles* or Noailles stop (entrance is at the intersection of La Canebière and boulevard Garibaldi, the extension of boulevard Dugommier) to the Rond Point du Prado stop. From there, walk south for a mile on the right side of boulevard Michelet. You'll see the building in the distance.

A mile from the same Métro stop—via avenue du Prado—is the **Plage du Prado**, the largest public beach in Marseille. For a circular and scenic route, bus #83 travels from this beach along the coast to the *Vieux Port*.

Restaurants

Brasserie New-York Vieux Port, 7 quai des Belges, moderate-expensive, tel. 91-33-60-98.

Maurice Brun-Aux Mets de Provence, 18 quai de Rive-Neuve, moderate, tel. 91-33-35-38.

Les Échevins, 44 rue Sainte (from the corner of quai des Belges and quai de Rive-Neuve, turn left onto cours Jean-Ballard, then right three blocks later), moderate-expensive, tel. 91-33-08-08.

La Charpenterie, 22 rue de la Paix-Marcel-Paul (narrow street off quai de Rive-Neuve) moderate, tel. 91-54-22-89.

Le Vaccares, 64 rue de la République (this street enters the corner of quais des Belges and quai du Port), inexpensive, tel. 91-56-16-76.

La Samaritaine, 43 quai du Port, inexpensive.

Chez Angele, 50 rue Caisserie (turn right off quai du Port onto avenue de St.-Jean before reaching *Fort St.-Jean*), inexpensive, tel. 91-90-63-35.

Chez Michel, 63 rue des Catalans (exit right from the *Parc du Pharo* on boulevard Charles Livon for a short distance, then left), moderate.

Flunch, 8-10 rue St.-Ferréol (facing away from the port, turn right off La Canebière a few blocks past the *Office de Tourisme*), inexpensive.

Chez Soi, 5 rue Papère (short street off La Canebière, one block before the Noailles Métro stop), inexpensive, tel. 91-54-25-41.

Le Jardin d' A Côte, 65 cours Julien (near the Notre-Dame-du-Mont-cours Julien Métro stop on Line 2), moderate, tel. 91-94-14-51.

Cousin-Cousine, 102 cours Julien, moderate, tel. 91-48-14-50.

La Dent Creuse, 14 rue Sénac-de-Meilhan (turn right off La Canebière two long blocks past the Noailles Métro stop), inexpensive, tel. 91-42-05-67.

Hotels

Relais Bleus St.-Charles, 5 boulevard Gustave-Desplaces (exit right from the *Gare St.-Charles* past place Victor-Hugo, then right for three blocks), moderate, tel. 91-64-11-17.

New Hôtel Select, 4 allées Léon-Gambetta (wide, divided street off boulevard Dugommier, two blocks from La Canebière), moderate, tel. 91-50-65-50.

Hôtel Lutétia, 38 allées Léon-Gambetta, moderate, tel. 91-50-81-78.

Hôtel Gambetta, 49 allées Léon-Gambetta, inexpensive, tel. 91-62-07-88.

New Hôtel Astoria, 10 boulevard Garibaldi (one block south of the Noailles Métro stop), moderate, tel. 91-33-33-50.

Hôtel Petit Louvre, 19 La Canebière (halfway between the *Vieux Port* and Noailles Métro stop), moderate, tel. 91-90-13-78.

Hôtel Rome, 7 cours St.-Louis (short block south of the cours Belsunce and La Canebière intersection; four blocks from the Noailles Métro stop), moderate, tel. 91-54-19-52.

Hôtel Alize, 7 quai des Belges, moderate, tel. 91-33-66-97.

Hôtel Sud, 18 rue Beauvau, moderate, tel. 91-54-38-50.

Novotel Marseille Centre, 36 boulevard Charles-Livon (between *Fort St.-Nicolas* and the *Parc du Pharo;* over two miles from the *Gare St.- Charles,* but excellent location and view), moderate-expensive, tel. 91-59-22-22.

Sights Worth Seeing Nearby
Take a 20-minute boat ride from quai des Belges to the tiny Ile Ratonneau to visit the **Château d'If,** a fortress built in 1524 by Francois I to defend Marseille. Later a prison, it was used as a setting in Alexandre Dumas' *The Count of Monte Christo.*

Just 19 miles north of Marseille, **Aix-en-Provence** is the sentimental capital of the Provence region. Home of artist Paul Cézanne (1839-1906), it has a much slower pace than Marseille. Non-TGV trains run there frequently.

Toulon

For centuries, Toulon has been one of the world's great naval ports. Surrounded by tall, terraced hills to the north and possessing one of the prettiest natural harbors on the Mediterranean, Toulon is the 13th largest city in France (182,000 residents) and the home port of France's Mediterranean fleet. Partly destroyed in World War II, this lively city resounds with the laughter and antics of sailors on leave and is worth a visit if only to see its harbor, filled with large naval boats and the local fishing fleet. More service-oriented than tourist-oriented, Toulon, on the western edge of the French Riviera, is an inexpensive base from which to explore the region.

TGV Travel from Paris
Three TGV trains travel daily from Paris to Toulon. The 526-mile trip takes five hours, 15 minutes. The *Gare SNCF* is at place de l'Europe on the north side of town, less than two miles from the harbor. Currently, the last TGV back to Paris leaves at 14:33.

Tourist Information Office
The *Office de Tourisme* and *Accueil de France* are at the corner of avenue Colbert and rue Victor-Clappier, not far from the *Gare SNCF.* To get there, exit left from the station on boulevard de Tessé for three blocks, then go right on avenue Colbert for one block.

Tour of Historic Sights & Major Attractions

To reach the port, walk south from the *Office de Tourisme* on avenue Colbert, crossing boulevard de Strasbourg to skirt around the left side (rue Molière) of the city theater to the left rear corner of the pedestrians-only place Victor-Hugo (behind the theater). From there, on the north edge of Toulon's picturesque **Vieille Ville**, follow rue Jean-Muraire-dit-Raimu past place Puget and the dolphin fountain, and take a right onto rue Hoche.

Halfway down, rue Hoche becomes **rue d'Alger**, the main business street in Toulon's old quarter. Lined with colorful shops, restaurants, and vendors, it's a fun street to explore during the day—but be very careful at night, since recent immigrants have overtaken much of this quarter. As in Marseille, unless you speak an Arabic language fluently, never walk alone there at night. Rue d'Alger eventually crosses avenue de la République, ending at quai Stalingrad and the **Vieille Darse** (old port).

After taking in the harbor sights, watching ships arrive and depart for Corsica, Malta, North Africa, and other destinations, venture down the quai to your right, passing the *Maritime Préfecture* to the **Musée Naval**, where you'll find ship models, paintings, mastheads, and mementos from Toulon's history. Next to the museum to the west is the **Arsenal Maritime**, Toulon's naval shipyard. Daily tours of the docks are available.

For a better view of Toulon and its harbor, climb the **Tour Royale**, a 16th-century tower three miles southeast of town on the Giens peninsula. To get there, backtrack on the quais past the old *Hôtel de Ville* to the entrance of the *Gare Maritime*. Turn right, following avenue de l'Infanterie-de-Marine/avenue des Tirailleurs-Sénégalais/rue du Polygone south beside the marinas until the road ends at the tower. An annex of the *Musée Maritime*, the tower's seven rooms have more maritime artifacts, including the first French submarine. Toulon's swimming beaches are to the east along the *Corniche du Mourillon*. Bus #3 from the *Gare SNCF* has several stops along this section of coastline.

After returning to the *Vieille Darse*, turn right in front of the small **Église St.-François** (off avenue de la République) onto the pedestrians-only **cours La Fayette**, where a large, noisy vegetable/flower market runs every morning. Halfway down this street in building #69, the **Musée du Vieux** illustrates the history of Toulon, including exhibits of items that belonged to Napoléon. Behind the museum, backtrack half a block to traverse de la Cathédrale and turn right for the 11th-century Romanesque **Cathédrale de Ste.-Marie-de-la-Seds**, which was expanded in the 17th and 18th centuries.

From the *Cathédrale*, exit to the right on rue Émile-Zola for four blocks to rue d'Alger. From there, retrace your steps to the theater, then turn left on boulevard de Strasbourg/avenue du Général-Leclerc, one of Toulon's main business streets, lined with department stores, chic shops, restaurants, and hotels. Or, armed with a good map, explore the *Vieille Ville*'s fascinating side streets, creating your own route to the destination below.

From the theater or points beyond, follow this street (or ride bus #191) to its intersection with rue Paulin-Guérin, where you'll find the **Musée d'Art et d'Archéologie** and **Musée d'Histoire Naturelle**. The fine arts museum has a good collection of Italian and modern paintings, including masterpieces by Fragonard, Vernet, David, Bacon, and Friesz. One room is devoted entirely to photography. Two rooms on the ground floor hold the small natural history museum.

To return to the *Gare SNCF* from there, walk a half-block further down avenue du Général-Leclerc to rue Chalucet, then go right along the pretty Jardin Alexandre 1er to boulevard Pierre-Toesca. The station is across the street to the right.

Before leaving Toulon, be sure to ride a cable car to the top of **Mont Faron** (three miles behind the *Gare SNCF*) for a marvelous panorama. The small **Musée du Débarquement** on the summit commemorates the Allied liberation of Toulon from the Nazis. You'll also find two restaurants, a zoo, and an abandoned fort.

The quickest way to reach the cable car, which is beside the three-star *Hôtel Altéa Tour Blanche*, is to take a taxi. By foot (only those in good shape should attempt this hilly climb), exit left from the *Gare SNCF* along boulevard de Tessé for a half-mile. When the boulevard forks right, turn left and cross the bridge over the railroad tracks, then angle right to follow avenue de Siblas past the cemetery. If you're wheezing by now, take bus #40 (which has a stop on this street) to the hotel. To continue walking, turn left one mile later at place Lieutenant-Lauret onto avenue Francis-Garnier. A half-mile later at rue Édouard-Perrichi, turn right and follow this street to the hotel.

Restaurants
Piano Crêperie, 45 rue Victor-Clappier, inexpensive, tel. 94-91-93-04.

Le Dauphin, 21 bis rue Jean-Jaurès (cross place de l'Europe to place Albert 1er, which narrows to avenue de Vauban/avenue Jean-Moulin; three blocks after crossing avenue du Général-Leclerc, turn right), moderate-expensive, tel. 94-93-12-07.

Restaurant Riny, 52 rue Jean-Jaurès (same directions as above, but go left on rue Jean-Jaurès), inexpensive, tel. 94-92-89-17.

La Ferme, 6 place Louis-Blanc (across from the *Église St.-François*), inexpensive, tel. 94-41-43-74.

Madeleine, 7 rue Tombardes (two blocks beyond the *Cathédrale Ste.-*

Marie, then right), inexpensive, tel. 94-92-67-85.

Pascal Chez Mimi, 83 avenue de la République, moderate.

Hotels

Nouvel Hôtel, 224 boulevard de Tessé (across from the *Gare SNCF*, two blocks to the left), moderate, tel. 94-89-04-22.

Le Grand Hôtel, 4 place Liberté (at intersection of rue Victor-Clappier and rue de Chabannes), moderate, tel. 94-22-59-50.

Hôtel La Residence, 18 rue Gimelli (the first street crossing avenue de Vauban), moderate, tel. 94-92-92-81.

Hôtel Maritima, 9 rue Gimelli, inexpensive, tel. 94-92-39-33.

Hôtel Dauphiné, 10 rue Berthelet (from the *Office de Tourisme*, turn left onto boulevard de Strasbourg, then right one block later), moderate, tel. 94-92-20-28.

Hôtel Molière, 12 rue Molière (across from city theater), inexpensive, tel. 94-92-78-35.

Sights Worth Seeing Nearby

The small fishing village of **St.-Tropez**, made famous by Brigitte Bardot and other jet-setters, is 43 miles east of Toulon. Several buses run there daily from the front of the *Gare SNCF.*

Two hours offshore from Toulon by motorboat, the **Iles d'Hyeres** is a picturesque series of islands first inhabited by a religious order and later a criminal colony that turned to piracy. Boats go out there twice a day from quai Stalingrad.

Cannes

Modern Cannes is synonymous with the glitzy world of the rich on elaborate yachts and glamorous movie stars in the latest films. With its large bay, sprawling beaches, luxury hotels, sub-tropical vegetation, and temperate climate, Cannes remains one of Europe's most popular vacation sites year-round. Once a Roman trading post and later a fortified fishing port, this town's constant festive atmosphere makes it fun place to visit, despite the high costs.

TGV Travel from Paris

Two TGV trains travel daily from Paris to Cannes. The 598-mile trip takes six hours, 28 minutes. The *Gare SNCF* is along rue Jean-Jaurès in the center of town. Currently, the last TGV back to Paris leaves at 13:24.

Tourist Information Office

The *Direction Générale du Tourisme et des Congrès* and *Accueil de France* are in the ultramodern *Palais des Festivals et des Congrès*, less than a mile from the train station at the east end of the *Vieux Port*. To reach this multi-level building (also the site of the International Film Festival), cross rue Jean-Jaurès to rue des Serbes. Stay on this street until you come to the palm tree-lined boulevard de la Croissette, Cannes' main road along the beaches. Across it to the right, at the end of esplanade Georges-Pompidou, is the *Palais des Festivals*.

Tour of Historic Sights & Major Attractions

From the *Direction Générale du Tourisme*, walk around the **Vieux Port** and watch the fisherman working, the yachts sailing into the small port, and the bustling flower market. From the port's southwest corner, ascend the narrow streets inland to Suquet hill, home of Cannes' **Vieux Ville**. At square Jean-Hibert, turn right onto rue du Port and left on the wide rue Georges-Clemenceau, and follow the steps of the *escalier de la Tour* on the right side of the street to rue Louis-Perrissol. From there, cross the street to the left, then go right on rue de la Castre to the Gothic **Église Notre-Dame-de-Bonne-Espérance**. Duck inside the church to see its lifelike statue of Ste.-Anne, then climb the 12th-century **Tour du Mont-Chevalier** (a.k.a. the "Suquet Tower" or "Lord's Tower") just south of the church for a marvelous view of Cannes. Next to the tower is Cannes' only museum, the tiny **Musée de la Castre**, containing temporary exhibits by local artists, regional archaeological relics, and collectibles from Africa, South America, and the Orient obtained in the travels of resident Baron Lycklama, who died in Cannes in 1900.

From the church, walk north on rue de la Castre to its end at rue Coste-Corail, and follow it to the right to a series of steps down to place de la Hôtel-de-Ville and the *Vieux Port*. After passing the port side of the **Hôtel de Ville**, follow the north edge of the port on allées de la Liberté to the *Palais des Festivals*.

From there, continue east for a long, leisurely stroll down boulevard de la Croisette. If you walk on the right side of this wide boulevard, you'll get a good view of body-to-body sunbathers on the private beaches owned by the hotels across the street. On the boulevard's left side, there are numerous luxury hotels, restaurants, art galleries, and designer boutiques. About halfway down, pause to admire the ultra-chic and luxurious **Hôtel Carlton Intercontinental**, an opulent haven for the jet-set. A little further down, the **Hôtel Martinez** rivals the Carlton. On the far east end of the boulevard is the **Port Canto**, where large ships anchor. Your walk will end at the **Palm Beach Casino** at *Pointe de la Croisette*.

To return to the *Gare SNCF*, retrace your steps on boulevard de la Croisette to rue des Serbes, or plot a new route on one of the many streets that connect the boulevard to rue Jean-Jaurès.

Restaurants

La Lorraine, 36 boulevard de Lorraine (extension of rue Jean-Jaurès, five blocks to the left beyond the *Gare SNCF*), Alsatian cuisine, inexpensive, tel. 93-38-51-39.

Le Monaco, 15 rue du 24-Août (street entering rue Jean-Jaurès to the right of the *Gare SNCF*), moderate, tel. 93-38-37-76.

Les Santons de Provence, 6 rue Maréchal-Joffre (exit right from the *Gare SNCF,* bear left three blocks later at rue Venizelos, then left again in two blocks), moderate-expensive, tel. 93-39-40-91.

Rescator, 7 rue Maréchal-Joffre, moderate-expensive, tel. 93-39-44-57.

Aux Bons Enfants, 80 rue Meynadier (pedestrians-only extension of rue Venizelos), inexpensive-moderate.

L'Olivier, 9 rue Rouguière (first left off rue Meynadier), moderate, tel. 93-39-91-63.

Au Mal Assis, 15 quai St.-Pierre (west side of the *Vieux Port*), moderate-expensive, tel. 93-39-13-38.

La Croisette, 15 rue du Commandant-André (two blocks off boulevard de la Croisette, extension of rue Teisseire from rue Jean-Jaurès), inexpensive-moderate, tel. 93-39-86-06.

Hotels

Hôtel du Nord, 6 rue Jean-Jaurès, moderate, tel. 93-38-48-79.

Roberts' Hôtel, 16 rue Jean-Jaurès, moderate, tel. 93-38-66-92.

Hôtel Modern, 11 rue des Serbes, inexpensive-moderate, tel. 93-39-09-87.

Hôtel de Bourgogne, 13 rue du 24-Août, inexpensive, tel. 93-38-36-73.

Hôtel des Congrès et Festivals, 12 rue Teisseire (walk left from the *Gare SNCF* three blocks, then right one block after passing the covered market), moderate, tel. 93-39-13-81.

Hôtel Arcade, 8 rue Marceau (turn left off rue Teisseire), moderate, tel. 92-98-96-96.

Hôtel Mondial, 77 rue d'Antibes and 1 rue Teisseire (one block further on rue Teisseire), moderate, tel. 93-68-70-00.

Hôtel France, 85 rue d'Antibes, moderate, tel. 93-39-23-34.

Sights Worth Seeing Nearby

For a spectacular view of Cannes, the Mediterranean coast, and the Maritime Alps, travel by taxi or rental car five miles north to the **Observatory of Super-Cannes.**

Two other sights just outside Cannes are **Grasse,** the perfume capital of the world, and **Vallauris,** the pottery capital of France, where local craftsmen trained Picasso in the ceramic arts. Several buses travel daily to these locations from the *Gare SNCF.*

From the *Gare Maritime* at the *Vieux Port,* you can take a 15-minute boat ride to the **Ile Ste.-Marguerite** or **Ile St.-Honorat.** On Ste.-

Marguerite, visit the *Fort de l'Ile* built by Spanish troops from 1635-37 and later remodeled by Vauban. Inside the fort, you can examine the cell of the prisoner immortalized by Dumas in *The Man in the Iron Mask* and visit the *Musée de la Mer*, containing Roman artifacts and the remains of a 10th-century Arab ship. The smaller Ile St.-Honorat is occupied primarily by monks, who built a monastery there in 410. Though the 19th-century abbey is open to all visitors, the older cloisters are open only to men.

Antibes

An ancient Greek trading post and former Mediterranean fishing village, Antibes today is a glamorous resort for the rich and famous and a major center for the commercial production of flowers. Preferred over neighbors Cannes and Nice for its small-town atmosphere, Antibes stays crowded in the warmer months, with tourists often outnumbering its 63,000 residents. With a superb beach, beautiful bay, colorful streets, posh shopping, and temperate climate, Antibes is a fun, albeit expensive, place to explore.

TGV Travel from Paris
Two TGV trains travel daily from Paris to Antibes. The 612-mile trip takes six hours, 39 minutes. The *Gare SNCF* is at place de la Gare on the northeast side of the city, a few blocks inland from the large *Port Vauban*. Currently, the last TGV back to Paris leaves at 13:14.

Tourist Information Office
The *Maison du Tourisme* is at 11 place Général-de-Gaulle in the center of town, about a half-mile from the *Gare SNCF.* To get there, exit right from the train station, walking parallel to the *Jardin René Cassin*. When the road splits, fork left across the street/traffic islands to avenue Robert-Soleau and follow this street until you reach place Général-de-Gaulle. The *Maison du Tourisme* is around the corner to the right.

Tour of Historic Sights & Major Attractions
Since Antibes is one of the prime resorts in Europe and a location historically linked to the Mediterranean Sea, most of the sights and attractions are on or near the waterfront. To reach the coast from the *Maison du Tourisme*, walk across place Général-de-Gaulle to boulevard Albert-1er, and go to its end eight blocks later at the small square Albert-1er. There are several excellent views of the city from the square, plus a good look at the coastline twisting east toward Nice. To the west is Antibes' largest beach, the *Plage de la Salis*, and the *Cap d'Antibes*. Turn around and you'll see the snow-capped mountains of the Maritime Alps.

From the square, follow Antibes' old coastal ramparts toward the city for more elevated views of the Mediterranean. Almost immediately, you'll come to the **Musée Archéologique.** Housed in the Bastion St.-André, a Vauban-designed fortification, this museum has over 300,000 items illustrating 4,000 years of area history, including Etruscan, Greek, and Roman artifacts excavated in the region, and coins, weapons, and tools salvaged from ships from the 10th- to 18th-century. The museum is closed in November.

Next, continue along the curvy ramparts and promenade Amiral-de-Grasse to the 16th-century **Grimaldi Castle,** easily identified by its square Romanesque tower. Built on a terraced cliff from the remains of a 12th-century castle (the original tower, two windows, and battlement walk remain), this building is most famous for being the first of many Riviera residences of Pablo Picasso. The **Musée Picasso** on the first floor contains several drawings, paintings, and ceramics the artist created while living there in 1946. The second floor offers works by contemporary artists, plus temporary exhibitions. From the castle's terrace, dotted with sculpture by Miro and Richier, you get more wonderful views of the coast.

Beside the castle, the **Église Immaculée-Conception** operated as a cathedral during the Middle Ages. With only the east wall still standing from its original Romanesque structure, this church features a 12th-century watchtower (now a belfry) and a 17th-century Classical façade and nave. There are interesting carvings inside, including an altar designed by Louis Bréa in 1515 and a wooden crucifix from 1447.

Beyond the museum and church, follow the coastal streets to the picturesque **Vieux Port,** filled with fishing boats, yachts, and a lively fish market. Larger commercial craft anchor at **Port Vauban** next door. Overlooking the other side of the ports, **Fort Carré** was built in 1578 on St.-Roch Hill, a peninsula dividing the bay of Nice from Antibes. During a war in 1746, the fort withstood a 46-day siege. In 1794, a local military commander—Napoléon Bonaparte—was imprisoned there briefly after the fall of Robespierre during the French Revolution.

Inland from the *Vieux Port* and these sights, the **Vieille Ville,** centered around place Nationale and rue de la République, is Antibes' most picturesque quarter, featuring interesting shops, cafés, restaurants, and a maze of narrow, pedestrians-only streets. The area has changed little over the centuries, and wandering evokes the days when traders, pirates, and troops explored the same streets for exotic bargains.

To get there, pass through the *Porte Marine* (old port entrance) to rue Aubernon, which leads to place Masséna, where a food and flower market runs daily. Buy a few items for your lunch, then turn right on rue Georges-Clemenceau. At the end of this street, veering to the left, you'll meet rue de la République and the rectangular place Nationale. (If you skip the *Vieux Port*, rue des Arceaux connects the *Église Immaculée-Conception* and *Castle Grimaldi/Musée Picasso* to place Masséna.)

To return to the *Gare SNCF* from there, stay on rue de la République for about a mile until it ends at place Général-de-Gaulle, opposite the *Maison du Tourisme*. A right turn there puts you back on avenue Robert-Soleau, which leads to the station.

Restaurants

La Marguerite, 11 rue Sadi-Carnot (near the *Gare SNCF,* turn left off avenue Robert-Soleau), moderate-expensive, tel. 93-34-08-27.

Du Bastion, 1 avenue Général-Maizière (turn left off boulevard Albert-1er one street before square Albert-1er), moderate, tel. 93-34-13-88.

Les Vieux Murs, promenade Amiral-de-Grasse (a few blocks before the *Musée Picasso*), moderate-expensive, tel. 93-34-06-73.

L'Armoise, 2 rue de la Touraque (beyond the *Musée Archéologique*, take the straight street instead of the ramparts and coastal road to the right), moderate, tel. 93-34-71-10.

Le Tire Bourchon, place Nationale, inexpensive, tel. 93-34-76-14.

L'Oursin, 16 rue de la République, moderate-expensive, tel. 93-34-13-46.

Le Romantic, 5 rue Docteur-Rostan (turn right off rue de la République beneath an overhead passage), moderate, tel. 93-34-59-39.

Hotels

Hôtel l'Étoile, 2 avenue Gambetta (at the eight-pronged intersection, turn right off avenue Robert-Soleau onto the last street entering from the right), moderate, tel. 93-34-26-30.

Hôtel Royal, boulevard Maréchal-Leclerc (three blocks to the right of square Albert-1er), moderate-expensive, tel. 93-34-03-09.

Hôtel Le Cameo, place Nationale, moderate, tel. 93-34-24-17.

Auberge Provençale, place Nationale, moderate, tel. 93-34-13-24.

Sights Worth Seeing Nearby

Southwest of Antibes, **Cap d'Antibes** is a rugged, curvy peninsula filled with luxury hotels and villas owned by the wealthy. At its far tip off avenue John-F.-Kennedy, the **Musée Naval et Napoléonien** offers an interesting collection of Napoleonic memorabilia and naval models. Unless you're training for the Olympics, take a taxi there, since it's about eight miles from central Antibes.

Fans of artist Fernand Léger, known for his tubular-shaped people and industrial landscapes, should take a bus to the village of **Biot**, home of the **Musée National Fernand Léger.** Created in 1957, two years after Léger's death, it was the first museum in France honoring a single artist. With over 300 paintings, the museum covers his entire oeuvre, with several polychrome ceramic works, including a massive design on the main façade. Biot is also known throughout Europe for its glassware artisans, and many of their studios are open to the public. Buses to Biot leave from the *Gare Routière* at place Guynemer, two blocks from the *Maison du Tourisme* off rue de la République.

Nice

With nearly 350,000 residents, Nice is the largest city on the French Riviera and the fifth largest in France. Although this capital of the Côte d'Azur may not be as quaint as the smaller towns on the Mediterranean coast, Nice is a beautiful city, set before the wide, sweeping *Baie des Anges* (Bay of Angels) that stretches several miles beyond the city limits in both directions. In the summer, its rocky beaches are lined with tanning bodies, and its crowded, lively streets are constantly festive. In the winter, when the weather is milder and the city less crowded, people retreat indoors—making it a good time to tour its fine museums and churches, relax in a café over an espresso, or share a bowl of *bouillabaisse* with a friend.

Nice was founded by the Greeks of Marseille in 350 B.C., and by 150 B.C., it had become a Roman colony of 20,000. Over the centuries, Nice endured many rulers, including the Counts of Provence and the House of Savoy, who returned it to France in 1860. By the end of the 19th century, Nice had become a popular resort frequented by the Queen of England and other wealthy Brits. The railroad, connecting Nice with the rest of Europe, spurred area growth. Today, with a modern airport and train station, Nice makes a good base from which to explore the French Riviera.

TGV Travel from Paris
Two TGV trains travel daily from Paris to Nice. The 624-mile trip takes six hours, 58 minutes. The *Gare Nice-Ville* is along avenue Thiers on the north edge of town, less than two miles from the beach. Currently, the last TGV back to Paris leaves at 13:00.

Tourist Information Office
Nice has two tourist information offices. The *Office de Tourisme* and *Accueil de France* are beside the *Gare Nice-Ville*. Another office is at 5 avenue Gustave-V, two blocks inland from the west corner of the Jardin Albert 1er and promenade des Anglais, the wide, congested road bordering the Mediterranean coastline (see below).

Tour of Historic Sights & Major Attractions
Most of Nice's sights are along the coast. To get there, exit left from

the *Gare Nice-Ville* to avenue Jean-Médecin, the city's main north-south business and shopping street, and walk to its end at place Masséna. Divided by pretty squares and promenades, the streets going east and west off place Masséna are lined with hotels, restaurants, and chic shops. Bus #12 travels between the station and the *Gare TN* (a.k.a. *Station Centrale*), the main city bus stop, two blocks east of place Masséna at 10 Félix-Faure and square Général-Leclerc.

From place Masséna, turn right on avenue de Verdun—which parallels the **Jardin Albert 1ᵉʳ**, filled with exotic flowers and palm trees—to the junction of avenue Gustave-V and **promenade des Anglais**, one of the prettiest streets in Europe. Lined with luxury hotels, designer outlets, and some of Nice's best restaurants, this beautiful avenue, designed in the early 1800's by the resident British colony, stretches five miles from the airport in the western suburbs to the *Tour Bellanda* at the base of Castle Hill. From the east end of the Jardin Albert 1ᵉʳ, the street narrows to become quai des États-Unis. Bus #9 and #10 travel from the old port along this avenue to the airport, if you get tired of walking.

Half a mile from this junction (facing the sea, turn right), you'll come to rue de Rivoli and the **Hôtel Négresco**, one of the most famous hotels in the world. On the outside, it looks like a cross between a French and Russian château, complete with a mansard roof and domed tower painted pink with turquoise trim. Inside, it's filled with antiques and luxurious furnishings.

On the same street, set back in a small park, the **Musée Masséna** combines art and history in the villa of Victor Masséna, Prince of Essling and grandson of Napoléon's Marshal Masséna. The collection focuses on regional and Italian art from the 15th- to 19th-century, including work by local artist Louis Bréa, plus 15th- to 17th-century sculpture, 13th-century ceramics, Niçois folk art and jewelry, and three galleries documenting area history.

About a mile beyond rue Rivoli, at 33 avenue des Baumettes (in a small municipal park), the **Musée des Beaux-Arts Jules Chéret** offers a fine collection of 17th- to 20th-century European art and sculpture, with an emphasis on French artists. Housed in the 1878 palace of Russian Prince and Princess Kotschoubey, the collection includes paintings by Fragonard, Renoir, Monet, Sisley, and Dufy, plus sculpture by Rodin, Rude, and Carpeaux. Jules Chéret (1836-1931), the museum's namesake, was a Nice artist and printmaker who had a big influence on Toulouse-Lautrec's poster art. When Chéret died, his personal art collection went to the museum.

To get there, continue west on promenade des Anglais to rue Honorè-Sauvan. Turn right, cross rue de France, then angle left through square Colonel-Bouvier to avenue des Baumettes. Follow this twisting street until you see the museum on the left. The stairs coming in from the left, shortly after you enter avenue des Baumettes, provide a shortcut to the museum.

From the museum, return to promenade des Anglais and backtrack (east) to the squat, circular **Tour Bellanda**, a 16th-century bastion at the foot of Castle Hill. Halfway to the tower, after the *Jardin Albert 1er* and the 19th-century Opéra building, take a detour by turning left at rue de la Terrasse, followed by an immediate right onto cours Saleya, where you'll find a lively flower and produce market from early morning until mid-afternoon. On the same street in building #3, the **Musée International de Malacolgie** showcases over 15,000 seashells from around the world, plus underwater flora exhibits and two aquariums.

Cours Saleya is also the south border of Nice's **Vieille Ville**. In this dilapidated old quarter, decorated mainly with laundry and flowers hanging from balconies, you can explore a maze of narrow streets and alleys, with a small church or inexpensive restaurant on nearly every corner. While some maintain it's a dangerous neighborhood—it has a reputation as a haven for drug traffickers, smugglers, and such—the *Vieille Ville* has the most character of any area in Nice. You'll be safe if you take the usual precautions and don't flash a wad of money around. Also, be hesitant to buy goods from anyone who approaches you on the street if they lack an official stand. Later in the tour, we'll walk this quarter from its north end.

Returning to the coast, take time to duck into the **Galeries d'Art Contemporain des Musées de Nice** at 59 quai des États-Unis. It usually has interesting exhibits of modern art (1960's to the present). When you reach the *Tour Bellanda*, check out the **Musée Naval** collection of weapons, ship models, nautical instruments, and other artifacts illustrating Nice's naval history. Used primarily by the military, the tower once had a celebrity resident: composer Hector Berlioz lived there while writing the music for "King Lear."

After the museum, take the elevator behind the tower to the top of **Castle Hill**, where you'll find the ruins of a 16th-century château and fortress destroyed in 1706 by order of Louis XIV. From the terraced hilltop, there are outstanding views of Nice, the *Baie des Anges*, and nearby Italy, with the snow-tipped Maritime Alps to the north. Castle Hill also contains the foundation of an 11th-century cathedral, some early Greek structures, lush gardens, an artificial waterfall, a cemetery, and several cafés. The energetic can take one of several paths to the summit instead of the elevator.

After returning to the *Tour Bellanda*, circle the south side of Castle Hill to the narrow **Bassin Lympia**, the old port of Nice. Opened for business in 1750, the port is filled today with small cruise ships and pleasure craft. Boats to Corsica leave from there.

From the northwest corner of the port, follow rue Cassini to the pretty place Garibaldi, an arcaded square with a statue of Giuseppe Garibaldi amid fountains and greenery. Garibaldi, born in Nice in 1807, was one of the leaders of the 1860 Italian Revolution and a valiant soldier in the French army in 1870 during the war against Prussia. A few blocks northwest on boulevard Risso is the **Musée Histoire Naturale.** Straight west of it, below the *Pont Garibaldi,* the **Musée d'Art Moderne** features important contemporary works. Not far south from the square on the narrow, pedestrians-only rue Neuve, the **Église St.-Martin-St. Augustin** is a small but elaborately decorated 17th-century Baroque church with a Pieta by Bréa and an interesting history: Martin Luther celebrated mass there in 1510, and Garibaldi was baptised there.

South of the church is the **Vieille Ville.** To get there, follow the steps west of the church to rue Pairolière, then go left to place St.-François, where a lively fish market runs every morning. One street west is boulevard Jean-Jaurès, which goes south to place Masséna and the bus station.

Just beyond place St.-François where the street splits, fork left on rue Droite to the **Palais Lascaris.** Built in the 1640's in the Italian Genoese-style for the Count of Vintimiglia, this small palace flaunts elegance throughout. There's interesting scrollwork around its doorway, a beautiful balustraded staircase, 17th-century paintings, Flemish tapestries, a *trompe l'oeil* ceiling in the salon, period furnishings, and a china/glassware collection. There are also several exhibits about Niçoise folk traditions and a re-created 18th-century pharmacy.

From there, continue south on rue Droite for half a block, then turn right at rue Rossetti, walking two blocks west to the **Cathédrale Ste.-Réparate.** Built in the Baroque tradition in 1650, the *Cathédrale* features a dome of glazed tiles and several outstanding carvings and decorative work in plaster and marble. The tower was added in the 18th century.

After this sight, explore the twisting, narrow streets and stepped passageways in the old quarter at random, or return to place Masséna via boulevard Jean-Jaurès (rue de la Préfecture two blocks south of the *Cathédrale* leads to this street). From place Masséna, follow avenue Jean-Médecin back to the *Gare Nice-Ville.*

If art is your passion, don't miss the following art museums in Nice's suburbs. West of Nice in Ste.-Hélène (near the airport), the **Musée International d'Art Naïf Anatole-Jakovsky** has over 600 drawings and paintings by artists from over 24 nations who paint in the naïf style popularized by Henri Rousseau. It's a long walk from central Nice, so take a taxi to it or bus #22 from place Masséna to the *Tour Sarrasine* stop, changing to bus #34, which stops at the museum.

The *Musée Marc Chagall* and the *Musée Matisse* are on the other side of the tracks from the *Gare Nice-Ville* in the elegant and hilly suburb of Cimiez. The **Musée Marc Chagall**, housed in a modern building on a tree-lined hill, opened in 1973 as the only national museum dedicated to a living artist (Chagall died in 1985). Among the numerous paintings, drawings, and sketches displayed, its greatest treasures are 17 of Chagall's Old Testament paintings from 1954-67. The museum also includes stained glass art, sculpture, lithographs, etchings, and tapestries.

To get there, exit left from the *Gare Nice-Ville* along avenue Thiers, then left on avenue Malausséna as it passes under the railroad tracks. Three blocks later, turn right on avenue Mirabeau/avenue George-V, forking to the right on avenue Paul-Dufourmantel. On the right side of the street just after the fork, look for a small set of steps leading to avenue Docteur-Ménard, the street the museum is on. If you miss them, continue a little further on avenue Paul-Dufourmantel, then turn right on avenue Docteur-Bergougnié, which intersects avenue Docteur-Ménard. It's about a 20-minute walk from the station.

From the middle of the city, bus #15 travels from the *Gare TN* to both museums. For the *Musée Chagall*, get off at the Docteur-Moriez stop, just south of the museum. For the *Musée Matisse*, exit at the Arènes stop. Other buses traveling to the *Musée Matisse* include #17 and #22 from place Masséna and bus #20 from the *Bassin Lympia*.

To reach the **Musée Matisse** on foot, exit the *Musée Chagall* to the right on avenue Docteur-Ménard to boulevard de Cimiez. Turn left and walk uphill to boulevard Édouard-VII (about a mile), turn right, then left on avenue Arènes de Cimiez. When you see the 1st-century **Roman Arena** on the right, stop. The *Musée Matisse* is behind it in the *Villa des Arènes*, a 17th-century home with *trompe l'oeil* frescoes on its exterior.

Henri Matisse (1869-1954), who lived in Cimiez for several years, is one of the greatest 20th-century artists and a major influence on modern art. When he died, his widow gave Nice a large body of his work. With oils, watercolors, and 50 bronze sculptures, this collection spans his entire oeuvre from the Impressionistic pieces of the 1890's to minimalistic line drawings of the 1950's. The museum also contains some of Matisse's personal art collection and belongings.

In the bottom floor of the villa, the **Musée Archaeologie** has an interesting group of ceramics, glass, coins, and tools from the Etruscans, Greeks, and Romans who occupied the area from 8 B.C.-A.D. 6. On the grounds are ancient Roman ruins, including a bathhouse that became a cathedral in the 5th century.

East of the museums in the *Parc Public*, the **Cimiez Monastery** was erected by Franciscan monks in 1546 to replace a 9th-century Benedictine monastery, which was built on the site of a Temple of Diana. The frescoes inside are from the 17th and 18th centuries. Next to the monastery, the **Musée Franciscan** tells the history of the order through exhibits on the monastic life. There are magnificent views of Cimiez's villas, Nice, and the coastline from the park and terraced gardens surrounding these sights.

Restaurants

L'Etoile, 3 rue de Belgique (directly across from the *Gare Nice-Ville*, angling left off avenue Thiers), moderate, tel. 93-87-35-24.

La Saëtone, 8 rue d'Alsace-Lorraine (cross avenue Thiers in front of the train station to avenue Durante, then take the second left), inexpensive, tel. 93-87-17-95.

Chez Davia, 11 bis rue Grimaldi (follow avenue Durante/avenue Baquis to boulevard Victor-Hugo, turn left for three blocks, then right), inexpensive, tel. 93-87-73-67.

St. Moritz, 5 rue du Congrès (extension of avenue Baquis from boulevard Victor-Hugo to promenade des Anglais), moderate, tel. 93-88-54-90.

Le Panda, 26 rue de la Buffa (crosses rue du Congrès), inexpensive, tel. 93-87-56-93.

Le Dalpozzo, 33 rue de la Buffa, inexpensive, tel. 93-88-11-11.

La Toque Blanche, 40 rue de la Buffa, moderate-expensive, tel. 93-88-38-18.

Flunch, 7 rue Halévy (short street off promenade des Anglais at the Casino Ruhl), inexpensive.

Le Cadaques, 8 quai des Docks (east side of the *Bassin Lympia*), inexpensive-moderate, tel. 93-89-41-76.

Le Gitane, place Rossetti (in front of the *Cathédrale Ste.-Réparate*), inexpensive, tel. 93-62-06-77.

Nissa Socca, 5 rue Ste.-Réparate (pedestrians-only street running south from the *Cathédrale Ste.-Réparate*), moderate, tel. 93-80-18-35.

Tocello, 6 rue Ste.-Réparate, moderate, tel. 93-62-10-20.

L'Univers, 54 boulevard Jean-Jaurès, moderate-expensive, tel. 93-62-32-22.

Hotels

Hôtel Durante, 16 avenue Durante, moderate, tel. 93-88-84-40.

Hôtel Excelsior, 19 avenue Durante, moderate, tel. 93-88-18-05.

Hôtel Trianon, 15 avenue Auber (one block west of avenue Durante), moderate, tel. 93-88-30-69.

Hôtel Oasis, 23 rue Gounod (two blocks west of avenue Durante), moderate, tel. 93-88-12-29.

Hôtel Gounod, 3 rue Gounod, moderate, tel. 93-88-26-20.

Nouvel Hôtel, 19 bis boulevard Victor-Hugo (turn left off avenue Baquis for two blocks), moderate, tel. 93-87-15-00.

Hôtel Cigognes, 16 rue Maccarani (turn left at boulevard Victor-Hugo, then right two blocks later), moderate, tel. 93-88-65-02.

Hôtel de la Mer, 4 place Masséna, inexpensive-moderate, tel. 93-92-09-10.

Hôtel Harvey, 18 avenue de Suède (north of the *Office de Tourisme*; turn right off avenue de Verdun or left off rue Maccarani), moderate, tel. 93-88-73-73.

Sights Worth Seeing Nearby

Thirteen miles east of Nice, the tiny country **Monaco** features the jet-set city **Monte Carlo.** Unless you spend a lot of time in its casino and museums, it's an easy half-day trip—time enough to take a short palace tour, view the harbor full of luxury yachts, admire the modern hotels and homes dangling over the sea, and explore the narrow, hilly streets.

Four miles beyond Monaco, **Menton** is a pretty city usually bypassed in favor of Italy (6.2 miles from Monte Carlo). The train station is just a half-mile from the seashore, so you can combine a walk along Menton's scenic coast with a half-day trip to Monte Carlo. Several non-TGV trains travel daily to these destinations.

A half-mile north of the *Gare Nice-Ville* at 33 avenue Malausséna is the *Gare de Provence* (a.k.a. the *Gare du Sud*), home of the private railway **Chemins de Fer de la Provence,** whose trains ascend a narrow-gauge track for a spectacular 103-mile trip through the northern hills of Nice up the Var River Valley to Digne. A one-way excursion, without getting off at any of the villages (**Annot** and **Entrevaux** are the most picturesque) along the route, takes three hours, 10 minutes. Some rail passes include a voucher for a free roundtrip ticket on this line.

CHAPTER 11

The Loire Valley & Environs

Vendôme

Nestled among several branches of the Loir River, Vendôme is a small town, featuring the ruins of a feudal château and an ancient abbey with a bell tower and museum. There's not a lot to see or do there, but if you want a break from the large TGV cities and a look at small-town life in France, Vendôme won't disappoint.

TGV Travel from Paris
Four TGV trains travel daily from Paris to Vendôme. The 106-mile trip takes 42 minutes. The modern *Gare Vendôme-Villiers-sur-Loire* is in the country, three miles west of town off the D957 highway. (The SNCF couldn't build high-speed tracks to Vendôme's old station, so it built a new station just for the TGV.) Currently, the last TGV back to Paris leaves at 21:26.

Tourist Information Office
The *Office de Tourisme* is at 47-49 rue Poterie in the *Parc du Lycée*. Unless you want a long walk from the station, take a taxi there.

Tour of Historic Sights & Major Attractions
From the *Office de Tourisme*, walk south on rue Poterie across a branch of the Loir River and go to the end of the street a half-mile later, where you'll find one of the town's original gateways and another branch of the river. Cross the river and turn left on rue Fermé, then right at the driveway leading to the hilltop **Château de Vendôme**.

Unfortunately, the *Château* is mostly in ruins. After severe damage during the Hundred Years War, it was dismantled as part of Vendôme's defense in 1589 and fell into disrepair, despite some 17th-century restoration. The only evidence left of its fighting past is an earth wall, fragmented ramparts, and a few decimated towers. The small **Musée de Château** on the grounds has a few artifacts documenting its history. There are good views of the city and surrounding countryside from the *Château's* adjacent park and terrace.

Returning to Vendôme, exit from the driveway entrance across rue Fermé to the right and cross the Loir River branch to rue St.-Bié. At place de la République or rue de l'Abbaye, turn right to visit the **Cloître de la Trinité**, a feudal abbey built from the 11th to early 16th century. The abbey church features an excellent Flamboyant Gothic façade and the "Virgin and Child" window, the oldest existing stained glass image of Mary as the Virgin Mother.

To the right of the church entrance, a 12th-century Romanesque belfry served as a model for one of the two spired towers of the cathedral in Chartres. After 5:00pm, you can climb it to watch the bells ring. The **Musée Municipale** (inside the monks' quarters) features Middle Ages and Renaissance religious art, including carved stonework from the church, some unexceptional pieces by French and Flemish artists, furniture, and Vendôme crafts.

If you have a few hours between trains, relax in the **Parc du Lycée**, located between two branches of the Loir River. The quickest way to get there from the *Cloître de la Trinité* is to turn left on rue de l'Abbaye to the pedestrians-only place St.-Martin, a lively market area and central meeting spot marked by the 15th-century **Tour St.-Martin**. Then, turn right on rue du Change (continuation of rue St.-Bié), which soon becomes pedestrians-only, too. After crossing a Loir River branch, turn left through an open area that leads to a short bridge over the river into the park. From the *Office de Tourisme* at the opposite end of the park, you can call for a taxi to return to the TGV station.

Restaurants

Le Darmier, 17 place de la République, moderate-expensive, tel. 54-77-70-15.

Chez Annette, 194 bis faubourg Chartrain (the continuation of rue du Change after it crosses the Loir River), inexpensive-moderate, tel. 54-77-23-03.

Jardin du Loir (also has nine inexpensive hotel rooms), place Madeleine (between the Loir River and its branch by the *Office de Tourisme*), moderate, tel. 54-77-20-71.

Hotels

Grand Hôtel St.-Georges, 14 rue Poterie (halfway to the *Château*), moderate, tel. 54-77-25-42.

Hôtel la Ville, 23 rue du Général-de-Gaulle (left off rue Poterie), inexpensive, tel. 54-77-25-70.

Hôtel Vendôme, 15 faubourg Chartrain (cross the Loir River bridge toward the *Gare SNCF*), moderate, tel. 54-77-02-88.

Sights Worth Seeing Nearby

Set on a high cliff above the Loir River next to the town of **Châteaudun** is the imposing castle and château of Dunois (a.k.a. "The Bastard of Orléans"), the faithful companion of Joan of Arc during the 15th-century wars against the English army. It's just 25 miles from Vendôme on a non-TGV train from the *Gare SNCF* (in north Vendôme off faubourg Chartrain).

Tours

Tours, the largest city in the Loire Valley (over 250,000 people), leads the region in commerce, culture, industry, and education. Although most tourists use it as a base to explore the 150-plus châteaux nearby, this former Gaul outpost offers its own historic sights, including an interesting old quarter, an ancient château, a Gothic cathedral, and numerous museums.

TGV Travel from Paris

Seven TGV trains travel daily from Paris to Tours. The 147-mile trip takes one hour, three minutes. The *Gare SNCF* is at place du Maréchal-Leclerc in the center of town.

In addition, nine TGV trains travel daily from Paris (a 56-minute trip) to the industrial suburb St.-Pierre-des-Corps, two miles east of Tours' *Gare SNCF.* (The seven trains to Tours stop in St.-Pierre- des-Corps, too.) When the high-speed rails were laid for the TGV Atlantique line, it was more convenient to place them a few miles east and south of the city, following the exisiting rail network, which included a stop in this suburb. By avoiding the heart of Tours (where the TGV must return to the old rail line), the TGV's service to southwest France is several minutes faster.

If you have a rail pass and get off at St.-Pierre-des-Corps, you need only to board one of the frequent commuter or *Grand Lignes* trains going into Tours. If you have a regular ticket, you must buy a transfer between these two stations.

Currently, the last TGV back to Paris leaves Tours at 20:59 and St.-Pierre-des-Corps at 22:07.

Tourist Information Office

The *Office de Tourisme* is in a small, self-contained building on the divided boulevard Heurteloup, halfway to the *Hôtel de Ville* (see below). To get there, follow rue de Nantes (the street bordering the left side of place du Maréchal-Leclerc) for one block, then go left at boulevard Heurteloup.

Tour of Historic Sights & Major Attractions

After you've had your fill of châteaux, take some time to explore Tours. The center of its social activity and business trade starts at **place Jean-Jaurès**, a large traffic circle where boulevard Heurteloup intersects rue Nationale/avenue de Grammont, Tours' main north-south street, which travels several miles between the Loire and Cher Rivers. On the corners of rue Nationale at place Jean-Jaurès, you'll find Tour's **Palais de Justice** and the large **Hôtel de Ville**, adorned with a domed bell tower, decorated clock, and sculpture at its roof line. Beyond these sights on the streets entering this congested circle are numerous banks, cafés, department stores, hotels, pastry shops, boutiques, and other businesses. Of particular interest to shoppers: the pedestrians-only rue de Bordeaux connecting the *Gare SNCF* (exit left across rue de Nantes) to avenue de Grammont. Some of this street's shops also have entrances on boulevard Heurteloup.

After exploring this area, walk north toward the Loire River (about a mile away) on the left side of rue Nationale. Halfway down the street, turn left on rue des Halles and walk four blocks to the **Tour Charlemagne** (on the right) and the **Tour de l'Horloge** (a few steps further on the left), two towers left from the 11th-century **Basilique St.-Martin**. The first church on this site, built over the 5th-century tomb of the Lord Bishop of Tours, was pulled down in 1802 after falling into disrepair. The current *Basilique* was built from 1887-1924.

Between the two towers, turn right on rue du Change and go north to Tours' **medieval quarter**, centered around the small place Plumereau. Surrounding this square on narrow, pedestrians-only streets are several restored houses and mansions. After exploring the area, follow rue du Commerce (which enters the upper right corner of place Plumereau) back to rue Nationale. You'll pass the **Hôtel Gouin**, a narrow, three-story, Renaissance mansion now housing the **Musée de la Société Archéologique Touraine**, with artifacts found in the Touraine region. (Although Tours is the capital of the Indre-et-Loire department within the Centre administrative region, it's still known in France as the capital of the Touraine region, one of three geographical areas designated long ago that form the 186-mile-long Loire Valley.)

Cross rue Nationale, then walk left towards the Loire River to the 13th-century **Église St.-Julien**, which today contains the **Musée des Vins de Touraine** (wine museum) in its ancient cellars. Wine aficionados searching for samples will have to look elsewhere—there's only a series of exhibits explaining winemaking and its importance to the region. Next door, the **Musée du Compagnonnage**, a crafts guild museum, traces the history, customs, and skills of area guilds and associations, many of which were responsible for building the region's elaborate châteaux and cathedrals.

After visiting these museums, continue down rue Nationale to quai d'Orleans, walking east (to the right) along its border with the Loire River. Because of the river's shallowness and erratic currents, commercial vessels no longer sail to Tours. The only action you'll see is the occasional fisherman heading to an island or a favorite fishing hole. (West of Angers, where the Maine River enters, the Loire River is again navigable for large boats.)

Opposite the narrow, pedestrians-only *Pont de Fil*, turn right off quai d'Orleans onto rue Lavoisier. On the corner, you'll find the **Château Royal de Tours** and **Tour de Guise**, remnants of the fortress built in 1160 by Henry II Plantagenet. Inside the restored château, a wax museum created by the Grevin Museum of Paris contains 165 wax figures that trace 1,000 years of Touraine history. For literature buffs, just down the street is the 15th-century **Cloître de la Psalette**, a location Balzac used in several chapters of *Curé de Tours*. Next to this sight, the twin-towered **Cathédrale St.-Gatien** is a massive display of Romanesque, Gothic, and Renaissance architectural styles. Begun in the 12th century on the foundation of the Gallo-Roman city wall, the *Cathédrale* was completed in the 1500's. Go inside to see its fine stained glass windows and the tombs of King Charles VIII's children. At its entrance, take note of the two square Romanesque towers topped by Renaissance domed lanterns and the elaborate decorations on its front façade, worthy of the Flamboyant Gothic period.

Just south of the *Cathédrale* at 18 place François-Sicard, the **Musée des Beaux-Arts**, located in a 17th-century archbishop's palace, contains works by Dutch, Flemish, French, and Italian artists from the 15th-20th centuries, including masterpieces by Caravaggio, Rembrandt, Rubens, Degas, Delacroix, and Monet. The only 20th-century work of any note is a mobile by Andrew Calder.

To return to the *Gare SNCF* from there, exit across the small place François-Sicard in front of the museum, then go left on rue Bernard-Palissy for a half a mile to its end at boulevard Heurteloup and place du Maréchal-Leclerc.

Restaurants
L'Odéon, 10 place du Maréchal-Leclerc (exit right from the *Gare SNCF*), moderate, tel. 47-20-12-65.

Le Lys, 63 rue Blaise-Pascal (exit left from the *Gare SNCF*, then left at the second street), moderate, tel. 47-05-27-92.

La Gourmandine, 49 rue Bernard-Palissy, moderate, tel. 47-05-13-75.

Flunch, 14 place Jean-Jaurès (half-block south of rue de Bordeaux), inexpensive.

Le Relais Buré, 1 place de la Résistance (one block to the left off rue Nationale, between rue du Commerce and rue des Halles), moderate, tel. 47-05-67-74.

La Rôtisserie Tourangelle, 23 rue du Commerce, moderate-expensive, tel. 47-05-71-21.

Les Gais Lurons, 15 rue Lavoisier, moderate, tel. 47-64-75-50.

Les Tuffeaux, 19 rue Lavoisier, moderate-expensive, tel. 47-47-19-89.

Ruche, 105 rue Colbert (street almost to the Loire River, connecting rue Nationale with rue Lavoisier), inexpensive, tel. 47-66-69-83.

Bigarde, 122 rue Colbert, moderate, tel. 47-05-48-81.

Hotels

Hôtel Terminus, 7-9 rue de Nantes, moderate, tel. 47-05-06-24.

Hôtel Europe, 12 place du Maréchal-Leclerc (exit right from the *Gare SNCF*), inexpensive-moderate, tel. 47-05-42-07.

Hôtel Bordeaux, 3 place du Maréchal-Leclerc (exit left from the *Gare SNCF*), moderate, tel. 47-05-46-44.

Hôtel l'Univers, 5 boulevard Heurteloup (a short distance left from place du Maréchal-Leclerc), moderate-expensive, tel. 47-05-37-12.

Hôtel Criden, 65 boulevard Heurteloup (to the right from place du Maréchal-Leclerc for a half-mile), moderate, tel. 47-20-81-14.

Hôtel Mirabeau, 89 bis boulevard Heurteloup (one block past the Hôtel Criden), moderate, tel. 47-05-24-37.

Hôtel Rosny, 19 rue Blaise-Pascal, inexpensive-moderate, tel. 47-05-23-54.

Hôtel l'Olympic, 74 rue Bernard-Palissy, inexpensive, tel. 47-05-10-17.

Sights Worth Seeing Nearby

Tours is in the middle of château country. For self-guided touring, you can take non-TGV trains and buses from Tours to **Amboise, Angers, Azay-le-Rideau, Beaugency, Blois, Chaumont** (depart at Onzain across the river), **Chenonceaux, Chinon, Langeais, Loches, Orléans**, and **Saumur**. If you rent a car, you'll be able to see even more.

When time and/or money are problems, try one of the best bargains in France: the half- or full-day bus tours offered by the *Services de Tourisme SNCF*. These inexpensive tours (with an English-speaking guide) depart daily from the *Gare Routière* (corner of place du Maréchal-Leclerc and boulevard Heurteloup) and visit three to five châteaux at one-third the cost of similar tours from Paris. Lunch is not included in the fee, but you get ample time to eat at a restaurant on the tour path. To book a tour, go to their small office by the main entrance of the *Gare SNCF*.

Le Mans

Though it's internationally known for the annual Grand Prix in mid-June, Le Mans is more than just a mecca for auto racing fans. A city rich in history, it offers an outstanding cathedral, remains of a Roman fortress, old mansions, a medieval quarter, and some good museums. Le Mans is also one of France's most prosperous cities. As the regional headquarters for many French companies (primarily in the automobile, banking, and insurance industries), it's a stable, growing city of over 150,000.

TGV Travel from Paris
Twenty TGV trains travel daily from Paris to Le Mans. The 131-mile trip takes 54 minutes. Two TGV trains also travel daily from Le Mans to Lyon (three hours, 21 minutes) via the feeder line at Massy that connects the TGV Atlantique to the TGV Sud-Est. The *Gare SNCF* is along boulevard de la Gare near the intersection of the Sarthe and Huisne Rivers on the south side of town. Currently, the last TGV back to Paris leaves at 21:54.

Tourist Information Office
The *Syndicat d'Initiative* is at 40 place de la République in the center of town, over a mile from the *Gare SNCF.* To get there, cross boulevard de la Gare to avenue du Général-Leclerc, follow this long street to place Franklin-D.-Roosevelt, then turn left on rue des Minimes, which ends at place de la République. The *Syndicat d'Initiative* is on the opposite side. If you'd rather not walk, bus #3 travels between the *Gare SNCF* and place de la République.

Tour of Historic Sights & Major Attractions
Le Mans' **Vieux Quartier**, not far from the *Syndicat d'Initiative*, is on a slight hill overlooking the Sarthe River. This historic area, anchored by the *Cathédrale de St.-Julien* at its north end and the Sarthe River on the west two streets away, is partially surrounded by rampart walls from a 3rd-century Roman fortress. Despite 20 separate sieges of Le Mans, 11 rampart towers are still standing. Within the walls are 15th- and 16th-century buildings occupied today by homeowners, antique dealers, artisans' studios, cafés, shops, and other businesses.

To reach the *Vieux Quartier*, exit right from the *Syndicat d'Initiative* and go around the corner for a block on rue du Cornet to place de l'Éperon. Cross this open place, walk around the block to the right, then angle left across rue des Poules to rue de la Truie-que-File, which leads to the south entrance of the ramparts. After the former rampart gate, the street widens into the Grand-Rue, the main street through the quarter to the *Cathédrale*.

If you only have a few hours in Le Mans, explore the Grande-Rue—which has the best architecture in the quarter—and the *Cathédrale*. Houses #9, 11-13, 18-20, 69, 71, 86, 105, and 108 have the most interesting façades. At 11-13 rue de la Reine-Bérengère (a short continuation of the Grande-Rue), the 15th-century **Maison de la Reine-Bérengère** now houses a small museum illustrating the cultural and historic traditions of the old Maine region (Le Mans is now a part of the Pays de la Loire region), plus arts and crafts by international artists.

For a full day of touring, explore the other streets in the *Vieux Quartier* and include a good look at the Roman ramparts. At square Dubois and the Grande-Rue, turn right onto rue du Pilier-Rouge to place du Hallai, where you'll find the 1760 **Hôtel de Ville**, the former residence of the Comtes du Maine. From this large town hall, follow rue du Hallai along its west side through place St.-Pierre to rue St.-Flaceau, where you'll see the east ramparts. Stay on this street and follow the outline of the ramparts, crossing the Grande-Rue where you first entered the quarter to rue de la Verrerie. The ramparts along this section feature four intact towers. A short distance later, you'll come to the *escalier Grande-Poterne*, a short series of steps through a narrow gateway to rue de la Porte-Ste.-Anne, one street from the Sarthe River quais. Linger to watch the river traffic, then follow the ramparts to rue des Pans-de-Gorron, where a right turn takes you to the *Cathédrale* entrance.

Begun in the 11th-century, the **Cathédrale de St.-Julien** is a fascinating conglomeration of architectural styles. The nave and façade are primarily a Romanesque inspiration, while the transept and choir come from Gothic leanings. The intricately carved statues surrounding the south entrance are reminiscent of the great Chartres cathedral south of Paris. The *Cathédrale* also contains outstanding stained glass windows and art dating from the-14th century, plus the tombs of Charles IV of Anjou (younger brother of Louis IX) and Guillame du Bellay (1491-1543), a Le Mans general and diplomat.

Not far from the *Cathédrale*, the **Musée de Tessé**, Le Mans' art museum, offers a diverse collection of Italian primitives and paintings by French, Flemish, Dutch, and Spanish artists from the 12th-20th centuries. The best part of the collection is the work of French artists, including an outstanding family portrait by David, and pieces by Vouet, Delacroix, and Géricault. The museum also has a good collection of sculpture, tapestries, and military medals.

To get there, exit right from the main entrance of the *Cathédrale* to rue Robert-Triger. Turn right and cross the avenue de Paderborn to the large park, the *Promenade des Jacobins*. Turn left and follow the edge of the park to the museum a few blocks down on the grounds of the

Jardin de Tessé.

To quickly return to the *Gare SNCF,* board bus #3 at the stop across the street from the museum. If you'd like to see another old church and public garden, get off the bus at the Préfecture stop, where you'll find the 11th-century **Église Notre-Dame-de-la-Couture.** This former abbey church, whose monastery now contains government offices for the Sarthe department, features a heavily sculpted front doorway and porch, semi-circular choir, 14th-century paintings and tapestries, a white marble sculpture of the Virgin, and the 6th-century shroud of St. Bernard. The adjacent **Jardin de la Préfecture** is one of the largest public parks in Le Mans.

Even if you miss the Le Mans 24-hour race, auto racing fans should not miss the **Musée de l'Automobile,** which has a collection of the winning cars from 1923 to the present, autos dating to 1914, and exhibits on the evolution of the automobile. Although it's about five miles south of the city, you can reach the museum by public transportation, coupled with a short walk. However, real fans should consider renting a car, since you may drive on the 8.36-mile race circuit when there isn't a race in progress. You might even encounter a challenger on the Hunaudières straightaway, where cars often exceed 200 m.p.h. during the race!

Unless a taxi ride is in your budget, get to the museum by taking bus #3 from the *Gare SNCF* to the Préfecture stop. There, change to bus #2 and take it to place Admiral-Tironneau, where you'll change to bus #6. Get off at the last stop (by the cemetery); the museum is less than a mile away on the D139 highway. Shortly after you pass under the N23 highway bypass, an underground entrance to the left of the D139 leads to the museum and the Bugatti race circuit, where tests are conducted.

Restaurants

Feuillantine, 19 bis rue de Foisy (one long block from the *Gare SNCF,* turn left off avenue Général-Leclerc onto rue de la Pelouse, left again two blocks later), moderate, tel. 43-28-00-38.

Le Grenier à Sel, 26 place de l'Éperon, moderate-expensive, tel. 43-23-26-30.

La Ciboulette, 14 rue de la Vieille-Porte (short street to the left off place de l'Éperon), moderate, tel. 43-24-65-67.

La Grillade, 1 bis rue Claude-Blondeau (from place St.-Pierre, go past the *Hotel de Ville* on rue des Ponts-Neufs, then take second left), moderate, tel. 43-24-21-87.

Grand Cerf, 8 quai Amiral-Lalande (from place de la République, cross rue du Cornet to rue Gambetta, following it across the Sarthe River, then left), moderate, tel. 43-24-16-83.

Hotels

Hôtel Anjou, 27 boulevard de la Gare, moderate, tel. 43-24-90-45.

Hôtel Commerce, 41 boulevard de la Gare, moderate, tel. 43-85-21-60.

Hôtel de Rennes, 43 boulevard de la Gare, moderate, tel. 43-85-00-70.

Hôtel Chantecler, 50 rue de la Pelouse, moderate, tel. 43-24-58-53.

Hôtel Moderne, 14 rue du Bourg-Belé (exit right from the *Gare SNCF* on boulevard de la Gare, then go left one block later), inexpensive-moderate, tel. 43-84-36-40 (good restaurant on premises).

Hôtel du Saumon, 44 place de la République, moderate, tel. 43-28-03-19.

Sights Worth Seeing Nearby

Tours and other **Loire Valley** towns, 50-60 miles south of Le Mans, are accessible via frequent non-TGV trains.

Laval

Often bypassed by tourists headed to Brittany, Laval is a pretty city, perfect for a half-day visit. The administrative capital of the Mayenne department and home to 55,000, the town has an appealing, relaxed pace and some terrific sights, including a 12th-century cathedral and château, and 16th-century mansions along the banks of the Mayenne River.

TGV Travel from Paris

Ten TGV trains travel daily from Paris to Laval. The 187-mile trip takes one hour, 34 minutes. The *Gare SNCF* is at place de la Gare on the northeast side of town. Currently, the last TGV back to Paris leaves at 20:37.

Tourist Information Office

The *Office de Tourisme* is on the corner of rue de Strasbourg and place du 11-Novembre in the center of the city on the west bank of the Mayenne River (which runs north-south through the middle of town). To get there, cross place de la Gare to the wide avenue Robert-Buron, walk almost a mile to the next large traffic circle, then go right on rue de la Paix, which ends three long blocks later at the Mayenne River and the *Pont Aristide-Briand*. Directly across the bridge is place du 11-Novembre, and the *Office de Tourisme* is on the opposite corner.

Tour of Historic Sights & Major Attractions

After visiting the *Office de Tourisme*, backtrack along the west edge of place du 11-Novembre, crossing slightly to the right to the post office and rue des Déportés. A few blocks later, you'll reach place de La Trémoille, where you'll find several 18th-century Classical mansions and the old **Palais de Justice** (1508-42) set back from the street. A few steps beyond, the forbidding **Vieux Château** features an enormous 12th-century keep topped by a wooden gallery and ramparts with good views of the city. The former residence of the Counts of Laval, its apartments are decorated with 14th- to 16th-century murals, sculpture, and large windows with intricately carved accents. Also worth seeing in the *Château* are the 12th-century Romanesque chapel, displays of artifacts from the area, and a collection of näif paintings dedicated to Henri Rousseau, who was born there. Unfortunately, the collection contains only one minor painting by Rousseau.

For excellent views of the *Château's* exterior and the 16th-century homes over the river quais, cross the *Pont Vieux* to the opposite side of the Mayenne River. The **Jardin Public de la Perrine**, a beautiful, terraced park overlooking the river a few blocks south of the *Château*, also offers good views, as well as Rousseau's grave.

However, before you cross the river, see the 12th-century **Cathédrale de la Laval**, easily reached by returning to place de La Trémoille, then taking a left onto rue Charles-Landelle for one long block. Built in 1185, it features a Romanesque nave, 17th-century Aubusson tapestries, a white stone/marble altar from 1640, and a 16th-century triptych of St. John.

Across from the *Cathédrale's* entrance, **Porte Beucheresse** is a remnant of Laval's original fortifications. Passing this gate on rue des Serruriers/rue de Chappelle/Grande-Rue brings you below the *Château* to the *Pont Vieux*. Cross the bridge, step onto the quai for a good look at the *Château*, then walk down rue du Pont-de-Mayenne for a few blocks to the **Église St.-Vénérand**, a 16th-century church featuring stained glass windows dating to 1521.

From there, backtrack to the Mayenne River to follow the river quais past the *Pont Aristide-Briand* and the *Pont de l'Europe* to rue Magenta, which runs from the river to the *Gare SNCF*. To return to the station from the church, continue a half-mile further on rue du Pont-de-Mayenne to boulevard Félix-Grat. Turn left, walk for half a mile until it ends at avenue Robert-Buron, then turn right to the station.

Restaurants

Bistro de Paris, 67 rue du Val-de-Mayenne (street starting at the river behind the *Vieux Château* and the *Palais* to place du 11-Novembre), moderate, tel. 43-56-98-29.

L'Antiquare, 5 rue de Béliers (behind the east side of the *Cathédrale*, follow rue Renaise two blocks, then go right), moderate, tel. 43-53-66-76.

La Beucheresse, 63 Grande-Rue, moderate, tel. 43-53-88-12.

Gerbe de Blé, 83 rue Victor-Boissel (one mile from the *Vieux Château*; cross the *Pont Vieux* and turn right on quai Paul-Boudet, left on rue d'Anvers, then right), moderate, tel. 43-53-14-10.

Hotels

Marin Hôtel, 102 avenue Robert-Buron at place de la Gare, inexpensive, tel. 43-53-09-68.

Hôtel St.-Pierre, 95 avenue Robert-Buron, inexpensive, tel. 43-53-06-10.

Hôtel Impérial, 61 avenue Robert-Buron, moderate, tel. 43-53-55-02.

Hôtel Arcade, 8 avenue Robert-Buron, moderate, tel. 43-67-19-25.

Sights Worth Seeing Nearby

The region of **Brittany** begins 12 miles to the west.

Angers

Located on the navigable Maine River in the western Loire Valley region, Angers is the former capital of the historic province of Anjou. Protected by a large fortress/château complex that still stands, it was one of the most powerful cities in France during the Middle Ages, the strongest link in a fortress chain erected throughout western France by the 11th-century Counts of Anjou.

Today, Angers has grown into a prosperous city of 143,000, with an economy revolving around the industries of slate quarrying, electronics, and umbrella manufacturing. It's also an important regional market for vegetables, fruits, and wines, and the administrative capital of the Maine-et-Loire department.

TGV Travel from Paris

Eighteen TGV trains travel daily from Paris to Angers. The 191-mile trip takes one hour, 33 minutes. Two TGV trains also travel daily from Angers to Lyon (four hours, five minutes) via the feeder line at Massy, which connects the TGV Atlantique to the TGV Sud-Est. The *Gare St.-Laud* is at place de la Gare on the south side of town. Currently, the last TGV back to Paris leaves at 21:14.

Tourist Information Office

The *Office de Tourisme* and *Accueil de France*, across from the *Château d'Angers*, are less than a mile from the station on the corner of boulevard du Roi-René and place du Président-Kennedy. To get there, follow rue de la Gare, which runs through place de la Gare, to the large open intersection at place Visitation, where several streets converge. There, follow the right side of the place to rue Talot. Two blocks later, turn left off rue Talot onto boulevard du Roi-René. A half-mile later, you'll see a statue of King René in the middle of the street as you enter place du Président-Kennedy.

Tour of Historic Sights & Major Attractions

The main attraction of Angers is the restored **Château d'Angers**—a misnomer, since it resembles a fortress more than the châteaux traditionally associated with the Loire Valley. It features 17 round towers of alternating black and white stone, ramparts, a drawbridge, prison cells, the apartments of King René, and a deep moat now hosting a formal flower garden, sculpted hedges, and grazing deer.

Built first in the 11th century on the side of a cliff overlooking the Maine River, then rebuilt from 1220-30, the *Château* was nearly destroyed during the Wars of Religion at the end of the 13th century. In the 15th century, King René built the palm-vaulted staircase, surrounding gallery, and hanging gardens in the royal apartments.

Today, the restored chapel and royal apartments house art and tapestries from the Middle Ages, including the "Apocalypse Tapestries," woven from 1373-80. If you are more interested in the *Château*'s architecture, its dungeon, ramparts, towers, and other buildings are open for full exploration. For a good view of Angers and the Maine River, climb to the top of the **Tour du Moulin** at the north corner of the fortress.

Nearby, the beautiful **Cathédrale St.-Maurice** features a 12th-century doorway decorated with Biblical characters, rare stained glass windows, several Gobelins tapestries, three exterior towers, and the widest nave (64 feet) of any cathedral in France. To get there, follow one of the narrow cobblestone streets away from the *Château d'Angers'* entrance to the *Cathédrale*. For an inspiring exterior view of the *Cathédrale*'s entrance, follow the steps (*montée St.-Maurice*) to the river, then walk back up.

You can also reach the *Cathédrale* from the *Office de Tourisme*. Follow rue Toussaint, which juts to the right off place du Président-Kennedy. In a few blocks, you'll see the rear of the *Cathédrale* on the left. Also on rue Toussaint, near the *Château*, the **Galérie David d'Angers**, housed in the 13th-century *Abbaye Toussaint*, features the work of Angers' sculptor Pierre-Jean David (1788-1856). Known for his busts and statues of famous 19th-century Frenchmen, the gallery has a complete collection of the plaster casts he made for his sculpture.

Connected to the abbey's south side, the **Logis Louis Barrault**, a lovely 15th-century palace, offers the town's **Musée des Beaux-Arts**. Created in 1804, the museum includes medieval religious artifacts and some good paintings from the 14th-20th centuries, including work by Watteau, Tiepolo, Corot, Géricault, and Fragonard.

North of these sights via rue Chaperonnière, the square **place du Ralliement** is a lively area filled with interesting shops, theaters, cafés, and restaurants. At its northwest corner off rue Lenepveu is the **Musée Hôtel Pincé**, an elegant Renaissance mansion with a collection of Greek and Roman antiquities, Oriental art, and a few drawings by European artists.

Tapestry connoisseurs should continue across the river. From place du Ralliement, follow rue de la Röe to quai Gambetta at the Maine River. Turn right and follow the quai to the *Pont de la Haute-Chaîne.* Cross it, and turn left on boulevard Arago, which leads to the 12th-century **Hôpital St.-Jean.** Founded in 1175 by Henry II of England as penance for the murder of Thomas à Becket, it now houses the **Musée Jean Lurçat**, named after a modern French artist and tapestry designer. Among the numerous tapestries exhibited—including many from the Gobelins factory in Paris—the focal point is a large, 10-piece work entitled *"Chant du Monde"* ("Song of the World"), created by Lurçat from 1957-66. The ancient hospital also features a 12th-century cloister and 13th-century chapel.

From there, follow boulevard Arago past the **École des Arts et Métiers** (School of Arts and Crafts), housed in the former Abbey of Le Ronceray and the 12th-century **Église La Trinité** (on the right up rue Beaurepaire). A left turn at this intersection will take you back to central Angers, crossing the Maine River on the *Pont de Verdun,* where you'll get a good view of the *Château d'Angers* high above the river.

From the bridge, turn right on quai Ligny, follow it past the *Château,* then go left up the hill to boulevard du Roi-René, where you can retrace your steps to the *Gare St.-Laud* or take bus #6 to the station.

Restaurants

Le Signal, rue de la Gare, inexpensive, tel. 41-87-49-41.

Rose d'Or, 21 rue Delaage (left off rue Talot), moderate, tel. 41-88-38-38.

Le Toussaint, 7 place du Président-Kennedy, moderate-expensive, tel. 41-87-46-20.

Le Quéré, 9 place du Ralliement, moderate, tel. 41-87-64-94.

Le Logis, 17 rue St.-Laud (a narrow, pedestrians-only street north of place du Ralliement beyond the *Musée Hôtel Pincé;* turn right off rue de la Röe), moderate-expensive, tel. 41-87-44-15.

L'Entracte, 9 rue Louis-de-Romain (turn right off rue Chaperonnière just before place du Ralliement), moderate, tel. 41-87-71-82.

Le Vert d'Eau, 9 boulevard Gaston-Dumesnil (cross the *Pont de la Basse Chaîne* past the *Château d'Angers* through a complex intersection, veer right when the street ends, then go left for a half-mile), moderate, tel. 41-48-52-86.

Hotels

Hôtel de France, 8 place de la Gare, moderate, tel. 41-88-49-42.

Hôtel la Coupe d'Or, 5 rue de la Gare, inexpensive, tel. 41-88-45-02.

Hôtel Univers, 16 rue de la Gare, inexpensive-moderate, tel. 41-88-43-58.

Hôtel Royal, 8 bis place Visitation (at top end of place at the corner of rue Hoche), inexpensive, tel. 41-88-30-25.

Hôtel Progrès, 26 rue Denis-Papin (crosses place de la Gare in front of the station; go left for two blocks), moderate, tel. 41-88-10-14.

Hôtel Champagne, 34 rue Denis-Papin, inexpensive-moderate, tel. 41-88-78-06.

Fimotel, 23 bis rue Paul-Bert (exit right from the *Gare St.-Laud* on rue Denis-Papin/rue du Haras across rue Paul-Bert, then go right for two blocks to the corner of rue Château-Gontier), moderate, tel. 41-88-10-10.

Sights Worth Seeing Nearby

Although there are many châteaux in the countryside near Angers, one of the best and most accessible in the western Loire Valley is the impressive château-fortress of **Saumur**, which overlooks the Loire River from a high cliff. On the other side of this small city, there's a cavalry-tank museum and its old cavalry school, where the best military riders in France trained. Several non-TGV trains travel daily to Saumur.

Brittany

Vitré

On the eastern border of Brittany, Vitré is one of the best preserved medieval towns in France. Part of a line of defensive strongholds separating Brittany from the rest of France during the Middle Ages, the town features a restored castle crowned by seven pointed towers—an impressive example of medieval military architecture. With a Gothic church, partially intact city ramparts, 15th-century houses, and narrow streets, Vitré makes for an interesting stop into the past.

TGV Travel from Paris

One TGV train travels daily from Paris to Vitré. The 209-mile trip takes one hour, 53 minutes. Unfortunately, the TGV to Vitré currently leaves Paris at 18:20. If you'd rather make Vitré a day trip, take an early TGV to Laval or Rennes, then transfer onto a non-TGV train.

The *Gare SNCF* is at place Général-de-Gaulle on the south side of town. Currently, the last TGV back to Paris leaves at 20:16.

Tourist Information Office

The *Office de Tourisme* is at the corner of place St.-Yves and rue Baudrairie. To get there, cross the *Gare SNCF* parking area to place Général-de-Gaulle, then go left for one block.

Tour of Historic Sights & Major Attractions

From the *Office de Tourisme*, walk into the heart of town on the narrow rue Baudrairie, a mostly pedestrians-only street filled with houses from the 15th-18th centuries. Halfway down, turn left on rue St.-Louis to get to the castle.

The triangular **castle**—with seven towers, a large circular keep, high machicolated walls, and a drawbridge—was built during the 14th and 15th centuries on the site of an 11th-century structure. From its formidable exterior, it's easy to understand why Vitré was never destroyed by enemy forces. Once inside the fortress, climb the ramparts and towers for commanding views of the town and countryside. The castle also has a small natural history museum and offices for the town government.

After exploring the castle, exit to the street entering the top left corner of the castle's parking lot and follow it to the Flamboyant Gothic **Église Notre-Dame**, an unusually large church for a town of Vitré's size. Built during the 15th and 16th centuries, it features studded gables, spires, an outdoor pulpit, and 32 Limousin enamel panels in its sacristy. A large market is held in front of the church every Monday.

Alongside the church, walk down rue Notre-Dame, lined with old, half-timbered houses, to the foot of place de la République. There, turn left on promenade du Val for a walk along the outside of the original city ramparts, following them around the corner. When the ramparts end, continue down rue du Val for an exterior view of the castle.

When the street ends, you have two sightseeing choices. First, you can circle the entire castle by continuing left on rue Pasteur, then going left on the street skirting the castle's south side. Or, you could take a right turn, which leads to the outskirts of town, past the Vilaine River, to the suburb of Rachapt, where you'll find a monastery and the 15th-century **Chapelle du St.-Nicholas**, with 16th-century frescoes. Across from the monastery, rue de Fougères (D178 highway) leads to the **Tertres Noirs**, a hilly overlook with excellent views of the entire town.

Returning to the town, follow the streets bordering the castle to a large open area that empties into rue de Brest. Take a left on rue de Brest to return to the *Gare SNCF.* Straight across the open area is the ancient rue d'Embas, where you can continue exploring Vitré's medieval streets. Vitré is small (13,491 residents), so indulge your whims, wander, and don't worry about getting lost.

Restaurants

Restaurant Petit-Billot, 5 place Maréchal-Leclerc (exit right from the *Gare SNCF* on rue de la Liberté for one block), moderate, tel. 99-74-68-88.

Taverne de l'Écu, 12 rue Baudrairie, moderate, tel. 99-75-11-09.

Le Chaperon Rouge, 12 boulevard des Jacobins (behind the *Gare SNCF*; exit right from the station, go right at place Maréchal-Leclerc, then take the first left after crossing the railroad tracks), inexpensive, vegetarian.

Hotels

Hôtel Chêne Vert, place Général-de-Gaulle, inexpensive-moderate, tel. 99-75-00-58.

Hôtel Petit-Billot, 5 place Maréchal-Leclerc, inexpensive, tel. 99-75-02-10.

Minotel, 47 rue Poterie (turn right off rue Beaudrairie), inexpensive-moderate, tel. 99-75-11-11.

Sights Worth Seeing Nearby

The **Château les Rochers-Sévigné**, home of the famous letter-writer Madame de Sévigné, is just four miles southeast of Vitré off the D88 highway. The 16th-century château, consisting of two buildings linked by a round tower, contains period furniture and some of the 1,500 letters Madame de Sévigné wrote to her daughter, in which she describes Paris and Versailles during the reign of Louis XIV. It's a nice walk out to the *Château*, or you can rent a car.

Another part of Brittany's old defense line is 19 miles north of Vitré at **Fougères**. This city's castle, built into a rocky outcrop overlooking the Nançon River, is larger than Vitré's. There is non-TGV train and bus service between the two towns.

Rennes

Rennes, the second largest city in Brittany, is the historic home of the region's struggle for independence. In the 15th century, Brittany formed its own parliament (in Rennes) and army to gain independence from France, but the upstart country was defeated in 1488 by the troops of Charles VIII. Ever since its official union with France in 1532, Rennes has been the political power center of Brittany.

Today, this active city of 200,000 is also the economic center of the region, a major university town (36,000 students), and the largest transportation hub in Brittany (most train travel to Breton sights [including two TGV lines] starts at Rennes). Despite a 1720 fire that destroyed much of the city, there are a few historic buildings, an outstanding art museum, and the region's best history museum.

TGV Travel from Paris

Twenty-eight TGV trains travel daily from Paris to Rennes. The 232-mile trip takes two hours, four minutes. Two TGV trains also travel daily from Rennes to Lyon (four hours, 39 minutes) via the feeder line at Massy that connects the TGV Atlantique to the TGV Sud-Est. The *Gare SNCF* is at place de la Gare on the town's south side. Currently, the last TGV back to Paris leaves at 21:19.

Tourist Information Office

Rennes has two tourist information offices. The *Syndicat d'Initiative* is at the corner of rue du Maréchal-Joffre and quai Émile-Zola next to the *Palais du Commerce*. The *Office de Tourisme* and *Accueil de France* are a little further west on a stretch of land built over the Vilaine River between quais Lamennais and Duguay-Trouin. Since both offices are past the first sight in the walking tour, directions to them are noted below.

Tour of Historic Sights & Major Attractions

From the *Gare SNCF,* cross place de la Gare to avenue Jean-Janvier and walk about a mile to quai Émile-Zola, where you'll find the **Palais des Musées**, home of the *Musée des Beaux-Arts* and the *Musée de Bretagne*. Buses #1 and #2 travel from the train station to this location.

The **Musée des Beaux-Arts** features a diverse art collection, ranging from da Vinci, Rembrandt, and Dürer drawings to 1960's abstract painters. Most of the paintings focus on Breton scenes, with the most notable work by George La Tour and the School of Pont-Aven, including a small still life by Gauguin. There are also masterpieces by Rubens, Chardin, Sisley, and Picasso. Since Brittany is famous for its ceramics, one room is dedicated to work by Rennes' potters from the 17th-19th centuries.

The smaller **Musée de Bretagne** focuses on the art, culture, history, and traditions of Brittany. Through a series of exhibits—including farm tools, furniture, costumes, jewelry, art, and audio-visual displays—you'll receive a good overview of Brittany's unique identity.

Across from the museums, the **Vilaine River** travels through the middle of town in a man-made, partly underground canal. From Rennes, it flows southwest to its intersection with the Nantes-Brest Canal at Redon, then on to the Atlantic Ocean. The river quais are lined with shops, restaurants, and offices.

Follow quai Émile-Zola west for three blocks to the *Syndicat d'Initiative* office at the corner of rue du Maréchal-Joffre, next door to the **Palais du Commerce**, a large building built 1886-1932 in the Louis XIV style. Directly across from the *Palais*, the open place de la République is a narrow strip of land used for parking and covering the river. The *Office de Tourisme* is in the middle of this place on the next block past the *Palais*.

After the *Office de Tourisme*, follow quai Duguay-Trouin west for a few blocks, turn right on rue Le Bouteillier for one block, and turn left on the curvy rue des Dames for two blocks to the **Cathédrale St.-Pierre**, which anchors the west side of **Vieux Rennes**. Built from 1787-1844, this cathedral's primary attraction is an Antwerp altarpiece from 1520.

Directly across from the *Cathédrale* entrance, astride the narrow rue des Portes-Mordelaise, the **Porte Mordelaise** is the last gatehouse left from the 15th-century ramparts that once circled the city. This historic sight was the main entrance for the Dukes of Brittany en route to the Parliament building a half-mile east. On the narrow streets surrounding the *Cathédrale*, there are a few half-timbered houses that survived the 1720 fire: 3 rue St.-Sauveur (a street heading east behind the *Cathédrale*) was built in 1557, and #5 on the same street is a good example of early 18th-century architecture in Rennes.

Continue east on rue St.-Sauveur, past the *Église St.-Sauveur* and through place St.-Sauveur, to rue Duguesclin and the **Hôtel de Ville**, built from 1732-62. An interesting, horseshoe-shaped town hall topped by a bell tower, its interior features an elaborate staircase and interesting tapestries. The circular place de la Mairie and the 1856 **Théâtre** are behind the *Hôtel de Ville*.

One long block north of the theater, across place du Palais, is Rennes' most famous building, the **Palais de Justice**. Built from 1615-55 for the Parliament of Brittany by Saloman de Brosse (the architect of Paris' Luxembourg Palace), the grey and white stone building is surrounded by Classical-inspired façades. Inside, every inch of its walls has decorative art and sculpted accents, elaborate paneling, decorated ceilings, paintings, and Gobelins tapestries. Painters who worked inside Versailles created much of the interior design.

After touring the *Palais de Justice*, backtrack across the left side of place du Palais to the pedestrians-only rue St.-Georges, a street featuring several homes and buildings dating to the 15th and 16th centuries. A block south (turn right on rue Derval), the 16th-century, Flamboyant Gothic **Église St. Germain** is an oddly-shaped church with exquisite ornamentation and fine stained glass windows.

When rue St.-Georges ends, turn left on rue Gambetta/rue de Fourgères (the north extension of avenue Jean-Janvier), and follow it past square de la Motte and the *Préfecture* to place St.-Mélaine. Set back from this place is the **Église Notre-Dame**, an abbey built in 1632, and the pretty **Jardin de Thabor**, the city's largest park.

To return to the *Gare SNCF* from there, retrace your steps to rue Gambetta, which goes to the station. After passing rue St.-Georges, note the **Palais St.-Georges** on the left, a 1650 building used by Benedictine monks. Nearby, at quai Émile-Zola, you can board bus #1 or 2 if you don't want to walk to the station.

Restaurants

Chouin, 12 rue d'Isly (exit left from the *Gare SNCF* on boulevard de Beaumont, then right for a half-mile), moderate-expensive, tel. 99-30-87-86.

Restaurant des Carmes, 2 rue des Carmes (turn left off avenue Jean-Janvier onto boulevard de la Liberté, then right), moderate-expensive, tel. 99-79-31-41.

Le Piré, 18 rue Maréchal-Joffre (right off boulevard de la Liberté), moderate-expensive, tel. 99-79-31-41.

L'Ouvrée, 18 place des Lices (from the *Cathédrale St.-Pierre*, cross to rue de Juillet, then go right to the north end of the place, across from the covered markets), moderate, tel. 99-30-16-38.

Piccadilly Brasserie, 15 Galeries du Théâtre (on north side of the city theater), moderate-expensive, tel. 99-78-17-17.

Palais, 7 place du Palais, moderate-expensive, tel. 99-79-45-01.

Le Boulingrain, 25 rue St.-Mélaine (runs west of place St.-Mélaine), inexpensive, tel. 99-38-75-11.

Au Jardin des Plants, 32 rue St.-Mélaine, inexpensive, tel. 99-38-74-46.

Hotels

Hôtel De Guesclin, 2 place de la Gare, moderate, tel. 99-31-47-47.

Hôtel Brest, 15 place de la Gare, moderate, tel. 99-30-35-83.

Hôtel President, 27 avenue Jean-Janvier, moderate, tel. 99-65-42-22.

Hôtel Voyageurs, 28 avenue Jean-Janvier, inexpensive-moderate, tel. 99-31-73-33.

Hôtel Sevigne, 47 avenue Jean-Janvier, moderate, tel. 99-67-27-55.

Hôtel le Magenta, 35 boulevard Magenta (narrow street running north from the *Gare SNCF,* one block west [left] of avenue Jean-Janvier), inexpensive, tel. 99-30-85-37.

Garden Hôtel, 3 rue Duhamel (two blocks before the Vilaine River, turn right off avenue Jean-Janvier), moderate, tel. 99-65-45-06.

Sights Worth Seeing Nearby

Mont St.-Michel, one of the most magnificent sights in France, is just 41 miles north of Rennes. This ancient abbey, still on the religious pilgrimage circuit, sits atop a small, mountainous island in the Atlantic, a mile from shore, on the border of Brittany and Normandy. Before 1879, pilgrims could get there only on foot, hopping from sandbar to sandbar when the tide was out. But since 1879, it has been linked to the mainland by a narrow causeway built just above the incoming tides. From Rennes, non-TGV trains leave four times a day for a one-hour ride to Pontorson, where you can take a bus or taxi for the final six miles. Or, take the *Courriers Breton* bus line direct from Rennes. (The *Gare Routière* is on boulevard Magenta.) If you rent a car, take the N175 highway to Pontorson, then the D976.

Fifty miles northwest of Rennes on the Atlantic is the fortified city of St. Malo. Between Rennes and St. Malo, the charming medieval village Dinan remains surrounded by its original ramparts. There are frequent non-TGV trains and buses to both locations.

Vannes

Midway between Rennes and Quimper, Vannes is a friendly Breton town with numerous old buildings, narrow streets, and ancient ramparts, plus a 15th-century cathedral. Though rather large (45,000 residents), it reflects provincial qualities that never fail to charm. Situated on the back of a narrow stretch of the Gulf of Morbihan, Vannes makes an excellent base for exploring south Brittany and its coastal islands. During the summer, expect crowds of French and European vacationers.

TGV Travel from Paris

Seven TGV trains travel daily from Paris to Vannes. The 311-mile trip takes three hours, one minute. The *Gare SNCF* is along rue Favrel-et-Lincy on the north side of town. Currently, the last TGV back to Paris leaves at 20:14.

Tourist Information Office

The *Office de Tourisme* is at 1 rue Thiers in a 17th-century building, about two miles from the *Gare SNCF*, on the west side of the *Vieille Ville*. Since most of Vannes' sights are east of the *Office*, directions to it are in the walking tour below.

Tour of Historic Sights & Major Attractions

Most of Vannes' sights are inside the ancient rampart walls of the **Vieille Ville**. To get there from the *Gare SNCF*, angle across rue Favrel-et-Lincy to the right to rue Olivier-de-Clisson. When it ends at rue St.-Symphorien, cross to rue Desgrès-du-Loû, follow it across boulevard de la Paix, then angle left to rue du Commandant-Maury. Take this street to the **Porte-Prison**, a 15th-century machicolated tower and the northeast entrance of the *Vieille Ville*.

Just beyond the tower entrance, the 15th-century **Cathédrale St.-Pierre** features a Flamboyant Gothic doorway with Renaissance recesses. Inside the *Cathédrale* lies the tomb of Saint Vincent Ferrier and a chapel with an early medieval wedding chest with exquisite figures painted on it. The half-timbered houses and buildings surrounding the *Cathédrale* are the oldest in Vannes.

Opposite the *Cathédrale* entrance and stretching to rue des Halles, the historic **La Cohue** is a restored covered market selling local crafts. It has also served as a court, assembly room, concert hall, prison, revolutionary tribunal, and theater. The small **Musée des Beaux-Arts** on the top floor of *La Cohue* has several small Rodin sculptures and paintings by local artists.

From the *Cathédrale* and *La Cohue*, head left down rue de la Monnaie across place Lucien-Laroche, where you'll run into the 15th-century **ram-**

parts. Crowned with several towers, the ramparts start at the port on the south side of the city, then run north-northeast along the east edge of the old town for a short distance beyond the *Porte-Prison*. The **Parc de la Garenne**, on the other side of the ramparts, is a pleasant spot for a picnic.

Following the ramparts, exit through the rue Porte-Poterne gateway, then go right on rue Alexandre-le-Pontois to the busy place Gambetta, where you'll find several cafés and the terminus of Vannes' **port**. This long, narrow, man-made inlet leads to a large bay at Conleau and the Gulf of Morbihan. From this island-filled gulf, commercial ships sail to the Bay of Quiberon and the Atlantic Ocean. On the port's west edge, the **Promenade de la Rabine** is a great place to relax and watch the boats.

Across from the port's terminus, head back to the *Vieille Ville* through the ornate **Porte-St.-Vincent**, built in 1704 to replace the medieval gates that guarded the south entrance to the city. After passing through the gate, walk on rue St.-Vincent past the covered market to place des Lices and follow its left side to rue des Halles. On these streets, buildings date to the 15th century, and some were homes of Breton Parliament members. A short block later, turn left onto rue Noë to reach the **Musée de Préhistoire-Archéologique**, housed in the **Château Gaillard**, the former seat of the 15th-century Brittany Parliament. The small museum has an extensive collection of prehistoric artifacts from Carnac (see below) and the Gulf of Morbihan area.

From the museum, exit to the right on rue Noë, then go right on rue Le Hellec, which ends at the intersection of rue Thiers and place de la République. The *Office de Tourisme* is just south, across the street and to the left. To the right, the 1700 **Hôtel de Limur** features a pretty garden, and at the north end of rue Thiers, set back from the street, the **Hôtel de Ville** is guarded by bronze lions.

From the *Hôtel de Ville*, you can return to the *Gare SNCF* by crossing the north end of rue Thiers to rue Joseph-Le Brix, then going left one block later onto rue Victor-Hugo/rue St.-Symphorien, which ends at rue Favrel-et-Lincy. Buses #4, 5, 6, and 7 travel between the *Gare SNCF* and place de la République.

Restaurants
Régis Mahé, across from the *Gare SNCF*, moderate-expensive, tel. 97-42-61-41.

La Morgate, 21 rue La Fontaine (south of the intersection of rue St.-Symphorien and boulevard de la Paix), moderate, tel. 97-42-42-39.

Restaurant la Mirage, 19 rue de la Boucherie (heading away from the station, turn right off avenue Victor-Hugo onto boulevard de la Paix, then left at rue de la Coutume, then next right), inexpensive, tel. 97-47-17-16.

Marée Bleue, 8 place Bir-Hakeim (outside the *Porte-Prison*, cross to rue Albert-le-Grand and follow it past the *Préfecture* on rue du Général-Leclerc for one long block), moderate, tel. 97-47-24-29.

Cafeteria les Arcades (faces the *Préfecture*), inexpensive, tel. 97-42-57-73.

La Paillotte, rue des Halles, inexpensive, tel. 97-47-21-94.

Chez Carmen, 17 rue Émile-Burgault (continuation northwest of rue de la Monnaie, by the *Cathédrale*), inexpensive.

Hotels
Hôtel d'Armor, 20 avenue Favrel-et-Lincy, inexpensive, tel. 97-66-20-60.
Hôtel Richemont, 24 avenue Favrel-et-Lincy, moderate, tel. 97-66-12-95.
Hôtel Clisson, 11 rue Olivier-de-Clisson, inexpensive, tel. 97-54-13-94.
Hôtel Anne de Bretagne, 42 rue Olivier-de-Clisson, moderate, tel. 97-54-22-19.
Hôtel Manche Océan, 3 rue Commandant-Maury, moderate, tel. 97-47-26-46.
Hôtel France, 57 avenue Victor-Hugo, moderate, tel. 97-47-27-57.

Sights Worth Seeing Nearby
The islands in the **Gulf of Morbihan** offer several good beaches and resorts, easily reached by boat from Vannes' port. You can also get to **Belle-Ile**, the largest island off the coast of Brittany, from the port. Belle-Ile attracts thousands of visitors a year.

There's an odd sight just 19 miles southwest of Vannes. Thousands of narrow, monolithic stones jut from the ground in the countryside near **Carnac**. Possibly a prehistoric assemblage, their exact history and purpose are a mystery. To see them, ride the TGV a short distance to Auray, then head south by rental car on the D768 highway, turning left 8-9 kilometers later on the D119 to the D196. You can see the monoliths by traveling in either direction on this narrow road.

Quimper

Ten miles inland on the southwest spur of Brittany, Quimper's renown comes from its decorative faïence-style ceramics. Although it has grown to over 60,000 people, this former capital of the ancient Cornouaille region has retained an old world ambiance, as many people still speak the ancient Breton language and older women still wear its traditional clothes.

TGV Travel from Paris
Seven TGVs travel from Paris to Quimper daily. The 386-mile trip from

Paris takes three hours, 51 minutes. The *Gare SNCF* is along avenue de la Gare on the southeast side of town. Currently, the last TGV back to Paris leaves at 19:24.

Tourist Information Office

The *Office de Tourisme* is at the large place de la Résistance on the south side of the Odet River, beyond the main tourist sights. To get there, cross avenue de la Gare in front the *Gare SNCF* and bear right. When the road splits, fork left onto boulevard Dupleix, following it along the river for about a mile.

Tour of Historic Sights & Major Attractions

Quimper's old quarter revolves around the **Cathédrale St.-Corentin**, created to honor a 6th-century Breton saint not recognized by Rome. Built in the 13th-15th centuries, this city landmark features Breton Gothic architecture and exceptional stained glass windows. There's also a wonderful statue of the legendary King Gradlon, a ruler of the Cornouaille region, between the two 250-foot spires.

Next to the *Cathédrale*, the **Musée Départemental Breton** showcases traditional Breton furniture, statues, tombstones, costumes, and pottery. On the grounds surrounding these two buildings are the *Cathédrale* gardens and the town's original ramparts.

To reach these sights from the *Gare SNCF*, exit right onto avenue de la Gare and fork right when the street becomes rue Jacques-Cartier. After crossing the Odet River, turn left onto boulevard Amiral de Kerguélen paralleling the river, then right at the narrow rue du Rois-Gradlon, which soon enters place St.-Corentin. From the *Office de Tourisme*, cross the Odet River, turn right onto rue du Parc bordering the river, then left at rue du Rois-Gradlon.

North of the *Cathédrale*, across a large parking lot, the **Musée des Beaux-Arts** offers a good collection of 17th-century Dutch, Flemish, and French paintings, including works by Rubens, Fragonard, Corot, and Boudin. It also features art from the Pont-Aven School, a group of late 19th-century artists influenced by Gauguin. Using Breton landscapes and people as their subjects, this group rejected the pure naturalism of Impressionism in favor of bright, irregular colors. The museum also has a room dedicated to Quimper author Max Jacob.

After visiting these sights, wander through the narrow streets of the old quarter, where very little has changed in 300 years. Most of the streets are too narrow for cars, making the area pleasant for a quiet stroll and a chance to see local women in the traditional Breton garb of black dresses and tall white bonnets.

Before you leave Quimper, take time to tour at least one of the famous ceramics factories—some have been operating since the 17th century. Two of the best are **Faïenceries Keraluc** and **Les Faïenceries de Quimper H.B.-Henriot**, found southwest of the city. To reach them, follow the south side of the Odet River (the *Cathédrale* is on north side) and the signs to Bénodet. The *Office de Tourisme* has directions to other factories in the area.

Restaurants

Camyflo Bar, 4 rue Ste.-Catherine (turn left off boulevard Dupleix), inexpensive, tel. 98-90-32-06.

Le Capucin Gourmand, 29 rue Réguaries (parallels boulevard Amiral de Kerguélen, one street further north), moderate, tel. 98-95-43-12.

Le Parisien, 13 rue Jean-Jaurès (cross avenue de la Gare from the *Gare SNCF* to rue Jean-Pierre Calloch, then turn right on rue le Déan/rue Jean-Jaurès), moderate, tel. 98-90-35-29.

L'Ambroisie, 49 rue Elie-Fréron (long, narrow street entering the north end of the parking lot by the *Cathédrale*), inexpensive-moderate, tel. 98-95-00-02.

Tritons, allées de Locmaria (along the Odet River beyond the *Office de Tourisme*), moderate-expensive, tel. 98-90-61-78.

Hotels

Hôtel le Terminus, 15 avenue de la Gare, inexpensive, tel. 98-90-00-63.

Hôtel Moderne, 21 bis avenue de la Gare, moderate, tel. 98-90-31-71.

Hôtel Dupleix, 34 boulevard Dupleix, moderate, tel. 98-90-53-35.

Hôtel Cornouaille, 46 rue Auguste-Briand (turn left off boulevard Dupleix), inexpensive, tel. 98-90-05-05.

Hôtel Tour d'Auvergne, 13 rue Réguaries, moderate, tel. 98-95-08-70.

Sights Worth Seeing Nearby

To discover the Pont-Aven artists fully, you must visit **Pont-Aven**, 19 miles southeast of Quimper. Painters found it around 1850, but Paul Gauguin's arrival in 1886 prompted a flood of aspiring artists, of which only a few achieved Gauguin's fame. Today, you can see Gauguin's studio and the locations that inspired specific paintings (marked by plaques throughout the town and countryside). The small *Musée Municipale* in the *Hôtel de Ville* displays some Gauguin drawings and letters, plus paintings by area artists from 1860-1940. The *Cars Caoudal* bus line travels to Pont-Aven four times a day from the *Café Nantais* on avenue de la Gare near the *Gare SNCF.*

Brest

The third-largest city in Brittany (175,000 residents), Brest is the farthest west the TGV travels. On the north end of a large, protected bay near the Atlantic Ocean, Brest began as a tiny Roman military outpost and stayed small until the 17th century, when Cardinal Richelieu encouraged large-scale exporting to boost France's economy.

Unfortunately, little remains from that glorious age. Bombed by Allied planes throughout World War II and besieged for 43 days during the D-Day invasion, Brest saw its old quarter mostly obliterated. Nonetheless, it's still an interesting city for a short visit. You can watch the international ships in the port, see the French Navy's large fleet, and visit its good museums.

TGV Travel from Paris
Ten TGV trains travel daily from Paris to Brest. The 387-mile trip takes three hours, 59 minutes. The *Gare SNCF* is at place du 19e R.I., between two *Gare Routière* terminals on the east side of town, a half-mile northeast of its port. Currently, the last TGV back to Paris leaves at 19:24.

Tourist Information Office
The *Office de Tourisme* is at 1 place de la Liberté at the corner of avenue Georges-Clemenceau. To get there, cross the narrow place du 19e R.I. in front of the *Gare SNCF* to square Président-John-Kennedy, then go right on avenue Georges-Clemenceau for two long blocks.

Tour of Historic Sights & Major Attractions
Walk around the corner from the *Office de Tourisme* and follow place du Général-Leclerc to the wide rue de Siam, going about a mile to its end at the Penfeld River and the *Pont de Recouvrance*. From the highest point of this bridge (92 feet above the water), you'll get excellent views of the port, the *Château*, and the city. Several buses leave from place de la Liberté on routes across the bridge to Brest's west suburbs.

When you reach the other side of the river, follow the steps down to **La Tour de La Motte-Tanguy**. Inside this 14th-century tower, the **Musée Brest** offers exhibits and artifacts from Brest's military history. Outside, there are fine views of central Brest and its *Château* along the corner of the river where it empties into the bay (*Rade de Brest*).

Return to the other side of the river and turn right on boulevard des Français-Libres to visit **Le Château**, a fortress built in 1465 on the site of a 4th-century Roman fort. Descend into its dungeon and climb its corner towers for good views of the city, river, and bay. The *Château* is also the home of the **Musée Naval**, which has a good collection of uniforms, weapons, and naval implements.

From the *Château*, follow rue Denver/rue Voltaire for a few blocks to rue Traverse, then go left for two blocks to the corner of rue Émile-Zola to the **Musée des Beaux-Arts.** This small art museum has paintings from Dutch, Flemish, French, and Italian schools, plus works from the Pont-Aven School. A World War II bombing casualty, the museum's collection was assembled through purchases and donations after 1958.

From there, follow rue Traverse back to rue Voltaire and cross to cours Dajot, an elevated promenade offering excellent views of the *Port de Commerce* dockyards. For a closer view of the ships, follow the streets down to the quais bordering the ship basins.

To return to the *Gare SNCF,* follow avenue Salaün-Penquer (on the south side of cours Dajot) to its end at the *Gare Routière.* The train station is around the corner to the right. Bus #7 travels from the quais and avenue Salaün-Penquer to the *Gare SNCF.*

Restaurants

Ruffé, 1 rue Yves-Collet (exit right from the *Gare SNCF* on avenue Georges-Clemenceau, then go right three blocks later), moderate, tel. 98-46-07-70.

Flunch, 20 rue Jean-Jaurès (same directions as above, except go two blocks further on avenue Georges-Clemenceau, then right at place de la Liberté), inexpensive.

Frère Jacques, 15 bis rue de Lyon (exit the *Gare SNCF* to the right side of square Président-John-Kennedy, follow rue du Château for two blocks, then right), moderate, tel. 98-44-38-65.

Crepes des Fontaines, 44 rue Jean-Macé (crosses rue du Château two blocks beyond rue de Lyon), inexpensive, tel. 98-43-30-33.

Le Vatel, 23 rue Fautras (from the corner of square Président-John-Kennedy and rue du Château, turn right to follow rue Colbert/rue d'Algésiras for eight blocks, then left), moderate, tel. 98-44-51-02.

Le Rossini, 16 rue de l'Amiral-Linois (about a mile from the *Gare SNCF*; turn right off rue du Château onto rue Monge for two blocks, then left), moderate, tel. 98-80-10-00.

Hotels

Hôtel Voyageurs, 15 avenue Georges-Clemenceau (on the corner of rue Yves-Collet), moderate, tel. 98-80-25-73.

Hôtel Altéa Continental, place la Tour d'Auvergne (off rue de Lyon), moderate, tel. 98-80-50-40.

Hôtel Paix, 32 rue d'Algésiras, moderate, tel. 98-80-12-97.

Hôtel Astoria, 9 rue Traverse (just off rue Voltaire), inexpensive, tel. 98-80-19-10.

Sights Worth Seeing Nearby
The **Ile d'Ouessant**, an isolated, windswept island 19 miles off the west coast of Brittany, is dotted with green pastures and small farms. It's a good place to view a part of the Breton culture that has yet to enter the modern age. There is regular service from Brest on the *Vedettes Armoricaines* ferry from *Port de Commerce*.

Nantes

The former capital of independent Brittany and the seventh-largest city in France (258,000 residents), Nantes experienced great prosperity and growth as France expanded its colonial empire in the 18th century. By the time the colonies had gained independence, Nantes had become a major European port.

Nantes is 30 miles east of the Loire River's junction with the Atlantic Ocean, along one of the few sections of the river deep enough for ocean-going vessels. Today, it ships over two million tons of natural materials and merchandise annually to worldwide locations. Despite its busy, industrial atmosphere, Nantes is a pleasant city to visit, filled with shady squares, interesting museums, elegant mansions, a large cathedral, and a military-style château.

TGV Travel from Paris
Twenty-five TGV trains travel daily from Paris to Nantes. The 246-mile trip takes one hour, 59 minutes. Two TGVs also travel daily from Nantes to Lyon (four hours, 42 minutes) via the feeder line at Massy that connects the TGV Atlantique to the TGV Sud-Est. The *Gare SNCF* is along cours John-Kennedy on the east side of the city. Currently, the last TGV back to Paris leaves at 21:48.

Tourist Information Office
The *Office de Tourisme* and *Accueil de France* are two miles west of the *Gare SNCF* on the south corner of place du Commerce. To get there, exit left from the station on cours John-Kennedy. After passing the *Château*, the street name changes to allée du Port-Maillard/de la Tremperie/Flesselles/Brancas before reaching place du Commerce. A tram line runs along these wide boulevards from the *Gare SNCF* to the *Bourse du Commerce* stop, just south of the *Office de Tourisme*.

Tour of Historic Sights & Major Attractions
(Note: Since half of the sights are located before you reach the *Office de Tourisme*, this tour starts from the *Gare SNCF*.) The first major sight, only a half-mile from the station on the right side of cours John-Kennedy, is the formidable **Château Ducal**, where King Henri IV signed the

1598 Edict of Nantes to end the Wars of Religion. Surrounded by a moat, this military fortress and residence of the Dukes of Brittany now houses three museums:

The **Musée des Arts Populaires Régionaux** in the *Tour de la Boulangerie* and former prison is a folk culture/art museum with a collection of colorful costumes, furniture, and recreated period rooms. The **Musée des Arts Décoratifs** in the former Governor's Palace features furniture, lace, ceramics, and exhibits of contemporary Breton artists. The **Musée des Salorges** documents the history of Nantes' commercial trade, including several exhibits on the brutal slave trade that brought vast wealth (an average 200% profit) to many merchants until it was outlawed in the mid-1800's. Fishing boats and maritime equipment are also displayed. After paying a small admission charge for the museums, you can explore the fort and ramparts free.

North of the *Château* entrance, go right onto rue des États, then angle left onto rue Mathelin-Rodier to the **Cathédrale St.-Pierre**. This large Gothic cathedral with a 121-foot soaring vault over the nave (higher than the one at the *Cathédrale Notre-Dame de Paris*) was built piecemeal from 1434-1893. It features 15th-century carvings on its interior façade, brilliant stained glass, and the intricately carved tombs of François II, one of the Dukes of Montfort who ruled Nantes, and of Marguerite de Foix, his second wife.

A few blocks east of the *Cathédrale* at 10 rue Georges-Clemenceau, the **Musée des Beaux-Arts** was stocked with art pillaged in Napoléon's foreign campaigns—the main reason it has one of the best collections of Italian paintings in France, as well as superb works by Rubens, Monet, Géricault, Delacroix, Kandinsky, and La Tour. To get there, walk from the rear of the *Cathédrale* to the spacious place Maréchal-Foch, cross it to the right past a small church, then go left at rue Georges-Clemenceau for one block.

West of the *Château*, at the intersection of allée de la Tremperie and place de la Commune-Libre-du-Bouffray, the small, 17th-century **Église Ste.-Croix** is surrounded by a pedestrians-only precinct with shops, cafés, and ancient half-timbered houses adorned with delightful carvings. To reach the church from the place, follow rue du Bouffray forking left, and veer around the corner to the right.

A few blocks west on allée Flesselles, you'll come to cours des 50-Otages, a busy commercial street packed with much of Nantes' retail, restaurant, and hotel trade. Built upon the destruction caused by World War II bombing (Nantes was liberated on August 12, 1944 by the U.S. army), this is one of the more modern sections of the city. The 40-story **Tower Bretagne** marks its north end.

Directly south, three east-west streets on a former island testify to the wealth of Nantes' 18th-century merchants and slave traders. Luxurious houses line allée Duguay-Trouin, rue Kervégan, and allée de Turenne. Marvel at these homes, then continue west on any of the streets to place de la Porte-Hollande. A right turn will take you to the *Office de Tourisme* and place du Commerce.

From the southwest corner of place du Commerce, follow the short rue François-Salières across rue de la Fosse to the **Passage Pommeraye**, a late 19th-century shopping arcade. Built with iron and glass, its elegant interior is decorated with ornate staircases and balconies, mirrors, statues, and colorful plaster work. Browse the boutiques and walk out the other end to the intersection of rues Santeuil, Boileau, and Crébillon.

About six blocks west on rue Crébillon (which becomes rue Voltaire after passing through place Graslin), you'll come to the **Musée d'Histoire Naturelle**, the first of four museums on Nantes' west end. This museum features displays of animals, minerals, reptiles, and insects native to the region. A few blocks further west, past place Jean V, the **Musée Archéologique** offers unique displays of rare Merovingian and Neolithic artifacts. At the other end of the street (north) on the same grounds is the **Musée Thomas Dobrée**, housed in a 19th-century, Romanesque-style mansion designed by Eugène Emmanuel Viollet-le-Duc, the architect who restored Carcassonne, Mont St.-Michel, the *Cathédrale Notre-Dame de Paris*, and other medieval monuments in France. Although Viollet-le-Duc is France's most renowned restorationist, his original work (like this building) is often rigid and austere with limited decoration, making the buildings appear ugly and gloomy. Inside, the museum has a hodgepodge collection: rare books, prehistoric and medieval antiquities, Greek pottery, 15th-century Flemish paintings, Breton costumes, the gold casket of Anne of Brittany (1477-1514), and a Roman-style sword designed by Jacques-Louis David (1748-1825), the Neoclassical artist famous for painting the major events of the French Revolution and Napoléon's reign.

To reach these museums directly from the east side of Nantes, take the tram from the *Gare SNCF* or the *Château* to the *Office de Tourisme* and transfer to bus #11 to the Jean V stop, or travel on bus #11 from the *Musée des Beaux-Arts* and the *Cathédrale*.

From the last two museums, cross rue Voltaire and place Jean V to rue des Cadeniers. You'll soon reach **cours Cambronne**, a long, rectangular area surrounded by elegant 18th- and 19th-century mansions, which runs to the southeast corner of place Graslin. Wealthy merchants operating in the African slave trade built most of the homes. There are even larger mansions a few blocks south along the river quais, as well as good views of the port of Nantes and the western tip of the *Ile Beaulieu*, an island where most of the ships dock.

Nantes is also the birthplace of author Jules Verne. The **Musée Jules Verne**, housed in a 19th-century townhouse, recreates the world of Captain Nemo and other characters through a collection of Verne's manuscripts, letters, photographs, and other memorabilia. For a glimpse of the heavens, the city's **Planétarium** is across the street on square Moysan.

The best way to reach these sights in the southwest corner of the city along the Loire River is to take bus #21 from the *Cathédrale* (an interesting ride through the city center) to the Garennes stop. Walk south toward the river to rue de l'Hermitage. The *Musée Jules Verne* is across this street in a triangular-shaped park with quai d'Aiguillon, the Loire River, and *Port Maritime* at its back. You can also get there by following the river about two miles from quai de la Fosse (or take the tram a mile along the river until it turns inland by the *Gare Maritime*). To get back to the *Gare SNCF* from these sights, board the tram at the quais or the *Office de Tourisme*.

When you return to the train station, save some time to visit the **Jardin des Plantes** across the street. It has many beautiful flowers and a collection of rare plants, similar to those found in Nantes during the colonial period.

Restaurants

Palombière, 13 boulevard Stalingrad (exit right from the *Gare SNCF* past the *Jardins des Plantes*), moderate-expensive, tel. 40-74-05-15.

Friterie de la Gare, 22 boulevard Stalingrad, inexpensive.

Coq Hardi, 22 allée Commandant-Charcot (across from the *Gare SNCF*, this street parallels cours John-Kennedy), moderate, tel. 40-74-14-25.

Auberge du Château, 5 place de la Duchesse-Anne (across from the east side of the *Château*; turn right off cours John-Kennedy onto rue Henri IV for a short distance), moderate, tel. 40-74-05-51.

Christiana, 3 rue Emery (after passing the *Château*, turn right on rue de Strasbourg and left one block later), inexpensive-moderate, tel. 40-89-68-31.

Le Change, 11 rue de la Juiverie (extension of rue Emery), inexpensive, tel. 40-48-02-28.

La Mangeoire, 16 rue des Petite-Ecuries (turn right off the allées du Port-Maillard before place de la Commune-Libre-du-Bouffay), inexpensive.

La Sirène, 4 rue Kervégan, inexpensive, tel. 40-47-0017.

Le Colvert, 14 rue Armand-Brossard (turn right at cours des 50-Otages, veering right seven blocks later by two small traffic islands after passing rue des 3 Croissants), moderate, tel. 40-48-20-02.

Flunch, 4-6 rue de Feltre (five blocks up cours des 50-Otages, turn left), inexpensive.

Margotte, 2 rue Santeuil, moderate-expensive, tel. 40-73-27-40.

La Cigale (circa-1900 *brasserie*), 4 place Graslin, inexpensive-moderate, tel. 40-69-76-41.

Hotels

Hôtel Astoria, 11 rue Richebourg (cross cours John-Kennedy to rue Stanilas-Baudry, the street alongside the *Jardin des Plantes*, then left at the second street), moderate, tel. 40-74-39-90.

Hôtel Richebourg, 16 rue Richebourg, inexpensive, tel. 40-74-08-32.

Hôtel Terminus, 3 allée Commandant-Charcot, inexpensive, tel. 40-74-24-51.

Hôtel de la Gare, 5 allée Commandant-Charcot, moderate, tel. 40-74-37-25.

Hôtel Vendée, 8 allée Commandant-Charcot, moderate, tel. 40-74-14-54.

Hôtel Bourgogne, 9 allée Commandant-Charcot, inexpensive-moderate, tel. 40-74-03-34.

L'Hôtel, 6 rue Henri IV (across from east side of the *Château*), moderate, tel. 40-29-30-31.

Hôtel Duchesse Anne, 3 place de la Duchesse-Anne, moderate, tel. 40-74-30-29.

Sights Worth Seeing Nearby

Located on the southeast tip of Brittany, Nantes makes a good base for exploring **Brittany** and the western **Loire Valley**. **Rennes**, 90 miles north on a non-TGV train, offers connections to two other TGV lines.

CHAPTER 13

Poitou-Charentes

Poitiers

Despite its proximity to the Loire Valley (62 miles from Tours) and its location on the popular Paris-Bordeaux rail line, Poitiers is usually bypassed by most tourists. Too bad, because Poitiers, one of France's most historic cities, will transport you to the nation's past—as far back as the 4th century.

Situated on a plateau above the Clain and Boivre Rivers, this ancient capital of Poitou has long been an artistic, political, religious, and intellectual hub. Coveted for its strategic location, Poitiers has seen numerous battles and was an important stop on the religious pilgrimage circuit. During the 14th century, 67 churches served its small population.

Today, this sprawling city of 83,000 is the business and government center of the primarily agricultural Poitou-Charentes region and home to 16,000 university students.

TGV Travel from Paris
Seventeen TGV trains travel daily from Paris to Poitiers. The 206-mile trip takes one hour, 28 minutes. The *Gare SNCF* is along boulevard du Grand-Cerf on the west side of town. Currently, the last TGV back to Paris leaves at 21:59.

Tourist Information Office
The *Office de Tourisme* is in the center of town at 8 rue des Grandes-Écoles. To get there, cross boulevard du Grand-Cerf to boulevard Solferino. Shortly after it turns left, you'll see steps on the right side of the street. Take these steps up to an open traffic area, and turn right on

the wide boulevard de Verdun (second street). About three blocks down, you'll reach place Aristide-Briand, in front of Poitiers' Préfecture. Follow the left side of the place to rue Victor-Hugo and walk two long blocks to its end at place du Maréchal-Leclerc. There, you'll find a thriving market, the *Hôtel de Ville*, and Poitiers' main business/shopping district. From the left side of the place, follow rue des Grandes-Écoles two blocks to its intersection with rue Paul-Guillon, where you'll find the *Office de Tourisme*.

If you'd rather not walk, buses #1, 2A, 3, 7, 8, 11, 16, and N1 travel from the *Gare SNCF* to a stop by the *Hôtel de Ville*.

Tour of Historic Sights & Major Attractions

With its vast religious heritage, Poitiers is still a city of churches, most of which are near the *Office de Tourisme* and the Clain River. To reach the first one, walk left for one block on rue Paul-Guillon to the pedestrians-only rue Gambetta, then left for a half-block to the 16th-century **Église St.-Porchaire**. After a brief look (there are better churches ahead), backtrack to rue Gambetta and follow it across rue Paul-Guillon to the pedestrians-only place Alphonse-Lepetit. To the right is the **Palais de Justice**, the former palace and residence of the Dukes of Aquitane. The building's Great Hall is most famous as the site of Joan of Arc's interrogation by a committee of bishops.

One block past the *Palais*, turn right at rue de la Regratterie for a two-block walk to the 12th-century **Église Notre-Dame-la-Grande**, a major sanctuary for pilgrims during the Middle Ages. This small, squat Romanesque church boasts detailed exterior ornamentation and an outstanding fresco on the vaulting in the choir. Just north, you'll find Poitiers' university and the spacious place Charles-de-Gaulle, where an open-air market runs daily.

If you have time, visit the 11th-century **Église St.-Jean-de-Montierneuf**, featuring an elegant, soaring apse supported by a flying buttress. It's a mile from the *Église Notre-Dame-la-Grande* on the north edge of the city—backtrack on rue de la Regratterie, go right on rue des Vieilles-Boucheries, then veer left across place Charles-VII to rue René-Descartes/rue de la Chaîne/rue Jean-Bouchet. Just before you reach the Clain River, you'll see place Montierneuf intersected by five streets and the driveway to the church on the upper right.

Nearby, the **Jardin Botanique** is a nice park for relaxation during warmer months. To reach it from the *Église St.-Jean-de-Montierneuf*, return to place Montierneuf, take a right on rue du Mouton and a right on boulevard Chasseigne bordering the river. The park is a half-mile away on the right.

Three must-see churches are less than a mile from the *Église Notre-Dame-la-Grande*, near the east side of the Clain River. If you visited the *Église St.-Jean-de-Montierneuf*, follow the boulevards along the Clain River to these sights. Otherwise, follow the Grand-Rue (beginning behind the *Église Notre-Dame-la-Grande*) to the river. Three blocks to the right along boulevard du Pont-Joubert, the 11th-century **Église Ste.- Radegonde** sits protected by a gate tower. Inside, its black marble crypt holds the tomb of Sainte Radegonde, the patron of Poitiers, who died in 587 A.D.

A few blocks behind this church is Poitiers' largest religious building, the 12th-century **Cathédrale St.-Pierre**, built on the ruins of a Roman basilica. The additions to the original structure make it one of the oddest-shaped cathedrals in Europe. Although it's not as striking as some of France's other Gothic cathedrals, go inside to feel its vastness and see its gorgeous stained glass windows. To reach it, turn right off boulevard du Pont-Joubert onto rue Jean-Jaurès, then go right at rue Ste.-Croix to place Ste.-Croix by the rear of the *Cathédrale*. To reach the main entrance, follow the building's outline to rue Ste.-Radegonde, then turn left to place de la Cathédrale et du Cardinal Pie.

One block further on rue Jean-Jaurès, France's oldest Christian building—the 6th-century, stone and brick **Baptistière St.-Jean**—has a 4th-century octagonal font sunk into the floor. This small building serves as a museum for Roman and early Christian decorations and antiquities found in the area. Next door, the **Musée Ste.-Croix**, built around the ruins of the *Abbaye Ste.-Croix*, features more relics from early Roman settlers, exhibits on local industries, and paintings by Dutch, Flemish, and French artists, including Vuillard, Boudin, and Sisley.

Across the Clain River from these sights, the unique **Hypogée Martyrium**, a 7th-century underground chapel, was built on the burial site of 72 Christians martyred by the Romans. Getting there requires a 20-minute walk uphill, so you may want to take a taxi. By foot, follow rue Jean-Jaurès across the river on the *Pont Neuf* to rue du Faubourg-du-Pont-Neuf. Half a mile later, turn left at rue de la Pierre-Levée. After another half-mile, turn left onto rue de St.-Saturin for a short distance. On the return, stop to view historic Poitiers from your lofty perch.

To return to central Poitiers or the *Gare SNCF* from the *Pont Neuf*, follow rue Jean-Jaurès/rue Paul-Guillon to the *Office de Tourisme*, then go left on rue des Grandes-Écoles to place du Maréchal-Leclerc. Bus #5 travels from the bridge to the *Hôtel de Ville*.

Before you go back to the station, two other sights merit a short visit: the elegant, 11th-century **Église St.-Hilaire-le-Grand**, where the 13-year-old Richard the Lion-Hearted was declared Count of Poitiers, and the **Parc de Blossac**, an English garden-style park designed over the original city ramparts. To reach them (a 10-15 minute walk from the lower right corner of place du Maréchal-Leclerc [facing the *Hôtel* *de Ville*]), follow rue Carnot/rue de la Tranchée to rue du Doyenné. Turn right and walk past the rear and side of the *Église* to rue St.-Hilaire, then turn left to the main entrance. You can enter the park on the left side of rue de la Tranchée, a few blocks past rue du Doyenné. There are good views of the Clain River on the opposite side of the park. Bus #9 travels between the park and the *Hôtel de Ville*.

To return to the *Gare SNCF* from the *Église*, exit left on rue St.-Hilaire. You'll soon reach a set of steps on your right that leads to boulevard de Pont-Archard. (This street also intersects the west end of the *Parc de Blossac*.) The train station is to the right, less than a mile away.

Restaurants
Aux Armes d'Obernai, 19 rue Arthur-Ranc (intersects boulevard de Verdun), moderate-expensive, tel. 49-41-16-33.

Jack Rolland, 16 rue Carnot, moderate-expensive, tel. 49-88-14-41.

Le Poitevin, 76 rue Carnot, moderate-expensive, tel. 48-88-35-04.

Maxime, 4 rue St.-Nicolas (turn left off rue Carnot), seafood and regional specialities, moderate-expensive, tel. 49-41-09-55.

Flunch, 2 rue du Petit-Bonneveau (turn left off rue Carnot, one long block past rue St.-Nicolas), inexpensive.

Chez Vladimar, 10 rue Jean-Macé (enters place Montierneuf), moderate, tel. 49-41-69-72.

Le Roy d'Ys, 51 rue de la Cathédrale (street leading away from the *Cathédrale St.-Pierre* main entrance), crêpes, inexpensive.

Hotels
Hôtel Continental, 2 boulevard Solferino, inexpensive-moderate, tel. 49-37-93-93.

Hôtel Terminus, 3 boulevard de Pont-Archard, moderate, tel. 49-58-20-31.

Hôtel du Poitou, 79 boulevard Grand-Cerf, inexpensive, tel. 49-58-38-06.

Hôtel Regina, 149 boulevard Grand-Cerf, moderate, tel. 49-58-20-38.

Hôtel Chapon Fin, place du Maréchal-Leclerc, moderate, tel. 49-88-02-97.

Hôtel Europe, 39 rue Carnot, moderate, tel. 49-88-12-00.

Hôtel le Carnot, 40 rue Carnot, inexpensive, tel. 49-41-23-69.

Sights Worth Seeing Nearby
If you are churched-out, venture five miles north of Poitiers for something completely different: **Futuroscope**, a science-oriented amusement park similar to Disneyworld's Epcot Center. The Innobus departs every morning from the *Gare SNCF* to this attraction, returning in the late afternoon and early evening. Admission to Futuroscope runs 85-130 francs, depending on your age.

La Rochelle

Founded in 1132, La Rochelle gained renown centuries ago as a Protestant stronghold. From there, the Huguenots sailed to freedom in Canada, eventually founding Montreal and other cities. In 1627, Cardinal Richelieu laid siege to the town, which was actively assisting the battles against Catholic ships. After a year's resistance, the city surrendered, mainly because of mass starvation: its pre-siege population of 30,000 had been reduced to a mere 5,000. Since the ruthless Richelieu leveled much of the town after the surrender, little of pre-1600's La Rochelle remains.

One of the oldest ports in France, La Rochelle's industry no longer revolves around maritime trade, which was devastated when Canada was lost to the English. However, it's still a principal fishing port, employing a large percentage of the city's 78,000 residents. It's also a popular tourist destination. With sandy beaches and island resorts nearby, La Rochelle attracts swarms of vacationers in the summer.

TGV Travel from Paris

In late 1993, a line from Poitiers will open TGV travel direct from Paris to La Rochelle, a rail distance of 298 miles. Until this line opens, you must transfer to a non-TGV train at either Poitiers or Nantes. The *Gare SNCF* is along boulevard Joffre on the southeast side of town, near the harbor.

Tourist Information Office

The *Office de Tourisme* is at place Petite-Sirène in the small *Gabut Quartier* on the south side of the *Bassin à Flot*, the city's main docking area, filled with small fishing boats. To get there, cross boulevard Joffre through place Pierre-Sémard, and follow avenue du Général-de-Gaulle to its end at place Commandant-de-la-Motte-Rouge. Cross avenue du 123eme on your left to quai du Gabut, then go left at the first street entering the quai, for two blocks.

Tour of Historic Sights & Major Attractions

To reach the compact **Vieux Port**, return to quai du Gabut, then go left to the 14th-century **Tour St.-Nicolas**, one of three defensive towers that once protected La Rochelle's harbor from invasion. Excellent views of the harbor, city, Atlantic Ocean, coastal countryside, and nearby *Ile de Ré* are available from the top of the tower. Descend the tower and view La Rochelle from the terrace, then walk across the narrow bridge over the *Bassin à Flot* to quai de Carénage, stopping briefly to view the colorful boats and active fish market. From this quai, follow the edge of the *Vieux Port* to the other side to visit the slightly shorter

Tour de la Chaîne. Finished in the late 14th century, this tower is also open for inspection. Its most interesting feature is a model of La Rochelle as it looked in the 1600's. The defense chain that once stretched across the narrow entrance of the *Vieux-Port* from tower to tower now connects low stone pylons a few steps north of the *Tour de la Chaîne* at place de la Chaîne.

From there, it's a short walk on rue Sur-Les-Murs to the third tower, the 15th-century **Tour de la Lanterne** (a.k.a. *Tour des Quartre Sergents*, for the four sergeants imprisoned and executed there). Topped by a 148-foot Flamboyant Gothic steeple, this tall tower has also served as a prison and lighthouse. Of course, its summit offers a splendid view. As you climb the stairs, be sure to read the graffiti carved in the walls by imprisoned English soldiers.

If you have time to spare, relax for a few hours in one of the city's parks. Just beyond the *Tower de la Lanterne* across a small stream, the **promenade de la Concurrence** offers a lovely tree-lined walk beside the harbor and beach that leads to the city's casino. Beyond the casino, there are two pretty parks back-to-back, the **Parc du Casino** and **Parc d'Orbigny**. To the north of the tower via chemin du Rempart, the long **Parc Charruyer** lies at the foot of the Vauban ramparts bordering the west side of the old city.

Day-trippers probably should skip the parks and proceed north beyond the *Tour de la Lanterne* to wander through the narrow, arch-covered streets behind the *Vieux Port*. Since La Rochelle is geographically small, you can't really get lost. If you do get turned around, ask a local for directions to the *Vieux Port*, where you can retrace your steps. After exploring the streets, head to the wide rue Léonce-Vieljeux (a few blocks inland from the *Vieux Port*), where you'll find the 14th-century **Porte de la Grosse-Horloge**, an elaborate Gothic gateway to the old city.

From there, stroll down rue du Palais/rue Chaudrier, a street lined with ancient wooden houses with beautiful doorways. Note the collonaded façade on the **Palais de Justice** at 10 rue du Palais. A few blocks further, you'll see the small **Église St.-Barthélemy**, built in 1152, and the city's uninspiring 18th-century cathedral. One block beyond, turn right on rue Gargoulleau to the **Musée des Beaux-Arts**, housed in the 18th-century *Hôtel Legoux*. Although this art museum has a few good Corot paintings and some Delacroix oil sketches, its mediocre collection ranks far below those at art museums in other TGV cities.

When rue Gargoulleau ends, turn right at rue St.-Yon, then take the next right on rue Fleuriau. At #10, behind a massive blue door, the **Musée du Nouveau-Monde** traces La Rochelle's role in North America and the French West Indies, beginning with La Salle's 1682 arrival in the Mississippi Delta to the settling of the Louisiana Territory.

The collection includes paintings, drawings, photographs, sculpture, and maps, plus 18th-century furniture and decorative arts. From there, cross rue St.-Yon to the tiny rue de Beur, then go right on rue des Merciers, a street filled with interesting old houses. At the end of the street on a triangular block, the **Hôtel de Ville** is an ornate building constructed in a Flamboyant Gothic style, complete with fortress walls. Supposedly, it has more chandeliers than any building in Europe. Behind the *Hôtel de Ville*, there's a maze of pedestrians-only streets filled with shops, cafés, and restaurants.

If you're interested in ceramics, visit the **Musée d'Orbigny-Bernon** at 2 rue St.-Côme. To get there, return to rue Chaudrier, turn left onto rue Aufrédy (where the *Église St.-Barthélemy* is located), then go left to the end of the street. And for something quite different, check out the **Musée Lafaille** at the corner of rue Albert 1er (extension of rue Chaudrier) and rue Alcide-d'Orbigny. This 18th-century building contains an eclectic collection of oceanographic items and other curiosities, including an idol from Easter Island, rare shellfish, and an embalmed giraffe!

To stay in the natural science mode, visit La Rochelle's **aquarium**, the largest collection of marine life in France. It's not far from the *Gare SNCF*, but it requires a circuitous route to reach it. From the station, turn left on boulevard Joffre, then right on avenue du 123eme. When you reach the first *bassin*, follow it all the way around to the left, cross the small bridge, turn right on rue des Minimes, then left a few blocks later onto rue La Désirée. The aquarium is two blocks away on the right. Next to the aquarium, the **Musée de la Voile** commemorates sailing ships. Bus #12 (board at the *Cathédrale*) travels along rue des Minimes.

Restaurants

Pizzeria-Grill don Arturo, 46 rue St.-Nicolas (a north-south street one block east of quai Valin, the extension of the avenue du Général-de-Gaulle), inexpensive.

Il Vesuvio, 24 cours des Dames (set back from the west side of the *Vieux Port*, near the *Tour de la Chaîne*), Italian, inexpensive.

Chez Serge, 46 cours des Dames, moderate-expensive, tel. 46-41-18-60.

Bar Andre, 5 rue St.-Jean-du-Pérot (one block north of the *Tour de la Chaîne* via the pedestrians-only rue de la Chaîne), moderate, tel. 46-41-28-24.

Assiette, 18 rue St.-Jean-du-Pérot, moderate, tel. 46-41-75-75.

L'Entracte, 22 rue St.-Jean-du-Pérot, moderate, tel. 46-50-62-60.

Toque Blanche, 39 rue St.-Jean-du-Pérot, moderate-expensive, tel. 46-41-60-55.

La Galathée, 45 rue St.-Jean-du-Pérot, inexpensive-moderate, tel. 46-41-17-06.

Les Quartre Sergents, 49 rue St.-Jean-du-Pérot, moderate, tel. 46-41-35-80.

Hotels

Hôtel Ibis, place du Commandant-de-la-Motte-Rouge, moderate, tel. 46-41-60-22.

Hôtel Terminus, 11 place du Commandant-de-la-Motte-Rouge, inexpensive-moderate, tel. 46-41-31-94.

Hôtel Bordeaux, 43 rue St.-Nicolas, inexpensive, tel. 46-41-31-22.

Hôtel St.-Nicolas, 13 rue Sardinerie (forks to the right off rue St.-Nicolas), moderate, tel. 46-41-71-55.

Hôtel Mercure Yachtman, 23 quai Valin, moderate, tel. 46-41-20-68.

Hôtel Tour de Nesle, 2 quai Louis-Durand (turn right off quai Valin), inexpensive-moderate, tel. 46-41-05-86.

Hôtel St.-Jean d'Acre, 4 place de la Chaîne, moderate, tel. 46-41-73-33.

Sights Worth Seeing Nearby

Two islands near La Rochelle, the **Ile de Ré** and **Ile d'Oléron**, offer miles of white, sandy beaches. The *Ile de Ré*, with 37 miles of coastline and several small villages, is two miles offshore from the suburb of La Pallice (north of La Rochelle), the Nazi's primary Atlantic submarine base during World War II. You can take a ferry there or cross a toll bridge one mile north of La Pallice's *Gare Maritime*. Bus #1 travels from the *Gare SNCF* through the center of the city to the *Gare Maritime*, and commercial buses from the *Gare Routière* (across from the *Cathédrale*) run to several island villages.

The slightly larger *Ile d'Oléron* (south of La Rochelle) is an 80-minute ferry ride from the *Gare Maritime* to the village of Boyardville in the middle of the island's east side. You can also get there by taking a non-TGV train to Rochefort and then a bus to the island's southeast corner via one of the longest toll bridges in France.

Ile d'Aix makes for another interesting excursion. One of the smallest islands in the Atlantic Ocean (just over a mile long), it retains a permanent place in French history as the last place in France to shelter Napoléon Bonaparte. In July of 1815, the ex-Emperor spent a week there before his exile on the British island St. Helena. The island's **Musée Napoléonien,** one of 12 provincial museums maintained by the national government, has a substantial collection of Napoléon memorabilia. From La Pallice, *Ile d'Aix* is 50 minutes away on the same boat to *Ile d'Oléron*.

Angoulême

Midway between Poitiers and Bordeaux, this bustling town of 51,000 plays a key role in the economy of western France. Despite the busy atmosphere and industrial overtones, Angoulême's old quarter, overlooking the Charente River, is worth a visit. There, you can walk into a medieval past of narrow, cobblestone streets, castle towers, and buildings dating from the 11th century.

TGV Travel from Paris
Fourteen TGV trains travel daily from Paris to Angoulême. The 277-mile trip takes two hours, 12 minutes. The *Gare SNCF* is at place de la Gare on the east side of town. Currently, the last TGV back to Paris leaves at 21:08.

Tourist Information Office
The *Office de Tourisme* is at 2 place St.-Pierre, across from the *Cathédrale de St.-Pierre*, about a mile from the *Gare SNCF.* To get there, follow the walking tour route described below.

Tour of Historic Sights & Major Attractions
To reach the old quarter and central Angoulême, exit right from the *Gare SNCF* on avenue Gambetta. At place Gérard-Pérot, where several streets converge, cross to rampe d'Aguesseau and bear right onto rue Marengo, which runs into the *Hôtel de Ville*. Buses #12 and 14 follow a similar route from the *Gare SNCF* to a parking area at place Bouillaud, opposite the west side of the *Hôtel de Ville*.

The 19th-century **Hôtel de Ville**, built to resemble a 13th-century Renaissance building, was constructed on the foundation of a castle belonging to the Counts de Angoulême. All that remains from the original castle are the 13th-century **Tour de Lusignan** and the 15th-century **Tour de Valois**. The towers are not open to the public, but you can tour the *Hôtel de Ville*'s salons.

From the west side of the *Hôtel de Ville*, cross through place Bouillaud, venture to the right down avenue Georges-Clemenceau, then turn right on rempart Desaix, one of a series of streets circling the old city along the site of the former town walls. From the rampart streets, you'll get excellent views of modern Angoulême, its suburbs, and the countryside.

Not far into your ramparts walk, you'll reach the *Office de Tourisme* and the **Cathédrale de St.-Pierre**. Built in 1128 and restored in the 19th century, this cathedral features two towers, each adorned with 75 statues representing the Last Judgment. Behind it, at the corner of rue de Friedland and rue de l'Évêché, the **Musée Municipal** (in a 12th-century Bishop's palace) now houses an interesting collection of European art, African art, and pottery. There's also a collection of original comic strips, which springs from the annual illustrator's convention held in town. Set in a futuristic room covered in chrome and mirrors (including the ceiling and floor!), it's one of the most bizarre arrangements of art anywhere.

From there, walk one block north on rue de l'Évêché, then go left on rue de Beaulieu, a street filled with buildings from the 15th-19th centuries, including a large boys' school and the *Hôtel-Dieu*. When the street ends opposite the entrance to the **Jardin Vert**, you have two options. First, for close-up views of the **Charente River**, follow the roads through the park to the *Pont de St.-Cybard*, or turn right on rempart de Beaulieu and follow it (it becomes boulevard Aristide-Briand after passing the open place Turenne) to the north side of the old city for an elevated view of the river, *Ile Marquais*, and the suburb St.-Cybard across the river. From there, the street curves around the old city past a large covered market, eventually running into rampe d'Aguesseau, which leads to the *Gare SNCF.*

For more variety, try this: After viewing the Charente River, explore the narrow streets in the middle of old Angoulême, between the rampart streets and the *Hôtel de Ville*. Since this is a fairly compact area, you can't get lost.

Restaurants

Terminus, place de la Gare, moderate, tel. 45-95-27-13.

La Chamade, 13 rampe d'Aguesseau, moderate-expensive, tel. 45-38-41-33.

Le Chat Noir, place des Halles (turn right off rue Marengo onto rue des Arceaux, which leads to the covered market), sandwiches and salads, inexpensive, tel. 45-95-26-27.

Le Margaux, 25 rue de Genève (crosses west side of place des Halles), moderate, tel. 45-92-58-98.

Halles, 11 rue Massillon (the street entering the west side of place des Halles and rue de Genève), moderate, tel. 45-92-65-24.

Brasserie Alsacienne, place du Champ-de-Mars (turn left off avenue Gambetta onto rue de l'Éperon), inexpensive, tel. 45-95-91-44.

Hotels

Hôtel les Messageries, place de la Gare, inexpensive, tel. 45-95-07-62.

Hôtel Pyrénées, 80 rue St.-Roch (extension of rue de l'Éperon, beginning at place Champ du Mars), moderate, tel. 45-95-20-45.

Hôtel du Cheval de Bronze, 7 rue St.-Roch, inexpensive, tel. 45-95-02-74.

Hôtel le Palma, 4 rampe d'Aguesseau, inexpensive, tel. 45-95-22-89.

Altéa Hôtel de France, 1 place des Halles, moderate (good restaurant on premises), tel. 45-95-47-95.

Sights Worth Seeing Nearby

Ten miles northeast of Angoulême, on the banks of the Tardoire River near the village of **La Rochefoucauld**, there's a large 11th-century château/castle with a dungeon, a chapel, and galleries. It's easily reached by bus or non-TGV train. The *Gare Routière* is at place du Champ-de-Mars.

Southwest Atlantic Coast

Bordeaux

Internationally famous for its namesake wines, Bordeaux is located on the Garonne River, 60 miles south of the Gironde Estuary, where the river meets the Atlantic Ocean. One of France's largest ports, with industry sprawling in every direction, it's not as quaint as other TGV cities, though it does have some outstanding churches, good museums, and pretty squares surrounded by 18th-century buildings. Most travelers use Bordeaux as a base for exploring the nearby vineyards and coastal cities to the south.

TGV Travel from Paris
Twenty-three TGV trains travel daily from Paris to Bordeaux. The 361-mile trip takes two hours, 58 minutes. The *Gare St.-Jean* is along rue Charles-Domercq near the Garonne River on the southeast side of town. Currently, the last TGV back to Paris leaves at 20:46.

Tourist Information Office
The *Office de Tourisme* and *Accueil de France* are in the center of the city at 12 cours du 30-Juillet, about three miles from the *Gare St.-Jean*. The quickest way to get there is by bus #7 or 8 from the train station. For a long, scenic hike past elegant buildings and old city gateways (*porte*), exit right from the station on rue Charles-Domercq, then go left on quai de Paludate, paralleling the river. Stay on this street as it changes name several times until you come to allées d'Orléans, two blocks past the 18th-century *Bourse du Commerce* building. Turn left there and walk

four short blocks to cours du 30-Juillet. Bus #1 travels along the river quais into the suburbs.

Directly across the street at 1 cours du 30-Juillet, the *Maison des Vins de Bordeaux* offers free samples of local wines and arranges vineyard tours. During the third week in June, this office and the city's hotels are jammed, as the world's wine buyers gather for the annual Vinexpo trade show.

Tour of Historic Sights & Major Attractions

Across from the *Office de Tourisme* along the allées d'Orléans, the 30-acre **Esplanade des Quinconces** is the largest municipal square in France. There's a 130-foot monument honoring the Girondins, the moderate revolutionary group opposed by Robespierre in 1789, on the square's west end. One block north (facing the river, turn left) via rue Foy, the **Musée d'Art Contemporain** features work by contemporary artists like Richard Serra, Sol Le Witt, and Julian Schnabel. You can also get there by turning left off quai Louis-XVIII onto rue Ferrére for one block.

Northwest of the *Esplanade des Quinconces* via cours du Maréchal-Foch, the 25-acre **Jardin Public**, vandalized during the French Revolution, was renovated in 1856 in the style of an English garden park. The **Musée d'Histoire Naturelle** is on its west end.

A block south of the *Office de Tourisme*, the 1773 Classical **Grand Théâtre** influenced the design of the Paris Opera. With a large colonnaded portico topped by statues of the muses and elaborate decorations inside, it is one of Bordeaux's most beautiful buildings.

From there, veer left across place de la Comédie in front of the theater to the pedestrians-only rue Ste.-Catherine, a main shopping street. A half-mile later at cours d'Alsace-et-Lorraine, turn right to the large **Cathédrale St.-André**, only 20 feet shorter in length than the *Cathédrale Notre-Dame de Paris*. Built from 1096 to the early 1500's, this primarily Gothic structure features an excellent Romanesque façade, numerous gargoyles and statues adorning its exterior, twin 266-foot spires, and decorated flying buttresses, including one resembling a ribbon of flames.

Separated from the church on its east side is the 155-foot **Tour Pey-Berland**, a 1440's belfry. On the north side, at the corner of rues Vital-Carles and des Trois-Conils, **Centre Jean Moulin** is a small museum documenting Resistance activity in Bordeaux during World War II.

Across from cathedral's west side, the **Hôtel de Ville** was the residence of the Archbishop of Bordeaux. Rue Montbazon (along the north side of this building) will lead you to two of Bordeaux's best museums. First, walk a block and turn right at rue Bouffard to the **Musée des Arts Décoratifs**. Housed in the 18th-century *Hôtel de Lalande*, this museum's collection includes French porcelain and faïence, furniture, glassware, animal sculpture, and prints of the city.

Second, backtrack to rue Montbazon, then go right briefly to the L-shaped **Musée des Beaux-Arts**. Located on the grounds of the *Jardin de la Mairie* behind the *Hôtel de Ville*, this fine arts museum features paintings and sculpture by Titian, Rubens, Corot, Delacroix, Renoir, Matisse, and many more. Buses #7 and 8 travel there from the *Gare St.-Jean*.

After getting a little culture, exit to the wide cours d'Albret at the far end of the museum, then turn left for a three-block walk to the *Palais de Justice*. After passing this building, turn left at place de la République and continue on rue de Cursol to cours Pasteur and the **Musée d'Acquitaine**. This history and archaeology museum explains the growth of Bordeaux and the Aquitaine region through a series of exhibits and artifacts on the region's agricultural, maritime, and commercial industries. Be sure to see the exhibits on the area's wine trade before you visit a vineyard.

After the museum, walk down cours Victor-Hugo (the continuation of rue de Cursol), filled with restaurants and shops for over a mile, to the **Pont de Pierre**, which spans the Garonne River. (Several buses follow this route.) Built in 1813 by order of Napoléon, it's one of the most beautiful bridges in France, its 17 arches glowing from the pink brick. Cross to the other side for excellent views of Bordeaux and the river. A variety of tour boats and dining cruises leave from quai Louis-XVIII.

Walk back across the bridge, turn left at quai des Salinières, then right when you see the 15th-century **Basilique St.-Michel**, noted for its triple nave and the **Tour St.-Michel**. Separated from the church, this 374-foot, hexagonal, Flamboyant Gothic bell tower erected in 1472 is the tallest belfry in southern France. Unfortunately, disrepair keeps it closed the public. (If you skip the *Pont de Pierre*, you can reach these sights by turning right off cours Victor-Hugo onto rue des Faures.)

Finally, walk past the right side of the church and follow rue Camille-Sauvageau to the 12th-century **Église Ste.-Croix**, a former Benedictine abbey laden with Romanesque arches and statues. Rue de Tauzia (to the right of the church entrance) ends at rue Charles-Domercq and the *Gare St.-Jean*.

Restaurants

Le Clavel Barnabet, 44 rue Charles-Domercq (exit left from the *Gare St.-Jean*), moderate, tel. 56-92-91-52.

La Tupina, 6 rue de la Porte de la Monnaie (connects rue Camille-Sauvageau to porte de la Monnaie/quai de la Monnaie), moderate, tel. 56-91-56-37.

La Flambee, 26 rue du Mirail (from the *Musée d'Acquitaine*, turn right off cours Victor-Hugo by a large school), inexpensive, tel. 56-92-71-02.

Le Vieux Bordeaux, 27 rue Buhan (turn left off cours Victor-Hugo), moderate, tel. 56-52-94-36.

Le Buhan, 28 rue Buhan, moderate, tel. 56-52-80-86.

La Ferme St.-Michel, 2 rue des Menuts (turn right off cours Victor-Hugo), moderate, tel. 56-91-54-77.

Les Plaisirs d'Ausone, 10 rue Ausone (turn left off quai Richelieu at cours d'Alsace-et-Lorraine, then take the first right), moderate, tel. 56-79-30-30.

La Forge, 8 rue du Chai-des-Farines (continuation of rue Ausone), moderate, tel. 56-81-40-96.

Les Provinces, 41 rue St.-Rémi (connects rue Ste.-Catherine with the riverside place de la Bourse), moderate, tel. 56-81-74-30.

Chez Philippe, 1 place du Parlement (from place de la Bourse, follow rue Fernand-Philippart two blocks to this small square), moderate, tel. 56-81-83-15.

L'Athenee, 44 rue des Trois-Conils, inexpensive, tel. 56-52-18-18.

Hotels

Hôtel Terminus, connected to the *Gare St.-Jean*, moderate-expensive, tel. 56-92-71-58.

Hôtel Royal St.-Jean, 15 rue Charles-Domercq, moderate, tel. 56-91-72-16.

Hôtel Le Faisan, 28 rue Charles-Domercq, moderate, tel. 56-91-54-52.

Hôtel Régina, 34 rue Charles-Domercq, moderate, tel. 56-91-66.07.

Hôtel Alliance, 30 rue de Tauzia, moderate, tel. 56-92-21-21.

Relais Bleus, 68 rue Tauzia, moderate, tel. 56-91-55-50.

Hôtel California, 47 Eugéne-Le Roy, moderate (directly in front of the *Gare St.-Jean*, cross rue Charles-Domercq through an open place to rue Fieffé and veer to the right when the street splits), tel. 56-91-58-97.

Hôtel Arcade, 60 rue Eugéne-Le Roy, moderate, tel. 56-91-40-40.

Hôtel Atlantic, 69 rue Eugéne-Le Roy, moderate, tel. 56-92-92-22.

Hôtel Normandie, 7 cours du 30-Juillet, moderate, tel. 56-52-16-80.

Sights Worth Seeing Nearby

Medoc, St.-Emilion, Sauternes, Graves, Libourne—all household names to wine connoisseurs. Near these small towns, north and east of Bordeaux, are the vineyards that produce over 70 million gallons of wine per year. For tours and further information, visit the *Maison des Vins de Bordeaux* at 1 cours du 30-Juillet.

Dax

After Aix-les-Bains, Dax is the second most popular spa city in France, with 13 thermal spas and several heated outdoor pools. Ever since the Roman Emperor Augustus and his family visited the town's hot springs between 27-25 B.C., Dax has attracted millions of people seeking relaxation and cures. Ruled by several regional nobles through its early history, with brief ownership by the English, Dax became an official city of France in 1451.

Located on a bend in the Adour River, 31 miles north of Bayonne, this small city is worth a brief stop to see the hot springs and explore the remains of a 4th-century Gallo-Roman fortification and arena. Two TGV lines intersect there, so Dax is an excellent base for exploring the Basque region and coastal cities of southwest France.

TGV Travel from Paris

Seven TGV trains travel daily from Paris to Dax. The 453-mile trip takes four hours, seven minutes. The *Gare SNCF* is at the east end of avenue de la Gare on the north edge of the city limits. Currently, the last TGV back to Paris leaves at 18:57.

Tourist Information Office

The *Office de Tourisme* is about two miles from the *Gare SNCF* on cours de Verdun, a few steps south of the Adour River. To get there, exit right from the station on avenue de la Gare for one block, then go left at avenue St.-Vincent-de-Paul for a long walk to the river. Immediately after crossing the Adour, you'll see the *Office de Tourisme* on the tip of a triangular block to the right, across from place Thiers.

Tour of Historic Sights & Major Attractions

After visiting the *Office de Tourisme*, cross through place Thiers to rue du Toro. You'll get your first look at Dax's chief attraction almost immediately, because straight ahead is the misty **Fountaine Chaude** (a.k.a. *Fontaine de la Nèhe*), a hot spring in the middle of an open traffic intersection. Flowing into a large pool covered by a Tuscan arcade, the water maintains a constant temperature of 147°F.

Walk past the right side of the fountain and down rue des Pénitents/rue de Borda until it ends at rue St.-Vincent, then veer left to the **Cathédrale Notre-Dame**. Rebuilt in the 17th century in the Classical style, this cathedral features a 13th-century Gothic doorway from the original sanctuary, plus furniture and paintings from the 17th-20th centuries. After visiting this sight, turn left at the cathedral's rear for a short walk down rue Cazade to a 17th-century mansion housing the **Musée Borda**, an art, archaeology, culture, and history museum on the Landes region.

From there, continue down rue Cazade to esplanade du Général-de-Gaulle, where you'll again see the *Fountaine Chaude*, now on your left. Turn right, then left off cours Julia-Augusta when you see a series of steps, which lead to a promenade along the city's former ramparts. The next set of steps to your right goes to the entrance of the **Parc Théodore-Denis**, built on a 4th-century Gallo-Roman fortification bordering the Adour River. The park road forking to the right takes you to a small Roman arena; the left fork goes to the middle of the park and paths along the river. Across from the park near the arena, there's a large sports complex where you can watch basketball, tennis, rugby, soccer, and other sports.

From the park, you can return to the *Gare SNCF* by crossing the *Pont des Arènes* at the north end, following its street to the avenue St.-Vincent-de-Paul, or by following the river back to the first bridge opposite the *Office de Tourisme* and retracing your steps to the station.

On your way back to the station, check out the interesting apse (altar end) of the **Église St.-Paul-les-Dax**, a small church half a mile from the *Gare SNCF* in the suburb of St.-Paul-les-Dax. Built in 1045 on the site of a Roman temple, the exterior of the apse (the only thing surviving of the original church) is laden with decorative Biblical scenes on its walls and buttresses. The rest of the church is from the 17th century, with a 19th-century tower. To reach this sight, follow avenue St.-Vincent-de-Paul past avenue de la Gare and the railroad tracks, then go left on rue Gambetta for three blocks.

Restaurants

Au Fin Gourmet, 3 rue Pénitents, moderate, tel. 58-74-04-26.

Taverne Karlsbrü, 11 avenue Georges-Clemenceau (south of the *Parc Theodore-Denis* via boulevard St.-Pierre; or, from the *Cathédrale*, the continuation of rue St.-Vincent/rue St.-Pierre), inexpensive, tel. 58-74-19-60.

L'Amphitryon, 38 cours Galliéni (from the rear of the *Cathédrale*, turn right on rue l'Eveche, then right again two blocks later), moderate, tel. 58-74-58-05.

Restaurant de Boulogne, allées Bois de Boulogne (a short distance outside the city; the lovely, wooded setting makes the taxi ride worth it), moderate, tel. 58-74-23-32.

Hotels

Hôtel Terminus, 163 avenue St.-Vincent-de-Paul, inexpensive, tel. 58-74-02-17.

Hôtel Nord, 68 avenue St.-Vincent-de-Paul, inexpensive, tel. 58-74-19-87.

Splendid-Hôtel, cours Verdun (connected to the *Thermes Splendid* near the *Office de Tourisme*), moderate, tel. 58-56-70-70.

Hôtel Parc, 1 place Thiers, moderate, tel. 58-74-86-17.

Hôtel Dax-Thermal (connected to the *Dax-Thermal*), boulevard Carnot (after crossing the Adour River, turn right on quai du 28th-Batillon-de-Chasseurs/allée des Baignots, then left on rue Le Vannier, then right), moderate, tel. 58-90-19-40.

Sights Worth Seeing Nearby

Dax is a TGV crossroads: Its line from Bordeaux continues south to **Bayonne, Biarritz, St.-Jean-de-Luz, Hendaye,** and **Spain;** another line heads east to **Pau, Lourdes,** and **Tarbes.**

Bayonne

Flanking the Adour and Nive Rivers in the southwest corner of France, Bayonne is a pretty town, with picturesque river quais, narrow streets, and several interesting sights. Since its discovery by the Romans in the 3rd century, Bayonne has been an important military outpost and a prosperous port. It may also be the most non-French city in France. Over 75% of its 43,000 residents are of Basque heritage, and many prefer *euskara*, the Basque dialect, over proper French.

TGV Travel from Paris

Five TGV trains travel daily from Paris to Bayonne. The 485-mile trip takes four hours, 36 minutes. The *Gare SNCF* is at place St.-Esprit, north of Bayonne and the Adour River in the suburb of St.-Esprit. Currently, the last TGV back to Paris leaves at 19:09.

Tourist Information Office

The *Office de Tourisme* is in the arcaded, 18th-century *Hôtel de Ville* on the west side of place de la Liberté. To get there, cross place St.-Esprit to the small *Église St.-Esprit* and pass it to the long *Pont St.-Esprit* over the Adour River to place du Réduit. From there, follow the right side of the place past a small park to the *Pont Mayou*, the first bridge over the narrow Nive River. The large, square building to your right is the *Hôtel de Ville*.

Tour of Historic Sights & Major Attractions

Separated by its two rivers, Bayonne is divided into three distinct areas. **Grand Bayonne** is south of the Adour River and west of the Nive River; **Petit Bayonne** is south of the Adour and east of the Nive; and the suburb **St.-Esprit** is north of the Adour. These titles are important, in case you need to ask for directions.

From the *Hôtel de Ville*, there are excellent views of the river traffic on the **Adour River.** Other good river views are available from place

Charles-de-Gaulle across the street and the riverside **Jardin Public,** one block further west. Beyond the park off allées Marine, the local port authority gives free tours of the river weekdays from 10:00-noon and 14:00-16:00.

After watching the action on the river, return to the *Hôtel de Ville* and walk south of place de la Liberté on the narrow, pedestrians-only rue du Port-Neuf (filled with boutiques, pastry shops, and cafés) to rue Orbe. Two blocks to the right on this street, the restored **Château-Vieux,** built in 1100 on the foundation of the original Roman ramparts, was the former residence of François 1er and other Bayonne rulers. From its four corner towers, there are fine views of Bayonne and its rivers. Looking west, you can see the elaborate ramparts (built by Vauban in the 17th century) that protected the west side of the *Château.* You can also see how the ramparts swing south of the city and resume across the Nive River to protect the east side of town. No longer used for defense, portions of the ramparts have been turned into a promenade as part of Bayonne's municipal park system.

After exploring the *Château,* continue south on rue des Gouverneurs to the **Cathédrale Ste.-Marie,** one of the finest cathedrals in southwest France and a Bayonne landmark. This 13th-century edifice, built in the northern French Gothic style, has soaring vaults, graceful lines, and twin spires. One of the pointed spires is from the original structure; the other was added in the 19th century. Although its stained glass windows are primarily restored works, the Renaissance window in the second chapel to the right of the entrance, picturing a woman kneeling before Jesus and his disciples, dates from 1531.

Petit Bayonne harbors the city's important museums. From the right rear side of the *Cathédrale,* follow rue Poissonnerie to the Nive River and cross on the *Pont Pannecau,* turning left on quai Galuperie to its intersection with rue Marengo. On this corner, the **Musée Basque,** the best museum in France for learning about Basque culture and history, showcases regional costumes, Basque architecture, paintings, an exhibit on Basque maritime activities, and a library with over 10,000 books, including nearly everything published about the Basques or written by Basque authors. On the top floor, the **Musée de la Pelote** focuses on the history of the popular game created by the Basques, similar to handball. You'll see people playing this lively game on outdoor courts throughout Bayonne.

From this museum, follow quai des Corsaires north along the Nive River to place du Réduit, then slant right to rue Frédéric-Bastiat, one street from the Adour River. One block later (at the corner of rue Jacques-Laffitte), you'll come to the **Musée Bonnat,** a small art museum named for Bayonne resident Léon Bonnat, a 19th-century portrait artist, art collector, and teacher whose students included Toulouse-Lautrec, Munch, and Braque. Bonnat's work, plus paintings by Degas, David, Goya, El Greco, Rubens, van Dyck, Rembrandt, Tiepolo, and da Vinci, are on display.

Wine connoisseurs can sample the heavy Basque liqueur *Izarra*, made from raspberries, every day except Monday from 14:00-17:00 at the **Izarra Distillery** in St.-Esprit. The distillery's official address is 9 quai Amiral-Bergeret, but the entrance for the tour is on rue Belfort, one street from the river. To get there from the north end of the *Pont St.-Esprit*, turn right at the tiny square Gambetta, follow the river for 3-4 blocks, go left on rue Ulysee-Darracq or rue de l'Este, then right on rue Belfort.

To return to the *Gare SNCF* from there, backtrack to the bridge, then head right past the *Église St.-Esprit*. If you have time, take a look at the six-pronged, Vauban-designed **citadel** (1680) behind the station. Its entrance is off rue Ste.-Ursule, which borders the tracks.

Restaurants

Le Taniere, 53 avenue du Capitaine-Resplandy (facing Petit Bayonne at the *Pont St.-Esprit*, follow the Andour River quais left for a mile), moderate, tel. 59-25-53-42.

Auberge Cheval Blanc, 68 rue du Bourg-Neuf (narrow street south of place Réduit in Petit Bayonne), moderate-expensive, tel. 59-59-01-33.

Restaurant Irintzinia, 9 rue Marengo (off quai des Corsaires in Petit Bayonne, opposite second bridge over the Nive River), inexpensive.

Euzkalduna, 61 rue Pannecau (opposite third bridge over the Nive River), moderate, tel. 59-59-28-02.

Beluga, 15 rue Tonneliers (off quai Galuperie in Petit Bayonne, between rues Marengo and Pannecau), moderate-expensive, tel. 59-25-52-13.

La Chistera, 42 rue du Port-Neuf, moderate, tel. 59-59-25-93.

Chez Jacques, 17 quai Amiral-Jauréguiberry (follow the Grand Bayonne quais along the Nive River almost to the fourth bridge, the *Pont du Génie*), inexpensive-moderate, tel. 59-25-66-33.

Le Saint Simon, 1 rue des Basques (at the south end of quai Amiral-Jauréguiberry, turn right to next street), moderate, tel. 59-59-13-40.

Hotels

Hôtel Côte Basque, 2 rue Maubec (exit left from the *Gare SNCF*), inexpensive-moderate, tel. 59-55-10-21.

Hôtel Bordeaux, 4 rue Maubec, inexpensive-moderate, tel. 59-55-04-07.

Hôtel Lousta, 1 place de la République (past the *Église St.-Esprit*), moderate, tel. 59-55-16-74.

Hôtel des Basques, 4 rue des Lisses (from place du Réduit, follow rue Bourg-Neuf in Petit Bayonne for five blocks, then go right; the modern *Église St.-André* and the fort *Château-Neuf* are across the street), inexpensive, tel. 59-59-08-02.

Hôtel des Arceaux, 26 rue du Port-Neuf, inexpensive, tel. 59-59-15-53.

Grand Hôtel Aux Deux Rivières, 21 rue Thiers (connects the *Hôtel de Ville* and place Charles-de-Gaulle with the *Château-Vieux*), moderate, tel. 59-59-14-61.

Sights Worth Seeing Nearby

The famed Atlantic Ocean resort of **Biarritz** is only six miles southwest of Bayonne. You can get there via TGV, non-TGV trains, bus #1 from the *Gare SNCF,* or bus #2 from the *Hôtel de Ville*. The *Office de Tourisme* has route maps and schedules.

Biarritz

A household word with the jet set, Biarritz offers fabulous beaches, luxurious casinos, beautiful people, fine wine, and exceptional food. What more could you need? A suitcase of money, maybe?

Surprisingly, no. Despite its reputation, you don't have to be rich and famous to enjoy Biarritz. People-watching is free, and so is walking on the soft, sandy beaches. And, believe it or not, the town has a few affordable hotels and restaurants for the budget traveler.

Before Biarritz turned to flash and glitter, it was a Basque fishing village made prosperous by the whaling industry. In 1854, Napoléon III built a palatial villa near Biarritz for his wife, the Empress Eugénie. Shortly thereafter, their friends were arriving for fun and sun, eventually building elaborate summer homes. Since then, this small city of 27,000 has been a magnet for the monied set and royal blood who prefer the Atlantic Ocean over the French Riviera.

TGV Travel from Paris

Five TGV trains travel daily from Paris to Biarritz. The 491-mile trip takes four hours, 46 minutes. The *Gare de Biarritz-la-Négresse* is off allée du Moura, four miles southeast of the city center. Currently, the last TGV back to Paris leaves at 18:59.

Tourist Information Office

The *Office de Tourisme* is at square d'Ixelles, just north of the *Hôtel de Ville*, at the intersection of avenues Édouard-VII, Louis-Barthou, and de la Marne. To get there from the train station, take bus #2 to the *Hôtel de Ville* stop. If you want to walk, follow avenue du Président-J.-F.-Kennedy/avenue du Maréchal-Foch/avenue Édouard-VII into the city.

Tour of Historic Sights & Major Attractions

The best way to view Biarritz is to follow the outline of its beaches. From the *Office de Tourisme*, walk west across avenue Édouard-VII to the Atlantic Ocean and the **Grande Plage**. In the summer, this beach is packed with sunbathers baking and surfers riding the large waves. Along quai de la Grande-Plage bordering the beach, there are numerous shops, cafés, souvenir stands, and the *Casino Municipal*. If you desire solitude, try several beaches to the north beyond Pointe St.-Martin, the narrow spur that juts into the ocean.

Halfway to Pointe St.-Martin at the north end of the *Grande Plage*, the beach-front **Hôtel du Palais** was the villa/palace built for Empress Eugénie. Complete with grand halls, marble columns, elaborate staircases, tapestries, chandeliers, and art nouveau decor, it continues to reflect its noble grandeur and remains Biarritz's most sumptuous hotel. But note: Dress up before visiting, since the management is not keen on non-paying tourist-types gawking about the property in shorts and flip-flops.

In the other direction from the *Grande Plage*, follow the quai south around a bend to the right. Across the street, you'll see the 1920's Art Deco **Casino Bellevue**. To enter, you'll need your passport and 100 francs (the entrance fee), which you can exchange for 50 francs in chips for the gaming tables.

Walk beyond the casino along boulevard du Maréchal-Leclerc to the picturesque fishing harbor **Port des Pêcheurs**, protected by rock jetties. Small boats dance on the water, and numerous bistros at the waterfront offer seafood and Basque specialties. Across the street from the port, in the oldest section of the city, the **Église Ste.-Eugénie** is dedicated to the empress.

From there, walk a little farther along the port, then turn right on esplanade de la Vierge, which leads to the **Rocher de la Vierge**, a small, rocky island connected to the mainland by a narrow footbridge. From its cliffs, you get great views of the Atlantic coastline. En route to the bridge, you'll pass the **Musée de la Mer**, a small museum with displays of North Atlantic marine life and models of Basque fishing vessels. Below you is the **Plage du Port-Vieux**, a rocky inlet with a sheltered beach, usually packed in the summer. Walk south beyond these sights via boulevard du Prince-de-Galles to another crowded summer beach, the **Plage de la Côte des Basques**. If you didn't pack your swimsuit, backtrack to the port to explore the maze of narrow streets entering place du Port-Vieux, the heart of the former fishing village.

To return to the *Gare de Biarritz-la-Négresse*, follow rue Mazagran or the narrow rue de Proutze behind the *Église Ste.-Eugénie* to place Georges-Clemenceau. At the end of this long place is avenue Maréchal-Foch, where you can catch a bus back to the train station.

Restaurants

L'Operne, 17 avenue Édouard-VII (near the *Office de Tourisme*), moderate, tel. 59-24-30-30.

Le Sully, square d'Ixelles at avenue Joseph-Petit, moderate, tel. 59-24-16-47.

La Gascogne, 11 avenue du Maréchal-Foch, inexpensive, tel. 59-24-43-84.

Café de Paris, 5 place Bellevue (behind the *Casino Bellevue*), expensive, tel. 59-24-19-53.

L'Alambic, 5 place Bellevue (shares kitchen with *Café de Paris*), moderate, tel. 59-24-53-41.

Belle Epoque, 10 avenue Victor-Hugo (street leading south from place Georges-Clemenceau), moderate, tel. 59-24-66-06.

Le Zouloo, 6 rue du Port-Vieux (street across from the beginning of esplanade de la Vierge), inexpensive.

Hotels

Hôtel Etche Gorria, 21 avenue du Maréchal-Foch (across from the *Jardin Public*), inexpensive-moderate, tel. 59-24-00-74.

Hôtel Président, place Georges-Clemenceau, moderate-expensive, tel. 59-24-66-40.

Hôtel Plaza, avenue Édouard-VII at avenue Joseph-Petit, moderate-expensive, tel. 59-24-74-00.

Hôtel Windsor, quai de la Grande-Plage, moderate-expensive, tel. 59-24-08-52.

Hôtel Océan, 9 place Ste.-Eugénie (on east side of the *Église Ste.-Eugénie,* across from the *Port des Pêcheurs*), moderate-expensive, tel. 59-24-03-27.

Hôtel Florida, 3 place Ste.-Eugénie, moderate, tel 59-24-01-76.

Hôtel Port Vieux, 43 rue Mazagran, inexpensive, tel. 59-24-02-84.

Sights Worth Seeing Nearby

The TGV continues south from Biarritz to the small fishing ports of **St.-Jean-de-Luz** and **Hendaye** at the Spanish border.

South Central France & the Pyrénées

Agen

Halfway between Bordeaux and Toulouse, this small market city is famous for two disparate items: prunes and a rugby team. With the large Garonne River on its west side, Agen is also a major port for the region's agricultural goods. Travelers will find it worth a brief stop to see the Goya and Corot masterpieces in its art museum and to watch a busy provincial city at work.

TGV Travel from Paris

Two TGV trains travel daily from Paris to Agen. The 446-mile trip takes four hours, three minutes. The *Gare SNCF* is at place Rabelais on the north side of town. Currently, the last TGV back to Paris leaves at 18:24.

Tourist Information Office

The *Office de Tourisme* is at 107 boulevard du Président-Carnot, a mile away on the street leading away from the *Gare SNCF.*

Tour of Historic Sights & Major Attractions

First, head straight for Agen's main sight: the set of five oil paintings by Goya (including a self-portrait) in the fine arts museum (simply called the **Musée**). Housed in four half-timbered, 16th-century townhouses in the center of the city, the museum also features Corot's famous painting *Pond at Ville d'Avray*, several pieces from 18th-century European artists, some good Impressionist work, paintings by lesser-known Cubist and Surrealist artists, and the *Venus du Mas*, a Hellenistic marble statue found in the region.

To get there, continue half a block down boulevard du Président-Carnot from the *Office de Tourisme* to rue de Raymond. Turn right, then veer left one block later onto rue des Droits-de-l'Homme. After passing the *Église Notre-Dame-du-Bourg*, the street becomes rue Chaudordy. It ends at place de l'Hôtel-de-Ville, and the *Musée* is on your right, with the 17th-century **Hôtel-de-Ville** on your left.

For a close look at the **Garonne River**, exit the Musée past the *Hôtel-de-Ville* to rue des Colonels-Lacuée. When this street ends, turn right and follow rue Mirabeau to cours Gambetta and the riverside **Esplanade du Gravier**. At this park's other end, step onto the narrow, pedestrians-only bridge for a distant view of the 1839 **Pont-Canal**, a special bridge that takes boats on the *Canal Latéral à la Garonne* across the Garonne River. The same canal parallels the railroad tracks. (Before you board the next train, take a closer look at the canal by crossing the tracks on the overhead walkway next to the station.)

Walk back to quai Baudin along the river, toward the canal bridge, until you come to rue Baudin. Turn right on this street, which widens two blocks later to become boulevard de la République, one of Agen's main business streets. A half-mile down, you'll pass the small place Laitiers, where a lively food market runs every morning.

Buy some treats for the next leg of your trip, then cross the street to rue des Cornières, which leads through the **Quartier des Cornières**, Agen's old quarter, filled with half-timbered, brick homes, some dating from the 13th century. When the street ends at rue des Augustins, a right turn takes you to the **Cathédrale St.-Caprais**, a Romanesque and Gothic structure built from the 12th-16th centuries.

From there, you can continue wandering through the narrow streets in the old quarter or return to the *Gare SNCF* by following rue Raspail (in front of the *Cathédrale* entrance) to its end at boulevard Sylvain-Dumon. The station is two blocks to the right.

Restaurants

Lamanquié, 66 rue Camille-Desmoulins (on the *Office de Tourisme* route, turn left on rue La Fáyette/rue Camille-Desmoulins), moderate, tel. 53-66-24-35.

L'Absinthe, 29 bis rue Voltaire (turn right off boulevard de la République), moderate, tel. 53-66-16-94.

Le Voltaire, 36 rue Voltaire, moderate, tel. 53-66-37-65.

Hotels

Hôtel Coq d'Or, 96 boulevard du Président-Carnot, inexpensive, tel. 53-66-05-33.

Hôtel Ibis, 105 boulevard du Président-Carnot, moderate, tel. 53-47-31-23.

Hôtel Provence, 22 cours du 14-Juillet (exit left from the *Gare SNCF* onto boulevard Sylvain-Dumon [soon bears to the right] for a half-mile to place du 14-Juillet, then right for two blocks), moderate, tel. 53-47-39-11.

Sights Worth Seeing Nearby

Several small towns in the scenic **Dordogne** region are under two hours north of Agen on non-TGV trains.

Montauban

The pretty city of Montauban, situated on a hill overlooking a wide bend in the Tarn River, 32 miles north of Toulouse, is best known in France as the birthplace of the 19th-century artist Jean-Auguste Dominique Ingres (1780-1867). Founded in 1144 by the Count of Toulouse, Montauban is also one of the oldest *bastides* in southwest France. Distinguished by a grid of streets surrounding a central square, *bastides* were planned communities (with their own militia) that a local noble or lord had built to maintain his power in the area.

With the Tarn River providing access to the Atlantic Ocean (via the Garonne River), Montauban quickly became a successful port, exporting silk and other textiles. Several centuries later, it was a hotbed of Protestant revolt in the Midi-Pyrénées region. After several unsuccessful sieges by Louis XIII's troops in 1621—which reduced much of the city to rubble—Montauban eventually returned to Catholicism in 1629, since all its allies were defeated. Today, with a population of 53,000 and the river no longer navigable by large boats, Montauban has settled for being a major market town, the administrative capital of the Tarn-et-Garonne department, and an important railroad junction.

TGV Travel from Paris

Two TGV trains travel daily from Paris to Montauban. The 489-mile trip takes four hours, 41 minutes. The *Gare Ville-Bourbon* is along rue Robert-Salengro in the small suburb of Ville-Bourbon, a short distance west of the Tarn River and Montauban. Currently, the last TGV back to Paris leaves at 17:48.

Tourist Information Office

The *Office de Tourisme* is on the north side of Montauban, almost two miles from the *Gare Ville-Bourbon* in the *Ancien Collège* building at the junction of boulevard Midi-Pyrénées, place Prax-Paris, and rue du Collège. Since all the town's sights are near the river and city center, you really don't need to visit the tourist office unless you want information on the region. Directions to the office are in the tour below.

Tour of Historic Sights & Major Attractions

Montauban's most important sight is the **Musée Ingres**, a fine arts museum and depository for several paintings and over 4,000 drawings the artist bequeathed to the city upon his death. Housed in a 1664 Episcopal bishop's palace, its best paintings are *Christ and the Doctors*, completed when Ingres was 82, and the pale blue *Dream of Ossian*, commissioned by Napoléon for his bedroom.

More important than the paintings, Ingres' drawings distinctly illustrate his techniques and the progression to a finished painting. Some are merely scribbled sketches, others are quite elaborate. Lacking space, the museum displays just a small selection of the drawings each month, but it does allow visitors to view the entire collection upon advance request.

The museum also has a few paintings by Ingres' contemporaries— David, Delacroix, Géricault, and Granet—from Ingres' personal collection. The ground floor of the museum is devoted primarily to the work of two other Montauban-born artists, sculptor Antoine Bourdelle (1861-1929), who has a museum of his sculpture in Paris, and Desnoyner, an unexceptional 20th-century landscape artist. In the basement, you'll find lapidary, historical, and archaeological collections, plus a set of medieval torture instruments.

To reach the *Musée Ingres*, cross rue Robert-Salengro in front of the train station to avenue Mayenne and walk a half-mile to the intersection of avenue Aristide-Briand, place Marty, and the Tarn River. Before crossing the river, admire the 14th-century, seven-arched *Pont Vieux*, with its diamond-pattern pavement that alternates between black basalt and granite stones. The museum is on the other side of the bridge and to the right, at 19 rue de la Mairie.

Just a few blocks past the Musée Ingres (exit right) is the *Hôtel de Ville*, and even farther down the same street is the large **Cathédrale de Notre-Dame**. This mid-1700's Classical cathedral, framed by two towers, is constructed from white brick, a unique contrast to the rest of the city, which was built primarily from the pink brick characteristic of the region. Although the *Cathédrale*'s exterior is quite plain, duck inside to see *The Vow of Louis XIII*, an interesting painting by Ingres commemorating the King's fight against the Protestants.

North of the *Cathédrale* entrance and place Franklin-Roosevelt, follow the narrow rue de la Résistance for two blocks to rue Michelet. If you turn right, then walk left three blocks later at boulevard Midi-Pyrénées to its end, you'll hit the *Office de Tourisme*. A left turn at rue Michelet takes you to Montauban's most intersting architectural sight, the semi-enclosed **place Nationale**. This square, with the buildings of each corner set at right angles, was rebuilt in the 17th-18th centuries. in the Classical Italian style, with a unique, triple row of covered arches now occupied by shops, restaurants, and cafés. Beginning with a lively fruit and vegetable market each morning, the square is a hub of activity throughout the day and evening.

From the lower west corner of place Nationale, follow a short sidestreet (continuation of rue Michelet) to the 14th-century **Église St.-Jacques**, the oldest church in Montauban. After the Catholics reclaimed the city in 1629, it was used as the city's cathedral until the *Cathédrale de Notre-Dame* was built. Cannon fire during the 1621 siege created the gouged holes in its belfry.

Just a few blocks south of the church, across square Général-Picard and bordered by a narrow park, you'll see the *Musée Ingres* and the *Pont Vieux*. To return to the *Gare Ville-Bourbon*, retrace your steps across the river to the avenue Mayenne.

Restaurants

Restaurant La Cuisine d'Alain, in the Hôtel Orsay across from the *Gare Ville-Bourbon*, moderate-expensive, tel. 63-66-06-66.

Le Ventadour, 23 quai Ville-Bourbon (at the *Pont Vieux* and place Marty, turn right), moderate, 63-63-34-58.

Chapon Fin, 1 place St.-Orens at the *Pont Neuf* bridge in Ville-Bourbon (cross rue Robert Salengro to the right from the train station and follow avenue Jean-Jaurès to the river), moderate-expensive, tel. 63-63-12-10.

Le Temps des Cerises, 20 rue d'Auriol (a short north-south street at the northeast corner of place Nationale), inexpensive, tel. 63-63-20-68.

Le Pitzou, 24 rue de la Comédie (turn left off rue d'Auriol), moderate, tel. 63-63-02-83.

Ambroisie, 41 rue de la Comédie (turn left off rue d'Auriol or follow rue Mary-Lafon north from the *Église St.-Jacques*), moderate-expensive, tel. 63-66-27-40.

Hotels

Hôtel Ingres, 10 avenue Mayenne, moderate, tel. 63-63-36-01.

Hôtel du Commerce, 9 place Franklin-Roosevelt, inexpensive, tel. 63-66-31-32.

Hôtel du Midi, 12 rue Notre-Dame (street along the north side of the *Cathédrale*), inexpensive-moderate, tel. 63-63-17-23.

Hôtel de la Poste, 17 rue Michelet, inexpensive, tel. 63-63-05-95.

Sights Worth Seeing Nearby

On a narrow bend in the Lot River, 38 miles north of Montauban, the small city **Cahors** features buildings dating to the 11th century and the 14th-century *Pont Valentré*, the best example in France of a medieval fortified bridge. There is frequent non-TGV train service to this location.

Toulouse

With easy access to the rest of France and Europe through its waterways, the Garonne River and the *Canal du Midi*, Toulouse has been an important commercial center for France from its earliest history as a 3rd-century Roman outpost. Today the fourth-largest city in France and the capital of the Midi-Pyrénées region, Toulouse leads the nation in scientific research, with many companies headquartered there in the aviation (the Airbus and Concorde are built there), electronics, biotechnology, and telecommunications industries. These prosperous companies have helped Toulouse become the fastest growing city in France. With a diverse population of over 355,000, which includes 60,000 university students and immigrants from Spain and North Africa, the city is eclectic and ever-changing.

Despite its big city problems, Toulouse projects a provincial atmosphere and relaxed pace, with leisure as important as work. Throughout the day, you'll see people strolling the tree-lined *allées*, relaxing along the river banks, and convening at sidewalk cafés for an afternoon beverage and conversation. Aside from the friendly residents, part of the city's warmth comes from its moderate climate, and the pastels cast by its red-brick buildings, which appear "pink at dawn, red in the noonday sun, and mauve at dusk."

TGV Travel from Paris

Two TGV trains travel daily from Paris to Toulouse. The 521-mile trip takes five hours, ten minutes. The *Gare Matabiau* is along boulevard Pierre-Sémard opposite the *Canal du Midi* on the northeast side of town. Currently, the last TGV back to Paris leaves at 17:21.

Tourist Information Office

The *Office de Tourisme* and *Accueil de France* are in the center of the city in a former dungeon, across from the *Capitole*. To get there, exit the *Gare Matabiau* across the *Canal du Midi*, then go left for three blocks on boulevard de Bonrepos along the canal until you come to allées Jean-Jaurès, the main business street, lined with fancy hotels, restaurants, and chic boutiques. Turn right and follow this wide, divided street until it ends at the traffic circle place Wilson (a.k.a. square La Fayette), where you'll find additional cafés and shops. Walk around the right side of the circle to rue Lafayette, which takes you a block later to square Charles-de-Gaulle on your left. The *Office de Tourisme* is on the other side at the top left corner of the square.

To help you avoid the temptation of all the fancy shops, buses #17, 21, and 22 travel from the intersection of boulevard de Bonrepos and allées Jean-Jaurès to the *Capitole*.

Tour of Historic Sights & Major Attractions

Across from the *Office de Tourisme* is the **Capitole**, the former seat and palace of the *capitouls* (city council members) of Toulouse. Still used as the *Hôtel de Ville*, it's also home to the city's symphony orchestra. Take a quick look inside to see the frescoes that illustrate the history of Toulouse, then skirt around the north side and turn right two blocks later onto rue du Taur. Just a few steps down this street is the 14th-century southern Gothic **Église Notre-Dame-du-Taur** (Our Lady of the Bull). The five-story belfry built into the façade inspired similar architecture in churches throughout the Midi-Pyrénées region, which were built for both religious services and defense from invaders.

At the end of the street, the brick-and-stone **Basilique St.-Sernin**, the city's oldest church, was named after the priest who introduced Christianity to Toulouse in the 3rd century. Unfortunately, he wasn't a big hit with the local population—he was executed by being dragged through the streets tied to a bull. (The place where the rope broke is the location of the *Église Notre-Dame-du-Taur*.) Built from 1080-96 and restored in the late 1800's by Viollet-le-Duc, the basilica is the largest existing Romanesque church in France. (During the Middle Ages, it was second in size to the church in Cluny.) Though Romanesque, it has the unusual feature of a double aisle with five naves, plus a 360-foot octagonal, double-arched, five-tiered bell tower crowned by a pointed roof. Stone carvings, 11th-century sculpture, and various paintings—as well as the tombs of the Counts of Toulouse and the relics of 128 saints, plus a thorn purportedly from the crown of Jesus—decorate the interior. Near the entrance of the church, the **Musée Raymond**, Toulouse's archaeological museum, contains one of the finest collections of Imperial busts outside Rome.

From there, return to the *Capitole* on rue du Taur, turn right on rue Romiguières, then left two blocks later at rue Lakanal. Halfway down, next to a large school, you'll find the **Église et Monastery les Jacobins** set slightly back from the street. You can reach the main entrance by following the driveway between the church and school to place des Jacobins. Founded in 1215 to train priests to fight the Cathar heresy, it features an aisle-less, 13th-century Gothic church, a coffer beneath the altar with the bones of Thomas Aquinas (1225-74), 14th-century frescoes decorating the cloister, and a 144-foot spireless bell tower that is yet another fine example of the southern Gothic architectural style. In the 1800's, the complex was used as a cavalry barracks, with horses stabled in the church.

Next, continue south on rue Lakanal and turn right on rue Jean-Suau to visit the **Église Notre-Dame-la-Daurade** on quai de la Daurade, opposite the Garonne River. This small church, one of the earliest in

Toulouse, was rebuilt in the 1700's on the site of its 5th-century foundation. Its tower is the second-highest (266 feet) in town. Directly across
the river, you can see the **Hôtel-Dieu St.-Jacques**, a 17th-century
hospital with a Classical dome.

From the church, follow quai de la Daurade south along the river
for a block and turn left by the *École des Beaux Arts* on rue Tabac,
which crosses rue Peyroliéres, to rue de l'Écharpe and the **Hôtel d'Assezat**. Architects consider this elegant mansion, built for a wine mer-
chant, to be the finest among 50 *Hôtel Particuliers* that have survived
the centuries. Built in 1555 during the Renaissance, when Toulouse was
one of the richest cities in Europe, it has a courtyard decorated with
several types of columns and a tower joining its two chief buildings.
Today, it's home of the **Académie des Jeux-Floraux**, Toulouse's
oldest literary society. The *Office de Tourisme* has a descriptive list of
other *Hôtel Particuliers* in the city, including the nearby **Hôtel d'Ol-
mières** (3 rue Peyroliéres), one of the city's oldest mansions.

From the *Hôtel d'Assezat*, exit to the left, then walk left around the
block on rue de la Bourse/rue Ste.-Ursule. Four blocks later, turn right
on rue du May, where you'll find the **Musée du Vieux Toulouse**,
a small museum documenting the history and culture of Toulouse. From
there, backtrack down rue de la Bourse until it ends, then turn left on
rue de Metz.

Three long blocks later at the corner of rue d'Alsace-Lorraine, you'll
come to the **Musée des Augustins**, Toulouse's fine arts museum.
Housed in a 14th-century cloister with a 19th-century addition designed
by Viollet-le-Duc, its outstanding collection of paintings includes works
by Toulouse-Lautrec, van Dyck, Rubens, Ingres, Delacroix, and Corot.
It also has a collection of sculpture, capitals taken from Romanesque
and medieval architecture, an early Christian sarcophagus, and a gallery
devoted to Toulouse artist Antoine Rivalz (1667-1735). (If you need to
return to the Capitole area, rue d'Alsace-Lorraine is a direct route.)

Walk along the other side of rue de Metz a few more blocks and take
a right on rue Boulbonne to the fortress-like **Cathédrale St.-Etienne**.
Built from the 11th-17th centuries, this cathedral reflects an unattractive
conglomeration of styles, though it does boast a 13th-century rose window copied from the *Cathédrale de Notre-Dame* in Paris, a Flamboyant
Gothic choir, and a 16th-century rectangular bell tower.

Explore the interior, then exit to the right on rue Riguepels, following
the streets bordering the left and rear of the *Cathédrale* to allées François-
Verdier, one of the wide boulevards circling the city. A right turn leads
to the **Grand Rond**, one of the prettiest traffic circles in France. The
formal **Jardin Royal** is on the right, and straight through the circle
and to the right (off allées Frédéric-Mistral) is Toulouse's prettiest park,

the **Jardin des Plantes**. The **Musée d'Histoire Naturelle** and the medical and pharmacy schools of Toulouse University border the park's north side.

If you turn left off the *Grand Rond* onto allées Paul-Sabatier and walk a long block, you'll come to the **Canal du Midi**. From Toulouse, the canal flows east to Carcassonne, Beziers, and its terminus at the Mediterranean Sea, and west as the *Canal Latéral à la Garonne*, joining the Garonne River a short distance south of Bordeaux. The *Gare Matabiau* is about two miles from there. To get there, just follow the canal or take bus #14, which stops two blocks away at the bridge crossing.

Restaurants

Flunch, 28 allées Jean-Jaurès, inexpensive.

Cafeteria Casino, place Wilson, inexpensive, tel. 61-22-52-62.

La Frégate, 16 place Wilson, expensive, tel. 61-21-59-61.

Vanel, 22 rue Maurice-Fonvielle (turn left off place Wilson [facing the *Capitole*] onto rue St.-Antoine, then take the first left), expensive, tel. 61-21-51-82.

Le Grand Café de l'Opéra, 1 place du Capitole (in the *Grand Hôtel de l'Opéra* off the square behind the *Capitole*), moderate, tel. 61-21-37-03.

Place du May, 4 rue du May (turn left off place du Capitole onto the pedestrians-only rue St.-Rome, then right), inexpensive, tel. 61-23-98-76.

Auberge Louis XIII, 1 bis rue Tripiere (two blocks beyond rue du May off rue St.-Rome), inexpensive.

Les Caves de la Marchale, 3 rue Jules-Chalande (turn left off rue St.-Rome opposite rue du May), inexpensive, tel. 61-23-89-88.

Au Coq Hardi, 6 rue Jules-Chalande, inexpensive, tel. 61-21-61-01.

Brasserie Beaux Arts, 1 quai de la Daurade (at the corner of rue de Metz), moderate, tel. 61-21-12-12.

La Barigourde, 8 rue Mage (one block past the *Musée des Augustins*, turn right off rue de Metz onto rue des Arts/rue Tolosane/rue Mage), moderate, tel. 61-53-07-24.

Rôtisserie des Carmes, 11 place des Carmes (from the *Musée des Augustins*, cross rue de Metz to rue du Languedoc and walk for a short distance until you see the covered market), moderate, tel. 61-52-73-82.

Hotels

Hôtel Victoria, 76 rue de Bayard (street leading away from the *Gare Matabiau* and *Canal du Midi* bridge), moderate, tel. 61-62-50-90.

Hôtel Le Concorde, 16 boulevard de Bonrepos, moderate, tel. 61-62-48-60.

Hôtel Terminus, 13 boulevard de Bonrepos, inexpensive-moderate, tel. 61-62-44-78.

Hôtel Orsay, 8 boulevard de Bonrepos, moderate, tel. 61-62-71-61.

Hôtel Bordeaux, 4 boulevard de Bonrepos, inexpensive, tel. 61-62-41-09.

Hôtel President, 45 rue Raymond-IV (at rue Bayard, turn right on boulevard de Bonrepos, then take the first left), moderate, tel. 61-63-46-46.

Hôtel Raymond IV, 16 rue Raymond-IV, moderate, tel. 61-62-89-41.

Hôtel Mermoz, 50 rue Matabiau (turn left off boulevard de Bonrepos, one block past rue Raymond-IV), moderate, tel. 61-63-04-04.

Hôtel Athénée, 13 rue Matabiau, moderate, tel. 61-63-10-63.

Sights Worth Seeing Nearby

If you make it to this region, you really should not miss either the fortress city **Carcassonne** (62 miles east), or **Albi** (47 miles northeast), with the *Musée Toulouse-Lautrec*, the southern Gothic *Cathédrale de Ste.-Cecile*, and the picturesque Tarn River. From Toulouse, there's frequent non-TGV train service to Carcassonne and two daily trains to Albi.

Pau

Situated in a valley on the Gave de Pau River within a prosperous agricultural region, Pau is a key component in the French economy, thanks to the large natural gas deposits nearby. It's also the largest city in the Pyrénées Mountains region (130,000 residents), the capital of the Pyrénées-Atlantique administrative department, a major university center for southwest France, home to one of France's largest army bases, and a cultural center for the region. For sightseeing, the city offers Henri IV's château, an interesting old quarter, good museums, a pretty park, and a casino. Despite its proximity to the mountains, the climate is usually mild, even in the winter.

TGV Travel from Paris

Five TGV trains travel daily from Paris to Pau. The 506-mile trip takes four hours, 57 minutes. The *Gare SNCF* is between the wide Gave de Pau River and the narrow l'Ousse River on the south side of town. Two short bridges from the station lead to avenues de la Gare and Gaston-Lacoste. Currently, the last TGV back to Paris leaves at 18:05.

Tourist Information Office

The *Office de Municipal de Tourisme* is next to the *Hôtel de Ville* across from the north end of place Royale. It's a short distance from the *Gare SNCF* via the free funicular (across from the station) that runs to boulevard des Pyrénées and the south side of place Royale. There are exceptional views of the Pyrénées Mountains from the boulevard.

Tour of Historic Sights & Major Attractions

Overlooking the river from Pau's highest point is the 12th-century, six-towered **Château de Pau**, where Henri IV was born in 1553. Known as the Protestant King of Navarre, Henry is most famous for invoking the Edict of Nantes, which gave Protestants the freedom to worship. After his assassination in 1610, France began two centuries of despotic rule. Enlarged in the 13th and 14th centuries, the *Château* was redecorated in the 1800's under orders of Louis-Phillipe and Napoléon III. Its interior features over 100 Gobelins and Flanders tapestries, painted ceilings, several ornate chandeliers, period furnishings, and two museums: The **Musée Nationale** consists of Henri IV memorabilia and the reconstructed apartments of Napoléon III and his wife Eugénie. The **Musée Bearnais** is a combination costume, crafts, archaeology, and natural history museum. To reach the *Château*, follow rue Henri IV from the *Office de Municipal de Tourisme* until it ends at the *Château*, or walk down boulevard des Pyrénées, which skirts its south side.

Nearby, Pau's restored **Hédas Quarter** features many restaurants and nightclubs in its old buildings. To travel through the heart of the *Quarter*, exit left from the *Château* on rue du Château, which soon curves to the right, then turn left on rue Bordenave-d'Abére, right on rue Tran, right on rue Fontaine, and left on the narrow rue Hédas, which passes beneath several streets. In the same quarter, at the tip of a triangular-shaped block where rue Tran ends, the **Musée Bernadotte** is dedicated to Napoléon's Maréchal Jean-Baptiste Bernadotte, who became King Charles XIV of Sweden in 1810. Housed in a two-story, 18th-century townhouse (Bernadotte's birthplace), the collection contains documents, pictures, medals, and other memorabilia about this French hero, plus Louis XVI furniture and period furnishings.

After touring the *Quarter*, follow rue des Cordeliers (past the museum across the street to the right) over rue Hédas (stairs at the bridge lead down to this street) to rue du Maréchal-Joffre. Turn left and follow the street across the left side of place Georges-Clemenceau, the heart of Pau's business district, to rue du Maréchal-Foch. A few blocks later, after the street becomes cours Bosquet, turn right on rue Mathieu-Lalanne, where you'll find the **Musée des Beaux-Arts**, a small art museum with excellent work by El Greco, Rubens, Velasquez, and Degas, plus an impressive collection of contemporary art. One interesting gallery ("*La Salle des Femmes*") is devoted to 19th-century paintings of women. Behind the museum, the city's **Bibliothèque** has an impressive collection of over 150,000 books, some from Henri IV's reign (1594-1610).

Before returning to the *Gare SNCF,* relax in the 30-acre, English-inspired

Parc Beaumont, reached by continuing down rue Mathieu-Lalanne from the *Musée des Beaux-Arts* until it ends at boulevard Barbanègre. One long block to the left from there, past the *boules* court, is a street entrance to the park. After entering the park, turn right on allée Alfred-de-Musset, passing the **casino** on the southwest corner of the park. To return to the *Gare SNCF* from there, walk out of the park to the east end of boulevard des Pyrénées. Just down this street, stairs on the left lead to avenue Napoléon-Bonaparte, which ends at avenue de la Gare, opposite the station. You can also follow boulevard des Pyrénées back to the funicular station.

Restaurants

Au Fin Gourmet, 24 avenue Gaston-Lacoste (across from the *Gare SNCF*), moderate, tel. 59-27-47-71.

Pyrénées, place Royale, moderate-expensive, tel. 59-27-07-75.

Au Fruit Defondu, 3 rue Sully (turn left off rue Henri IV, three blocks from place Royale), inexpensive, tel. 59-27-26-05.

Chez Maman, 6 rue du Château, inexpensive, tel. 59-27-59-88.

Chez Olive, 9 rue du Château, moderate, tel. 59-27-81-19.

Restaurant, O'Gascon, 13 rue du Château, inexpensive, tel. 59-27-64-74.

Le St.-Jacque, 9 rue du Parlement (turn right off rue du Château), moderate, tel. 59-27-58-97.

La Gousse d'Ail, 12 rue du Hédas, moderate, tel. 59-27-31-55.

Flunch, 2 rue Maréchal-Joffre (from the *Office de Tourisme*, follow rue St.-Louis along the *Hôtel de Ville* to rue du Maréchal-Joffre), inexpensive.

L'Agripaume, 14 rue Latapie (off the southeast corner of place Georges-Clemenceau), moderate, tel. 59-27-68-70.

Hotels

Hôtel Ronceraux, 25 rue Louis-Barthou (near place Royale on the east extension of rue Henri IV), moderate, tel. 59-27-08-44.

Hôtel Ossau, 3 rue Alfred-de-Lassence (one long block from place Royale on rue Louis-Barthou, then left; the other end of the street is place Georges-Clemenceau), inexpensive, tel. 59-27-07-88.

Hôtel Central, 15 Léon-Daran (turn left off rue Louis-Barthou a half-mile from place Royale), moderate, tel. 59-27-72-75.

Hôtel le Bearn, 5 rue du Maréchal-Joffre, inexpensive, tel. 59-27-52-50.

Grand Hôtel du Commerce, 9 du Maréchal-Joffre, moderate, tel. 59-27-24-40.

Hôtel le Bourbon, 12 place Georges-Clemenceau, moderate, tel. 59-27-53-12.

Hôtel Continental, 2 rue du Maréchal-Foch, moderate, tel. 59-27-69-31.

Sights Worth Seeing Nearby

For a closer view of the **Pyrénées Mountains**, travel south by rental car for 35-40 miles on the N134/D934 highways to the west edge of the **Parc National des Pyrénées Occidentales**, one of France's six national parks. With altitudes from 3,200-11,000 feet above sea level, the park has hiking trails for every skill level—including the GR 10, which traverses the entire east-west length of the Pyrénées Mountains from the Mediterranean to the Atlantic. During the winter, several ski resorts in the area offer slopes as challenging as any found in the more crowded Alps. Pau's *Office de Tourisme* has general trail maps and more information about the park.

At the conflux of three mountain rivers in the foothills of the Pyrénées, the ancient Basque village **Oloron-Ste.-Marie** is 32 minutes southwest of Pau on a non-TGV train. This small town has a few 12th-century churches, an old quarter with 15th-18th-century houses, and several lovely mountain views. And don't leave without buying a béret there, since béret-making is one of the local industries.

Lourdes

Today the site of one of the world's most famous religious pilgrimages, Lourdes was once a nondescript village in the foothills of the Pyrénées Mountains. Its personality changed dramatically on February 11, 1858, when 14-year-old Bernadette Soubirous claimed to have had visions of the Virgin Mary in a nearby cave. As word spread, the Catholic Church turned the cave into a shrine, and people began to arrive seeking healing and other miracles. Though over 5,000 "miracles" were reported between 1878-1978, the Church recognizes only 64 as genuine. But this hardly discourages the faithful: over five million people travel to Lourdes each year, making it a gold mine for the townspeople who run the hotels and sell tacky souvenirs and religious icons by the truckload.

The prime pilgrimage months are April-October, with August 15th the busiest day, when over 100,000 people come for the Marian Feast of the Assumption. The second busiest day is September 30, the anniversary of St. Bernadette's death. (She gained sainthood in 1933.)

TGV Travel from Paris

Five TGV trains travel daily from Paris to Lourdes. The 530-mile trip takes five hours, 23 minutes. The *Gare SNCF* is at the east end of avenue de la Gare on the north side of town. Currently, the last TGV back to Paris leaves at 17:39.

Tourist Information Office

The *Office Municipal de Tourisme* is in the center of the city on the south end of place du Champ-Commun. Since it is far from the main sights, a visit there is unnecessary unless you desire more information about the region. To get there, exit right from the *Gare SNCF* on avenue de la Gare for one long block, then go left for about two miles on the main north-south street, chaussée Maransin (listed on some maps as avenue Général Baran-Maransin)/rue St.-Pierre/rue Lafitte.

Tour of Historic Sights & Major Attractions

From the *Gare SNCF,* cross chaussée Maransin (or just follow the crowd) and fork left on boulevard de la Grotte to its intersection with place Jeanne-d'Arc. From there, bear right on boulevard de la Grotte to the *Pont St.-Michel* and cross over the Gave de Pau River to the **Cité Religieuse.** Past the statue of St.-Michel, take either fork of the tree-lined *Esplanade des Processions* to the **Grotto des Apparitions.** At the back of the Grotto, to the left of the altar, is the "healing spring" that welled up during Bernadette's ninth vision. Its water is collected in giant reservoirs for the public to sample, believers hoping a mere touch will cure their ailments. If you're staying overnight, don't miss the evening service, a captivating sight of thousands of pilgrims carrying candles on the route to the Grotto and churches.

To your left on the way to the Grotto, you'll pass the massive, modern **Basilique-souterraine Missions St.-Pie X,** completed in 1958 to celebrate the centenary of the visions. Resembling a stadium, this oval, semi-underground building is the largest church in the world, with seating for over 20,000.

Next to the Grotto, the **Basilique Supreme du Rosaire,** a Roman-Byzantine-inspired church built from 1876-1908, seats over 4,000 and has 15 chapels dedicated to the rosary. Just east, the **Rosaire,** a 230-foot-high bell tower, was built in 1876 to resemble a 13th-century Gothic tower.

From these sights, follow rue Monseigneur-Théas to the right to place Monseigneur-Laurence, where you'll find the **Musée Bernadette,** containing exhibits documenting the saint's life. Not far from there, as boulevard de la Grotte begins to curve left, the **Musée Notre-Dame** offers more relics from Bernadette's life.

After visiting the museums, follow boulevard de la Grotte back across the *Pont St.-Michel* to the east side of Lourdes. At rue du Bourg, turn right, then turn right soon again up the narrow rampe du Fort. At the top of this driveway, the **Château-Fort de Lourdes** protected the town during the 12th-century Wars of Religion and other Middle Ages battles, only to be drastically remodeled for use as an army prison from 1820-80. Little remains of the original structure, but visit for the panoramic view of the *Cité Religieuse* across the river and the Pyrénées Moun-

258 / South Central France & the Pyrénées

tains to the south. Inside the fort, the **Musée Pyrénéen** showcases regional crafts and costumes, including dolls in various nuns' habits. Scale models of the varieties of architecture in the region are displayed in the courtyard.

To return to the *Gare SNCF* from there, follow rampe du Fort down to rue Bourg/place Jeanne-d'Arc and retrace your steps to the station.

Restaurants

L'Ermitage, boulevard de la Grotte at avenue Bernadette-Soubirous (after crossing the *Pont St.-Michel*, bear left), moderate, tel. 62-94-08-42.

Taverne de Bigorre, 21 place du Champs-Commun, moderate, tel. 62-94-75-00.

Please note: Most hotels in Lourdes, including those listed below, have a restaurant on their premises.

Hotels

Hôtel Beauséjour, 16 avenue de la Gare, moderate, tel. 62-94-38-18.

Hôtel Lutétia, 19 avenue de la Gare, moderate, tel. 62-94-22-85.

Hôtel Majestic, 9 chaussée Maransin, moderate, tel. 62-94-27-23.

Hôtel Acropolis, 5 boulevard de la Grotte (just across chaussée Maransin), moderate, tel. 62-94-23-18.

Hôtel Ambassadeurs, 66 boulevard de la Grotte (near the *Pont St.-Michel*), moderate, tel. 62-94-32-85.

Hôtel Excelsior, 83 boulevard de la Grotte, moderate, tel. 62-94-02-05.

Hôtel Gallia, 26 avenue Bernadette-Soubirous (a few steps south of the *Cité Religieuse*), expensive, tel. 62-94-35-44.

Hôtel Notre-Dame de France, 8 avenue Peyramale (a short distance south of the *Cité Religieuse*; turn left at the *Pont St.-Michel*, follow quai St.-Jean for a mile, cross the *Pont Vieux*, then go left for a block), moderate, tel. 62-94-91-45.

Hôtel Gave, 28 avenue Peyramale, moderate, tel. 62-94-90-11.

Hôtel Christina, 42 avenue Peyramale, moderate, tel. 62-94-26-11.

Sights Worth Seeing Nearby

Five miles west of the *Gare SNCF,* **Lac de Lourdes** is a scenic country spot—great for escaping the crowds and enjoying some water sports. To get there, turn right on chaussée Maransin, then, after passing beneath the railroad tracks, left on boulevard Commandant-Célestin-Romain. Stay on this street until you turn left on chemin du Lac. This is the D940 highway to Pau, so you might consider trying to hitch a ride.

Some of the highest peaks of the **Parc National des Pyrénées Occidentales** are accessible 25-30 miles south of Lourdes by rental car on the N21, D920, and D921 highways. The *Office de Tourisme* has basic trail maps for the park and information about ski resorts. If you don't have a car, you can still get a good view of the mountains by taking a taxi or following avenue Maréchal-Foch/avenue Francis-Lagardère south of the *Office de Tourisme* for about three miles to the funicular station. The cable car goes to the 3,110-foot summit of the *Pic du Jer* for a magnificent view of the mountains—all the way into Spain.

Tarbes

One of the Pyrénées region's economic leaders and the birthplace of World War I hero Ferdinand Foch, Tarbes is located in the upper valley of the Ardour River, where the rich soil yields bountiful harvests of wheat and maize. It is the major agricultural market for the area as well as an industrial center, with several engineering and chemical companies. With its lush valleys, Tarbes is also famous for breeding championship race horses. A compact town with 54,000 residents, Tarbes makes a delightful half-day's exploration.

TGV Travel from Paris
Five TGV trains travel daily from Paris to Tarbes. The 543-mile trip takes five hours, 41 minutes. The *Gare SNCF* is along avenue du Maréchal-Joffre on the north side of town. Currently, the last TGV back to Paris leaves at 17:22.

Tourist Information Office
The *Syndicat d'Initiative* is in the middle of the triangular place de Verdun in the center of town. To get there, cross avenue du Maréchal-Joffre to rue Victor-Hugo, follow it half a mile, then turn left on rue Georges-Lassalle for three blocks to place de Verdun.

Tour of Historic Sights & Major Attractions
From the *Syndicat d'Initiative*, backtrack up rue Georges-Lassalle, then turn left on rue Raymond. The 18th-century mansion at the end of this short street (at the corner of rue de la Victoire) is the **birthplace of Maréchal Ferdinand Foch**, the most popular military hero of World War I. (Almost every city in France has a street named after him.) Opened in 1951 as a public museum, the exhibits and memorabilia in each room show a different period of his life, with special emphasis on his illustrious military career. His study and battle room show his plans for recapturing the Alsace and Lorraine regions from Germany. Another room is devoted solely to the gifts he received after the war from the grateful French people.

From Foch's home, cross rue Victoire, then turn right onto the wide rue de la Abbé-Torné. The 12th-century **Cathédrale Notre-Dame-de-la-Sede**, a few blocks down, features excellent Gothic vaulting and furnishings from the 1700's.

A few blocks south of the *Cathédrale*, the **Haras National** is the national stud farm, where some of the best racing horses in France are raised and trained. To get there, turn right off rue de la Abbé-Torné at the rear of the *Cathédrale* onto rue des Ursulines, which leads to promenade du Pradeau, overlooking the farm's race track and pasture. To reach the main entrance of the farm for a tour of the stables, turn left (facing the farm) on promenade du Pradeau, walk to a narrow passageway that leads to rue des Pyrénées, then go right for a half a mile.

From the stud farm, follow rue des Haras away from its entrance to allées Général-Leclerc, a large promenade featuring a statue of Foch at its south end. From there, cours Gambetta dividing the promenade travels to place de Verdun. Walk along its left side to rue Massey, and three long blocks later you'll come to the west side of the beautiful **Jardin Massey**. Designed during the Middle Ages, it's one the oldest public parks in France. From there, follow the park's paths to the **Musée International des Hussards**, housed in an 18th-century Italianate villa. Dedicated to the history of the modern cavalry, the museum has an interesting collection of uniforms, swords, and equipment from the U.S., France, and other European countries.

From the north end of the *Jardin Massey*, the *Gare SNCF* is a few blocks down the street to the left.

Restaurants
Buffet de la Gare, 21 avenue du Maréchal-Joffre, moderate, 62-93-16-22.
L'Isard, 70 avenue du Maréchal-Joffre, moderate, tel. 62-93-06-69.
Panier Fleuri, 74 avenue du Maréchal-Joffre, moderate, 62-93-10-80.
Toup' Ty, 86 avenue Bertrand-Barère (another street leading away from the *Gare SNCF*), moderate, 62-93-32-08.
L'Amphitryon, 38 rue Larrey (crosses cours Gambetta at the top end of allées Général-Leclerc), moderate, tel. 62-34-08-99.

Hotels
Hôtel Excelsior, 38 avenue du Maréchal-Joffre, moderate, tel. 62-93-05-84.
Hôtel Terminus, 42 avenue du Maréchal-Joffre, moderate, tel. 62-93-00-33.
Hôtel Henri IV, 7 avenue Bertrand-Barère, moderate, tel. 62-34-01-68.
Hôtel Foch, 18 place de Verdun, moderate, tel. 62-93-71-58.

Sights Worth Seeing Nearby
Lourdes is 12 miles south.

CHAPTER 16

Northern France & Normandy

Amiens

The administrative capital of the Picardy region, Amiens has been a prosperous textile town since the Middle Ages. Since 60% of the city was destroyed by World War II air raids, it's one of France's more modern cities, evident in the utilitarian skyscrapers dotting the landscape and some haphazard urban planning. But who cares? It's the cathedral—the largest in France—you came to see.

TGV Travel from Paris

Currently, there are no TGV trains from Paris to Amiens. Rather, Amiens is on the direct TGV line to Lyon (and several locations in the French Alps), which bypasses Paris. As in Tours, where most of the TGV trains skirt around the city because of better rail access, in Amiens the TGV never enters the city. Instead, it stops three miles southeast in the suburb of **Longueau**.

Four TGV trains travel daily from Longueau to Lyon's *Gare de la Part-Dieu*. (Three of these trains stop at Lyon's *Gare de Perrache* as well.) The 380-mile trip takes three hours, 24 minutes. A fifth TGV train travels daily from Longueau to Grenoble (four hours, 28 minutes), Albertville, Bourg-St.-Maurice, Modane (five hours, 50 minutes), and other alpine villages (see Chapter 5). The *Gare SNCF* in Longueau is on rue Pierre-Sémard.

Railpass holders departing the TGV at Longueau can take one of the frequent commuter trains or other *Grand Lignes* trains to Amiens' *Gare du Nord*, located at place Alphonse-Fiquet. If you don't have a railpass, you must purchase a transfer between these two stations. Bus #9 also provides transportation between Longueau and the *Gare du Nord*. Currently, the last TGV back to Lyon leaves at 15:07.

Tourist Information Office

The *Office de Tourisme* is in the *Maison de la Culture* building near the intersection of rue Jean-Catelas and place Léon-Gontier, four blocks from place Gambetta (see tour below) via rue Delambre/rue Gresset. Buses #1, 2, 3, 4, and 8 travel from the *Gare du Nord* to the *Hôtel de Ville* on rue Delambre/rue Gresset. This office is two miles from the *Gare du Nord* and beyond the major sights, but there is a small annex at the train station entrance and at place Notre-Dame, opposite the *Cathédrale*.

Tour of Historic Sights & Major Attractions

The **Cathédrale de Notre-Dame**, built primarily from 1220-69, is the largest cathedral in France: 1,469 feet long, 230 feet wide, and topped by a 368-foot spire. One of the best examples of Gothic cathedral architecture in Europe, it miraculously escaped destruction during World War II; buildings surrounding it were reduced to rubble.

A thorough examination of its beauty and complex structure would take days, but you can get a satisfying taste in an afternoon. Start at the main entrance: Exterior highlights include three deeply recessed doorways elaborately decorated with statues and bas-relief sculpture of Biblical figures, including a 13th-century statue of Christ and an interpretation of the Last Judgment. Above the doorways are two galleries—the upper one, with statues of 22 French kings, is crowned in the center with a circular, 16th-century stained glass window flanked by two large towers. The north side of the *Cathédrale* offers more complex decorations and statues.

Inside, this marvel features a 141-foot-high vaulting supported by 126 pillars, bronze funeral effigies of the founding bishops, excellent 13th-century stained glass windows, over 4,000 Biblical figures carved by 13th-16th-century craftsmen, outstanding iron grill work, a 16th-century choir stall featuring 110 intricately carved spaces, and goldsmithing from the 12th century in the treasury.

The quickest way to reach the *Cathédrale* from the *Gare du Nord* is to exit across place Alphonse-Fiquet to the right on boulevard d'Alsace-Lorraine for one block, then turn left at rue Gloriette. Four blocks later (note that this street changes its name at every block: rue de l'Oratoire, rue Lefevre, and rue Cormont), you'll come to the rear of the structure.

Though you could leave Amiens' satisfied having seen only the great cathedral, the city does have other interesting sights. North of the *Cathédrale*, the **Quartier St.-Leu** is the oldest section of Amiens, flanked by the Somme River and several crisscrossing canals. The 15th-century buildings that line the narrow streets of the area (plus modern university buildings) fell into disrepair after World War II. Recently reclaimed by real estate developers, they are being restored for housing and businesses.

To reach the *Quartier*, exit the *Cathédrale* to the short rue André, which enters place Notre-Dame from the right corner, then turn right on rue Flatters/rue St.-Leu, or wander through any of the streets north of the *Cathédrale*. The small *Église St.-Leu* on rue St.-Leu, about a mile from the *Cathédrale*, is considered the center of the *Quartier*.

The **Hortillonages** (market garden), northeast of the *Cathédrale* across the Somme River from port d'Amont, is an interesting sight, where fruit and vegetables are grown and irrigated by branches of the Somme, tended by farmers from small punts. To get there from the *Cathédrale*, backtrack two blocks down rue Cormont/rue Lefevre, then turn left at rue des Augustins. Three long blocks later, the street ends at port d'Amont. For better views, turn right past the port, then left across the wide Somme River bridge, then right along chemin de Halage bordering the river.

To get there directly from the *Gare du Nord*, exit right on boulevard d'Alsace-Lorraine, which crosses the river. For a scenic trip, board bus #6 at the *Gare du Nord*, which travels down this boulevard past the Somme River, then west through the *Quartier St.-Leu*, with its final stop on rue des Sergents, near the *Cathédrale*.

The **Musée d'Art Local**, a few blocks south of the rear of the *Cathédrale* at 36 rue Victor-Hugo in the former Hôtel de Berny (a 1634 mansion), features art by local and regional artists, 17th-century furniture, and exhibits on the region's history. From November-April, the museum is open only on Wednesday, Saturday, and Sunday. The large building across the street is the city's *Palais de Justice*.

Further south, at 48 rue de la République, the **Musée de Picardie** is one of the best fine arts museums in northern France. Housed in a 19th-century building set back from the street, its collection features sculpture by Rodin, Bourdelle, and Barye, and paintings from the 15th-20th centuries, including works by El Greco, Tiepolo, Delacroix, Gauguin, Matisse, and Picasso. There's also has an interesting collection of 16th-century paintings on wood and some archaeological exhibits.

To get there, exit left from the *Cathédrale* entrance across place Notre-Dame to rue Dusevel. Stay on the left side of this street as it skirts through two major traffic intersections (rue des Sergents and place Gambetta) to become rue de la République heading south. (A right at place Gambetta onto rue Delambre leads to the *Office de Tourisme*.)

From the art museum, science fiction fans need to visit the **Musée Jules Verne**, devoted to the author who lived in Amiens most of his life. To reach the house where he lived and wrote most of his novels, exit right from the *Musée de Picardie* on rue de la République, then left on the wide *mail* (another name for "avenue") Albert-1er. One block later, turn right at the open parking area of place Longueville, then left at boulevard Jules Verne. The museum is four blocks away at the corner of rue Charles-Dubois. Verne is buried in the *Cimetière de la Madeleine* on the north edge of the city.

To return to the *Gare du Nord* from there, cross boulevard Jules Verne to the triangular place du Maréchal-Joffre (bus #8 goes to the station from there) and veer left through a short street opening to boulevard de Belfort. Turn right there and follow the street as it curves left to the north. The modern, 26-story *Tour Perret*, across from the station, is the most visible landmark to head toward.

Restaurants

Le Mermoz, 7 rue Jean-Mermoz (exit right from the *Gare du Nord*, then right two blocks later), moderate, tel. 22-91-50-63.

Couronne, 64 rue St.-Leu, moderate, tel. 22-91-88-57.

Les Marissons, 68 rue des Marissons (past the right side of the *Église St.-Leu*, over a canal, then right), moderate, tel. 22-92-96-66.

Le Prieure, 17 rue Porion (street south of the *Cathédrale*), moderate, tel. 22-92-27-67.

La Mangeoire, 3 rue des Sergents (intersects rue Dusevel near the *Cathédrale*; turn right), inexpensive, tel. 22-91-11-28.

Migmi, 44-50 rue des Trois-Cailloux (turn left off rue des Sergents at place Gambetta, past its intersection with rue Dusevel), inexpensive, tel. 22-91-48-27.

Josephine, 20 rue Sire-Firmin-Leroux (turn left off rue des Trois-Cailloux), moderate, tel. 22-91-47-38.

Hotels

Le Grand Hôtel d'Univers, 2 rue de Noyon (street entering boulevard de Belfort, south of the *Tour Perret*; exit left from the *Gare du Nord*), moderate, tel. 22-91-52-51.

Hôtel Carlton-Belfort, 43 rue de Noyon, moderate-expensive, tel. 22-92-26-44.

Hôtel Normandie, 1 bis rue Lamartine (turn right off rue de Noyon), moderate, tel. 22-91-74-99.

Sélect-Hôtel et Rhin, 69 place René-Goblet (west end of rue de Noyon), moderate, tel. 22-91-32-16.

Hôtel des Voyageurs, 7 rue Jean-Mermoz, inexpensive, tel. 22-91-50-63.

Sights Worth Seeing Nearby

If you're fascinated by Amiens' *Cathédrale*, don't miss the Gothic cathedrals in **Beauvais** (37 miles south of Amiens) and **Rouen** (50 miles south). There are non-TGV trains to both cities from Amiens and Longueau.

Arras

For centuries, Arras has been a place of prosperity and conflict. Just 32 miles south of Lille, it was an important center of tapestry manufacturing and other cloth industries during the Middle Ages. As these industries evolved, war erupted in Arras in the early 1400's. During the next five centuries, the town was in or near numerous battles and was bombarded and captured by half the armies of Europe. The wars finally ended when the Allies crushed the Nazis in 1945.

Despite the damage from these wars—especially in World War I, when Arras was an integral part of the front lines—much of this small city's historic architecture has survived. An aggressive post-World War II rebuilding program modernized the town, and its older buildings were restored to their Old World splendor. Today, after nearly five decades of peace, Arras is a modern city of 45,000 and one of northern France's economic leaders.

TGV Travel from Paris

There are currently no TGV trains from Paris to Arras. Rather, Arras is on the direct TGV line to Lyon (and several locations in the French Alps), which bypasses Paris. Four TGV trains travel daily from Arras to Lyon's *Gare de la Part-Dieu*. (Three of these trains also go to Lyon's *Gare de Perrache*.) The 398-mile trip takes three hours, 52 minutes. A fifth TGV train, which bypasses Lyon, travels daily from Arras to Grenoble (five hours, six minutes), Albertville, Bourg-St.-Maurice, Modane (six hours, 46 minutes), and other alpine villages (see Chapter 5).

The *Gare SNCF* is at place du Maréchal-Foch on the southeast side of town. Currently, the last TGV back to Lyon leaves at 14:37.

Tourist Information Office

The *Office de Tourisme* is in the *Hôtel de Ville* on the west end of place des Héros. To get there, cross to the left of the monument on place du Maréchal-Foch to the wide rue Gambetta. Walk two blocks, then turn right at the pedestrians-only rue Ronville/rue Wacquez-Glasson. Two blocks later, opposite the *Église St.-Jean-Baptiste*, turn left onto rue de la Housse, which empties into place des Héros, a smaller version of *Grande Place* (see tour below), lined with cafés, bars, restaurants, and shops in Flemish-inspired townhouses. The *Hôtel de Ville* is at the opposite end. Bus D travels from the *Gare SNCF* to this sight.

Tour of Historic Sights & Major Attractions

After visiting the *Office de Tourisme*, explore the **Hôtel de Ville**. This 15th-century building, which resembles a cathedral more than a town hall, was rebuilt in 1918 after a fire and other war damage. Set amid many Flemish-style buildings, it was built in the Gothic style, found throughout most of France, of its time. Inside, many of the ornate rooms are open for viewing, and an elevator will take you to the top of the 246-foot belfry for a great view of the city. And don't miss the basement, where you can take a tour of the intersecting tunnels and large caves beneath the building and place des Héros. Originally created to house chalk miners, they were later used as a shelter and hospital during both World Wars.

Just north of the *Hôtel de Ville*, connected by rue de la Taillerie at the other end of place des Héros, is the truly grand **Grande Place**. This large, cobblestone square, surrounded by 155 tall, narrow townhouses made from brick and stone with ornate gables, is the best example of 15th-18th-century Flemish architecture in France. At street level, arcades supported by sandstone pillars offer shade to patrons of the hotels, restaurants, cafés, and shops now occupying most of the lovely homes. Behind many pillars, trap doors lead to cellars used as hiding places during the various wars. A lively market runs there every Saturday, but otherwise this graceful square is usually empty. During World War I, the occupying German forces placed a barbed wire down the middle of the square to divide their front line from the French.

From its northwest corner, exit the *Grande Place* on rue Ste.-Croix and pass along the left side of place Guy-Mollet to rue du Marché-aux-Filet. Follow this street as it curves to the right, eventually running into the rear of the **Cathédrale St.-Vaast**. Built from 1783-1833, this huge structure is one of the best examples of Neoclassical architecture in France. Enter the *Cathédrale* from rue du Marché-aux-Filet or the main entrance off rue des Teinturiers, and examine the statues of the saints, a 17th-century bust of Christ in wood, and other 17th-18th-century art and sculpture.

Next door, stretching across the large square St.-Vaast to rue Paul-Doumer, the **Palais St.-Vaast** has quite a history. An 11th-century abbey, it was built on the foundations of a 7th-century monastery constructed to honor the 6th-century evangelist Saint Vaast. Destroyed by the Vikings in the 9th century and rebuilt three times after fires, the 11th-century structure was redesigned by Benedictine monks from 1741-80. Today, it houses the **Bibliothèque Municipale** and **Musée des Beaux-Arts**, whose collection includes interesting medieval sculpture, 16th-century triptychs, and some exceptional work by French artists Corot, Delacroix, and Dufy. Unfortunately, despite the city's fame for tapestry manufacture, the museum has only one 15th-century tapestry produced in Arras.

To return to the *Gare SNCF* from there, go to the far end of square St.-Vaast (where the museum ends), then left on rue Paul-Doumer/rue Émile-Legrelle/rue Pasteur to boulevard de Strasbourg. From there, angle right across the street to rue Chanzy, which ends at place du Maréchal-Foch, opposite the station.

Restaurants

Ambassadeur, in the *Gare SNCF*, moderate, tel. 21-23-29-80.

Chanzy, 8 rue Chanzy, moderate, tel. 21-71-02-02.

La Coupole, 26 boulevard de Strasbourg, moderate, tel. 21-71-88-44.

Restaurant la Modernite, 5 boulevard Carnot (wide boulevard angling into the *Gare SNCF* from the far left), inexpensive.

Victor Hugo, 11 place Victor-Hugo (turn left off boulevard Carnot onto boulevard Vauban, then right on rue Victor-Hugo to this circular place with an obelisk in its middle), moderate-expensive, tel. 21-71-84-00.

La Rapière, 44 Grande Place, moderate, tel. 21-55-09-92.

La Faisanderie, 45 Grande Place, expensive, tel. 21-48-20-76.

La Gare, 50 Grande Place, inexpensive, tel. 21-58-53-84.

Hotels

Hôtel Astoria, 12 place du Maréchal-Foch, moderate, tel. 21-71-08-14.

Hôtel le Rallye, 9 rue Gambetta, inexpensive, tel. 21-51-44-96.

Hôtel Moderne, 1 boulevard Faidherbe (wide street angling into the *Gare SNCF* from the right) moderate, tel. 21-23-39-57.

Hôtel les Grandes Arcades, 12 Grande Place (turn left off boulevard Faidherbe onto rue Paul-Périn), inexpensive, tel. 21-23-30-89.

Hôtel les 3 Luppars, 46 Grande Place, moderate, tel. 21-07-41-41.

Hôtel Univers, 3 place de la Croix-Rouge (turn left on the short rue des Jésuites off rue Gambetta/rue Ernestale), moderate, tel. 21-71-34-01.

Sights Worth Seeing Nearby

Five miles north of Arras at **Vimy Ridge**, 75,000 Canadian soldiers died fighting the Germans for over two years in World War I. To commemorate Canada's sacrifice, the battlefield has been preserved as it was during the war, including meandering trenches through grassy plains, underground shelters, and shell holes. Canadian students provide guided tours of the battlefield. To get there, rent a car and take the the N25 highway.

Lille

Just 15 miles from the Belgium border, Lille is the largest city in northern France (1.1 million in the greater metropolitan area) and the third-largest urban area in the country (behind Paris and Lyon). Formerly the capital of Flanders, Lille—or L'Isle, as it was known during the Middle Ages—was ceded to France in 1667 after nine days of siege by Louis XIV's troops.

Devastated by at least 11 sieges in its history and during the World Wars, Lille today is the most modern big city in France. It's also one of the country's most prosperous cities. Surrounded by thriving manufacturing facilities in its suburbs, Lille exports its goods worldwide.

TGV Travel from Paris

There are currently no TGV trains from Paris to Lille. Rather, Lille is on the direct TGV line to Lyon (and several locations in the French Alps), which bypasses Paris. Four TGV trains travel daily from Lille to Lyon's *Gare de la Part-Dieu.* (Three of these trains also go to Lyon's *Gare de Perrache*). The 424-mile trip takes four hours, 41 minutes. A fifth TGV train (which bypasses Lyon) travels daily from Lille to Grenoble (five hours, 45 minutes), Albertville, Bourg-St.-Maurice, Modane (seven hours, seven minutes), and other alpine villages (see Chapter 5).

Lille's *Gare SNCF* is at place de la Gare in the center of town. To coincide with the opening of the TGV Nord line in mid-1993, a new station will open off rue Le Corbusier, which runs along the north side of the current station.

Currently, the last TGV back to Lyon leaves at 13:59.

Tourist Information Office

The *Office de Tourisme* and *Accueil de France* are at place Rihour in the remains of the 15th-century *Palais Rihour*, not far from the *Gare SNCF*. Diagonally across from this office, the *Comité de Régional de Tourisme Nord-Pas de Calais* has more information about regional sights. To reach these offices, cross place de la Gare to rue Faidherbe. When this streets ends two blocks later at place du Théâtre, follow the sidewalk around the place to the left (the building to your right is the *Vieille Bourse*), then through a short, pedestrians-only street to place Rihour.

You can also get to place Rihour by boarding Lille's modern, fully automated subway. It stops at the *Gare SNCF*, place Rihour, place de la République (near the *Musée des Beaux-Arts*), and the suburbs.

Tour of Historic Sights & Major Attractions

According to art experts, Lille's **Musée des Beaux-Arts** is the second best art museum in France, behind the Louvre. Housed in a gorgeous 19th-century building, it has masterpieces primarily by Dutch, French, Italian, and Spanish artists from the 15th-20th centuries: Donatello, El Greco, Watteau, David, Monet, Renoir, Delacroix, Rousseau, Picasso, and many more. It also has two enormous altarpieces by Rubens, a fine collection of ceramics, and several Rodin sculptures.

To reach the museum directly from the *Gare SNCF,* exit to the left side of the station and cross rue de Tournai to rue du Molinel. Follow this street until it ends at the intersection of boulevard de la Liberté and place de la République. The museum is a block to your left. You can also get there on the subway.

To get there from the *Office de Tourisme,* follow rue Jean-Roisin one block north from place Rihour to rue Nationale. Turn left and stay on this street until you reach boulevard de la Liberté, where you'll turn left again. The *Musée des Beaux-Arts* is a mile down this street. You can also travel to the museum on the subway from place Rihour to the République stop, or on bus #68A along boulevard de la Liberté.

A half-mile south of the art museum, the **Musée d'Histoire Naturelle** features a large Egyptian mummy display, a weird mutant animals exhibit, an exhibit about the various geological forms found in Europe, and the usual stuffed animals. To get there, exit to the right of the art museum onto boulevard de la Liberté, walk one block, turn right on rue Jeanne d'Arc, then left on rue Malus.

To see an interesting monument, follow the left side of boulevard de la Liberté south for about six blocks to a large open intersection at boulevard Papin. Around the corner to the left, in the middle of the street, is the **Porte de Paris**, the second-largest triumphal arch in France, erected in honor of Louis XIV—despite protests from revolutionary residents. Bus #13 from the *Gare SNCF* stops at this location. Just beyond this monument to the right, the city's 1933 **Hôtel de Ville** features two giant statues at its doorway and a 459-foot bell tower, which you can climb for a panoramic view of the city.

In the opposite direction, one mile north of the *Musée des Beaux-Arts* (exit left on boulevard de la Liberté), Lille's large, star-shaped **Citadelle** was restored in the 17th century by Vauban. Considered by military historians to be Vauban's masterpiece, each side of the fortress is protected by earthworks, a moat, and a canal. Today, the outer grounds are used as a promenade and park, and there's a zoo near its entrance. Since the French army still uses the fortress, you must sign up for a group tour at the *Office de Tourisme* to see the interior. Bus #68A travels down boulevard de la Liberté from place de la République to boulevard Vauban, a block from the *Citadelle* entrance.

After touring the *Citadelle,* exit left from its entrance onto avenue Cuvier (before crossing the canal) and turn right one long block later across *Pont du Ramponneau*, then through square du Ramponneau to rue Léonard-Danel/rue d'Angleterre. Four blocks later, turn right on rue des Trois-Mollettes, which leads to the **Cathédrale de Notre-Dame-de-la-Treille**, an unfinished, 19th-century, Neo-Gothic structure. Although the architecture is hardly awe-inspiring, don't bypass it. Otherwise, you'll miss the **Musée Diocésain d'Art Religieux**, a small museum in the cathedral's crypt, with sacred art from the 17th-20th centuries.

One street behind the *Cathédrale* at 32 rue de la Monnaie is the **Musée de l'Hôspice Comtesse**, which you can enter free with your *Musée des Beaux-Arts* ticket. This 13th-century hospital contains a collection of old furniture, paintings, and interesting Flemish tile work on the walls. Outside, rue de la Monnaie (the former main street of old Lille) and neighboring streets feature brick and stone houses from the 17th and 18th centuries.

After exploring this area, you can return to the *Gare SNCF* on buses #3, 6, or 9, which travel in the neighborhood. By foot, exit left from the museum on rue de la Monnaie and veer around the corner to the right, where the street becomes rue des Chats-Bossus. At the next block, turn left onto rue de la Grande-Chaussée, which ends a block later at the intersection of rue Lepelletier and the north end of place du Théâtre. From there, follow the left side of the place past the city theatre to rue Faidherbe, which ends at the train station.

For a last-minute detour, turn right one block before you reach the station at rue des Ponts-de-Comines, then take the next left at the short, pedestrians-only rue Schepers to visit the **Église St.-Maurice**, a small Gothic church featuring five naves of equal height and a 14th-century tower. The *Gare SNCF* is behind the church to the right.

Restaurants

Le Féguide, place de la Gare, inexpensive, tel. 20-06-15-50.

Lutterbach, 10 rue Faidherbe, inexpensive-moderate, tel. 20-55-13-74.

Brasserie Jean, corner of rue Faidherbe and rue de Paris at place du Théâtre, inexpensive.

Alcide, 5 rue des Débris St.-Étienne (short street north of the *Vieille Bourse*), moderate, tel. 20-55-06-61.

Bistro Romain, 20-22 place Rihour, inexpensive, tel. 20-54-53-69.

Le Varbet, 2 rue de Pas (continuation of rue Jean-Roisin off place Rihour), moderate-expensive, tel. 20-54-81-40.

Le Club, 16 rue de Pas, moderate-expensive, tel. 20-57-01-10.

Le Flambard, 79 rue d'Angleterre, expensive, tel. 20-51-00-06.

La Petite Taverne, 9 rue du Plat (near the *Musée des Beaux-Arts*; turn left off rue du Molinel), moderate-expensive, tel. 20-54-79-36.

Flunch, rue de Béthune (turn right off rue du Molinel onto rue d'Amiens, then left two blocks later), inexpensive.

Hotels
Hôtel Paris Nord, 14 rue du Molinel, inexpensive, tel. 20-06-27-54.

Hôtel Ibis, avenue Charles-St.-Venan (turn right off rue de Tournai), moderate, tel. 20-55-44-44.

Hôtel Carlton, 3 rue de Paris (turn left off rue Faidherbe onto rue des Ponts de-Comines, then right), moderate-expensive, tel. 20-55-24-11.

Hôtel Paix, 46 bis rue de Paris (across the street from rue des Ponts de-Comines), moderate, tel. 20-54-63-93.

Hôtel Monte Carlo, 17 place des Reignaux (one block down rue Faid-herbe away from the *Gare SNCF,* turn right), inexpensive, tel. 20-06-06-93.

Hôtel l'Univers, 19 place des Reignaux, moderate, tel. 20-06-99-69.

Grand Hôtel Bellevue, 5 rue Jean-Roisin, moderate, tel. 20-57-45-64.

Hôtel de Strasbourg, 7 rue Jean-Roisin, inexpensive-moderate, tel. 20-57-05-46.

Sights Worth Seeing Nearby
About 70 miles west of Lille on the Atlantic coast, **Calais** is a major French shipping port and currently the most popular port for passenger ferries and Hovercraft to England—at least until the English Channel tunnel is completed. (Calais will become a TGV city when the TGV Nord line begins service through the English Channel Tunnel in late 1993.) If you have a long layover there, see Rodin's famous bronze sculpture *The Burghers of Calais,* in front of the city's *Hôtel de Ville.* Across the street in the *Parc St.-Pierre,* a camouflaged Nazi blockhouse is used as a war museum. Both sights are near the *Gare Centrale* (exit right). Over 20 non-TGV trains leave daily from Lille to Calais.

Versailles

One of the most awesome sights in France is the Palace of Versailles, the residence of the kings of France from 1682-1789 (Louis XIV, XV, and XVI). From the sumptuous living quarters to the meticulous land-scape of statue-lined paths, fountains, forests, canals, and gardens, the Palace displays almost unimaginable wealth. It's so big, you'll need at least two (and possibly more) days to tour all the buildings and grounds. If your time is limited, arrive early for a tour of the main Palace, then explore the grounds on your own until closing time.

TGV Travel from Paris
There are currently no TGV trains from Paris to Versailles. Rather, Versailles is on the direct TGV line to Lyon. Two TGV trains travel daily

from Versailles to Lyon's *Gare de la Part-Dieu* and *Gare de Perrache.*
The 274-mile trip takes two hours, 40 minutes. The *Gare Versailles-Chantiers* is off rue des Chantiers/rue des États-Genéraux, about a mile southeast of the Palace. Currently, the last TGV back to Lyon leaves at 15:16.

Tourist Information Office

The *Office de Tourisme* is at 7 rue des Réservoirs, a street alongside the north wing of the Palace. To get there, turn right before entering the Palace courtyard and follow the wrought iron fence and north minister's building along rue Robert-de-Cotte to the Palace building where the street turns right. The office is two blocks away at the intersection of rue Carnot. Maps of the Palace and grounds are available at the Palace ticket office.

Tour of Historic Sights & Major Attractions

To reach the **Palace of Versailles**, exit across the *Gare Versailles-Chantiers'* parking area to rue des États-Genéraux, then go left for half a mile to avenue de Paris. A left there takes you to place d'Armes, the huge square in front of the Palace. From there, you pass through a wrought iron gateway decorated with King Louis' coat-of-arms into a cobblestone courtyard.

After taking a guided tour of the Palace interior, examine the exterior and stroll through the main garden and forest, especially the **Neptune Basin** (to the right of the Palace), with its interesting fountain, and the **Apollo Basin** at the end of the wide esplanade leading away from the Palace. Then, if you have time, stroll along the **Grand Canal** and head for the smaller but elaborate **Petit** and **Grand Trianon Palaces** and Marie Antoinette's "Hamlet" play area, on the far corner of the Palace grounds.

Since Versailles is such an elaborate complex, deserving far more descriptive text than this book can include, you really should get a guidebook written specifically about it.

Restaurants

There are a few outdoor restaurants and food/beverage stands on the Palace grounds, plus a cafeteria inside. Since you'll probably spend the whole day there, pack a picnic lunch to avoid lunch-time crowds and gouge-the-tourists prices. For a better lunch/supper meal, try the restaurants below, all located between the Palace and train station.

Brasserie du Théâtre, 15 rue des Réservoirs, moderate, tel. 39-50-03-21.

Le Quai #1, 1 avenue de St.-Cloud (facing away from the Palace entrance, angle left across place d'Armes to this wide, divided street), moderate, tel. 39-50-42-26.

Le Pot au Feu, 22 rue de Satory (angle right across place d'Armes to avenue de Sceaux, then take the next right), moderate-expensive, tel. 39-50-57-43.

Potager du Roy, 1 rue du Maréchal-Joffre (extension of rue de Satory), moderate-expensive, tel. 39-50-35-34.

Hotels

Hôtel Paris, 14 avenue de Paris, inexpensive-moderate, tel. 39-50-56-00.

Bellevue Hôtel, 12 avenue de Sceaux (turn left off rue des États-Genéraux onto rue de Noailles to the foot of avenue de Sceaux), moderate, tel. 39-50-13-41.

Residence du Berry, 14 rue Anjou (from the foot of avenue de Sceaux, follow rue Charton for one block, then take the next right), moderate, tel. 39-49-07-07.

Hôtel Home St.-Louis, 28 rue St.-Louis (three blocks further on rue Charton, then right), inexpensive-moderate, tel. 39-50-23-55.

Sights Worth Seeing Nearby

Versailles is just 13 miles from **Paris**, accessible via non-TGV train from the *Gare Versailles-Chantiers* or a fast RER commuter train (C-5 line) from the *Gare Versailles-Rive Gauche*. To reach the RER station from the Palace, turn right off avenue de Paris onto avenue Général-de-Gaulle by a small park (one block before rue des États-Genéraux).

Chartres, 41 miles south of Versailles, is the home of the most outstanding Gothic cathedral in Europe. With an intricately sculpted doorway at its main entrance and two sharply spired towers, the 26,000-square-foot marvel features the largest collection of intact 12th-13th-century stained glass windows in Europe. Frequent non-TGV trains leave from the *Gare Versailles-Chantiers* to Chartres.

Rouen

The capital of the Haute Normandy region, Rouen is one of France's most historic cities. Just 87 miles west of Paris, Rouen has been home to Romans, Normans, and Vikings, plus William the Conqueror, Joan of Arc, Flaubert, and Monet. Though much of its medieval quarter was destroyed during World War II bombing raids, the town has been restored to its original look, with many of its streets turned into pedestrian malls.

Always valued for its strategic location on the Seine River, which bisects the city and empties into the Atlantic Ocean 20 miles away, Rouen is France's third-largest port and an important cog in the French economy. The large labor force in industries lining the river to the ocean has pushed the metro area's population to over 380,000.

TGV Travel from Paris

There are currently no TGV trains from Paris to Rouen. Rather, Rouen is on the direct TGV line to Lyon (and several locations in the French Alps), which bypasses Paris. Two TGV trains travel daily from Rouen to Lyon's *Gare de la Part-Dieu* and *Gare de Perrache*. The 352-mile trip takes three hours, 56 minutes. A third TGV train travels daily from Rouen to Albertville (five hours, 40 minutes), Moutiers, Aime-la-Plagne, and Bourg-St.-Maurice (six hours, 50 minutes), bypassing Mantes-la-Jolie, Versailles, and Lyon.

Rouen's *Gare Rive Droite* is at the triangular place Bernard-Tissot on the north side of town, two miles north of the Seine River. Currently, the last TGV back to Lyon leaves at 14:31.

Tourist Information Office

The *Office de Tourisme* and *Accueil de France* are at 25 place de la Cathédrale, across from Rouen's cathedral. Since most of the historic sights are between this office and the train station, directions are below in the walking tour.

Tour of Historic Sights & Major Attractions

Rouen's historic and restored **Vieux Quartier** is just over a mile from the *Gare Rive Droite*. To get there, cross place Bernard-Tissot to rue Jeanne-d'Arc (several buses travel down this street from the station), which gently slopes down to the Seine River. When you reach rue du Gros-Horloge, a narrow and crowded pedestrians-only street lined with half-timbered buildings, shops, cafés, and restaurants, turn right for two blocks to place du Vieux-Marché, where you'll find the modern **Église Ste. Jeanne-d'Arc**. The bronze cross and mosaic in the pavement identify the spot where Joan of Arc was tied to a stake and burned alive on May 30, 1431, after being indicted by an English-led court for heresy. Though they accused her of witchery for her religious visions, the English feared her even more for inspiring and rallying French knights to victory over their armies. The **Musée Jeanne-d'Arc** on the south end of the square traces her short life with a series of wax figures. On the last Sunday in May, the museum hosts an annual feast to commemorate her execution. At the west end of the square, the small **Musée Corneille** houses the works of Rouen-born playwright and poet Pierre Corneille.

Backtracking to rue Jeanne-d'Arc, cross the street to the other half of rue du Gros-Horloge, where you'll find the **Gros Horloge**, a large clock set into a wall above an archway. Placed there in 1527, this ornate, gilded Renaissance clock dating to 1390 is connected to a Louis XV sculpted fountain and bell tower, which you can climb for good views of the quarter. The clock still keeps accurate time, and at night, the bells ring.

Three blocks past the clock, rue du Gros-Horloge ends at the large, open place de la Cathédrale. The *Office de Tourisme* is around the corner to the right. In front of you across the place, the awesome **Cathédrale de Notre-Dame** was made world-famous by Claude Monet's impressionistic paintings. Built from 1201-1514, this massive Gothic edifice suffered some damage in World War II, but restorationists have done a remarkable job rebuilding it to resemble the original structure. The west façade of the *Cathédrale*, adorned with carved sculpture, is particularly interesting, with its two irregular towers rising high above the main entrance. The octagonal *Tour de Beurre* (right), erected in the 15th century, contains a carillon of 56 bells, while the *Tour St.-Romain* on the left (north) side is part of the original structure, as are two of its recessed doorways. The 500-foot, iron-and-bronze spire, placed atop the *Cathédrale* in the 19th century, is the tallest spire in France.

Inside, there are more elaborate Gothic decorations, excellent stained glass windows, and a medieval crypt with the tombs of ancient Rouen heroes: Rollo, Richard the Lionheart, Henri the Young King, Duke of Normandy William Longsword, and two Cardinals of Amboise. A coffer embedded in one wall holds the heart of King Charles V.

After exploring this sight, follow the pedestrians-only rue St.-Romain, filled with well-preserved 15th-18th-century homes, along the north side of the *Cathédrale* to rue de la République. Across this street, set back on a hidden square with crooked-timbered homes, is the **Église St.-Maclou**, built in 1200. Partially destroyed and rebuilt from 1437-1517, then heavily restored after World War II, this small church features 16th-century door panels that depict Biblical scenes and animals in the sculpted, semi-bas-relief style popular in the Renaissance. Behind it (via rue de Martinville), the **Aître St.-Maclou**, former charnel house of the church, is now a fine arts school. The wooden beams in this building have carvings from the 1400's.

From there, walk down rue de la République to the **Seine River**, where you can view the industrious river traffic. On the *Pont Pierre-Corneille*, cross the tip of the *Ile Lacroix* to the more modern side of Rouen. Steps at the bridge lead to the waterfront for a closer view of the river.

After a good look at the river, retrace your steps to the *Église St.-Maclou* and walk past it on rue de la République to the 14th-century **Église St.-Ouen**, a well-known Gothic building that's as big as many cathedrals. Actually an extension of a Benedictine abbey built in 535 (only a wing of the cloister remains), this church features a 375-foot Gothic, octagonal lantern tower and four turret towers. With decorations and stained glass windows from the 14th-18th centuries and a towering vault second only in height to one in the cathedral at Beauvais, it rivals the city's *Cathé-*

drale de Notre-Dame in beauty and is an important sight for students of Gothic architecture. The entrance is off rue des Faulx (turn right off rue de la République) through the Marmouset Portal. North of this church, in the abbey's former dormitory, is the **Hôtel de Ville**.

From the *Église St.-Ouen*, cross rue de la République to the pedestrians-only rue de l'Hôpital/rue Ganterie. Four blocks later at rue l'Écureuil, turn right for one block and cross rue Thiers to the small **Musée Le Secq des Tournelles**, where you'll find a unique wrought iron collection housed in the 15th-century *Église St.-Laurent*. Named after a Parisian aristocrat who started the collection in 1870, the museum has over 14,000 pieces of wrought iron and related metal work—from utensils to a balustrade from Madame de Pompadour's country mansion.

Across the street at 26 bis rue Thiers on the east end of the square Verdrel, the **Musée des Beaux-Arts**, an excellent art museum that opened in 1800, contains masterpieces primarily by French, Spanish, and Italian artists, including La Tour, David, Delacroix, Ingres, Velasquez, Caravaggio, Rubens, Fragonard, Corot, and Monet (including one of his famous Rouen Cathedral paintings). Separate galleries showcase the work of Rouen natives Théodore Géricault (1791-1824), one of the founders of the Romanticism art movement; Jacques-Emile Blanche (1861-1942), who painted portraits of 19th-20th-century intellectuals, writers, and musicians; and the Duchamp family (Marcel, Raymond, and their half-brother Jacques Villon), early 20th-century artists who influenced Cubism and modern art forms.

Ceramics was a major craft and industry for Rouen and the Normandy region during the 16th-18th centuries, so the city is the perfect locale for the **Musée de la Céramique**, one of the best ceramic collections in Europe. Housed in a 17th-century mansion one block west of the *Musée des Beaux-Arts* on rue du Bailliage, the museum features over 6,000 items, representing every French region and a few foreign countries. Individual galleries highlight Chinese ceramics from 1699-1745 and master faïence artists Masseot Abaquesne (1500-64) and Louis Poterat (1673-96). Your ticket for the *Musée des Beaux-Arts* also allows entry to this museum.

Two other museums to consider, each less than a mile north of the *Musée des Beaux-Arts* and *Musée Le Secq des Tournelles*, are the **Musée des Antiquities** and **Musée d'Histoire Naturelle**. To reach them, backtrack two short blocks down rue Thiers to rue Beauvoisine. Turn left and walk until you see the *Musée des Antiquities* at building #198. Housed in a 17th-century convent, this museum's collection is dominated by religious treasures dating back to the Middle Ages, plus medieval and Renaissance furniture and some Greek, Roman, and regional ceramics. The natural history museum is next door.

Fans of author Gustave Flaubert (*Madame Bovary*) may want to visit his birthplace, which has been turned into the **Musée Flaubert et d'Histoire de la Medecine.** Located at 51 rue de Lecat on the west side of town (next to the *Hôtel-Dieu*), this small museum unfortunately has few of Flaubert's possessions. Instead, it has family furniture and the medical paraphernalia that his father used as director of the adjacent hospital. To get there, follow the left side of rue Thiers (from square Verdrel) across rue Jeanne-d'Arc for about six blocks to place Cauchoise. Three blocks later, turn left at rue de Lecat, passing the horseshoe-shaped *Hôtel-Dieu* to the intersection with rue du Contrat-Social.

From all the museums, the easiest way to return to the *Gare Rive Droite* is to follow rue Jeanne-d'Arc from the west end of square Verdrel. One final sight, halfway between this square and the station via rue du Donjon (turn right), is the **Tour Jeanne-d'Arc,** where Joan of Arc was held during her trial. The authorities feared an escape attempt—she had already leapt over the wall of another castle where she was imprisoned, only to suffer several injuries—so she was chained to a heavy log in the dungeon and watched round-the-clock by five guards. Today, the three-story tower, set in a small garden surrounded by a moat, is the only structure left from a massive, 13th-century castle that occupied this location. In the dungeon, you can see the torture instruments Joan's accusers threatened her with and view exhibits on her life. There are also fine views of Rouen from the top of the tower.

Restaurants

Auberge de Vieux Carré, 34 rue Ganterie (turn left off rue Jeanne-d'Arc), moderate, tel. 35-71-67-70.

Pascaline, 5 rue de la Poterne (second right off rue Ganterie), moderate, tel. 35-70-56-65.

Flunch, 60 rue des Carmes (turn right off rue Ganterie; continuing south on this pedestrians-only street takes you to the *Cathédrale*), inexpensive.

Maison Dufour, 67 rue St.-Nicolas (street one block north paralleling the *Cathédrale*, connecting rue des Carmes with rue de la République), moderate, 35-71-90-62.

Les Flandres, 5 rue des Bon-Enfants (turn right off rue Jeanne-d'Arc; continuation of rue Ganterie), inexpensive, tel. 35-98-45-16.

Au Bois Chenu, 23 place de la Pucelle-d'Orleans (turn right onto rue du Gros-Horloge, then left at rue de la Vicomté), moderate, tel. 35-71-19-54.

Brasserie du Vieux-Marché, 2 place du Vieux-Marché, moderate, tel. 35-71-59-09.

La Vieille Auberge, 37 rue St.-Étienne-des-Tonneliers (turn left off rue Jeanne-d'Arc onto rue Général-Leclerc, take the first right at rue du Docteur-Rambert, then first left), moderate, tel. 35-70-56-65.

Marine, 42 quai Cavelier-de-La Salle (cross over the Seine River on the *Pont Jeanne-d'Arc*, then go right), moderate-expensive, tel. 35-73-10-01.

Hotels
Hôtel Astrid, place Bernard-Tissot, moderate, tel. 35-71-75-88.

Hôtel Dieppe, place Bernard-Tissot, moderate, tel. 35-71-96-00.

Hôtel Normandy, 32 rue du Cordier (at end of rue du Donjon past the *Tour Jeanne-d'Arc*, cross place Docteur-Alfred-Cerné to rue du Cordier), inexpensive, tel. 35-71-46-15.

Hôtel Carmes, 33 place des Carmes (heading south toward the *Cathédrale*, turn left off rue des Carmes), moderate, tel. 35-71-92-31.

Hôtel Gros-Horloge, 91 rue du Gros-Horloge, moderate, tel. 35-70-41-41.

Hôtel de Paris, 12 rue de la Champmeslé (almost to the Seine, turn left off rue Jeanne-d'Arc onto rue Général-Leclerc, then go right three blocks later), moderate, tel. 35-70-09-26.

Hôtel le Cardinal, 1 place de la Cathédrale, inexpensive, tel. 35-70-24-42.

Hôtel de la Cathédrale, 12 rue St.-Romain, moderate, tel. 35-71-57-95.

Sights Worth Seeing Nearby
Honfleur, 47 miles from Rouen on the Atlantic coast, is the most painted village in France. It's not served by regular train service, so the best way to get there is by rental car. Or, take the TGV (or other train) to Le Havre and transfer to bus #20 of the *Bus Verts du Calvados* line, which travels the Normandy coast eight times daily between Le Havre, Deauville, and Caen. Le Havre's *Gare Routière* is next to its *Gare SNCF.*

Halfway to Paris from Rouen, **Giverny** is a small village with Claude Monet's home and beautiful gardens. You can get there easily via a non-TGV train to Vernon, then take a taxi or a bus, rent a bicycle, or walk to Monet's home, four miles from the train station.

The Future of the TGV

There are four things certain about the TGV's future. First, it will break its current high-speed record. Second, it will expand its high-speed track network throughout France. Third, it will expand its network beyond France to other European countries. And, fourth, by accomplishing the above three, it will remain the best train system in the world.

With European countries beginning to merge economies and boundaries, the TGV will become increasingly important for travel in France and throughout the rest of the continent. Already serving five cities in western Switzerland, the TGV has lines being completed for travel in Spain and through the English Channel Tunnel ("Chunnel") to London. By 2015, experts estimate that the European train system will have over 12,000 miles of new high-speed track. With this network, all the major cities of Europe will be just a few hours away.

Listed below are various TGV projects, approved by the French government, that will be built during the next 20 years at an estimated cost of $31.5 billion.

These plans have specific dates for completion:

1. In early 1993, the TGV Atlantique will begin service from Paris to La Rochelle.

2. In mid-June 1993, the TGV Nord will begin service from Paris and the Roissy-Charles de Gaulle Airport to Longueau, Arras, Douai, Lille, and Calais.

3. In mid-June 1993, a 31-mile extension line running south of Paris will link the TGV Sud-Est and TGV Atlantique lines to the TGV Nord line.

4. In late 1993, the TGV Nord will travel through the English Channel Tunnel to Folkstone and London, England.

5. In early 1994, the TGV Sud-Est's new high-speed rail bypass will go around Lyon to Valence, with a stop at the Lyon-Satolas Airport.

6. In June 1994, the TGV Nord will stop at the Euro Disney Resort in the Paris suburb Marne-la-Vallée.

These plans have been approved and are in various stages of implementation:

7. Extension of the TGV Sud-Est high-speed line from Valence to Marseille to reduce travel time from Paris to three hours (high priority).

8. Extension of the TGV Sud-Est high-speed line from Avignon to the border of Spain.

9. New TGV Sud-Est high-speed spur line from Lyon to Chambéry.

10. New TGV Est route to provide direct service from Paris to Strasbourg, where the EEC has its headquarters (high priority).

11. New TGV Rhine-Rhône route to provide direct service from Mâcon to Dole, Besançon, Belfort, and Mulhouse.

12. New TGV Picardie route to provide direct service from Paris to Amiens (not Longueau) and Calais.

13. New TGV Normandy route to provide direct service from Paris to Rouen and Caen.

14. New TGV Riviera route to provide direct service from Aix-en-Provence to Frejus (near St.-Raphäel, currently served by the TGV).

15. New TGV Auvergne route to provide direct service from Paris to Nevers and Clermont-Ferrand.

16. New TGV Limousin route to provide direct service from Paris to Limoges, with a possible TGV spur line from Limoges to Poitiers.

17. New TGV Sud route to provide direct service from Bordeaux to Toulouse, Carcassonne, and Narbonne, and to link the TGV Atlantique with the TGV Sud-Est.

18. Extension of the TGV Atlantique high-speed line from Le Mans to Rennes.

19. Extension of the TGV Atlantique high-speed line from Le Mans to Angers.

20. Extension of the TGV Atlantique high-speed line from Tours to Bordeaux and Dax.

21. Using TGV technology, Spain recently opened high-speed rail travel from Madrid to Seville, with plans for a line from Madrid to Barcelona.

22. Extension of the TGV Sud-Est route to Barcelona, Spain.

23. Extension of the TGV Nord route to Belgium, The Netherlands, and northern Germany.

24. Extension of the TGV Est route to Luxembourg, central and southern Germany, and Zurich, Switzerland.

25. Extension of the TGV Sud-Est spur line (see #8) from Chambéry to Turin, Italy—through a 15-mile tunnel beneath the Alps.

26. Selling TGV technology elsewhere. Currently, customers include Spain, South Korea, and Texas in the U.S. Many other countries are looking to the TGV as a possible solution for their transportation problems.

About the Author

Mark Beffart is a writer and photographer in Atlanta. When he is not exploring France via the TGV, he writes articles about art, business, and travel for national magazines. He also writes corporate communications for several Atlanta companies and operates a stock photography business, selling his photographs to advertising agencies, books, magazines, and other publishers.

Index to Cities,
Towns & Islands

More Great Travel Books
from Mustang Publishing

Let's Blow thru Europe by Neenan & Hancock. The ultimate guide for the "15-cities-in-14-days" traveler, this is the funniest, most irreverent, and definitely most honest travel guide ever written. With this book, you can blow off the boring museums and minor cathedrals and instead find the great bars, restaurants, and fun stuff in all the major cities of Europe. *"A riot!"* —The Daily Northwestern (Northwestern U.). **$10.95**

Festival Europe! Fairs & Celebrations throughout Europe by Margaret M. Johnson. What's the best—and least expensive—way to interact with Europeans and their cultures? Attend their myriad festivals, celebrations, fairs, and parades, most of which are free! From the somber Holy Blood Procession in Bruges to the wild Oktoberfest in Munich, this guide will help any traveler have a terrific, festive time in Europe. *"An excellent book for the serious traveler."* —Bookviews. **$10.95**

Europe on 10 Salads a Day by Mary Jane & Greg Edwards. A must for the health-conscious traveler! From gourmet Indian cuisine in Spain to terrific take-out pizza in Italy, this book describes over 200 health food/vegetarian restaurants throughout Europe. *"Don't go to Europe without it"* —Vegetarian Times. **$9.95**

Europe for Free by Brian Butler. If you're on a tight budget—or if you just love a bargain—this is the book for you! With descriptions of thousands of things to do and see for free all over Europe, you'll save lots of lira, francs, and pfennigs. *"Well-organized and packed with ideas"* —Modern Maturity. **$8.95**

Also in this series:
London for Free by Brian Butler. **$7.95**
DC for Free by Brian Butler. **$6.95**
Hawaii for Free by Frances Carter. **$6.95**

The Nepal Trekker's Handbook by Amy R. Kaplan. This book guides trekkers through every aspect of planning and enjoying a trek through Nepal—one of the world's most magnificent adventures. From medical advice to cultural *faux-pas*, it's an essential guide. *"A must"* — Midwest Book Review. **$9.95**

Australia: Where the Fun Is by Goodyear & Skinner. From the best pubs in Sydney to the cheapest motels in Darwin to the greatest hikes in Tasmania, this guide by two recent Yale grads details all the fun stuff Down Under—on and off the beaten path. *"Indispensable"* — Library Journal. **$12.95**

Northern Italy: A Taste of Trattoria by Christina Baglivi. For the most delicious, most authentic, and least expensive meals in Italy, skip the *ristoranti* and head straight for *trattorie*, the small, unassuming cafés known only to locals. This guide, describing over 10 *trattorie* from Rome to Milan, is a must for the hungry traveler. *"A tasty tidbit of a tour guide"* —Quick Trips Travel Letter. **$9.95**

Bet On It! The Ultimate Guide to Nevada by Mary Jane & Greg Edwards. What does it mean when there's a cup over the handle of a slot machine? When should you buy "insurance" in blackjack? Which hotels have the best deals in Las Vegas? Is there good fishing near Reno? **Bet On It!** can answer all those questions and more. It's a complete handbook on all the casino games, plus an up-to-date guide to Nevada's best—and best-avoided—hotels, attractions, and tourist activities. A sure bet for anyone going to Nevada! *"Amusing and useful"* —New York Daily News. **$10.95**

Mustang books should be available at your local bookstore. If not, send a check or money order for the price of the book, plus $1.50 postage per book, to Mustang Publishing, P.O. Box 3004, Memphis, TN 31173 U.S.A.

Allow three weeks for delivery. For rush, one-week delivery, add $3.00 to the total. *International orders*: Please pay in U.S. funds, and add $5.00 to the total for Air Mail.

For a complete catalog of Mustang books, send $1.00 and a stamped, self-addressed, business size envelope to Catalog Request, Mustang Publishing, P.O. Box 3004, Memphis, TN 31173.